PRAISE FOR
THE INDIAN HERITAGE OF
AMERICA

"THE BEST SINGLE VOLUME YET PRODUCED FOR QUICK AND COMPREHENSIVE GUIDANCE TO THE WHOLE PAN-ORAMA OF THE AMERICAN INDIAN."
—San Francisco Chronicle

"FINE, INTENSELY INTERESTING, WELL ILLUSTRATED."
—Wall Street Journal

THE
INDIAN
HERITAGE
OF
AMERICA

ALVIN M. JOSEPHY, JR.

THE INDIAN HERITAGE OF AMERICA
A Bantam Book

PRINTING HISTORY
Alfred A. Knopf edition published September 1968
2nd printing ....September 1968
3rd printing ....December 1968
History Book Club edition published October 1968
Bantam edition published September 1969
2nd printing

*Bantam Books are published by Bantam Books, Inc., a National
General company. Its trade-mark, consisting of the words "Bantam
Books" and the portrayal of a bantam, is registered in the United
States Patent Office and in other countries. Marca Registrada.
Bantam Books, Inc., 666 Fifth Avenue, New York, N.Y. 10019.*

PRINTED IN THE UNITED STATES OF AMERICA

THIS BOOK IS DEDICATED, *with affectionate memory,*
to my first teachers, my mother and father,
SOPHIA K. *and* ALVIN M. JOSEPHY, SR.

Acknowledgments

To a great extent this book rests on the writings and studies of a very large number of people, professionals and laymen, who, since the time of Columbus, have contributed to our knowledge of the Indians of the Americas. I have listed the works of many of them in my bibliography, and wish to acknowledge with gratitude the great debt I owe to all of them. A more personal note of appreciation is due Clifford Evans, John C. Ewers, and Betty J. Meggers, all of the Smithsonian Institution; Frederick J. Dockstader of the Museum of the American Indian, Heye Foundation; my cartographer, Mr. Jean Paul Tremblay; and the various individuals and institutions, acknowledged individually elsewhere, who kindly provided the illustrations for this book. I am deeply grateful also to the John Simon Guggenheim Memorial Foundation for a Fellowship which facilitated research for part of this volume, and to my wife, Betty, for her understanding love and support.

A.M.J., Jr.

Greenwich, Connecticut
January 1968

Contents

Illustrations

PORTFOLIO I / *Before the White Man*

Folsom spear point
Lovelock Cave duck decoy
Tlatilco figurine
The Castillo, Chichén Itzá
Mayan pottery figure
Tlaloc, the rain god
Mayan writing
Mochica pottery
A quipu
Peruvian fringed tapestry

Machu Picchu
Hohokam ball court
Casas Grandes effigy vessel
Mimbres bowl
Hopewell figurine
Mississippian temple-mound
  village
Spiro Mound shell gorget
Key Marco carving

PORTFOLIO II / *The People*

Eskimo using a bow drill
A Tsimshian Indian
Kwakiutls
Interior of Micmac lodge
Timucua chief
Blood Sun Dance
Paiute woman

Navahos
Hupa White Deerskin Dance
Drawing of an Indian, 1529
Lacandón Maya
Wai Wai Indian
Tehuelches
Yahgan shaman

PORTFOLIO III / *Indian-White Contact*

Depiction of cannibalism, 1505
Indian canoe, 1572
Brazilian hammock, 1625
Aztecs attacking Alvarado
Mexican Indian petition
  to Spanish government
Capture of Atahualpa
Incident of the Canadian
  fur trade, 1715
Massacre at Lancaster, Penn-
  sylvania, 1763

Treaty of Greenville, 1795
Red Cloud
Set-Tainte (Satanta)
Custer at the Washita
Chief Joseph
Geronimo
The Little Bighorn
Pine Ridge Sioux reservation,
  1896

Maps

The Indian Heritage of America

A PRIMITIVE PEOPLE *is not a backward or retarded people;
indeed it may possess a genius for invention or action that
leaves the achievements of civilized peoples far behind.*

CLAUDE LÉVI-STRAUSS

1

Stereotypes and the Real Indian

FOR ALMOST FIVE HUNDRED YEARS THE AMERICAN INDIAN
has been one of the principal symbols of the New World.

To many persons, the mention of Brazil, Peru, Bolivia, or
almost any South American state evokes an image of its
original native inhabitant, whether a river dweller in a dugout
in the jungle basins of the Orinoco and Amazon, or a pon-
choed descendant of the Incas tending llamas in the highlands of the Andes. Mexico, Guatemala, and the other countries of Central America are still synonymous in the popular
mind with visions of the Mayan, Aztec, and other glittering
pre-Columbian civilizations and with the present-day arts and
handicrafts of their inheritors. And in Washington, D.C.,
the United States Travel Service of the Department of Commerce, established to attract visitors from other countries to
the modern, industrialized U.S., testifies to the great interest
foreign tourists have to this day in the storied Iroquois,
Apaches, and Sioux of other times by using the symbol of
the warbonneted Plains Indian on much of its official travel
literature. Even the Eskimo and his igloo and kayak come
readily to mind at the thought of Alaska and parts of
Canada.

In truth, the beliefs, ways of life, and roles of the American Indians are interwoven so intimately with the cultures
and histories of all the modern nations of the Americas that
no civilization of the Western Hemisphere can be fully
understood without knowledge and appreciation of them.
And yet, from the time of the Europeans' first meeting with
the Indians in 1492 until today, the Indian has been a
familiar but little known—and, indeed, often an unreal—
person to the non-Indian. What has been known about him,
moreover, frequently has been superficial, distorted, or false.

3

What the white man calls him is itself the result of an error. When Christopher Columbus reached the New World, he had no idea that a land mass lay between Europe and Asia; the islands at which he touched he thought were those known at the time as the Indies, which lay off the coast of Asia, and the people he found on them he called *los Indios*, the people of the Indies, or the Indians. Other early navigators and chroniclers used the same name mistakenly for the various peoples they met at the end of each westward voyage, and by the time the Europeans discovered their error and realized that they were still far from Asia, it was too late. The name had taken hold as a general term of reference for all the inhabitants of the newly found lands of the Western Hemisphere.

Errors of far greater significance—and seriousness—stemmed from fundamental cultural differences between Indians and non-Indians. Deeply imbedded in the cultural make-up of the white man with a European background were the accumulated experiences of the Judeo-Christian spiritual tradition, the heritages of the ancient civilizations of the Near East, Greece, and Rome, and the various political, social, and economic systems of western Europe. The Indians did not share any of these but, on their part, were the inheritors of totally different traditions and ways of life, many of them rooted in Asia, some of them thousands of years old, and all as thoroughly a part of Indian societies as European ways were a part of the white man's culture.

Meeting peoples with such different backgrounds led white men to endless misconceptions. Beginning with Columbus, the whites, with rare exceptions, observed and judged natives of the Americas from their own European points of view, failing consistently to grasp the truths and realities of the Indians themselves or their backgrounds and cultures. In the early years of the sixteenth century educated whites, steeped in the theological teachings of Europe, argued learnedly about whether or not Indians were humans with souls, whether they, too, derived from Adam and Eve (and were therefore sinful like the rest of mankind), or whether they were a previously unknown subhuman species. Other Europeans spent long years puzzling on the origin of the Indians and developing evidence that they were Egyptians, Chinese, descendants of one of the Lost Tribes of Israel, Welshmen, or even the survivors of civilizations that had once flourished on lost continents in the Atlantic and Pacific oceans.

In the lands of the New World, white men who came in contact with Indians viewed Indian cultures solely in terms that were familiar to themselves, and ignored or condemned what they did not understand. Indian leaders were talked of as "princes" and "kings"; spiritual guides and curers were called wizards, witch doctors, and medicine men, and all were equated as practitioners of sorcery; Indian societies generally—refined and sophisticated though some of them might be—were termed savage and barbaric, often only because they were strange, different, and not understood by the whites.

Many of the differences brought friction and, on both continents, fierce, interracial war. Conflicts resulted from misconceptions of the nature of Indian societies, the limits of authority of Indian leaders, and the non-hostile motives of certain Indian traits. Differing concepts concerning individual and group use of land and the private ownership of land were at the heart of numerous struggles, as were misunderstandings over the intentions of Indians whose actions were judged according to the patterns of white men's behavior rather than those of the Indians.

Through the years, the white man's popular conception of the Indian often crystallized into unrealistic or unjust images. Sometimes they were based on the tales of adventurers and travelers, who wove myths freely into their accounts, and sometimes they were reflections of the passions and fears stirred by the conflicts between the two races. Described by early writers as a race of happy people who lived close to nature, the Indians of the New World were first envisioned by many Europeans as innocent, childlike persons, spending their time in dancing and equally pleasurable pursuits. From this image in time sprang Jean Jacques Rousseau's vision of the natural man, as well as arguments of liberal philosophers in Europe who influenced revolutionary movements, including those of the United States and France, with comparisons between the lot of Europeans "in chains" and Indians who lived lives of freedom.

This idealistic version of the Indian as a symbol of the naturally free man persisted into the nineteenth century, sometimes being advanced by admiring observers like the artist George Catlin who visited many tribes and found much to admire in their ways of life, but generally being accepted only by persons who had no firsthand contact with Indians. On each frontier, beginning along the Atlantic coast, settlers who locked in conflict with Indians quickly conceived of them as bloodthirsty savages, intent on murder, scalping, and pillage. As the frontier moved west, and the Indian menace vanished from the eastern seaboard, generations that did not know Indian conflict at firsthand again thought of the native American in more tolerant terms. James Fenimore Cooper's version of the Noble Red Man helped gain sympathy among easterners for Indians who were hard pressed by the whites elsewhere. Thus, throughout much of the nineteenth century people in the northeastern cities often gave support to movements for justice for the southern and western tribes.

But as long as conflicts continued, the border settlers regarded the Indians in terms that had been familiar to the New England colonists during King Philip's war in the seventeenth century, and echoed the sentiment that "the only good Indian is a dead Indian." Only with the defeat of tribes did that point of view change—and then, inevitably, it was succeeded by still another image, which also moved from one border to another as settlers took over lands from which they had dispossessed the natives. It was the cruel conception of the Whisky Indian, the destroyed and impoverished survivor who had lost his home, tribal life, means of sustenance, and cultural standards; and lacking motivation—and often even the will to live—sought escape in alcohol. Unfeeling whites, failing to recognize the causes of the Indians' degradation, forgot their past power, pride, and dignity, and regarded them as weak and contemptuous people.

Only rarely did astute observers try to understand Indian life and depict Indians realistically. One of them, Edwin T. Denig, an American fur trader living among still-unconquered tribes on the upper Missouri River during the first half of the nineteenth century, wrote angrily on the white man's lack of knowledge about Indians at that time.

> It would be well for the public if everyone who undertook to write a book was thoroughly acquainted with the subject of which he treats.... This is particularly the case in most of the works purporting to describe the actual life and intellectual capacity of the Indians of North America; much evil has been the consequence of error thus introduced, bad feelings engendered, and unwise legislation enforced, which will continue until our rulers are enlightened as to the real state of

their Government, character, organization, manners and customs, and social position ... a hastily collected and ill-digested mass of information form the basis of works by which the public is deceived as to the real state of the Indians. Even foreigners who have possibly passed a winter at some of the trading posts in the country, seen an Indian dance or two or a buffalo chase, return home, enlighten Europe if not America with regard to Indian character; which is only the product of their own brains and takes its color from the peculiar nature of that organ. Hence we find two sets of writers both equally wrong, one setting forth the Indians as a noble, generous, and chivalrous race far above the standard of Europeans, the other representing them below the level of brute creation.

It might be assumed that much has changed since the time when Denig wrote. But despite vast study by scientists and a voluminous literature of modern knowledge about Indians, still common are ignorance and misconceptions, many of them resulting from the white man's continuing inability to regard Indians save from his own European-based point of view. Today most Indians on both continents have been conquered and enfolded within the conquerors' own cultures; but the span of time since the various phases of the conquest ended has been short, and numerous Indians still cling to traits that are centuries, if not millennia, old and cannot be quickly shed. Many Indians, for instance, still do not understand or cannot accept the concept of private ownership of land; many do not understand the need to save for the future, a fundamental requirement of the economies of their conquerors; many find it difficult, if not impossible so far, to substitute individual competitiveness for group feeling; many do not see the necessity for working the year-round if they can provide for their families by six months of work, or the reason for cutting the earth-mother with a plow and farming if they can still hunt, fish, and dig roots. Many yet feel a sacred attachment to the land and a reverence for nature that is incomprehensible to most whites. Many, though Christian, find repugnance in the idea that man possesses dominion over the birds and beasts, and believe still man is brother to all else that is living.

Such ideas, among a multitude that continue to hold numerous Indians apart from non-Indians, are either unrecognized or frowned upon by most whites today. Those who are aware of them are more often than not irritated by their

persistence, yet the stubbornness of the white critics' own
culture to survive, if a totally alien way of life, like that of
the Chinese Communists, were to be forced upon them,
would be understood.

More common among most whites are the false under-
standings and images which they retain about Indians. For
many, the moving pictures, television, and comic strips have
firmly established a stereotype as the true portrait of all
Indians: the dour, stoic, warbonneted Plains Indian. He is
a warrior, he has no humor unless it is that of an incongru-
ous and farcical type, and his language is full of "hows,"
"ughs," and words that end in "um." Only rarely in the
popular media of communications is it hinted that Indians,
too, were, and are, all kinds of real, living persons like any
others and that they included peace-loving wise men, mothers
who cried for the safety of their children, young men who
sang songs of love and courted maidens, dullards, statesmen,
cowards, and patriots. Today there are college-trained Indians, researchers, business and professional men and women,
jurists, ranchers, teachers and political office holders. Yet so
enduring is the stereotype that many a non-Indian, especially
if he lives in an area where Indians are not commonly seen,
expects any American Indian he meets to wear a feathered
headdress. When he sees the Indian in a conventional business suit instead, he is disappointed!

If Indians themselves are still about as real as wooden
sticks to many non-Indians, the facts concerning their present-day status in the societies of the Americas are even less
known. Again, stereotypes, like those of "the oil-rich Indian"
or "the coddled ward of Uncle Sam" frequently obscure the
truth. A few Indians have become wealthy, but most of them
know poverty, ill health, and barren, wasted existences. Some
have received higher education, but many are poorly educated or not educated at all. Some are happily assimilated in
the white man's societies; others are in various stages of
acculturation, and many are not assimilated and do not wish
to be anything but Indian. In the United States, in addition,
it often comes as a surprise to many otherwise well informed
whites to learn that the Indians are citizens and have the
right to vote; that reservations are not concentration camps
but are all the lands that were left to the Indians, and that
are still being guarded by them as homes from which they
can come and go in freedom; that the special treaty rights
that they possess and that make them a unique minority in

the nation are payments and guarantees given them for land they sold to the non-Indian people of the United States; that Indians pay state and federal taxes like all other citizens, save where treaties, agreements, or statutes have exempted them; and that, far from being on the way to extinction, the Indian population is increasing rapidly.

Finally, there are facts that should be obvious to everyone after five hundred years but are not, possibly because Columbus's name for them, Indians, is to this day understood by many to refer to a single people. Despite the still commonly asked question, "Do you speak Indian?" there is neither a single Indian people nor a single Indian language, but many different peoples, with different racial characteristics, different cultures, and different languages. From Alaska to Cape Horn, in fact, the Indians of the Americas are as different from each other as are Spaniards, Scots, and Poles— and, in many cases, as will be seen, they are even more different.

2

The Diversities
of Indians

To the average person all Indians may seem physi-
cally alike, and in truth they do share certain characteristics. Although the term "redskin" is as much an
exaggeration as is "paleface" for the flesh color of a Cauca-
sian, the skin coloration of Indians ranges from a coppery
brown to a yellowish brown. Most Indians also have prominent cheekbones, which make their faces appear broad and
large, although their chins often seem somewhat receding.
They are generally dark-eyed, and their hair is black and
straight, growing thickly on their heads but usually only
sparsely on their faces and bodies. It is untrue that they cannot grow mustaches and beards; some of them did, but most
of them plucked hairs from their faces.

At the same time, any perceptive observer who has seen
Indians in different regions of the Americas, or even in different parts of the United States, knows also that there are
great physical differences among them, marked variations
in size, features, and head and body shape that provide one
of the most readily recognized indications that Indians are
not all one people. Some Indians are extremely tall, some
medium-sized, and some very short. Some are round-headed,
some long-headed. Some have coarse features, and some have
delicate features. The shape of the nose varies from group to
group, as does the thickness of the lips. Some persons think
of Indians as "looking Asiatic"; yet if by that they mean
slant-eyed, only a relatively small number of Indians—although most Eskimos—have the slanting-eyed look that
comes from the so-called Mongoloid fold of the eyelid. In
general, from one end of the hemisphere to the other,
Indians exhibit many physical variations; there is not the
slightest resemblance between a New York Iroquois and a

Brazilian Cayapó, between a Montana Crow and a Mexican Maya.

The question of the relationship of the various American Indian peoples to the races of mankind has puzzled generations of scientists. Some of the characteristics that have been enumerated as being shared by most Indians are typical also of physical traits of the Chinese, Japanese, and other Mongoloid peoples of parts of Asia, and have led to Indians being classified as a subdivision of the Mongoloid race. But the many differences among the Indians, as well as their possession of various features that are not common to present-day Mongoloids, have given rise to numerous theories concerning their ancestry.

It is accepted as certain today that Indians are of Asiatic origin, but the solution of the racial problem rests to a considerable extent on still-unanswered questions of where in Asia the different peoples came from and when. One theory suggests that in the remote past peoples who may have been the first to enter the Western Hemisphere had drifted away from a "proto-Mongoloid" stock in Asia, from which there later evolved the modern-day Asian Mongoloids. According to this theory, the descendants of these immigrants to the Western Hemisphere multiplied and spread across the Americas, evolving differently not only from the peoples who had remained behind in Asia but also among themselves, depending on various influences, including environment, ways of life, and unions among groups. There may have been much later migrations of parent groups of Eskimos and Aleuts and of people who became the Athapascan Indians, all showing more features of modern-day Mongoloids, but by the time the white man reached America, the forces of evolution, working on the descendants of the original arrivals in the hemisphere, would have accounted for the great physical diversities of most of the different groups on the two continents. Still another theory proposes that there were two or more migrations from Asia into the Western Hemisphere, the earlier one of people of a "proto-Mongoloid" stock, and the second or later ones of people who possessed features that had become more like those of present-day Asian Mongoloids. Still another theory suggests multiple migrations of peoples who came at different times from different parts of Asia and thus introduced the various physical characteristics of the individual groups that the white men found living in the Western Hemisphere.

The great variety of Indian languages—although it is

known that they diverged through the millennia from a smaller number of parent tongues of very ancient times— also bespeak many peoples. It has not been possible so far to determine how many different languages and dialects have been spoken in the Americas. Many tongues have become extinct. But linguistic scholar Morris Swadesh believes that when the whites arrived in the New World, Indians were speaking some 2,200 different languages, many of them possessing regional variations. Other students have estimated that there were at least 200 mutually unintelligible languages among the native peoples north of Mexico, at least another 350 in Mexico and Central America, and considerably more than 1,000 in the Caribbean and South America.

Despite the disappearance of many of the tongues, a great number of Indian languages and dialects still exist, and millions of people in the Americas still use them in daily conversation. On reservations in the western part of the United States, visitors may still hear Sioux, Crows, Blackfeet, Pueblos, Navahos, and other Indians conversing in their own languages. In South America more than 5 million people still use Quechua, the language of the Peruvian Incas, while more than half of Paraguay's population of almost 2 million speaks another Indian tongue, Guaraní, which, with Spanish, is an official language of the country.

At the same time, if one has the idea that all Indian languages sound alike, he has only to read the journals of Lewis and Clark. As the explorers traveled from tribe to tribe across the North American continent, they remarked again and again on the phonetic differences among the languages of the various Indian peoples they met. Some of the tongues sounded harsh and guttural, others liquid and melodious. Phonetically, the differences are numerous. In many of the Indian languages, certain consonants are whispered or are not pronounced. In some, the sounds of *k*, *p*, or *t* are uttered with constricted throat muscles, as if the speaker were being choked. Some Indian tongues possess tonal characteristics like those of the Chinese; changes in the pitch of a vowel, for instance, completely alter the meaning of a word or an expression.

The grammars also vary greatly from language to language, although many of them have a number of traits in common. Nouns and pronouns are often combined in a single word. A sentence's subject or object, or both, is frequently contained in the verb. Many of the languages convey an entire image or idea by modifying the stem of a word, by adding other sounds to it so as to make it into a very long word, or by running it together with other words in a word phrase. The Nez Perce name, *Tawis Geejumnin*, for instance, was translated to mean "Horns Worn Down Like Those on an Old Buffalo," and a Southern Paiute word phrase, *wiitokuchumpunkuruganiyugwivantumu*, cited by Edward Sapir, the noted student of Indian languages, meant "they-who-are-going-to-sit-and-cut-up-with-a-knife-a-black-cow-   (or bull-) buffalo."

No Indian tribe possessed an alphabet, but the Mayas, Aztecs, and other highly advanced peoples of Middle America developed various systems of written communication. The Mayas and some Mexican peoples employed picture symbols, or glyphs, some of which probably represented syllables. On Mayan carvings and codices approximately 400 different glyphs have been identified, although up to now only some 150, including symbols for time periods, numbers, astronomical bodies, and zodiac signs, have been deciphered. The Aztecs used a less sophisticated system of stylized pictures, but by the time of the Spanish Conquest some of the symbols were apparently beginning to stand for syllabic sounds, and Aztec writers were beginning to combine pictures to form words. In other parts of the New World various devices, like wampum belts among the Iroquois and other tribes in the eastern part of North America and knotted strings among the Incas in Peru, were used as memory aids to assist in the recalling of events, and here and there simple picture-writing existed among different bands. On the plains of North America, moreover, Indians learned to use a sign language, comprised of numerous hand signs, so that without uttering a word peoples of many different tribes could communicate with each other.

The study of Indian languages, a field of scholarship that with the assistance of modern data-processing systems has made considerable progress in recent years, has shown that many of the tongues derived from the same parental language stocks or superstocks of long ago. Attempts to classify the various languages into related groups have been numerous and full of problems. One of the best-known classifications was made as long ago as 1891 by Major John Wesley Powell, the explorer of the Green and Colorado rivers who became director of the Bureau of Ethnology of the Smithsonian Institution. Powell confined his study to the Indian languages north of Mexico and, by identifying relationships among them, grouped them into 56 separate linguistic families. His major divisions—Algonquian, Iroquoian, Athapascan, Siouan, and others—are still used by many persons today. But work by more recent scholars has revealed abundant evidence of relationships even between members of Powell's major divisions, and new attempts at classifications have grouped the languages under a smaller number of parental stocks and superstocks. One of the more startling classifications—although admittedly highly tentative—has come from Morris Swadesh, who suggests that every known native language in the Americas save four can be traced back to no more than five basic "phyla," or parental superstocks. He lists the five (in the order of their possible arrival in the Americas from Asia) as Macro-Carib, including Ge; Macro-Arawakan; Macro-Quechuan; Macro-Mayan; and a portion of Bask-Dennean (the rest of that phylum being distributed throughout Eurasia). Other proposals include a list of six totally unrelated family superstocks for all languages north of Mexico, and, for South America, a suggestion by the anthropologist and linguistic scholar Joseph Greenberg that all native languages in that continent can be grouped under three superstocks. None of these simplified classifications has yet been fully accepted, however, although it appears that in time some satisfactory system will be devised that will link all the languages of the world, including those of the Americas, and trace them back to a minimum of common parental tongues in the Old World.

Among Indians there is little relationship between language groups and culture. Many contrasting ways of life, as well as sharply different cultural levels, existed among peoples who spoke the same or related tongues. The rich, powerful Aztecs of Mexico and the poor, timorous Gosiutes of the Utah-Nevada desert were members of the same language family. At the same time, peoples like the Flatheads and Nez Perces, who spoke entirely different languages, could band together and lead the same type of life. The study of Indian languages, however, can be extremely valuable in the knowledge it provides of the backgrounds and prehistoric origins, movements, and cultural developments of individual tribes and bands. As already stated, the many different languages and dialects emerged from original superstocks. Through the millennia, the diverging tongues underwent numerous evolutions and changes that included borrowings from other languages. Studies of the languages can throw considerable light on what happened to the people who spoke them. Language characteristics, for instance, provide clues to early links between different peoples, help indicate the approximate time and place in which people were once located, point to centers of dispersion, and illuminate migrations, divisions. contacts, past associations. and content of prehistoric cultures. And language borrowings from other tongues—or the lack of them—can often clarify relationships between stronger and weaker groups and between more developed peoples and those with less advanced cultures.

Under the circumstances previously stated no list of languages, with their evidence of the diversity of Indian groups, can be considered complete or final at this time. One classification of tribal groupings by languages may be preferred to another. Until a proposal such as that of Swadesh is more widely accepted, however, it seems that the following framework, adhering generally to the classification of North American language groups compiled by Harold E. Driver in *Indians of North America* (Chicago, 1961), and the South American classification proposed by Joseph Greenberg may be helpful in showing the principal languages spoken by the different native American groups at the time of white contact with them:

I. ESKIMO-ALEUT

Eskimo, Aleut in the Aleutians, western and northern Alaska, northern Canada, and Greenland.

II. NA-DENE

A. ATHAPASCAN

Ahtena, Bear Lake, Beaver, Carrier, Chipewyan, Dogrib, Han, Hare, Ingalik, Kaska, Koyukon, Kutchin, Mountain, Nebesna, Sekani, Slave, Tanaina, Tanana, Tuchone, Yellowknife in the Subarctic area of northwestern Canada and Alaska.

Chilcotin, Nicola on the Northwest Plateau, western Canada.

Hupa, Mattole in southern Oregon and northern California.

Sarci on the northwestern Canadian plains.

Kiowa-Apache on the southern U. S. Plains.

Apache, Navaho in the U. S. Southwest.

B. RELATED

Haida, Tlingit on the Northwest Pacific Coast.

Toboso in northern Mexico.

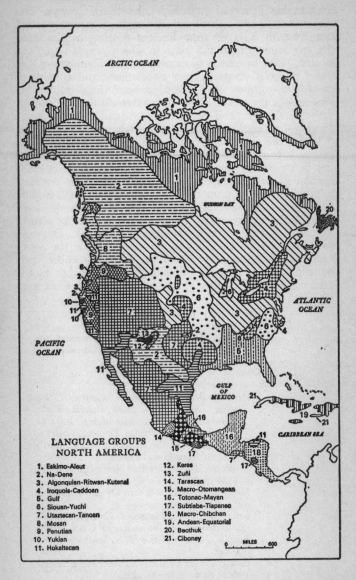

LANGUAGE GROUPS
NORTH AMERICA

1. Eskimo-Aleut
2. Na-Dene
3. Algonquian-Ritwan-Kutenai
4. Iroquois-Caddoan
5. Gulf
6. Siouan-Yuchi
7. U␣aztecan-Tanoan
8. Mosan
9. Penutian
10. Yukian
11. Hokaltecan
12. Keres
13. Zuñi
14. Tarascan
15. Macro-Otomanguean
16. Totonac-Mayan
17. Subtiaba-Tlapanec
18. Macro-Chibchan
19. Andean-Equatorial
20. Beothuk
21. Ciboney

III. ALGONQUIAN-RITWAN-KUTENAI
   A. ALGONQUIAN
      Cree, Montagnais, Naskapi in the Subarctic
      of eastern Canada. *Abnaki, Chickahominy,
      Delaware, Lumbee, Malecite, Massachuset,
      Mattapony, Micmac, Mohegan, Nanticoke,
      Narraganset, Nipmuc, Pamlico, Pamunkey,
      Passamaquoddy, Pennacook, Penobscot, Pe-
      quot, Powhatan, Shawnee, Wampanoag,
      Wappinger* in the Eastern Woodlands from
      Nova Scotia to the Carolinas.
      *Illinois, Kickapoo, Menominee, Miami, Ojibwa
      (Chippewa), Ottawa, Peoria, Potawatomi,
      Sauk and Fox* in the Midwest and around
      the Great Lakes.
      *Arapaho, Atsina (Gros Ventre), Blackfoot
      (Blood, Piegan, Siksika), Cheyenne, Plains
      Cree* on the Plains.
   B. RITWAN
      Wiyot, Yurok in northern California.
   C. KUTENAI
      Kutenai on the Canadian border with Idaho
      and northwestern Montana.
IV. IROQUOIS-CADDOAN
   A. IROQUOIS
      *Erie, Huron, Iroquois (Cayuga, Mohawk,
      Oneida, Onondaga, Seneca), Neutral, Sus-
      quehannock (Conestoga), Tionontati (To-
      bacco)* in the Eastern Woodlands of Canada
      and the U.S.
      Cherokee, Nottoway, Tuscarora in the Caro-
      linas.
   B. CADDOAN
      Caddo, Kichai, Tawakoni, Waco, Wichita
      bordering on the Plains in the Southeast.
      Arikara, Pawnee on the eastern Plains.
V. GULF
   A. MUSKOGEAN
      *Apalachee, Alabama, Chickasaw, Choctaw,
      Creek, Hichiti, Houma, Mobile, Seminole,
      Tuskegee, Yamasee* in the Southeast.
   B. RELATED
      *Atakapa, Calusa, Chitimacha, Natchez, Timu-
      cua, Tunica* in the Southeast.
VI. SIOUAN-YUCHI
   A. SIOUAN
      *Assiniboine, Crow, Dakota Sioux (Santee,
      Teton, Yankton), Hidatsa, Iowa, Kansa,*

> *Mandan, Missouri, Omaha, Osage, Oto,*
> *Ponca* on the Plains.
> *Winnebago* in Wisconsin.
> *Biloxi, Quapaw* in the Southeast.
> *Catawba, Tutelo* in Virginia and the Caro-
> linas.
>
> B. YUCHI
> *Yuchi* in the southern Appalachians.

VII. UTAZTECAN-TANOAN
> A. UTAZTECAN
> *Bannock, Chemehuevi, Gosiute, Kawiisu,*
> *Mono, Paiute, Panamint, Paviotso, Sho-*
> *shoni, Ute* in the Great Basin and Rocky
> Mountains.
> *Comanche* on the Plains.
> *Cahuilla, Serrano* in southern California.
> *Hopi, Pima, Papago* in the Southwest.
> *Acaxee, Cahita, Concho, Cora, Huichol,*
> *Jumano, Mayo, Pima Bajo, Opata, Tara-*
> *humara, Tepehuan, Tepecano, Yaqui* in
> northern Mexico.
> *Nahuatl (Aztec, Tlaxcalan)* in central Mexico.
>
> B. TANOAN
> *Picurís, San Ildefonso, San Juan, Taos Pueblos*
> in New Mexico.
>
> C. KIOWA
> *Kiowa* on the southern Plains.

VIII. MOSAN
> A. SALISHAN
> *Bella Coola, Chehalis, Coast Salish, Tillamook*
> on the Northwest Pacific Coast.
> *Coeur d'Alene, Colville, Cowlitz, Flathead,*
> *Kalispel, Lilooet, Nisqually, Okanogan,*
> *Puyallup, Sanpoil, Shuswap, Spokan, Thomp-*
> *son* on the Northwest Plateau and in the
> Puget Sound area.
>
> B. WAKASHAN
> *Kwakiutl, Makah, Nootka* on the Northwest
> Pacific Coast.

IX. PENUTIAN
> A. CHINOOK-TSIMSHIAN
> *Chinook, Tsimshian* on the Northwest Pacific
> Coast.
>
> B. COOS-TAKELMAN
> *Coos, Kalapuya, Takelma* on the Northwest
> Pacific Coast.
>
> C. KLAMATH-SAHAPTIN
> *Cayuse, Klickitat, Molala, Nez Perce, Palouse,*

Umatilla, Wallawalla, Yakima on the Columbia River Plateau.

D. CALIFORNIA PENUTIAN
   Costanoan, Maidu, Miwok, Wintun, Yokuts in California.

X. YUKIAN
   Yuki in California.

XI. HOKALTECAN
   A. HOKAN
      Chumash, Karok, Pomo, Salinan, Shasta, Yana in California.

      Achomawi, Atsugewi, Washo in the Great Basin.

      Havasupai, Maricopa, Mohave, Walapai, Yavapai, Yuma in the Southwest.

      Cochimi, Pericu, Seri, Tequistlatec, Waicuri in northern Mexico.

   B. COAHUILTECAN
      Coahuiltec, Karankawa, Tamaulipec, Tonkawa in Texas and northern Mexico

XII. KERES
   Acoma, Cochiti, Keres, Santa Ana, Zia Pueblos in New Mexico

XIII. ZUÑI
   Zuñi in the Southwest.

XIV. TARASCAN
   Tarascan in Mexico.

XV. MACRO-OTOMANGEAN
   Chinantec, Mazatec, Mixtec, Otomí, Pame, Zapotec in Mexico.

XVI. TOTONAC-MAYAN
   A. TOTONACAN
      Totonac in Mexico.

   B. MIZOCUAVEAN
      Huave, Mixe, Zoque in Mexico.

   C. MAYAN
      Huastec, Maya (Lacandón, Quiche, and others) in Mexico, Guatemala, and El Salvador.

XVII. SUBTIABA-TLAPANEC
   Tlapanec in Mexico.
   Subtiaba in Nicaragua.

XVIII. MACRO-CHIBCHAN
   A. CHIBCHAN
      Cara, Chibcha (Muisca), Cuna, Guaymí, Lenca, Mosquito in Central America, Colombia, and Venezuela.

   B. PAEZAN
      Cañari, Jirajara, Puruhá in northern South America.

LANGUAGE GROUPS
SOUTH AMERICA

1. Macro-Chibchan languages
2. Ge-Pano-Carib languages
3. Andean-Equatorial languages
4. Uncertain

MILES   1000

Atacameño in northern Chile.

Mura on the upper Amazon River.

XIX. GE-PANO-CARIB

 A. GE

  Bororo, Botocudo, Caingang, Canella, Cayapó, Shavante, Sherente in central and southern Brazil.

  Manasí in eastern Bolivia.

 B. PANOAN

  Conibo, Shipibo in the Peruvian Montaña.

 C. CARIBAN

  Arara, Arma, Calamari, Camaracotó, Carib, Catio, Motilon, Quimbaya in the West Indies and northern South America.

  Yagua in the Peruvian Montaña.

 D. GUAYCURUAN

  Abipón, Matacoan, Mbayá, Payaguá in the Paraguayan Gran Chaco.

  Charrua in Uruguay.

XX. ANDEAN-EQUATORIAL

 A. QUECHUAMARAN

  Quechua, Aymará in the Peruvian and Bolivian highlands.

 B. ARAUCANIAN-CHON

  Araucanian, Chono, Ono, Puelche, Tehuelche, Yahgan in southern Chile and Argentina.

 C. ZAPAROAN

  Zaparoan in the Peruvian and Ecuadorean Montaña.

 D. ARAWAKAN

  Taino in the West Indies.

  Goajiro, Guayapé, Palicur in northern South America.

  Campa in the Peruvian Montaña.

  Chané, Guaná in the Paraguayan Gran Chaco.

  Bauré, Mojo, Paressí in eastern Bolivia.

 E. TUPÍ-GUARANÍ

  Camayurá, Mundurucú, Parintintin in the Amazon Basin.

  Tupinambá on the Brazilian coast.

  Guaraní in Paraguay.

  Chiriguano, Sirionó in Bolivia.

 F. JÍVAROAN

  Jívaro, Palta in the Peruvian and Ecuadorean Montaña.

 G. OTHERS

  Timotean in Venezuela.

  Zamucoan in the Paraguayan Gran Chaco.

3

"Indianness"

A S STATED EARLIER, THE OUTWARD MANIFESTATIONS OF
Indian cultures have been apparent to white observers
since 1492, but not often have they been understood
or accurately interpreted.

To a large extent, Indian cultures reflected the environments in which they were shaped. As the various peoples
who preceded the white man to the Western Hemisphere
spread through the Americas and occupied different portions
of both continents, they adopted the traits and techniques
necessary for their survival. There were local and regional
adjustments to extremes in temperature and climate, to
mountain, desert, jungle, woodland, grassland, and coastal
topography, and to the availability of various kinds of food
resources. According to the supply, men at different times
hunted and trapped different species of large and small game,
and adapted their weapons, methods of hunting, and even
their manner of living and social customs and beliefs to the
pursuit of food. Those who lived where game was scarce
developed cultures based more on the gathering of wild
plant foods or shellfish, or on fishing. With the rise of
agriculture, farming spread into areas that could sustain it
and changed many peoples' ways of life. Some lived almost
entirely on agriculture, while others combined hunting,
gathering, farming, and fishing. The different economies
gave rise to diverse customs and to many different social,
religious, and political systems. Many traits and patterns of
existence, carried from group to group by migrations, inter-
marriage, fighting, or trade contacts, spread across large
areas often being adopted by people far distant from the
originators. For instance, the idea of making pottery may
have moved by steps from the coast of Ecuador to the
coasts of Florida, Georgia, and South Carolina. But "borrowed" techniques and systems were frequently also modified

and adapted to meet the specific needs of the "borrower," and throughout the hemisphere there came to exist a huge range and variety of Indian cultures.

This kaleidoscope of different—and often altering—native ways of life makes little more than a figure of speech the term "Indianness," which, more aptly, is a modern-day reference to traits by which Indians today retain recognition for themselves as Indians. But while it is difficult, if not impossible, to cite any cultural patterns that existed in every Indian society after the earliest stage of big-game hunters, some traits were common to many Indian cultures, and a number of generalizations can be made about many different groups. At the same time, it is well to begin with the realization that much of what the white man today often thinks of as peculiarly American Indian is not, in fact, exclusively Indian at all. Bows and arrows, the use of war paint, and so-called medicine men, or shamans, all existed among other peoples in the world; so did the mythical thunderbird, rain dances, and the practice of scalping.

Like numerous groups in Africa, Asia, and Oceania, the social organization of many American Indians was based on family and clan units. Small family units dominated the life of many of the more primitive bands, while in the more advanced groups people were organized frequently in clans composed of persons who traced themselves back through either the male or the female line alone to a common ancestor. The clans were sometimes named for animals known as *totems* (derived from an Algonquian word meaning approximately "brother"), which were regarded as their supernatural ancestors or spiritual guardians. Clan relationships and activities were usually important parts of a group's daily existence. A clan might share with the family the responsibility for the raising of children, overseeing the discipline of the youths when it was necessary—although rarely meting out physical punishment. Often clans had specific tribal or village rights and duties. Many supervised and conducted intricate ceremonies that attended the initiation of young people into adulthood. Among some tribes the clans were separated into two different encompassing bodies referred to by anthropologists as moieties (halves), which competed in games and divided between themselves the carrying out of various village functions and activities.

The life of almost all Indian societies was colored by a deep faith in supernatural forces that were believed to link human beings to all other living things. To many Indians, each animal, each tree, and each manifestation of nature had its own spirit with which the individual could establish supernatural contact through his own spirit or that of an intermediary. In some societies, the combined total of the people's spiritual powers was believed to be the unseen force that filled the world. It was a sum supernatural force that shaped and directed life. The Iroquois called it *orenda*, the Algonquians *manitou*, the Sioux *wakan*, and the South American Incas *huaca*. Various Indian groups believed in gods, ghosts, and demons. Some believed in personal guardian spirits and sought to establish contact with them through dreams and vision quests. Several tribes worshipped a single creator force, or Supreme Being, which white men taught them to call "the Great Spirit," but some groups, while acknowledging such a force or presence, regarded it as dead or disassociated from human affairs and dismissed it from consideration in daily life.

Common to most of Indian life were shamans, individuals with especially strong supernatural powers. Among many peoples, they were the "medicine men," but their functions often went far beyond curing the sick. Able to establish direct contact with the spirit world, they could call on aid from a supernatural helper or be possessed themselves by spirits. Sometimes they interceded for individuals, sometimes for the whole group. They could ensure good crops, a good hunt, or success in war. Or they could bring harm to an enemy or a rival. They occupied different roles and assumed different stations among different peoples, ranging from soothsayers, magicians, and hypnotists to members of hierarchies of trained priests who presided over formal cults and rituals. Some shamans exercised political power in bands or tribes; the Hunkpapa Sioux Sitting Bull was a notable example. Others, like the Mayan priest-rulers, dominated the total apparatus of statecraft of huge and complex civilizations. These differences reflected many diverse religious systems. Some peoples observed no formal religious practices. Others had small priesthoods that presided over carefully taught rites. Still others, like the Aztecs, were led by powerful religious hierarchies in paying homage to large pantheons of deities with specialized characteristics and functions.

Two mythical figures, the so-called culture hero and the trickster, were widespread in Indian lore, appearing in different guises among various tribes. The former figure was regarded as the person who had taught the members of the tribe their way of life in the distant past, while the latter, a fabulous jokester, was partly a sacred being and partly a humorous character who frequently managed to outsmart himself and get into trouble. Both figures, sometimes combined into one person, who might be an animal like the coyote, or a human, were the subjects of many tales told by grandmothers to children, and repeated from one generation to the next. Among the most common stories were those that related how mankind had been created. Typical of such tales was one told by the Achomawi, a group of Pit River Indians of northeastern California: One day Coyote watched Silver Fox gather some serviceberry sticks and start to whittle them down. Silver Fox told him he was going to make people. The finished sticks would be chiefs and warriors; the shavings would be common people. After a night and a day of whittling, Silver Fox turned the sticks and shavings into people. Coyote decided he would make people too. So, copying everything he had seen Silver Fox do, he gathered some serviceberry sticks and whittled them down. After a night and a day, he too turned the finished sticks and shavings into people. Then Coyote ran after some of the women he had created and at length caught them. But when he touched them, they all turned back into shavings.

Indian rituals and celebrations were often accompanied by dancing, drumming, and singing. Dances, many of them sacred but others done simply for pleasure, varied in all parts of both continents. Songs also differed greatly; some related people's experiences, extolled exploits, or merely expressed a thought, while others were sung to nonsense words or to sounds that had no meaning. The drum was used by almost all tribes. Two of the most common types were the double-headed drum and the water drum, the latter possessing a single head of skin and being filled with water. Some drums were held in the hand and beaten with a short stick; others, especially those used for dances in many parts of the present-day United States, were large round drums that rested on the ground, hung from sticks, or were held by chanters. Many drums could be heard for long distances and were used to transmit signals or messages. Among some tribes an eagle-bone whistle was also employed in ritualistic dances and ceremonies like the Sun Dance. The flute, blown at one end rather than at the side, was used by some peoples, often by young men who were courting maidens. Almost all tribes, also, employed rattles made either of gourds or turtle shells and various types of crude instruments, including notched sticks that were rubbed across each other to make rasping sounds.

Many Indians held in common certain fundamental ideas. A concept concerning the right of land ownership, basically different from that of the white man, was shared by most Indians. To them, land and its produce, like the air and water, were free to the use of the group. No man might own land as personal property and bar others from it. A tribe, band, or village might claim certain land as its territory for farming, hunting, or dwelling, but it was held and used communally. No clash of concepts caused more friction than this one between Indians and white men in the United States, for Indians frequently found it difficult to accept an individual's right to own land and keep others from using it. Some tribes, moreover, regarded the earth as the mother of all life and thought it impossible to sell their mother. The concept is still strong among some Indians today. At Taos Pueblo in New Mexico, Indians may still be seen taking shoes off horses and walking about in soft-soled shoes themselves in the spring, for at that time of the year, they believe, the earth is pregnant and they must not harm her body. Taos Indians, also, are not alone among Indians who still resist or avoid the use of modern agricultural implements, such as steel-bladed plows, which would slice open the breast of their earth-mother.

Generally, most Indians had respect, if not reverence and awe, for the earth and for all of nature and, living close to nature and its forces, strove to exist in balance with them. If harmony with nature were disturbed, illness, pain, death, or other misfortunes would result. To most Indians, also, life after death was regarded as a continuation of existence in another world. Few thought of it, however, specifically as a hunter's paradise. The expression "happy hunting ground," a white man's invention, merely symbolized the belief of some Indians that it was a good land where everything, including the securing of food, was easier for people than it had been before.

Warfare was common on both continents and was a principal preoccupation among some Indian societies. But it is either false or exaggerated to conceive of all Indians as warriors or as war-motivated people. Certain groups like the Hopis were among the most peaceful on earth, and many

Indians abhorred warfare and the misery and violent death that it brought. White men publicized images of the Indians as savage and "bestial" warriors, but Indian warfare was often no more savage than the type of war Europeans introduced to the hemisphere and waged against the natives. In fact, Indian warfare was often stimulated and intensified by the impact of the Europeans.

Few Indian groups, for example, were wealthy enough at any time to maintain a standing army. Warfare, even after the arrival of the whites, usually consisted of sporadic raids, conducted in defense of tribal lands and hunting grounds, or for honor, revenge, slaves, horses or other booty. There were few sieges, protracted battles, or wars of conquest. Quite often an attacking side believing that nothing was worth the loss of its own people, would break off fighting as soon as it had suffered casualties. Among various plains tribes in North America, counting coup, touching a live enemy and getting away unharmed, was the main goal of a warrior and the highlight of war, even more honorable an achievement to some than slaying an enemy.

Here and there on both continents, Indians indulged in cannibalism, although the reasons for its practice differed considerably among various tribes. Some groups in the Caribbean and South America, like the Brazilian Tupinambás, prized human flesh as a food and made war to obtain victims (the word itself comes from Carib Indians, among the first the Europeans observed practicing the custom). On the Northwest Pacific Coast, however, most Indians regarded cannibalism as a fearful and repellent act, to be indulged in only in rituals and while under the influence of supernatural powers. Elsewhere, some Indians ate the heart and other portions of enemies in the belief that they would thus acquire the courage or other qualities of the victim.

Many Indians could also be characterized in common by a number of implements and material objects that were associated with almost all of their cultures. Their weapons throughout the hemisphere included spears, spear throwers, and bows and arrows. Knives, scrapers, cordage, netting, and baskets were also in use almost everywhere. Some items, employed widely but not by everyone, included fishhooks, digging sticks, pottery, and canoes. Indians who became farmers developed corn, squash, and many varieties of beans, and these crops were cultivated in many different parts of the New World. In addition, Indians developed numerous other agricultural articles unknown to Europeans; grown in various regions, they included white and sweet potatoes, tobacco, peanuts, peppers, vanilla, tomatoes, pumpkins, cacao, avocados, and pineapples.

Indians are sometimes characterized, also, by what they did not possess, but even here there are many misconceptions. Most tribes made no effective use of metal. But metallurgy did exist among the higher Indian civilizations of Middle and South America; the Mexicans, Central American Indians, and Incas, among others, smelted gold and silver; and in various places groups made useful and decorative objects of beaten copper. No Indian group ever made practical use of the wheel; but some peoples were familiar with it, for in Middle America it was used on toys. The question of the domestication of animals also needs explanation. Although horses had existed in the New World for more than 60 million years, they became extinct in the Western Hemisphere after the Ice Age ended. Indians thus had neither horses nor cattle to domesticate until white men brought them over from Europe. Nevertheless, some Indians used domesticated dogs to drag or carry their burdens. People in Middle America and the Andes domesticated ducks, and the Andeans kept guinea pigs about their homes and employed the partly domesticated llama, alpaca, and vicuña for wool, food, and to carry loads. Turkeys were also domesticated for their feathers and for food in parts of the Southwest of the present-day United States and in Middle America, and honey and wax were harvested from bees by some Indian beekeepers.

Modern Pan-Indian movements in Latin America and organizations working toward unity among present-day United States and Canadian Indians have a tendency to list other qualities and characteristics as common attributes of "Indianness." Many of the traits cited, however, were typical only among some Indian groups. Democratic political institutions, an individual's freedom of choice, and the right to have a say in one's own affairs—frequently referred to as peculiarly "Indian"—were, indeed, a part of the pattern of life among some native peoples. But in many Indian societies authoritarianism prevailed, and the world perhaps never experienced a more totalitarian state than that of the Incas of Peru. Nevertheless, in the case of the United States particularly, there is some justification in citing these traits, for colonial records show that many of the Indian peoples of the Atlantic seaboard taught the European settlers much with regard to freedom, the dignity of the individual, democracy, representative government, and the right to participate in the settling of one's affairs.

The Pan-Indianism of today, particularly in the United States, has resulted from numerous forces, including relocation, education, government programs, social gatherings, and political strivings, that bring Indians of different tribes and backgrounds into contact with each other, and from the modern means of transportation which have encouraged and eased mobility. Youths from different tribes meet at schools and eventually marry; intertribal powwows, dances, and other social events attract participants from tribes in all parts of the country, and even from Canada and Latin America; religious convocations, nationalistic movements, and conferences on Indian economic and political problems bring together leaders from many tribes; and relocated Indians in urban areas find companionship and comfort at Indian centers in the cities. These associations have led gradually to an increasing feeling of unity among many Indians and an emphasis on recognition that they are Indians as well as members of particular tribes. Pan-Indianism has been felt strongly in parts of Oklahoma, where many tribes dwell, but it has grown also among Indians elsewhere. It is reflected at powwows where Indians of different tribes now dance the same dances and wear somewhat identical dance costumes; by the adoption by many Indians of such items as the Plains tribes' eagle-feather headdress as a symbolic article of garb for all Indians; by joint political action of many tribes in behalf of one or a few of them; and by efforts of relocated Indians, students, and others away from reservations to retain Indian identification in the midst of white society by finding new pride, dignity, and self-assuredness in their "Indianness." The forces of the world around the Indian have also had an effect: the ideals of the United Nations; the independence of countries that were formerly colonies in Africa and Asia; and the "war" on poverty and the Negroes' civil rights struggle in the United States have all tended to encourage the emergence of a unifying spirit among the Indians that transcends tribal affiliations or traditions.

4

The White Man's
Debt to Indians

FEW PERSONS TODAY RECOGNIZE, OR ARE APPRECIATIVE OF,
the vast contributions made to contemporary life by the
American Indians. All aspects of Indian existence—agriculture, government, religion, trade, mythology, economics,
and arts and crafts—influenced white men at one time or
another and helped to shape the destiny of each of the countries of the Western Hemisphere.

From the moment of Columbus's landfall in the Ba-
hamas, the Indian made possible the European's first precarious footholds in every part of the Americas. He supplied
the newcomer with Indian foods that were new to him,
taught him to plant, fish, and hunt with Indian methods,
guided him through the wilderness over Indian trails and
in Indian-style watercraft, and introduced him to Indian
implements, utensils, tools, clothing, and ways of life that
made existence easier and more secure. By friendly trade
he supplied the white man with furs and other goods that
helped revolutionize styles and materials in the Old World;
and his art forms, crafts, and cultural objects heavily influenced certain aspects of European artistic and intellectual
life. Indian gold and other treasures built up the courts,
armies, and navies of European rulers and nations, and
financed intrigues, rivalries, and wars among imperial powers
for generations. Finally, Indian social and political concepts
and structures profoundly influenced settlers and Old World
philosophers alike and played a significant role in the evolution of many modern institutions of government and daily
life.

Among the world's total food supply today, almost half
the crops grown were first domesticated by American Indians

and became known to white men only after 1492. Two of
those crops, corn and potatoes, are now—with rice and
wheat—the most important staples in the world. Not far
behind them in present-day importance are two other In-
dian-developed crops—manioc, which has become a staple in
parts of Africa, and the American sweet potato. In addition,
Indians introduced to the white man more than eighty other
domesticated plants, including peanuts, squashes, peppers,
tomatoes, pumpkins, pineapples, avocados, cacao (for choco-
late), chicle (for chewing gum), many kinds of beans, and
other vegetables and fruits that are common to most people
today. All cotton grown in the United States, as well as the
long-fiber cotton raised in Egypt and in other parts of
Africa, is also derived from species cultivated by the American Indians; tobacco—first seen in use by Columbus in the
form of cigars in Cuba—came from the Indians; and at least
fifty-nine drugs, including coca (for cocaine and novocaine),
curare (a muscle relaxant), cinchona bark (the source of
quinine), cascara sagrada (a laxative), datura (a pain-
reliever), and ephedra (a nasal remedy), were bequeathed to
modern medicine by the Indians.

In addition, people today make use of numerous Indian
devices, including canoes, snowshoes, moccasins, hammocks,
kayaks, smoking pipes, ponchos, rubber syringes, dog sleds,
toboggans, and parkas. Indian designs have affected many
manufactured goods, from beach backrests to jewelry, and
both the rubber ball and the game of lacrosse were adopted
from Indians. Thousands of names for cities, states, lakes,
mountains, rivers, and other geographical sites and features
in the Western Hemisphere are Indian, and European languages contain many words, like the French *apache*, that
derive from American native tongues. Indian contributions
to the English language include wigwam, succotash, tobacco,
papoose, chipmunk, squash, skunk, toboggan, opossum, tomahawk, moose, mackinaw, hickory, pecan, raccoon, cougar,
woodchuck, hominy, and hundreds of other words. Many
other common expressions came from translations of Indian
ideas, including war paint, Indian file, bury the hatchet,
paleface, warpath, big chief, Indian summer, and happy
hunting ground.

Literature, music, art, the drama and dance, motion pictures, and television programs have all reflected the influence
of Indians, although their interpretations of Indian culture
and history have often been far from accurate, and they have

only rarely as yet made use of the vast resources of Indian cultures. Indian mythology and folklore—the unwritten oral literature of the different tribes—provide a rich and diverse heritage that is still largely ignored by most non-Indians. Rooted deeply in antiquity, folktales and myths permeated all of Indian life, being intertwined with religious, social and political systems, habits and beliefs of the peoples, and daily codes of conduct. The folk tales explained the nature of the universe and its various inhabitants, laid down rules of behavior, described migrations and early history, related traditions concerning features of nature and geographical terrain, and told of Creation and of the time before humans. These thousands of tales and myths of the Indians of both continents, a resource as rich as the mythology of ancient Greece and Rome, were expressed, moreover, in Indian ceremonial dances, sacred rituals, songs, and arts and crafts. To some extent, they have had an impact on non-Indians. But such works as Longfellow's *Hiawatha* and Charles Cadman's "From the Land of Sky Blue Waters" only suggest the vast treasure of Indian themes awaiting the use of discoverers in each field of creative expression.

In other ways, also, Indians have influenced modern life. Many woodcraft skills were derived from Indians, and the international Boy and Girl Scout movements were inspired, in great part, by the lessons of Indian life. More recently, in a world faced by exploding populations, air and water pollution, overcrowding, and the disappearance of green space, open land, and wilderness, conservationists are recalling the Indians. "It is ironical that today the conservation movement finds itself turning back to ancient Indian land ideas, to the Indian understanding that we are not outside of nature, but of it," wrote Secretary of the Interior Stewart L. Udall in his book, *The Quiet Crisis*, in 1963. "From this wisdom we can learn how to conserve the best parts of our continent. In recent decades we have slowly come back to some of the truths that the Indians knew from the beginning: that unborn generations have a claim on the land equal to our own; that men need to learn from nature, to keep an ear to the earth, and to replenish their spirits in frequent contacts with animals and wild land. And most important of all, we are recovering a sense of reverence for the land." In other words, instead of "conquering" nature, white men are finding value in the Indian's lesson of learning to live in harmony with nature.

In the field of medicine, Indian shamans in early days were frequently called upon to minister to pioneer whites who were without the benefit of nearby white physicians. Several Indian curers became celebrated in New England and the Midwest, and Indian herbs and drugs were adopted whole-sale by grateful whites, some of whom exploited the popular reliance on Indian medicines by concocting and peddling worthless nostrums under such labels as "Seneca Oil" and "Kickapoo Juice." In recent times, with the emergence of psychiatry and psychosomatic medicine, attention has been paid to the practices of Indian curers that were designed to restore a patient's health by ministering to his mental state and bringing him back into harmony with his universe. The curing ceremonies of such peoples as the Navahos are being studied anew, and, in general, a greater respect than formerly is being accorded the roles and methods of some of the Indian shamans.

In other ways, too, aspects of Indian culture, long ignored by non-Indians, are receiving new awareness: child psychologists are studying Indians' methods of raising, educating, and disciplining youths; administrators of government poverty and self-help programs are drawing lessons from ancient methods of Indian group-directed activities; and cooperatives follow patterns of organization developed long ago by Indians.

The political traits and institutions of some Indians, it has already been mentioned, also had an impact on whites. The League of the Iroquois was particularly influential on the thinking of some of the leaders of the American Colonies. Benjamin Franklin had great respect for the organization of the League and, when making his proposals for a union of the Colonies at Albany in 1754, wrote: "It would be a strange thing if Six Nations of ignorant savages should be capable of forming a scheme for such an union, and be able to execute it in such a manner as that it has subsisted ages and appears indissoluble; and yet that a like union should be impracticable for ten or a dozen English colonies, to whom it is more necessary and must be more advantageous, and who cannot be supposed to want an equal understanding of their interests." In time, the structure of the League had an indirect influence not only on the union of the Colonies, but on the government of the United States as it was constituted in 1789. In such forms as the methods by which congressional Senate and House conferees work out bills in compromise sessions, for instance, one may recognize similarities to the ways in which the Iroquois League functioned.

Finally, white men saw—although they often misinterpreted—Indian ways of life that seemed utopian. Descriptions of Indians who lived in a Golden Age of virtue and innocence began with the writings of Peter Martyr in the sixteenth century. ". . . If we shall not be ashamed to confess the truth," he wrote, "they [the Indians] seem to live in that golden world of which old writers speak so much: wherein men lived simply and innocently without enforcement of laws, without quarrelings, judges and libels, content only to satisfy nature, without further vexation for knowledge of things to come." Such passages were widely circulated, and by the eighteenth century their impact had reached its height, affecting not only the courts of Europe which found delight in masques and balls whose participants played at being happy, innocent American Indians, but more serious philosophers. The latter, from Montaigne to Rousseau, compared what they understood to be the lot of free Indians with the state of men in Europe who were living in want under various forms of tyranny. Everywhere, Rousseau wrote, with his eye on the Indians as white men first discovered them, "man is born free, and everywhere he is in chains." The powder keg the philosophers ignited erupted eventually into revolutions that changed the world.

The deductions of the philosophers about the Indians were not entirely wrong. Belief in the freedom and dignity of the individual was deeply ingrained in many Indian societies. In some tribes it was observed to such an extent that at any time—even when his people were fighting for their lives— a man could go his own way and do whatever seemed right to him. Among many tribes, also, councils decided on courses of action by unanimous, rather than majority, agreement; the feelings and opinions of each person were considered too important to override. Such influences, reflecting the equality of individuals and respect for their rights, made their mark on the European philosophers. In the New World, they undoubtedly played a strong role in helping to give the colonists new sets of values that contributed to turning them from Europeans into freedom-loving Americans.

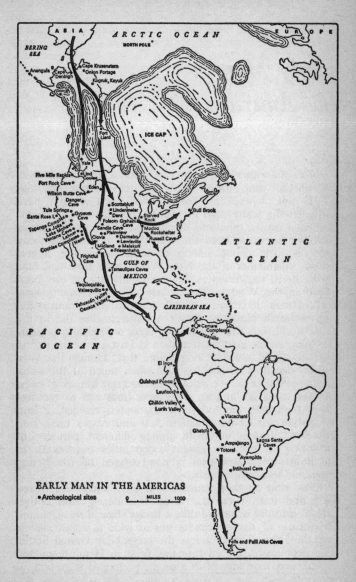

EARLY MAN IN THE AMERICAS
• Archeological sites   0   MILES   1000

5

Early Man in
the Americas

THE QUESTIONS OF WHO THE AMERICAN INDIANS ARE, whether they evolved in the Western Hemisphere, and, if not, where they came from (and when), have intrigued the white man ever since the time of Columbus. As stated earlier, questions of race and of precise places and times of departure from the Old World persist, but today there is little doubt among scientists where the earliest known inhabitants of the New World came from and how they entered the Americas. Since no remains have ever been found in the Western Hemisphere of a pre-*Homo sapiens* type of man, it is now generally accepted that humans did not evolve in North or South America as they did in the Old World, but that the first of them crossed into present-day Alaska from northeastern Asia at least 12,000 to 15,000 years ago, and possibly long before that. During the Wisconsin glaciation of the Ice Age, when much of the water of the oceans became congealed in the great icepack glaciers, the sea levels fell and at times were from 250 to 300 feet lower than they are today. As the waters receded, a land bridge connecting northeastern Asia and Alaska came into existence, varying in width during different periods but extending on occasion almost 1,000 miles from north to south across an area that is now covered by the Bering Strait and its adjoining seas.

From time to time, animals and men could have passed back and forth with ease across this Bering land bridge, which in reality was more than a bridge since at its maximum its expanse of treeless tundra was as wide as approximately one third the distance across the present-day United States. The people who moved into the Western Hemisphere, and stayed, may have arrived in a single, protracted migration, in two or more migrations at widely separated times, or in many different groups at different periods over a long span of time. They were small hunting groups, simply following herds of game animals, and unaware that they had passed from one large land mass to another. It is still not possible to date the arrival of the very first people. Some experts have speculated that the earliest migrants could have reached North America during the Sangamon Interglacial period before the Wisconsin glaciation. That would have been 75,000 years ago! But most scientists, while not ruling out the possibility of such an early entry into the Western Hemisphere, are more conservative and provide estimates that range from 12,000 to 35,000 years ago or slightly earlier.

What happened after man first reached Alaska is related to the question of when he arrived there, and is the subject of continuing studies of the Bering land bridge and the Ice Age itself. One theory suggests that an early migration, perhaps the first, occurred prior to 25,000 years ago, peopling the land bridge and ice-free parts of Alaska. From the latter region, according to this theory, hunting groups moved slowly along the northern coast of Alaska or up the Yukon and other river valleys, carrying with them stone age implements that had derived from those in use that early on the plains of Eurasia. The great ice sheet, spreading westward from the Hudson Bay area, would have stopped the nomadic peoples in the neighborhood of the Mackenzie River Valley, but there, as well as at places farther west, they and the game animals they were following would have been able to turn south and from time to time find ice-free valleys, which acted like avenues, drawing them on. Eventually, the different groups moved down the eastern side, or perhaps both sides, of the Continental Divide, hunting game along the cordillera into Central and South America and wandering eastward after animals across the plains and through the forests and lowlands of both continents. These people, it is suggested, gradually developed the unique spear points of the early big game hunters of the Western Hemisphere. Meanwhile, behind them, according to the same theory, glacial action sealed the routes they had followed south from Alaska and isolated them for thousands of years from the people who had remained in that northern region. During that time, the Bering land bridge was submerged and then reappeared. When the land was again above water, new peoples bringing more advanced material traits from Asia may have crossed into Alaska. By about 15,000 to 12,000 years ago, passage

was again opened between Alaska and more southern areas
of the continent, and migrations south (or from north to
south) may have occurred again in northwestern North
America. Other theories suggest a variety of different occurrences: that the big-game hunting ancestors of the American
Indians crossed the interior of the Bering land bridge about
15,000 years ago (although there may have been earlier
crossings by previous migrants) and the maritime-oriented
ancestors of the Eskimos and Aleuts occupied the southern
coast of the land bridge at approximately the same or a later
period; that there were two major periods of human migration, the first one witnessing the crossing by the ancestors
of most American Indians more than 25,000 years ago and
the second the arrival of the ancestors of the Eskimos and
Aleuts about 10,000 to 11,000 years ago; and, finally, that
there were a number of separate migrations by different
groups over a long span of time. Whenever the first peoples
came, however, all overland travel from Asia to America
would have ended by 10,000 years ago when the land bridge
disappeared for the last time.

The inhabiting of the New World was a long and gradual
process, requiring, according to some authorities, perhaps
as much as 25,000 years for man to spread from Alaska to
Cape Horn at the southern tip of South America. During
much of that time different groups may have been making
their way south from Alaska. Although population would
have been sparse, and much distance would have separated
many of the nomadic bands, some of the newcomers no
doubt collided here and there with earlier arrivals, sometimes
combining with them and sometimes forcing them into less
desirable or accessible parts of the country. It is noteworthy,
for example, that some linguistic scholars believe that the
oldest extant Indian languages in the hemisphere are those
of the Nambicuaras and others in relatively inaccessible areas
of central South America.

In succeeding millennia, more arrivals from Asia may have
reached different parts of the Western Hemisphere by other
routes. Long after the Ice Age ended, when men had learned
to make open-water crossings in boats, they may have crossed
to Alaska by way of St. Lawrence Island. About 3000 B.C.,
according to recent discoveries, transpacific travelers, perhaps blown or carried eastward involuntarily, seem to have
arrived on the coast of Ecuador with a style of pottery prevalent at that time in parts of Japan and maybe, also, with
domesticated cotton. Thereafter, other contacts with Asia

may have occurred. Chinese junks may have been blown eastward, as they were in historic times. Certainly, by at least 1500 B.C., Asians were capable of making long sea trips. Much later, perhaps as late as A.D. 500–1000, when the islands of Polynesia were first populated, other long-distance oceanic voyages may have been made in one or both directions between America and the Pacific islands. Although no proof exists of such contacts, various authorities have cited evidence that suggests their occurrence, and Norwegian anthropologist Thor Heyerdahl sailed his raft *Kon-Tiki* successfully across the Pacific from South America to show that Indians, at least, could have reached the islands of Polynesia.

Despite the existence of many seriously considered theories in the past, no convincing evidence has ever been produced to prove that there were transoceanic migrations or contacts across the Atlantic between the Old World and the New prior to the time of the Vikings. Even less acceptable to scientists today are a host of once-popular ideas concerning the precise place of origin of the Indians. Before the development of modern dating methods that established beyond doubt the great antiquity of early man in America, it was believed that the Indians were offshoots of known civilizations of the Old World. Some scholars argued that they had come from Egypt, others that they had broken away from the Chinese, and still others that they were descendants of Phoenician or Greek seamen. Viscount Kingsborough, a nineteenth-century Irish nobleman, spent many years and a fortune trying to prove that the Mayas of Middle America had descended from members of one of the Lost Tribes of Israel. Another belief, more legend than theory, held that various light-skinned tribes possessed the blood of Welshmen who had come to America in the remote past with a Welsh prince named Madog. Even as a legend, however, it died hard; although Lewis and Clark and others quashed the story, many persons as late as the mid-nineteenth century believed that the Mandan Indians of the upper Missouri River were Madog's Welsh descendants, and the tale continues to be examined in serious books that are yet being written.

Still other investigators insisted from time to time that the Indians had come to the Western Hemisphere via the supposed Lost Continents of Atlantis in the Atlantic Ocean or Mu in the Pacific, making their way safely across from the Old World before the continents sank beneath the oceans. These, and other fanciful ideas, have all been proven unsound by modern scientists who have established that there were no lost continents and that man was present in the Western Hemisphere at least 10,000 years ago, long before the rise of Egypt, China, or other civilizations of the Old World. Members of the Church of Jesus Christ of Latter-Day Saints, or Mormons, nevertheless, maintain a different belief; the Book of Mormon relates that Indians are descended from Lamanites, a degenerate element of the Jews who migrated to the New World prior to the Christian era.

Large gaps, at the same time, still exist in present-day knowledge of the continuity of man's occupation of the Americas, and it is not yet agreed that any modern-day Indians are directly descended from the earliest arrivals in the New World. But in recent years significant archeological discoveries and new dating techniques have begun to fill in important gaps and have tended to illuminate the existence of various distinct cultures and the chronologies of their developmental stages, commencing with the first peoples known so far to have been in the Western Hemisphere and continuing, hazily at least, to historic times.

For years scientists relied generally on geology and dendrochronology (counting tree rings) for help in dating the age of archeological remains. Since World War II, a more accurate tool, the technique of radiocarbon dating developed by Willard F. Libby, has helped to establish more precisely the age of plant and animal remains, including such things as bits of charcoal from ancient fires, as well as bone, shell, wood and textile fragments. The method cannot be applied to all finds, and the age of many discoveries is still in doubt. But where it has been employed successfully, it has often established dates that have pushed back dramatically the time of man's known presence in the Americas.

Although some archeologists, using this new technique, as well as a more recent one—dating by determining the hydration of obsidian finds—have worked out tentative sequences for cultures of early man in individual areas of the New World, few have attempted to correlate the sequences of the different areas and propose a history of the cultural progression for the hemisphere as a whole. One interesting framework, advanced recently by archeologist Alex D. Krieger, suggests a series of stages of development through which early man advanced, although, as Krieger makes clear, certain stages existed at different times—beginning later or lasting longer—in various areas of the hemisphere, so that on both continents the timing of the development from stage to stage was uneven in different regions, and the stages themselves were marked by numerous local and regional variations.

Krieger's earliest stage, which he terms a Pre-Projectile Point Stage, reflects the archeological discoveries of sites suggesting not only the greatest age, but the presence of people who could not yet thin and flatten materials into knives and projectile points. The people of this first stage are characterized by their possession of bone implements and large, crudely made stone tools and implements. In many areas, according to Krieger, this stage, called by some a Paleolithic or Lower Lithic Stage, existed more than 20,000 years ago, but it may have begun later or persisted for a longer period of time in some areas than in others.

To most persons, the discoveries that Krieger groups in this earliest stage of man's occupation of the New World are perhaps the most intriguing because they suggest the greatest antiquity. But it is well to remember, also, that all of these finds are still in the realm of controversy, none of them as yet being accepted by all archeologists, and some still being debated seriously as to age and other problems. In the group are finds of charred vegetal remains at Lewisville, Texas, which may have been left by men more than 37,000–38,000 years ago; stone and bone artifacts at Tule Springs, Nevada, possibly 28,000 to 32,000 years old; artifacts and carvings on bones of extinct animals found near Valsequillo Reservoir, central Mexico, that have been dated tentatively by their discoverer as about 30,000 years old; remains of extinct bison, showing evidence of having been killed by men more than 30,000 years ago near American Falls on the Snake River in southern Idaho; mammoth bones apparently burned by men on Santa Rosa Island, California, perhaps as long ago as 29,500 years; and flint artifacts associated with remains of extinct animals, dated from the period of the Wisconsin glaciation, at Friesenhahn Cave, central Texas. In addition, Krieger places a number of other discoveries of suspected similar antiquity in this Pre-Projectile Point Stage, the sites of such finds stretching from Anaktuvuk Pass in the Brooks Range of northern Alaska to the southern part of South America. Although some of these sites have been dated at considerably later times than others, an accepted age of 25,000 years or more for any of the sites in the present-day United States or farther south would tend to support the premise that man had indeed entered Alaska from Asia at a time close to 40,000 to 50,000 years ago.

Krieger terms his second stage of development the Paleo-Indian Stage, during which man, having now learned to make relatively thin and flat artifacts, fashioned stone knives and projectile points for his spears and darts. The projectile points were usually lanceolate or leaf-shaped and, because so many of the types were fluted, some persons have called the stage, or a portion of it, the Fluted Point Stage, although still others use the term Upper Lithic or Paleo-American. Of whatever shape or type the points were, however, Krieger notes that they were the first to appear in any area, thus marking the end in that area of a Pre-Projectile Point Stage. His Paleo-Indian Stage, which may have occurred in various places between about 10,000 and 20,000 years ago, existing at different times in different areas, was characterized also by better work in percussion chipping of stone artifacts and by the absence, save in rare instances, of food-grinding implements, a characteristic of his next stage, in which the gathering of wild plant foods became important.

By noting many of the different regional cultures that existed during his Paleo-Indian Stage, Krieger also suggests clarity in correlating some of the cultural sequences in different areas on the two continents. The first group of sites in this overall stage are those of what has been called the Llano Culture, which extended generally from eastern New Mexico and the Great Plains to the Midwest, the Great Lakes, and the Northeast and Southeast, and was characterized by the use of Sandia-type and Clovis-type points, some of which have been found in association with the remains of mammoths and other extinct animals. Among the oldest of the Llano Culture finds may be some long, unfluted Sandia spear points, slightly incut on one edge at the bottom, named for Sandia Cave, New Mexico, where Frank C. Hibben discovered them, together with bones of camels, mastodons, and prehistoric horses, in 1936. Although the radiocarbon dating technique has not been able to establish their age, it is believed as the result of other efforts to date them that they may have been fashioned by men as long ago as 20,000 years. Since Hibben's initial discovery, other points of the same type and perhaps the same age have been found elsewhere in the Southwest and in such widely separated areas as Alberta and the eastern seaboard.

The somewhat similar and probably less ancient Clovis-type grooved, or fluted, points of the Llano Culture were found originally near Dent, Colorado. Discoveries of points

like them have been made since then across most of the
present-day United States, from California, Oregon, and
southern Arizona to the East, as well as in parts of Mexico
and on the central Canadian plains. Principal sites of these
finds include Naco and the Lehner Ranch, Arizona; Blackwater Draw, New Mexico; and numerous locations in the
Midwest and East, where, because of the abundance of the
finds of fluted points, some persons believe the type was
invented. Dates of Clovis-type points have ranged from 7,000
to 12,000 years in age, but they seem to have been in widespread use by men who hunted mostly mammoth about
11,000–12,000 years ago.

The oldest human skeletal remains yet discovered in the
hemisphere, believed to be those of a thirty-year-old woman,
were found in 1953 near Midland, Texas, in a deposit of
sand that also included Llano Culture chipped-stone tools
and the remains of extinct horses, bison, and antelope. The
human bones were originally estimated to be 8,000 to
10,000 years old, but recent tests of the sand using a new
dating technique, the so-called Rosholt method, a refinement of a "uranium clock" process for dating rocks, have
hinted at a much older age.

A second culture falling within Krieger's Paleo-Indian
Stage is the Lindenmeier Culture, named for a discovery
site at Lindenmeier, Colorado, and characterized by Folsom-
type fluted points. Used by men who principally hunted the
huge, extinct bison rather than the mammoth, they were
smaller than the Sandia and Clovis points and came into
use at a later time, generally about 10,000–11,000 years ago.
The discovery of the first Folsom point, occurring in 1927
near Folsom, New Mexico, was a spectacular one. The point
was found embedded between two ribs of a Pleistocene bison,
and was the first discovery to provide proof that man had
been present in the Western Hemisphere when Ice Age
animals had still been alive. Folsom-type fluted points have
since been found abundantly in many different areas of the
United States, as well as in part of Canada and Mexico,
and in 1965 what appeared to be a more than transient occupation site of Folsom Culture hunters was discovered near
Albuquerque, New Mexico. Consisting of roughly circular
depressions over which shelters of branches and skins may
have been built, the site, whose "lodges" housed perhaps
some twenty families—identified by leavings of more than
8,000 Folsom-type spears points and other relics—may prove
to be the oldest village location yet found in the hemisphere.

Krieger's Paleo-Indian Stage also enfolds the Old Cordilleran Culture, which spread down the Pacific Northwest along the cordillera from Alaska to the Great Basin and Southwest—and perhaps beyond, into South America. It was characterized by the Cascade point, shaped like a long, narrow leaf pointed at both ends, and its principal sites in North America, ranging in age from about 9,500 to 12,000–13,000 years, include the Flint Creek and Ford Liard complexes in the Yukon; Yale on the Fraser River in British Columbia; Five Mile Rapids on the Oregon side of the Columbia River; and Fort Rock Cave, Oregon. At the latter site were found almost one hundred pairs of sandals made of shredded sagebrush and dated at more than 9,000 years of age.

Many other sites on both continents may also be classified in Krieger's Paleo-Indian Stage, although the periods of their existence differ from region to region. Among important finds are those of Wilson Butte Cave in south-central Idaho, occupied apparently as long ago as approximately 15,000 years; Danger Cave, Utah, and the Lake Mohave complex in California, both some 9,500 to 12,000 years old; various sites in the eastern part of the United States, including Bull Brook, Massachusetts, dated at about 10,000 years of age; the Lerma complex in northern Mexico, the stone points and mammoth remains at the Santa Isabel Iztapán site in central Mexico, and the Lagunas complex in Venezuela, the latter at least 11,000 years old; and the artifacts and remains of humans and extinct fauna at the Lagoa Santa caves in Brazil, dated at approximately 10,000 years of age; the projectile points, scrapers, and other artifacts found in Peru's Lauricocha caves and Ichuna Rock Shelter, at El Inga in the Ecuadorean highlands, in the Chillón Valley in Peru, in the Intihuasi Cave and at the Ayampitín site in Argentina, and at Ghatchi and Zuniquena in Chile, most of them perhaps 8,000 years old, or older. The projectile points discovered at some of the South American sites were large, long, and flat, and suggest to some persons a relationship to the Cascade point of the Old Cordilleran Culture of North America. Many of the South American sites, also, have revealed in lower layers the relics of an earlier, Pre-Projectile Point Stage. Chopping tools found in northwestern Venezuela, in Peru's Chillón Valley, at Ampajango, preceding the Ayampitín stage in Argentina, and at other places suggest an age of as much as 14,000 years.

Krieger's third stage, which he terms the Protoarchaic

Stage, and which approximates what others have called the Early Archaic Stage, is characterized in his classification system by the appearance for the first time of food-grinding implements. The gathering of wild plant foods, supplementing hunting, had undoubtedly existed earlier, but had not been too important in the economy. Now, with the Ice Age ending and the glaciers retreating, the Pleistocene big animals began to disappear, and food gathering became more important to replace the dwindling meat supply. Krieger notes that while the use of fluted points disappeared in North America about 10,000 years ago, milling stones and manos appeared at about the same time.

Nevertheless, some species of Pleistocene mammals, such as big bison on the plains, prehistoric horses, antelopes, and ground sloths in several areas, and perhaps mastodons in the eastern United States, lingered on and were trapped and hunted for a while. In most places new types of unfluted, lanceolate points, some with stems or corner notches, came into use. Parallel flaking was done by pressure; a greater variety of stone and bone artifacts, including drills, awls, shaft smoothers, and eyed needles, was made; caves and rock shelters were occupied more intensively; and the dead were often buried in graves.

As in the previous stage, the Protoarchaic embraced several regional cultures. Among them was the Plano Culture, which extended across southern Idaho, the Great Plains, the United States, and the Great Lakes area (where it is sometimes termed the Aqua-Plano Culture). Principal sites, ranging from approximately 8,000 to 10,500 years in age, and marked by food-grinding implements as well as a number of different types of stone points, include: the Cody complex at Eden, Wyoming; sites at Scottsbluff, Nebraska, and Plainview, Texas; the Modoc Rock Shelter, Illinois; and Russell Cave, Alabama. Farther west, a Desert Culture in the Great Basin and the Southwest (possibly succeeding the Old Cordilleran Culture and including the plateau and other peripheral areas) also falls in this stage, its principal sites including Gypsum Cave, Nevada, where various artifacts, including painted shafts of spear throwers known as *atlatls*, were found among 9,000-year-old ground sloth remains; Ventana Cave, Arizona, where artifacts and late Pleistocene animal remains seem to be almost 12,000 years old and place the site more properly perhaps in the preceding Paleo-Indian stage; Frightful Cave in northern Mexico; and complexes of the Cochise culture, almost strictly a wild-plant-food-gathering culture in southeastern Arizona, with long sequences that began approximately 9,350 years ago.

Again, since the Protoarchaic was a stage in man's development rather than a particular time in prehistory, it occurred at different times in different regions, beginning later in some areas and enduring longer in others. On both continents, Krieger includes numerous other finds, 5,000 to 9,000 years old, in his Protoarchaic Stage. Among the more important are the Topanga complex and La Jolla complex sites in California, belonging to what has been called a California Early Milling Stone Culture; the Denbigh Flint complex and Kayuk complex sites in Alaska; Lind Coulee and Cougar Mountain Cave in eastern Washington; the Chalco complex in central Mexico; levels II and III of the Lauricocha caves in Peru; and the Palli Aike and Fell's caves in southern Chile, the former about 9,000 years old.

In summation, it may be said that, however one chooses to organize the sequences of early man's cultures in the New World, the many archeological finds already made, and still being made, are beginning to provide a panorama of development that starts with nomadic hunters moving through parts of the hemisphere in pursuit of Pleistocene animals more than 10,000 years ago. Gradually, after about 8500 B.C., the mammoths, mastodons, and other Ice Age mammals became extinct, most of them disappearing apparently prior to 7500 B.C. in Middle America, perhaps about 6500 B.C. in the western part of the United States, and still later in the north. As the big animals vanished, and big game hunting came to a close, the period of early man ended, and an Archaic Stage began. It was characterized by the pecking, and then the grinding and polishing of well-shaped stone artifacts, and by men turning increasingly to the more intensive use of deer, rabbits, birds, small game, fish, shellfish, and wild plant foods. For the first time, during this stage also, certain other developments appeared: pottery was made by some peoples, beginning in Ecuador and Colombia, apparently about 5,000 years ago; lumps of copper in the region of the westernmost Great Lakes were hammered into spear points, tools, and decorative objects by people of what is called the Old Copper Culture, which reached a height from about 4,000 to 3,000 years ago; and—commencing more than 7,000 years ago—incipient agriculture, stemming from increased reliance on vegetal foodstuffs, began.

6

Agriculture and the Rise of Population

THE BEGINNINGS OF AGRICULTURE IN THE NEW WORLD are still the object of intensive archeological study. For some time, various authorities have believed that Indians at several different places, independently of each other and at different times, may have learned to domesticate some of the same wild plants. At the same time, the cultivation of certain agricultural products possibly began in individual regions from which they eventually spread Pumpkin domestication, for instance, appears to have gotten its start in northeastern Mexico, and the cultivation of certain squashes may have begun in the highlands of central and southern Mexico and Guatemala—or, as some botanists believe, in the lowlands of Central America. Indian maize, or corn, was first cultivated from wild corn in central Mexico, while various root crops, like manioc and the sweet potato, were undoubtedly domesticated originally in the Caribbean area or in parts of South America.

In 1948 tiny cobs of domesticated corn, between 4,000 and 5,000 years old, were found by archeologists both at Bat Cave in New Mexico and at La Perra Cave in Tamaulipas in northeastern Mexico. Since then, archeological work directed by Richard MacNeish in two regions of Mexico has thrown important new light on the entire subject of the start of New World agriculture. In the Cañon del Infiernillo in Tamaulipas, discoveries by MacNeish revealed an initial stage of experimentation with plant cultivation (bottle gourds, pumpkin, peppers, and a sort of runner bean) 9,500 to 7,500 years ago. The innovators, MacNeish pointed out, were still essentially gatherers of wild plant foods, who complemented their food supply by hunting

47

and trapping. Cultivation increased, however, and common beans were being grown in the area some 5,000 to 6,000 years ago; a pod-pop type of corn about 4,500 years ago; cotton and squash soon afterward; and about 3,000 years ago agriculture, with fully developed corn, was established in the region as the principal source of food.

Farther south, in caves and rock shelters about Tehuacán in the arid highlands of the central Mexican state of Puebla, a team of experts in many sciences, working with MacNeish, laid bare a sequence of cultural development of the inhabitants in that area, with few interruptions, from approximately 12,000 years ago until A.D. 1500, or historic times. The work was unprecedented and revealed, among many other things, the origination and development of agriculture in that region. Until about 9,000 years ago, the studies showed, the sparse population in the neighborhood lived predominantly by trapping and hunting small animals, birds, and turtles, by killing occasionally the remaining species of Pleistocene antelopes and horses, and by gathering wild plant foods. Between about 9,000 and 7,000 years ago, the people shifted considerably more to the collecting of wild plants, and during that period began the domestication of certain products, including squashes and avocados. By about 6,000–7,000 years ago a new phase of development was well underway. Although only about 10 per cent of the people's food came from cultivated products, many different plants, including corn, the bottle gourd, squash, amaranth, certain beans, and peppers, had already been domesticated, and by about 5,400 years ago some 30 per cent of the people's food came from agriculture. At the same time, the first fixed settlements (small pit-house villages) appeared, and dogs were domesticated. Reliance on the products of agriculture, especially more productive hybridized types of corn, increased steadily thereafter; pottery appeared about 4,300 years ago; population expanded, especially after 2,500 years ago; and cultures became more sophisticated and complex. Since those studies of the MacNeish group, a somewhat similar sequence of development, beginning almost 10,000 years ago, was also revealed by other archeologists working in central Mexico's Oaxaca Valley.

Thus, it may be summarized that discoveries made so far reveal domesticated pumpkins and peppers 9,500 to 7,500 years old (perhaps the oldest agricultural remains yet found in the Americas) in northeastern Mexico, and domesticated squash and corn 7,000 years old in central Mexico. It cannot yet be said that they were the first areas in which these products were grown, or that the inhabitants of those areas were the only peoples cultivating the products at those early dates. Further finds may disclose still earlier dates elsewhere for these and other products, and ultimately it may be possible to pinpoint with some degree of accuracy the dates and places of the first domestication of various plants.

As yet, no evidence has been found of corn prior to about 3,500 years ago in South America, where it is presumed that agriculture commenced with other crops and that corn was introduced from Middle America. In sites at Chilca and Nazca on the southern Peruvian coast both bottle gourds and lima beans, the oldest agricultural remains found so far on the southern continent, have been dated at about 6,700–5,000 years of age, placing incipient cultivation in that region at a time somewhat after that of the earliest sites discovered in Middle America. Some 5,000 years ago also, it appears, linted cotton was present on the west coast of South America, the result, possibly, of an even earlier hybridization of cultivated Peruvian lintless cotton and a strain introduced in some still-unknown fashion from Asia. The 5,000-year-old date is the New World's oldest so far for cotton; at a later time, it appeared in Middle America and regions farther north.

Significant other developments, which needed agriculture as a base, but which did not occur inevitably everywhere that agriculture became established, mark the period from about 7,000 to 3,000 years ago. Generally, some writers view this time span as the one in which groups and their traits in most parts of the hemisphere changed from those of early man to those of the ancestors of the modern-day Indians. In Middle America, the first domestication of plants, occurring close to the time of the disappearance of Pleistocene animals in that area, did not immediately provide the basis of peoples' economies. As MacNeish's studies confirmed, there was no sharp and sudden shift to agriculture. For a long time, economies were based primarily on the gathering of wild plants, with supplementary hunting and trapping providing an important second source of food, and the cultivation of wild plants being more of an experimental additive. Gradually, cultivation became more important, but the emergence of the first economies based primarily on agriculture occurred no less apparently than thousands of years after the start of cultivation.

Wherever farming ultimately took over and groups settled down permanently to till their fields, however, population began to increase and, in time, tended to become concentrated. A more plentiful and secure food supply provided the base for these changes. In addition, surpluses of agricultural products gave people more leisure, and with an increasing esthetic sense they began to fashion utilitarian objects, as well as articles of decoration and spiritual meaning that pleased and aided them. Some of the people began to accumulate possessions and objects of wealth; and in various areas social distinctions, specialists, and a division of labor appeared, and religious, social, and political systems required by the growing concentrations of population increased and became more complex.

The two most intensive regions of agriculture were in Middle America and in the central Andes. There, in southern and central Mexico (where, around Tehuacán, MacNeish indicated a starting date of some 5,300 years ago for village life), Guatemala, Ecuador, and Peru, village life, based on clusters of farming peoples, was already well underway by about 1500 B.C. Eventually, from some of those villages arose important cultures that led, in time, to the highest civilizations ever developed by American Indians. From those centers, also, were diffused or carried influences that gradually affected other peoples elsewhere in the hemisphere and helped to shape many of the vast variety of Indian cultures which the white men eventually found throughout the Americas.

Although many persons have tried to estimate how many Indians inhabited the New World by 1492, there is no agreement on the figure. In the past some have believed that there were as many as 75 million, others a maximum of only 8 million. Until recently, the most knowledgeable students estimated that there were somewhere between 15 and 20 million Indians in the hemisphere when Columbus arrived, agreeing also that probably only some 850,000 lived within the present boundaries of the contiguous states of the United States, and considerably fewer farther north in Canada and Alaska. The bulk of the population was found below the Rio Grande, concentrated most heavily in the regions of the most intensive practice of agriculture; and it was thought that perhaps 7 million or more people were in Mexico, Central America, and the Caribbean prior to the white man's arrival, and at least 10 million throughout South America, more than half of them in the Andean highlands. Recent demographic studies in various areas, however, indicate that earlier data are inaccurate and suggest that population estimates be revised upward. It is now more thoroughly recognized, for instance, that the first white contacts with tribes were often made after great epidemics, introduced from the Old World but sweeping ahead of the white explorers and settlers, had claimed the lives of large numbers of Indians. Some students believe that the estimates, cited above, may have to be increased possibly as much as ten times. This may be too high. A sounder projection might be suggested by a study made of California's Indian population: until recently, it was thought that somewhat more than 130,000 Indians were in present-day California before the appearance of white men; now it appears more probable that they were in excess of 350,000.

During the course of the white man's conquest of the New World, Indian numbers changed greatly. Many native peoples were entirely exterminated; many were almost wiped out; others approached the brink of extinction and then "came back." The Indian population within the United States (excluding Alaska) declined rapidly until by 1860 there remained only some 340,000. By 1910 the figure had declined to 220,000, and the Indian had taken on the popular image of the "vanishing American." About that time, the trend reversed, and today, with a rapidly decreasing death rate and a high Indian birth rate, Indians are increasing in number at a rate 10 per cent faster than that of the overall United States population. Agreement differs on how many Indians are now in the United States, for there are differences over some of the definitions of what now constitutes an Indian. In 1960, the United States Bureau of the Census reported an inclusive total of 552,228 Indians, Eskimos, and Aleuts in the contiguous states and Alaska. But the Census Bureau, listing as an Indian any "person of mixed white and Indian blood . . . if enrolled in an Indian agency or reservation roll, or if not so enrolled, if the proportion of Indian blood is one-fourth or more, or if the person is regarded as an Indian in the community where he lives," undoubtedly overlooks many Indians of more than one quarter Indian blood living in cities or elsewhere off of reservations. In 1950, a study group at the University of Chicago, making its own count and including isolated Indian "communities" in urban areas, as well as individuals who possessed some degree of Indian culture, arrived at that time at a total figure of 571,784. Although some of the criteria differ in the various counts, however, it is generally agreed that the Indian population has increased by more than 350,000 in the last half century, and that the total is now beyond 600,000, which would be only some 250,000 fewer Indians than were thought, until recently, to have been in the same area in 1492. At the rate of increase, sociologists believe that there may be between 720,000 and 1 million Indians in the United States by 1975, posing enormous subsistence and other problems for tribes on or near reservations—a population which in 1965 numbered about 380,000.

Canada, meanwhile, counts 225,000 Indians today, but the figures for Latin America are difficult to agree upon. Under Spanish and Portuguese rule, Indian populations declined steadily in many of the Latin American countries. One hundred years after the arrival of Cortés in Mexico, the native population of that country is estimated to have fallen to about 2 million. In the last century, however, the number rose again, and in 1950 more than 2.5 million Mexicans were speaking Indian languages. Elsewhere, Indian population figures are a problem to assess because of difficulties in taking a census and a lack of agreement over who is and who is not an Indian. Generally, in most Latin American countries, the definition of an Indian is based on whether a person lives like an Indian. In many states, those with both Indian and white blood are listed as mestizos, rather than Indians, but it is possible for mestizos living in Indian villages to be regarded as Indians while their relatives in cities are looked upon as mestizos. On the basis of reports of those who "live like Indians," there are probably from 7 to 14 million Indians in Latin America south of Mexico today. But certain groups, including the Inter-American Indian Institute, which use blood as a criterion, estimate the figure to be closer to 30 million.

In modern times, anthropologists have classified the different Indian groups into cultural areas, really geographic divisions of the Americas containing tribes that displayed numerous similarities in their ways of living, as well as sharp differences from tribes that dwelled in other areas. It is a good way to become familiar with the backgrounds and ways of life of the native peoples of the different parts of the hemisphere. Schemes for making such divisions have differed, however, and no single proposal for drawing boundary lines between the tribes can be considered absolutely correct. Culture areas to a great extent must be approximate, since the lines between neighboring peoples were often vague and changing, and some features of life in one culture area frequently existed in others. People of the same language family, moreover, were often found in more than one culture area, and, conversely, individual areas contained groups that spoke different languages.

The backgrounds, ways of life, and traits of the Indians in the various cultural areas that are most generally accepted, however, will be described in the chapters that follow.

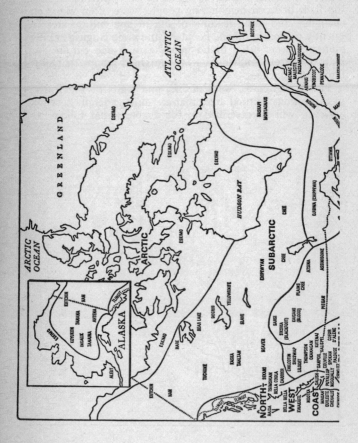

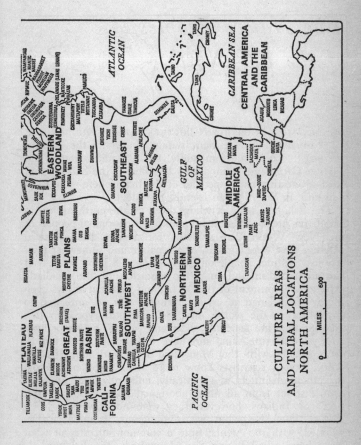

CULTURE AREAS
AND TRIBAL LOCATIONS
NORTH AMERICA

0   MILES   600

7

The Native Peoples of the Far North

THE MOST NORTHERN CULTURE AREA, THE ARCTIC, embracing the Aleutian Islands, almost all the Alaskan coast, except the Panhandle, the Canadian Arctic, and western Greenland, is inhabited by some of the hardiest and most interesting native peoples of the hemisphere—the Eskimos and, in the Aleutian Islands, the Aleuts.

The Eskimos, some of whom dwell on the northeastern tip of Siberia, are so different from all other aboriginal peoples of the New World that students for a long time puzzled whether they were Indians, or a separate and somewhat mysteriously distinct people on earth—a species, as it were, that had originated in, and under the conditions of, the peculiarly extreme environment of the Arctic, and that had always been there. Their language, as an example, seemed unrelated to any other in the world, and their physical type appeared unique: they are generally short and plump, possess a fatty layer beneath the skin, and have flat, broad faces, narrow eyes, usually with the Mongoloid fold, and long, narrow noses. Today, scientists know more about them and recognize them definitely as genetically, culturally, and linguistically distinct from all other aboriginal New World people. Like the Indians, however, they were not always in their present homelands, but were immigrants from Asia. Descended, with the Aleuts, from a common ancestry of what some have called Bering Sea Mongoloids, the Eskimos are inheritors of Siberian and earlier Arctic cultures to which they added their own adaptations and innovations.

In terms of time, Eskimo culture, as it exists today, is comparatively young. Both on the Arctic coast and in the interior, archeologists have discovered sites of pre-Eskimo

56

hunters of great antiquity. The dates vary, and the peoples appear to have possessed different technical abilities and traits, stemming apparently from various areas in Siberia. Hunters of what has been termed a British Mountain technical tradition left certain types of scrapers, knives, crude projectile points, and other artifacts in association with remains of caribou and extinct bison on the Arctic coasts of Alaska and the Yukon possibly between 13,000 and 18,000 years ago, when that region was more moderate in climate than it is today. Other British Mountain tradition sites have been found in Alaska's Brooks Range (perhaps 8,000–10,000 years old) and possibly at Cape Krusenstern on the Chukchi Sea (c. 5,000–11,000 years old). Many projectile points of another tradition, resembling the points of the Old Cordilleran Culture of the Pacific Northwest, have also been found in much of the western Arctic and Subarctic, ranging in age from about 8,500 to 13,000 years. In addition, fluted points, possibly prototypes of the Clovis fluted point, and Plano-type points have been found at various northwestern Arctic sites. On Anangula Island in the Aleutians small blades, called microblades, and other artifacts, dated between approximately 7,700 and 8,500 years of age, are assigned to a so-called Aleutian Core and Blade Industry that persisted in the Aleutians for a long time and provided sources for the eventual development of Eskimo cultures in that region. During the Ice Age, some scientists have noted, Anangula Island was part of the southern coast of the Bering land bridge. The extreme age of the artifacts found there suggests to them the presence of maritime-oriented Bering Sea Mongoloids, who may have migrated from Asia along the southern coast of the land bridge. When the bridge disappeared, some of them may have stayed on the newly created Aleutian Islands and become the Aleuts; the others, according to the theory, moved north along the new coastline and became the Eskimos.

The dates of many of the pre-Eskimos finds in the Arctic are still a matter of conjecture. Although much of the coastal region frequented by early man during the Ice Age must now be under water, some of the sites discovered may be as old as any yet found in the hemisphere, and may be of nomadic peoples whose descendants gave rise to the big game hunting cultures farther south. The various projectile points, including those of Old Cordilleran- and Plano-type, possibly spread southward in a connected cultural bond from

Alaska. On the other hand, some persons believe that the Plano-type points, particularly, came from the south in a south-to-north drift of bison hunters who were already on the continent, and thus appeared in the Arctic later than in the more southerly areas of the Great Plains and the Great Lakes. At the same time, it has been noted that many pre-Eskimo traits resembling those found farther south persisted in the north for longer periods of time: Plano-type projectile points used by the Pleistocene bison hunters on the Great Plains almost 10,000 years ago, for instance, were still used on Alaska's Arctic coast by men who hunted caribou about 1500 B.C.

Beginning about 8,000 years ago and enduring for several millennia was another tradition, which is known as the Northwest Microblade. Characterized by the use of numerous microblades, it was probably a development of hunters who lived in interior forests, and its sites have been found in several places in Alaska and northwestern Canada. Before it had ended, it was overlapped and succeeded, about 5,500 years ago, by an important new tradition, the Arctic Small Tool, which began in the western Arctic and gradually extended its influence across the Far North, from Alaska to Greenland. In time, some of its elements were retained in the various developing Eskimo cultures.

Recent archeological studies by the late J. L. Giddings and others around Norton Sound on Alaska's northwestern coast and at Onion Portage in the Brooks Range have shed light on the coming of later peoples, and the transition, beginning about 3,000 years ago, to Eskimo culture. Prior to 7,000 years ago, those two regions were occupied by pre-Eskimo hunters. About 6,000 years ago, Arctic Small Tool people of the Denbigh Flint Culture (named for Cape Denbigh, Alaska, discovery site) spread into Alaska from Asia, "pushing aside or overriding" the more Indian-like culture of the hunters who were already there. The new culture, becoming established at Norton Sound about 5,000 years ago, possessed a stone industry as well as material traits that included small, delicate end blades, side blades, and microblades.

The Denbigh Flint Culture evolved to Eskimo culture through several sequences of succeeding cultural phases in the Arctic. Around Kotzebue Sound on Alaska's northwest coast, have been listed, in order, stages of development that include the Old Whaling Culture (about 4,000–3,500 years ago); the Choris Culture (about 3,000 years ago); the Norton Culture (from about 400 B.C. to shortly after the beginning of the Christian era); Near Ipiutak; and Ipiutak (about A.D. 300). The last, based at Point Hope, was a unique culture of a people who lived in a settlement of some 600 houses, the largest Eskimo site found in the Arctic; possessed a rich array of well-made artifacts; and overran or influenced the cultures of many other Eskimo groups in the western Arctic.

In the region of the Bering Strait, a second sequence of stages bears the coloration of another group of migrants who came from northeastern Siberia about 2,000 years ago and, like the Ipiutaks from the American side, overwhelmed already existing local forms of culture. Known as the people of the Northern Maritime, or Bering Sea, Culture, their development at sites like those on St. Lawrence Island can be traced through related sequential stages that include Old Bering–Okvik (about 250 B.C.); Birnirk; and Punuk and Thule, the latter two occurring about the same period. This culture, from its Birnirk phase on, became the most influential of all Eskimo cultures, spreading the maritime, sea-mammal-hunting way of life across the entire Arctic to Greenland. Other centers of early Eskimo development have been revealed on the south Alaskan coast and in the Aleutians, in the central and eastern Canadian Arctic, and in Greenland. Archeological work in what is known as the Pacific Eskimo-Aleut province of the Aleutian Islands and south Alaska has yielded a find about 3,000 years old on Umnak Island in the Aleutians and another, dated at 748 B.C. and showing influences from Indian cultures to the south and from Asia, at Kachemak Bay on Cook Inlet. In the central and eastern Arctic, sites have been found as old as 4,000 years of predecessors of a Dorset Culture people who occupied that portion of the Far North during the first millennium before the Christian era and the first after.

The early history of the Eskimos is still imperfectly known, and much remains to be learned of the influences and links between different cultures, the variants that occurred at different sites, and the origins of individual groups. Better known are the broad outlines of occurrences in more recent times that brought all Eskimo life throughout the Arctic closer to synthesis. In the first millennium after Christ, people of the Northern Maritime's Thule Culture of western Alaska, encompassing traits developed in the stages that had followed the Old Bering Sea Culture, as well as influences from other western Arctic centers, spread eastward across the Canadian Arctic coast, implanting the Thule Culture throughout the Arctic, from northern Alaska to Greenland. In more recent times, Thule Culture peoples returned westward, further solidifying their influences along their route of migrations. On the western Alaskan coast conformity was similarly spread from about A.D. 1200 to 1650 by people of the Nukleet Culture, the direct ancestors of the modern Eskimos in that area.

By about A.D. 1000, the peoples of the entire American Arctic, it may be said, had become what we call and think of as Eskimos. But many of the material traits that mark their culture, even today, had come into use among the peoples of the Arctic long before that time. By 2,500 years ago, at least, they had developed the kayak, a one-man canoe made of a driftwood frame covered with sewed skins, and the larger umiak, which was also used to carry goods. For at least 2,000 years, they are known to have employed harpoons, specialized fishing gear, ice picks, floats of inflated bladders, bows and arrows, dog-drawn sleds, bone and ivory hobnails on boots to help in walking over the ice, and goggles, made first with holes and then with slits, to protect them against snow blindness. Another Eskimo possession, lamps made of moss wicks in stone trays and fed with blubber or oil, had several variations, but they were the only lamps ever used by pre-Columbian peoples of the New World and probably originated in Asia.

To many persons, the unique image of the Eskimos is of a people who, by ingenious inventions that helped make like endurable, adapted themselves to a stern and almost uninhabitable environment. Living in small, isolated units of families and family groups, all of them speaking related dialects, the Eskimos maintained a rich and full existence and, despite the rigors of Arctic life, were industrious and happy. From ancient times until late in the nineteenth century, life in the Arctic changed slowly and almost imperceptibly, but during the first millennium A.D. the artistic work of some of the people reached high levels. In various regions at that time, roughly contemporary cultures, including Ipiutak and Old Bering Sea in northwestern Alaska, Kachemak Bay in southern Alaska, and late Dorset and early Thule around Hudson Bay and in the eastern Arctic and western Greenland, produced beautiful works in carved ivory and bone. In the same period some pottery appeared, and the Alaskan Eskimos developed their skill at whaling from small boats.

Eskimos were essentially a hunting people. Sometimes they are classified in two groups, those who lived along the coasts and hunted seal, walrus, and whale, and those who dwelled inland and pursued caribou and other land game. A great number of them, however, did both at different seasons, although the hunting routines might have varied from group to group. In the spring, Eskimos generally killed seals basking on the shores; in summer, they harpooned them from kayaks in the open water, and in the winter, they caught them through breathing holes in the ice.

Eskimos built their homes from whatever materials were available. In the summer, almost all the groups lived in tents made of poles covered with skins. In the winter, families in the eastern part of the Arctic built houses of stone, while many in the west and in Alaska used driftwood and sod. The unique domed igloo (the word refers to any type of house) was found most commonly in northern Canada and was rarely seen in Alaska. Cold as it looked, it was actually warm, and even stuffy, inside. Making use of the principle that hot air rises, it had its entrance usually below the level of the ground so that the warm indoor air could not escape via the door. Sometimes the vaulted rooms of these snow houses, with long passageways to keep out the cold, could hold up to sixty people. They were also insulated with furs and could admit light through openings on top sealed with translucent gut.

People wore clothing that was well adapted to the harsh climate. Both men and women wore fur trousers and shirts, usually made of caribou hide, but sometimes of polar bear or other fur. Hooded parkas, or outer jackets, were added in winter, the woman's being cut fuller so that a mother could carry her baby inside the garment or within the hood. Stockings, boots, and mittens were also fashioned from fur, and sinew was used for thread. Women made the clothing, which the people wore loosely, except at the neck and extremities, in order to let the wearer be warmed by air heated by one's own body.

Eskimo life was marked by simple social and governmental organization. Routines revolved around the life of families or groups of families and the annual cycle of securing food. Daily existence was full of taboos. People had great faith in the power of shamans to cure sicknesses, produce seals or other sources of food supply in times of scarcity, secure revenge, or otherwise restore balance and harmony to the world after a taboo had been violated. Both men and women could be shamans. There were few rituals, but Eskimo lore was full of legends and mythical characters. A powerful figure of myth was a great sea goddess called Sedna, "She Down There," who could keep sea creatures far from shore to punish hunters who had sinned or offended her. Usually in winter, annual gatherings were held, when Eskimos indulged in dances, singing contests, and gymnastics. Dancers often wore masks impersonating various deities and mythical characters and acted out the plots of legends. One of them, still performed by masked dancers at Point Hope, facing across the icy Chukchi Sea toward Siberia, concerns Ooyalu, "the contrary woman." "Once there was a woman," the tale goes, "a flinty-hearted woman, whom many a man courted. But she would have none of them. One by one, as they pressed their suits, she rejected them. They gave her presents, but it was of no use. She turned them all away. Finally the woman was taken by a monster. It was her punishment for being contrary." In the dance, the masked Eskimos act out every nuance of the plot. Sometimes, singers settled quarrels by ridiculing each other in their songs and letting the audience judge who had won.

The Aleuts, who were a slightly different people from the Eskimos (although they apparently shared a common ancestry), inhabited many of the islands of the long chain of Aleutians. They had received a number of influences from the Choris, Norton, and Near Ipiutak cultures of the northwest Alaskan coast, but, like the south Alaskan Eskimos, possessed also some culture elements that had come to them directly from Asia and from contact with Indians of the Northwest Pacific Coast. Aleuts wore carved wooden hats, wove beautiful basketry, and in their death rites and ceremonial distributions of property, showed a tendency to social divisions—all traits of the Northwest Coast Indians. They used kayaks and hunted sea mammals like the Eskimos, but many of them relied principally on salmon and birds for food.

Eskimos were the first inhabitants of the New World known to Europeans. Norse seamen came on them in Greenland after about A.D. 850. From that contact developed still another local Eskimo culture, Inugsuk, a modified form of the Thule Culture, that flourished, with some adaptations of northern European traits, during the thirteenth and fourteenth centuries in Eskimo villages in western Greenland. The Europeans were familiar to the Greenland Eskimos until the middle of the fourteenth century, when the white settlements were abandoned. In the sixteenth century, European explorers discovered the Eskimos again in the northern seas, but by that time there was little evidence that the native peoples had ever had previous contact with whites. In the eighteenth century, Russians crossing from Siberia came on the Aleuts and Eskimos of Alaska and, pressing some of them—particularly Aleuts—into the fur trade, added numerous traits, including ironware and the beliefs and rituals of the Russian Orthodox Church, to their culture.

Today Eskimo and Aleut life has been even more greatly influenced—and, in some places, drastically altered or even eliminated—by the white man's civilization. Some natives have been educated and have taken leading roles in modern commercial and political life in Alaska. An Eskimo, William E. Beltz, was elected president of Alaska's first state senate after achieving statehood, and other Eskimos have served in the state legislative and executive branches. Many villages, from Alaska to Greenland, have received as neighbors air bases, radar warning stations, and other installations with advanced technological equipment, and Eskimos have been given specialized training in order to qualify for employment at them. Young Eskimos pilot planes, man computers and electronic apparatus, service heavy earth-moving equipment, and do other specialized and skilled jobs that reflect a sharp break with the past. A newspaper, *The Tundra Times*, is edited and published by an Eskimo, carrying news and features of interest to Eskimos and Alaskan Indians. Other Eskimos and Aleuts, who continue to pursue the old hunting life, have adopted outboard motors, rifles with telescopic sights, and plastic equipment. In both Alaska and Canada, the pace of change is becoming increasingly rapid, with consequent cultural dislocations and confusions to many of the peoples. The governments of the United States and Canada are aware of the problem, but so far efforts designed to help the natives adjust to the increasing pressures of change have, in the opinion of many, been inadequate.

8

The Indians of the Subarctic

THE BROAD, SPARSELY POPULATED EXPANSE OF WOODS, waterways, mountains, and treeless tundra, or barrens, that stretches across North America south of the Arctic from interior Alaska and the Canadian Rockies to Labrador and Newfoundland, has been termed the Subarctic Cultural Area. Its native peoples have lived in a hard, severe environment, and their culture—varying only slightly in different regions and, here and there, from influences of neighbors in adjoining cultural areas—reflects the sternness of their existence.

Hudson Bay divides the Subarctic tribes roughly into two major language families, the Algonquians and the Athapascans, the latter living across the vast country west of the Bay. Named originally for a single band that dwelled in the vicinity of northwest Canada's Lake Athabaska, Indians of the various Athapascan-speaking tribes lived mostly in small, independent hunting and fishing groups in the great basins of the Yukon and Mackenzie rivers and in the valleys of other streams that empty in the Arctic and Pacific oceans or the Gulf of Alaska. In Alaska and neighboring parts of Canada, their tribes include the Ahtena (on southeast Alaska's Copper River); Koyukon (in the Yukon Basin in Alaska); Kutchin (a group of tribes extending from Alaska's upper Yukon Valley across the central portion of the Yukon Territory and down the valley of the lower Mackenzie River); Tanana (centered about the confluence of the Tanana and Yukon rivers in Alaska); Tanaina (about Cook Inlet and on the Kenai Peninsula on Alaska's southern coast); Ingalik (along the lower Yukon); Han (the upper Yukon in east central Alaska and the Yukon Territory); and

Nabesna (in the valleys of the Nabesna, Chisana, and other rivers in southeastern Alaska above the Panhandle).

In the Canadian interior, Athapascan tribes include the Beaver (the lower Peace River Basin in northern Alberta); Carrier (the valleys of the upper Fraser, Blackwater, Nechako, and other rivers, inland from the coast in western British Columbia); Chipewyan (extending westward from Hudson Bay, and north of the Churchill River, to the eastern edges of Athabaska and Great Slave lakes); Dogrib (between Great Slave and Great Bear lakes); Hare (west and northwest of Great Bear Lake and on the upper Mackenzie River); Kaska or Nahani (in the mountains west of the upper Mackenzie River); Sekani (in the basins of the Parsnip, Finlay, and upper Peace rivers, mostly in British Columbia); Slave (about Great Slave Lake); Tahltan (on the upper Stikine River and on headwaters that feed the Nass River in northwestern British Columbia); Tuchone (in the southern Yukon Territory); and Yellowknife (northeast of Great Slave Lake).

The Algonquian-speaking tribes of the Subarctic, living generally south and east of Hudson Bay, are fewer in number. They include the Naskapi (in most of interior Labrador); Montagnais (southwest of the Naskapi, in a large area north of the lower stretch of the St. Lawrence River); and Cree (circling about the southern side of Hudson Bay and extending northwestward to the Churchill River and westward beyond the north side of Lake Winnipeg). In Newfoundland, Beothuks, now extinct, spoke a tongue seemingly unrelated to any other known Indian language.

Although many of the tribes in the area have had long associations with French and British fur traders, they are among the least-studied aboriginal peoples in North America, and knowledge of their history and culture is comparatively meager. The Algonquian-speakers, related to numerous tribes that practiced agriculture in cultural areas farther south, are probably descendants of peoples who have been in the eastern portion of the Subarctic for many thousands of years. The Athapascans are believed to be later arrivals in the New World, the first of them having entered Alaska from northeastern Asia perhaps about 5,000–6,000 years ago. This is still a debatable question, however, and some scientists suggest that members of the Northwest Microblade tradition, whose artifacts in interior Alaska and northwestern Canada date back some 8,000 years, may have crossed from Asia via the interior of the Bering land bridge at least 2,000 years earlier and have been the ancestors of the Athapascan peoples.

In the centuries immediately preceding the arrival of the white man, the Athapascans, possibly seeking more hospitable country where winters were not so long or severe, seem to have been pressing southward. Some of them did break away from the northwest in a migration that took them down the Great Plains, or through the Great Basin, to New Mexico, where they arrived not long before the appearance, in the same region, of the Spaniards. These Athapascan peoples are today's Apaches, Kiowa-Apaches, Lipans, and Navahos of the U.S. Southern plains and Southwest and Tobosos of northern Mexico. Another Athapascan group, the Sarci, also moved south to the Canadian plains just before the coming of the Europeans and, attaching themselves in alliance with the buffalo-hunting Blackfeet tribes, took on the coloration of a plains tribe. In the west, some Athapascans fingered their way southward to establish enclaves among other tribes from Alaska to southern California. But in the southeast the hostility of the Crees seems to have held them back.

None of the Indians of the Subarctic practiced agriculture. All were hunters and fishermen, pursuing the animals most common in their individual territories (moose, caribou, musk oxen, bear, elk, beaver, porcupine, rabbits, and other small game); using bows and arrows, clubs, spears, but quite often snares of various kinds; catching fish, sometimes at every season of the year; and supplementing their diets with waterfowl and other birds, and berries and roots. Some of the tribes preferred hunting to fishing; the Sekani, who possessed a club fashioned from the jawbone of a moose, resorted to fishing only when necessary. Others, like the Slave Indians who refrained from venturing onto the open barrens after caribou herds but sought moose and caribou only in the woods, relied on fish for half of their diet. And in parts of the far west, where tribes lived along salmon-filled rivers and could secure fish through lake ice in the winter, the products of the waters supplied the principal staple of diet throughout the year.

Hunting and fishing routines varied. The Carriers (named for their custom of compelling widows to carry the charred bones of their dead husbands on their backs) lacked snowshoes and toboggans and so were rarely able to hunt in the winter. In the extreme North, where some of the traits of the tribes closely resembled those of the neighboring Eskimos, the Indians hunted caribou on the barrens in the summer, snaring them in pounds and spearing them in lakes; in the winter, they tracked them in the woods. In Labrador, the Naskapi hunted caribou on the open, grass-covered plateau of their country during the winter; in the spring, some of the people went down toward the coast to fish, while others remained inland, fishing and hunting small game. Their neighbors, the Montagnais, hunted moose in winter, but in spring went down the rivers to spear salmon and eels and to harpoon seals on the shores of the lower St. Lawrence. Throughout the area, tribes used bone hooks, nets, and spears to fish, and some fished at night from canoes, using the light of jack-pine torches.

As a rule, the Subarctic tribes made less use of stone than of wood, bone, horn, and antler for implements. Spruce and birchbark, as well as wood, were employed in the making of many utensils (cooking vessels were often made of birchbark), and ropes and thongs were made of rawhide and the fibers of roots. Canoes of various types were used in the summer, and toboggans, sleds, and snowshoes in the winter. Dwelling styles differed: in far western Canada and in parts of Alaska, Athapascans sometimes had plank houses similar to those of their neighbors, the Northwest Pacific Coast tribes. The southernmost Carriers, influenced by the interior Salish peoples of the Plateau area south of them, built their houses underground in the winter. In the summer, they often lived in shelters, roofed with spruce bark, but without walls. In winter, the Kutchins used enlarged domed sweathouses, banked with snow around the outside walls, and with an opening for a smoke hole; in the summer, they lived in tents. Elsewhere across the Subarctic, homes were usually conical frameworks of poles, covered with brush, bark, or skins, the ancestor of the Plains tipi. The Crees, reflecting influences from farther south, used both conical and dome-shaped wigwams, covered with birchbark, pine bark, or caribou skins.

Life, as in the Arctic, centered mostly on family units and around the routines of securing food. There was little, or no, tribal cohesion. People usually lived and hunted in independent groups that roamed over separate hunting territories and, during fishing seasons, occupied regular fishing sites which they regarded as their own. Leaders of the groups rarely had any authority. Among some groups, women and old people were treated harshly. The women dragged the toboggans, built the shelters, gathered firewood, and sometimes ate only after the men were finished. Old people, among such groups, were the special victims of the severe environment. If they were too infirm to keep up, they were killed or abandoned and left to starve. The Chipewyans, Kutchins, Hares, Crees, and Montagnais were among those noted for their sternness to the elderly. Among the Kutchins, mothers often killed their girl babies to spare them from what they themselves were enduring, and old people sometimes asked to be strangled rather than to be deserted. On the other hand, the Slave Indians treated their wives kindly; the men prepared the lodges, gathered wood, and did the heavy work; and their groups never abandoned the aged. The Beavers and Dogribs also placed their women on a higher scale; their men were among those of several tribes who, when contending for a certain woman as a wife, wrestled for the right to claim her.

Most elements of dress were similar among the Subarctic peoples, but there were tribal variations. Clothing was made from the skins of moose, caribou, and other animals; rabbit skins were fashioned into robes; and leggings and moccasins, sometimes joined in one piece, were often decorated with quillwork or beadwork in bright floral designs. The Hare Indians, who were named so because much of their economy was based on that animal, used the hare's fur for their clothes. The Slaves' clothing was heavily bordered with fringes and was decorated with porcupine quills and moose hair. In some of their ceremonies, the Carriers used handsome Chilkat blankets, which they had traded from their Pacific coastal neighbors, while the dress of both the Kutchins in Alaska and the Yukon and the Naskapi in Labrador reflected the influence of the Eskimos. Among the Kutchins, the caribou-skin shirt was short-waisted and had long tails in front and back. Sometimes Kutchin women enlarged the back of the shirt so that they could carry babies within it, in the style of the Eskimo women. Kutchin men also wore headbands, necklaces, and nose pendants of shells, and painted their faces and placed feathers in their hair; the women tattooed their chins like Eskimo women. The Naskapi adopted the tailored shirt of the Labrador coast Eskimos, but ornamented it with painted geometrical designs usually in red, yellow, or blue. Other tribes, including the Chipewyans and Yellowknives, also tattooed their faces, and the Beothuks of Newfoundland gained the name "Red Indians" because they smeared their bodies and clothing with red ocher, possibly as a protection against insects.

The most notable "outside" influences were found among the far western Athapascan tribes, including the Carriers and Tahltans, that bordered the peoples of the Northwest Pacific Coast culture area. Influences from the coastal Tsimshians, for instance, permeated the social and political life of the Carriers, whose population was divided into "nobles," commoners, and slaves—although slaves were not numerous. A commoner could often attain the status of a nobleman by giving potlatches, or proud give-away feasts (also "borrowed" from the Tsimshian culture), and taking on an appropriate title. The Carriers were organized, moreover, into clans, each of which claimed individual hunting territories and fishing sites. Poaching could lead to serious friction. The Tahltans, also adopting traits from the coast, had six clans divided into two bodies, Raven and Wolf, and the population, again, was divided into "nobles," commoners, and slaves.

Warfare was more common in some parts of the Subarctic than in others. The Tahltans engaged in frequent petty wars with neighbors, killing male prisoners, and enslaving women captives. The Carriers, like the coastal tribes, wore armor made from slats of wood or from moose hide coated with pebbles, and protected further by oval shields, fought with clubs, knives, lances, and bows and arrows. The Chipewyans could be fierce to enemies, plundering the weak, and massacring helpless groups; but although the Chipewyans were the largest and strongest of the Athapascan tribes (numbering an estimated 3,500 people when the Europeans first encountered them), they were eventually bested by the even more numerous Crees who, armed with guns provided by fur traders, terrorized the Chipewyans and ultimately invaded and laid claim to large parts of their territory. On the other end of the scale were the timid Slaves and Hares, the latter so timorous that they fled from all strangers and were despised for their cowardice by their neighbors, the Eskimos, Kutchins, and Yellowknives.

The harshness of the Subarctic land, the loneliness of its vast reaches, and the cold winds, long winters, and other natural phenomena of its northern environment contributed to making its people particularly susceptible to fear and awe of the supernatural. Mysteries were numerous and ever-present; rapids and lakes were haunted by spirits; ghosts and demons lurked in the woods, traveled with the winds, and waited everywhere to do mischief. Few tribes had any well-formed religious beliefs. Some acknowledged the existence of a vague supreme sky-god or sun-god but paid little attention to him, appealing, instead, to a multitude of spirits in nature around them—usually animals or birds—with whom they tried to establish contact through dreams or visions, and whose assistance they sought through shamans and rituals. The shamans, or medicine men, were particularly important, often the only person in a group with authority of any kind. Sometimes they were soothsayers, practitioners of magic, curers, or casters of spells; their strong powers could heal or inflict diseases, could intercede with the spirits for good or evil fortune, could weave protection or doom. In some tribes, the shamans were the link between men and animals, able to invoke and join the spirits of the two. Some peoples had no shamans, but established contact with spirits through their own dreams. With or without the shaman, belief in witchcraft was strong, and often all ills, calamities, and deaths were ascribed to the unseen world. The Kutchins, constantly haunted by spirits, burned fat in the fire to obtain supernatural aid for success in the hunt. The Crees, sometimes reduced by starvation to cannibalism (which, like the other tribes of the area, they viewed with horror), lived in fear of legendary *windigos*—human beings who had eaten human flesh and been transformed into supernatural man-eating giants.

From the seventeenth to the nineteenth centuries French and British traders enlisted many of the Subarctic peoples in the fur trade. In time, the presence of the Europeans was disastrous for the natives. As the various tribes acquired guns and ironware, their economies changed. But intertribal warfare was intensified, invasions and annihilations, wrought with firearms, occurred, and native populations declined. Epidemics of smallpox, influenza, and other diseases brought by the white men completed the demoralization and disintegration of most of the tribes. By 1829, the Beothuks were extinct; the Chipewyan population had declined by two thirds, and many of the Crees had expanded so far westward that large numbers of them were on the plains of Canada and had changed their culture to that of plains Indians. They were twice hit by smallpox epidemics, however, and the survivors, finally halted in their expansion, became pockets of people among other tribes. In Alaska, the Athapascans had a longer period of grace; some Indians only saw their first whites during the Klondike gold rush of 1898.

Today, many of the Subarctic peoples engage in trapping for white buyers and serving as guides for sportsmen, but their subsistence to a great extent still depends on hunting, fishing, and the gathering of berries. Large numbers of Alaskan Athapascans still inhabit the Yukon Basin, trying to maintain their traditional way of life, but feeling increasing pressure from the white developers of the new state. A proposed hydroelectric dam at Rampart on the Yukon would flood out thousands of natives, inundating their ancestral hunting and fishing territories on the Yukon flats, and forcing the people to find new lives for themselves elsewhere. As if bowing to what they consider inevitable, however, some natives are already receiving education and vocational training and are readily adopting the ways of their white neighbors. In Canada, such a wholesale change may be longer in coming; yet even there, the opening of the Canadian north by mineral-seeking industries has already drawn numerous natives toward the white man's way of life.

9

The Tribes of the Northwest Pacific Coast

ALONG THE MISTY, FORESTED SHORES OF THE PACIFIC
Northwest, inhabiting a generally narrow coastal area,
hemmed between mountains and the sea and extending from Alaska's Prince William Sound to northern California, are a number of tribes that once possessed a dramatic
and vigorous culture that included wealth-conscious societies,
class distinctions, technical specializations, and exciting,
highly skilled art traditions. Commencing in the north, the
tribes include the Tlingits (from Prince William Sound to
the lower portion of Alaska's Panhandle); Haidas (on Queen
Charlotte Island); Tsimshians, Bella Coolas, and Kwakiutls
(on the British Columbia coast); Nootkas (on the west side
of Vancouver Island); various Coastal Salish tribes, including Duwamish, Klallams, Lummis, Muckleshoots, Nisquallys,
Puyallups, Skagits, Snohomish, Snoqualmis, Swinomish, and
Tulalips (around Puget Sound); Makahs, Quinaults,
Quileutes, Chehalis, Chinooks, Tillamooks, Umpquas, Coos,
Takelmas, and others (on the Washington and Oregon
coasts); and Wiyots, Hupas, Yuroks, Karoks, and Tolowas
(in northwestern California).

Although agriculture, normally a basis of the more advanced cultures in the hemisphere, was absent (as was
pottery), the Northwest Coast peoples developed remarkably
stable societies of splendor and complexity, the foundation
of which in their case was an abundant and easily obtained
supply of food from the waters and forests around them.
Salmon, halibut, cod, shellfish, and, among some tribes,
whales were harvested from the sea and the coastal rivers
along which the people dwelled, and berries and game were

plentiful in the nearby woods. The mild winters of the fog-shrouded islands and fiords of the area, together with the advantage of having much leisure time, gave them opportunities to develop crafts and artistic skills, as well as rich social and religious systems, marked by traits that included an intense, and at times almost a paranoid, competition for status by the ostentatious acquisition and spending of wealth—something unusual among most American Indians.

Due to the many difficulties of archeological study in the area (absence of pottery remains, the people's use of wood and other perishable materials for implements, the scarcity of flaked stone tools, the accumulation of shell debris at sites, and other problems), knowledge of the prehistory of the Northwest Coast inhabitants is still relatively scanty. Because of the series of mountain ranges that separate it from the interior, the region is an isolated one, and at first glance suggests development independent of contact with the other streams of Indian life in the hemisphere. But access to the coastal area was possible to peoples using boats, and to others who moved from the north or the south along the coast or who crossed mountain passes from the interior plateau and came down the various river valleys from the cordillera. Although archeological investigations are increasing, little, however, can be said yet concerning how the first peoples arrived in the area, when they came, or how the different cultural systems developed. There is some evidence of the presence of what has been called an initial Coastal Land Hunting Period, beginning perhaps more than 8,000 years ago, when hunters, coming presumably by land, across passes, down rivers, or up from more southerly regions, occupied parts of the area. A few chipped stone points of the Clovis and other types have been found. These may have been left by hunting and gathering peoples of the Old Cordilleran Culture (falling within Krieger's Paleo-Indian Stage), who killed Pleistocene game. The culture, it is thought, was based originally along the cordillera, from where it spread eventually down such rivers as the Fraser and Columbia toward the coast.

The next oldest finds date from much later periods, commencing about 1000 B.C., and show the presence by that time of sea-oriented cultures in parts of the area. The oldest, termed Early Maritime, and characterized by the traits of people who fished extensively, hunted sea mammals with harpoons, and used ground slate more than stone for points and implements, has suggested to some that there was an intrusion into the area of Eskimo influences from the north. More recently, however, it has been proposed that these influences reached the area from Asia, via the interior of northwestern North America, bypassing the Eskimos, who, instead of doing the influencing, were themselves influenced by this culture of the Northwest Coast, which spread north toward them. Others believe that a combination of influences interacted on the Northwest Coast, that hunting peoples from the interior plateau who had moved down to the coast had gradually developed a maritime-based culture which, as time passed, received additional influences both from Asia (via the interior plateau) and from the Eskimos. The time span after the Early Maritime Culture has been divided by some into an Intermediate Period, characterized by the integrating of the traits and ways of life of the maritime peoples and land hunters, and a third period, called Late, marked by an emphasis in the adaptation of economies and cultures to the maritime environment. At any rate, it seems that during the last 2,000 years, economies oriented to fishing, supplemented by gathering and hunting, existed in much of the area, and that within at least the last 700 years, with additional influences arriving perhaps from the north or the interior, there developed the various cultures found along the coast in historic times, with their intricate societies and special traits, ranging from caste systems to extraordinary skills with woodworking tools.

When they were first met by the whites, the peoples of the Northwest Coast exhibited various tribal differences, but all were obsessed with property and prestige. The property, accumulated by individuals, included items of material wealth, such as blankets, baskets, canoes, beautifully carved boxes, decorated hides, and slaves, as well as the ownership of certain valued rights, like a heraldic crest, a particular name, a guardian spirit, or even a song that no one else might sing. Especially treasured by some peoples, after the arrival of white sea traders, were large panels of hammered copper, which were sometimes equal in trade value to several thousand blankets.

A unique institution known as the potlatch (from the Nootka expression *patshatl*, meaning "giving") was a prominent feature of tribal life and gave owners of property an opportunity to compete for prestige and status. At a potlatch, a feast given usually to celebrate some important event, such as a marriage or the naming of an heir, or even to remove the stain of a personal humiliation, the host sought greatness

and position by giving away his wealth, or ostentatiously
destroying it in front of his guests. On such an occasion he
would free or kill his slaves, cut up or throw away his large
plates of copper, distribute piles of blankets, and burn his
store of fish oil and perhaps his own house. The more
wealth he divested himself of, the greater was his prestige and
that of his clan. All the while he would sing songs that
boasted about himself, proclaimed his own greatness, and
insulted his rivals. Those persons would suffer humiliation,
but they would have to endure it until they, in turn, could
give potlatches of their own that outdid that of the taunter
in the amount of property given away or destroyed. Thus,
the round of accumulating and squandering wealth continued. Persons who gave a certain number of potlatches and
impressed others with their wealth were classed as chiefs
and "nobles"; everyone else was a commoner or a slave. To
many whites who, in later days, witnessed potlatches, the
institution seemed strange and wasteful; but the wealth
distributed at potlatches often passed into the hands of
many people who, eventually, would give potlatches themselves, so that some of the property went round and round.
Moreover, some of the wealth was usually surplus property
that had no trading value, for there was little that it could
purchase or that could be done with it.

Most of the clans and villages of the tribes engaged in
frequent raiding and warfare. Men on war parties wore
wooden helmets and slat armor and fought with clubs, bows
and arrows, daggers, and spears. Among the fiercest of the
raiders were the Tlingits of Alaska's Panhandle, but one of
their stories tells of the making of a peace. The Tlingits
frequently experienced drawn-out periods of interclan raiding
for slaves and loot. Once, according to the tale, uninterrupted
struggle continued for so long that the villagers on both
sides were prevented from securing food for the winter. As
the weather became colder, everyone could sense the ap-
proaching crisis when no one would have anything to eat.
The headman of one of the sides finally decided on an act of
sacrifice. Walking out between the warring camps, he called
to the enemy," You know my rank and importance. I am
the chief. Take me, make peace, and go gather food." After
a moment, the enemy accepted his offer. They seized him,
slew him, and made peace with his people. Then everyone
on both sides hurried to gather food.

A principal object of most raids was to secure slaves, one
of the main elements of wealth. Many villages contained

large numbers of slaves; in one of them it was said that almost a third of the population were slaves.

War parties—and most of the people generally—traveled by water. In addition to raids, frequent trips were made to trade or simply to visit. The people were excellent canoe builders, fashioning craft that varied in length, size, and decoration. The largest vessels, which could be used for harpoon whaling and other trips on open water, were up to sixty feet in length, hollowed by fire and adz from single trees, and carved with various figures. The Nootkas of Vancouver Island and the Makahs of Cape Flattery were accomplished whalers; most other tribes stayed closer to shore and made less frequent long distance sea trips.

In almost all the villages the people had a rich and significant religious life, full of dramatic rituals, dances, and ceremonies. They believed in many spirit beings, including those of the eagle, beaver, raven, bear, and whale, whose protection they continually sought. Sometimes the spirits were unfavorable, withholding protection or good fortune, and then they might be reviled and cursed. There were numerous shamans who employed magic and elaborate trickery to enhance their prestige and often engaged in competitive displays of magic to defeat and humiliate rivals. Secret societies, each one with particular religious rituals and functions, existed among the tribes; one of the best known was the Kwakiutl Cannibal Society, whose initiates were possessed by the Cannibal Spirit at the North End of the World. Working up to a frenzy, the dancers bit flesh from the arms of those watching them, and then ate of the body of a specially killed slave or of an animal masked to resemble a human. There were, in addition, numerous ceremonies participated in by dancers in symbolic masks.

The richly carved and ornamented masks were part of a great outpouring of artistic works by skilled woodworkers and other craftsmen and artisans among the tribes. All of the work was functional or meaningful in the daily lives of the people. The many products, with imaginative designs based on stylized birds and animals, including the beaver, bear, whale, and mythical Thunderbird, comprise one of the world's most vigorous and easily recognized art styles. The adz, and perhaps the skills of carving, came to the coast from the interior. Among the Kwakiutls and Haidas, carvers, sometimes working with shell and slate as well as wood, turned out decorative boxes, hats, and utilitarian objects in addition to magnificent masks. Tlingits and

Tsimshians produced beautiful Chilkat blankets, woven of cedar bark and the hair of mountain goat, and containing forceful and striking designs. Hats and baskets were also woven, and hides were painted. Skilled craftsmen, in addition, built large, gabled houses of planks, adorning them with carved house posts and door poles, painted, like the house walls, with the owner's crests—the animal spirit guardians and ancestors of his clan.

After white traders arrived on the coast and provided the Indians with iron-edged tools, the imagination of the native carvers increased with their new capabilities, and the art of wood carving reached its highest level. Especially after the middle of the nineteenth century tall trees were felled, and after being carved into monumental totem poles—which had no religious significance but were merely symbols of prestige, bearing the crests or narrative histories of the men who paid for the making of the poles—they were erected in front of houses. Many villages were sometimes marked by lines of such poles standing before the rectangular houses, and in time the dramatic totem pole with its column of carved animals and birds, one above another, became a visual symbol, like a trademark, for all American Indians among white men in many parts of the world.

The clothing worn by the peoples of the Northwest Coast was simple and was usually made of shredded cedar bark. In summer men wore only breechcloths or went naked, but women always wore plant-fiber skirts. Robes and shirts were also in use, and in cold weather furs and hides served as cloaks. People rarely used moccasins, but cone-shaped basketry hats with wide rims to protect against the frequent rains were commonly worn. Sometimes the hats were painted or woven with designs. Men pierced their noses to hold decorative pieces of shell or wood in their septums, and sometimes they wore mustaches and beards, a trait that was rare among American Indians, although it did exist elsewhere among some tribes. In the central part of the area, infants' heads were flattened by being pressed with bindings against the cradleboard. Flattened heads were considered marks of nobility and beauty, and slaves could be easily identified by their unflattened heads. Both sexes also practiced tattooing.

In the more southerly portion of the area, the culture was less splendid, and tribes possessed less wealth than those farther north. Instead of the copper plates (traded from whites for sea-otter furs, usually, and called "coppers") and the finely designed blankets, such items as the skins of albino deer and blades of obsidian, a volcanic glass, were prized among the Hupas, Yuroks, and other northwestern California peoples. Rather than destroying their wealth, the California tribes were generally content to show it off in ceremonies. From Vancouver Island to California, small, tusk-shaped dentalium shells, used as decorations, standards of value, and objects of barter, were especially valued by the different tribes. Although all the tribes maintained contact and some trade relations with neighboring peoples of other culture areas in the interior, the more southerly tribes conducted a regular and important intercourse with their neighbors. The Chinooks of Oregon and Washington became known as middlemen in a busy commerce that carried articles back and forth between coastal tribes and those of the interior Plateau Culture. The Dalles fishing center on the Columbia River was one especially important trading center where Chinookan-speaking tribes met and traded regularly with Plateau Indians. At such places in western Washington and Oregon, which were frequented later also by white men, there developed what was termed the Chinook Jargon, a mixture of Chinookan, Salishan, and white men's words and expressions that was used as a medium of communication in the Northwest.

The first whites to reach the Northwest Coast were Russian fur traders who arrived in the eighteenth century. They introduced manufactured goods, including ironware, as well as certain artistic and design influences. Spanish mariners and English and American sea-otter traders appeared toward the end of the century, accelerating the impact of civilization on the tribes. Many of the Indians perished in conflicts with the traders or from diseases which the white introduced. The Indian culture, however, held its own for a while, even reaching a climax in wood carving after the white men's tools became plentiful. But in time the culture degenerated, and its brilliance dimmed and disappeared. Indian villages still exist, and a few carvers here and there have tried to keep alive or revive old skills; but their work, even including an occasional totem pole, is usually done today as an attraction for tourists or on assignment for some non-Indian purchaser. Meanwhile, non-Indians in Alaska, failing to take steps to protect the truly creatives poles and houseposts of the past, are allowing these monumental carvings to rot away in the damp climate and disappear.

10

The Tribes of the Northeast Woodlands

A DISTINCT CULTURAL AREA EXISTED IN THE EASTERN PART
of North America from the St. Lawrence River and
the Great Lakes to the Carolinas and the Ohio River
drainage and westward to the Mississippi River. In this
region, which included the Atlantic Coast, interior rivers,
lakes, and woodlands, as well as Midwest prairies, lived a
large number of tribes, speaking principally Algonquian,
Iroquoian, and Siouan languages. There were no sharp
borders to the area: in the north, hunting bands shared
some traits with neighboring peoples of the Subarctic area;
in the west, the prairie peoples had various traits in common with some of the tribes of the eastern fringe of the
Plains cultural area; and in the south, the ways of life of
many of the agricultural groups were not wholly dissimilar
from those of neighboring tribes of the Southeastern United
States.

Along the Atlantic Coast, extending from Canada's St.
Lawrence Valley to the Carolinas, generally on the eastern
side of the Appalachians, were the first North American
Indians known to the white colonists. In the north,
French and English met Micmacs, Abnakis, Penobscots,
Passamaquoddys, and Malecites in Nova Scotia, New Bruns-
wick, and Maine. Those Indians were principally forest
hunters and fishermen, but many of them also gathered
maple sugar, and those farthest south did some farming.
In New England and the lower Hudson River Valley lived
Algonquian-speaking Pennacooks, Nipmucs, Massachusets,
Wampanoags, Nausets, Niantics, Narragansets, Pequots,
Mahicans, Mohegans, Wappingers, and several smaller
groups. To their south were Delawares (also known as Lenni

Lenapes), Nanticokes, Conoys, Pamlicos, Powhatans, and Shawnees, all members of the Algonquian-language family, as well as Monacans, Saponis, Catawbas, and Tutelos, who spoke Siouan tongues; Tuscaroras and Nottaways, who were Iroquoian; and other less numerous groups. South of Maine all of these Atlantic coastal peoples depended principally on agriculture for their food, although they also hunted and fished and many of them gathered shellfish and various wild foods.

In the northern interior, Iroquoian-speaking tribes dominated territory extending from the St. Lawrence River to Georgian Bay in Canada and from the western side of the Hudson River in New York, across a large part of Pennsylvania, to eastern Ohio in the present-day United States. In Ontario, on the eastern side of Georgian Bay and Lake Huron, were the Hurons and their relatives, the Tionontatis, also called the Tobacco People or Petuns; together, they are believed to have had a population of between 45,000 and 60,000 when white men first encountered them. To their south was a confederacy of Iroquoian settlements that became known as the Neutrals, because they tried to avoid entanglements in the wars between the Hurons and the New York Iroquois. Susquehannocks, or Conestogas, dwelled in central Pennsylvania, and Eries, also called "People of the Panther," were to their west. Across upper New York, from Lake Champlain to the Genesee River, were the most powerful and best known Iroquois tribes: from east to west they were Mohawks, Oneidas, Onondagas, Cayugas, and Senecas. Together they constituted the confederacy of the Five Nations, known as the League of the Iroquois, later changed to the Six Nations, when the Tuscaroras joined them.

In the Midwest, beyond the Iroquoian settlements, a number of other tribes, almost all of them Algonquians, lived around Lakes Michigan and Superior. They included Sauk and Foxes, Potawatomis, Ottawas, Menominees, Kickapoos, and Ojibwas. The latter, whose name Europeans corrupted into Chippewa, had an estimated population of 25,000, most of them nomadic hunters and fishermen who lived too far north to depend to a great extent on agriculture. The region also included Siouan-speaking Winnebagos who lived in the Green Bay area of Wisconsin, and whose ancestors seem to have left other Sioux and migrated to that area from the upper Mississippi Valley about A.D. 1000.

South of the Great Lakes, in Indiana and Illinois, were

still more Algonquian-speaking tribes. They included Kas-kaskias, Peorias, and other tribes of the Illinois Confederacy, and Miamis, who were related to nearby Weas and Pianka-shaws. All of them were hunters and farmers, but they were not as numerous as the more northerly tribes. West Virginia and Kentucky were used as hunting grounds by many tribes, particularly by the Shawnees who lived in numerous sepa-rated groups from the Kentucky-Tennessee border to the Southeast. They made long treks paralleling the Appalachian spine to hunt, visit, and make war, and after the Atlantic colonists began pushing coastal tribes into their country, their bands gradually concentrated in the Ohio Valley.

Man is know to have been in the Northeast area for at least 11,000 years. Even while the Ice Age still existed, small groups of nomadic hunters, using Clovis-type spear points and chipped-stone implements similar to those of the fluted-point big-game hunters of the Southeast and Plains, were in the Northeast, probably having spread into it from the West or South after migrations from Alaska. Although no human relics have yet been found in the area in association with remains of extinct Pleistocene animals, archeologists have discovered lanceolate points, knives, scrapers, and other artifacts with remains of barren ground caribou, about 11,000 years old, in southeastern Michigan and a site of early hunters in Nova Scotia, dating back to at least the same time. In addition, many other ancient relics, including fluted points, scrapers, and knives, have been found in nu-merous areas, and it is assumed that hunters of the North-east killed mastodons, musk ox, and giant beaver and elk, in addition to smaller game and, in the north, moose and caribou.

About 10,000 years ago, as the Ice Age ended and mastodons and other Pleistocene big game began to disap-pear, the fluted-type spear points, associated with hunters of those animals, went out of use through most of the area, although they continued to be employed for a longer time in the north and extreme northeast, where the big game animals persisted for a lengthier period. The older points were gradually replaced by various Plano-type points, and their users went through a long stage of transition and devel-opment, often referred to as the Early Archaic and lasting, in different regions, for approximately 3,000 to 5,000 years. In the region of the Upper Great Lakes, where people lived in an environment of glacial and postglacial lakes, much of this era is referred to as the Aqua-Plano Stage. During the period the different peoples throughout the area were influenced increasingly by a gradual change in climate and plant life, as the glaciers retreated, the weather warmed, and ecological zones crept northward. Although the people were still essentially nomadic hunters, they came to depend more on gathering and collecting wild foods and on fishing, and the development of the various groups reflected such influences as the availability of different foods and raw materials and the ability to move from one area to another. Material traits, methods, and techniques changed also. Ground-stone mortars, pestles, adzes, and other objects came into use and in the region of the Upper Great Lakes the first form of crude boats, perhaps dugout canoes hollowed from logs, may have been developed.

The period from about 5,000 to 3,000 years ago, sometimes termed the Late Archaic, was marked by the emergence of a number of regional cultures, many, if not most, of them related possibly to a single parent culture or to each other, but in ways that are not yet fully clear. One generalized culture that was parent perhaps to others over most of the area has been called Boreal Archaic. The culture extended from the Upper Great Lakes to the Atlantic Coast and has been characterized as forest-adapted, not unlike other early boreal cultures that existed in the northern forested regions of Asia and Europe. Some persons believe that the boreal culture was brought to the Northeast by migrants from a similar habitat in northeastern Asia, who, after crossing to North America, moved south, skirted the Great Lakes on the west, and then moved into the Northeast. It was during this period, perhaps, that persons speaking a tongue parent to the Algonquian languages of later times entered the Northeast, but little is actually known yet concerning movements of peoples at this time.

However the Boreal Archaic Stage developed, it thrived in the pine and hardwood forests of the area. The people possessed woodworking tools, making stone adzes, axes, gouges, and other implements by newly introduced techniques of pounding and pecking, followed by grinding and polishing. In the Upper Great Lakes region, people employed grooved axes more than other tools and, by this time, definitely made dugout canoes. Farther east, where the period has been divided by some persons into Early and Late stages, relics, including ground-stone tools and grooved stones for nets with which to snare birds, have been found in northern New England and the lower St. Lawrence Valley and ascribed to people who lived during the Early stage. The Late stage, beginning about 4,000 years ago and lasting for approximately a thousand years (although longer in the north), was marked by an increase in the variety and number of implements made and by the employment of new and better techniques.

During the same period, beginning about 4,500 years ago or more, western New York was the scene of a relatively short-lived Lamoka Culture whose people used projectile points related possibly to others found in several places from eastern Michigan to the Atlantic Coast and bone-implement and ornament types found also in the Ohio Valley. The Lamoka people, who may have been a link between those on the coast and others in the Ohio Valley and farther west, utilized bone and antler intensively for the production of knives, scrapers, awls, fishing tools, whistles, and pendants, but also produced tools and such implements as mortars and pestles by grinding and polishing stone. A longer-lived Laurentian Culture, also a manifestation of the Boreal Archaic Stage, existed about the same time, or slightly later, in eastern New York, the St. Lawrence Valley, and New England. Characteristic of that culture were gouges, adzes, harpoons, and ground slate points and knives. There were a number of regional variants of the culture, and projectile points similar to those of the Laurentian peoples have been found also from the Ohio Valley to the eastern part of the northern prairies.

In the area of the western Great Lakes, centering from northern Illinois to Lake Superior, people began to hammer, grind, and shape pieces of raw copper into utilitarian and decorative forms, making spear points (both socketed and with tangs), knives, wedges, awls, beads, gouges, celts, axes, pendants, and bracelets. The first workers of metal in the Americas (and perhaps the world), they also learned the process of annealing, and developed what has been called the Old Copper Culture. An offshoot possibly of an early stage of boreal culture, it reached a height from about 4,000 to 3,000 years ago. Its people made containers and other objects of birchbark and possessed domesticated dogs, wooden dugouts, and perhaps birchbark canoes. Why the culture ended is not known. Possibly the retreat of glacial ice and the northward move of the boreal forest and animals drew some of the Old Copper people northward from the region where the copper existed. Other persons may have stayed and been assimilated into new cultures, or they may have altered their own culture in the changing climate and environment. The use of copper, however, gradually declined in the region, although some groups continued to employ it in making knives, small awls, and a few other objects up to historic times.

Generally, the Boreal Archaic Stage reflected a link in the continuous change throughout the area from the original hunting culture to the emergence of differentiated Woodland groups possessing more stable economies and more sedentary ways of life. The Late Archaic Stage saw the beginning of transition to Early Woodland cultures. In that period, beginning approximately 3,500 years ago, people of what is referred to as the Glacial Kame burial complex, whose sites have been found so far in southern Ontario, Vermont, southern Michigan, and northern Indiana and Ohio, exemplified an increasing custom of burying the dead in high places, such as sandy knolls or ridges, away from settlement sites. With the dead were placed various objects, including tools and ornaments of stone, copper, and shell, as well as powdered red ocher.

By approximately 3,000 years ago, a so-called burial complex, overlapping the latter stages of the Boreal cultures, had become widespread across a large part of the Northeast. It was marked by great attention to forms and rituals that accompanied the burying of the dead. Goods buried with the deceased included many new items, and some traits, like an increase in cremation, which occurred almost everywhere, seem to hint at links between the different regions. Yet the various sites also show distinct regional characteristics and suggest the spread of ideas and customs among different local groups rather than the existence of some sort of unifying bond among them. In the western part of the area people began raising dome-shaped mounds of earth above the burials. In addition, the period was marked by the first appearance of pottery in the Northeast. Its origins are disputed. It has been suggested by some persons that its distinctive cord-marked style resembled ceramic work done by people of the forest zones of Europe and Asia, and that it was introduced in the Northeast at this time by migrants who had come originally from Siberia. Others theorize, instead, that it developed independently within the area, that it had been developed in the Southeast (where a different pottery, derived apparently from South or Middle America, had been present since about 2500 B.C.) and had diffused north, or that it had come from Mexico. All that seems definitely known, however, is that archeological studies show that it appeared in the eastern part of the Northeast (about 1200 B.C.) before the rest of the area, and that for a long time it was of relatively little importance in the places in which it existed.

The period from about 3,000 years ago until approximately 500 years before the beginning of the Christian era has been characterized as the Early Woodland Stage of development in the Northeast, and is marked particularly by the rise and growth of mound-building cultures. Beginning about 1000 B.C. and lasting to perhaps A.D. 200, the most important burial mound culture of the period, the Adena, developed and flourished in the Ohio Valley, from where migrants seem to have spread it eventually to the Chesapeake Bay region and thence northward into New York and New England. During this same period, simple agriculture, which had originated millennia earlier in northern and central Mexico, spread gradually into the Northeast—probably after having been introduced to the lower Mississippi Valley by migrants from Mexico. It was an incipient stage of agriculture in the Northeast, and people still relied principally on hunting, gathering, fishing, and the collection of shellfish. In the region of Salts Cave, Kentucky, however, people of about 1190 B.C. seem to have been relying already on cultivated squash, gourd, and possibly sunflower and marsh elder for 45 per cent of their food, and on wild foods for the rest of their diet, thus suggesting, if recent archeological studies in that region have been assessed correctly, that agriculture was already well advanced in at least parts of the Northeast by 3,000 years ago.

As it had done elsewhere, agriculture in time permitted the acceleration of population growth and the establishment of fixed settlements, the development of culture and trade, and the adoption of increasingly complex and sophisticated social and religious systems in the Northeast. The Adena Culture, with roots in the simple burial-mound cultures of the Late Archaic and transitional stages, reflected the beginnings of all these changes. In its early stages, it was characterized by simple low burial mounds and relatively simple burial objects. The later Adena sites are marked by circular earthworks and large, elaborately constructed mounds, showing the labor of many people under some overall direction, and also by artistic objects of mica and copper, incised pottery, engraved tablets, pearl beads, and various items of ornamentation, different cloth weaves, and an art style of a high level. These later Adena sites also reflect evidence of an increasing population, a more sedentary life, status differentiation among the people, the use of rectangular houses, and, generally, a broad cultural development. Elsewhere in the Northeast, development was somewhat similar, although apparently not as fulsome or flamboyant. In a number of regions, the study of sequences of Early Woodland cultures shows influences of Adena traits and the development of Adena-like cultures, but the original Adena sites in the Ohio Valley seem to form the central and most important cultural complex in the Northeast during the period.

In that same Ohio Valley heartland, after about 100 B.C., arose one of the most impressive "golden ages" of native peoples that ever existed on the continent north of Mexico. Termed Hopewellian, for the name of the owner of one of the principal of its 75–100 sites found in the Ohio Valley, it had roots in the Adena stage, and its centers were also in the central Mississippi and Illinois river valleys. Moreover, it received influences from time to time from various other groups in both the Northeast and Southeast, and also—via the Southeast—from Mexico.

The Hopewell stage lasted until about A.D. 500–700, and the period is designated as Middle Woodland. Hopewellian villages and ceremonial centers were built along rivers and were characterized principally by large conical or dome-shaped burial mounds, up to 30 feet or more in height and 200 feet in circumference, as well as by great, elaborately constructed earthen walls enclosing large circular, oval, or rectangular areas. Although the growth of agriculture provided the base for the development of the Hopewellian stage, and the people raised corn, squash, and presumably beans and tobacco, farming was still not as fundamental to the economy as it would become later in the Northeast. Hunting was still of major importance, and the villagers fished the streams and, in certain areas, gathered shellfish. The dwellings of the people were probably different types of round or oval wigwams with dome-shaped roofs of bent saplings covered with skins, mats, or sheets of bark. Few of the people, it is believed, lived in the ceremonial centers, but rather in nearby semi-permanent villages that had neither mounds nor earthen walls.

One of the principal factors that contributed to the growth and vitality of the Hopewellian Culture was the existence of a remarkable network of trade, almost continent-wide, that brought to Hopewellian settlements a great variety of objects and exotic materials, including such things as grizzly bear teeth and obsidian from the Rocky Mountains, conch shells from the Gulf Coast and other shells from the Atlantic Coast, mica from the Appalachians, and copper and lead from the Great Lakes and upper Mississippi Valley. A primary aim of the trade network—which, at the time, spread Hopewellian traits—seems to have been to acquire materials from which to fashion ceremonial objects to deposit in the mounds with the dead. But articles of all kinds and for many uses were produced in profusion and with artistic excellence. Tools were made of copper, stone, bone, and antler. Ornaments, including bead necklaces, arm bands, pendants, and ear and breast decorative pieces, were fashioned from metal, shell, bone, and stone. Fine pottery of several styles, including some of the best made at any time by Indians in the Northeast, was produced; spoons and other utensils were made of various materials, including shells; cloth was woven with thread made from the soft inner bark of certain trees; and stone bowls of tobacco pipes were sculptured beautifully in the form of humans and animals. Artistic abilities reached a climax in the making of effigy forms of copper and mica, the sculpturing in stone and bone, and the engraving on bone, shell, and wood. Musical instruments, including panpipes, various types of rattles, and, probably, drums, were also made.

Many beautiful objects were buried with the dead of high rank; after the burial, the large mounds of earth were erected over the corpse and the objects that had been placed with it. The mounds and other archeological evidence suggest that the Hopewellians had a highly developed social organization that included class structure and a division of labor, with specialists like metal workers, artists, and traders; leaders of hereditary rank and privileges; a strong religious system; and direction over cooperative labor. The culture, as a whole, must have been vital and dynamic to have maintained the far-flung exchange system. Some persons have suggested that the Ohio Hopewell sites reflect the existence of a single cultural group with an expansionist society that was dominated and directed by an elite element. But although other societies with Hopewellian traits existed in the Northeast and Southeast areas during this period—their cultures being modified generally by various local traditions and different external influences—there is no evidence that the Ohio Hopewellians, despite their aggressive and widespread trade, were bent on overcoming neighbors and implanting their ways on others. The Illinois Hopewellians were more expansionist; they spread their culture, both by migrations and influence, into many Midwestern regions, including parts of the Upper Great Lakes and across Missouri to the vicinity of present-day Kansas City.

Elsewhere, the Hopewell way of life was a distinctive stage of development across much of the Northeast area, although no group equalled the Ohio people's levels of accomplishment. An important sequence of northern cultures, termed Point Peninsula and centered in parts of New York and Ontario, had no agriculture, at least in its early stages, but possessed an interesting type of pottery found also from Alberta and northern Minnesota to the Atlantic Coast. The ceramic type seems to have originated in Asia, and some archeologists think it was brought directly by migrants who moved through the Canadian forests from the Northwest, and whose arrival in the Northeast cultural area during the Adena period contributed a stimulus to the development of the Hopewellian Culture. That may be true; but evidence is also strong that the Hopewell Culture, instead, influenced later stages of Point Peninsula, which after a long sequence of changes, and under additional influences, went on to become the Owasco Culture of about A.D. 1200–1300, and then the initial stage of eastern Iroquoian culture.

After A.D. 500 the Hopewell zenith faded. What happened is not known; perhaps the trade network so necessary for the acquisition of raw materials collapsed. At any rate, fewer of the huge burial mounds were built, and artistic abilities declined. Many of the Hopewellian traits disappeared, and new cultural groups developed gradually throughout the whole Northeast area. The underlying way of life was now generally the same everywhere, but the many separate groups, all on a somewhat similar cultural level, differed among themselves in details of life according to the persistence of local ideas, the degree of the importance of agriculture, and the strength of influences coming to them from new sources, particularly from a developing Mississippian Culture centered in the Mississippi Valley and characterized by a strong agricultural base. That culture seems to have arisen about A.D. 700 in the Mississippi Valley between the present-day vicinities of Memphis and St. Louis and to have been stimulated, about two hundred years later, by agricultural and other influences that reached it from the Huastec area of northeastern Mexico. It spread aggressively through the present-day U.S. Southeast, giving rise there to the advanced temple mound-building societies, and then by migrations and the diffusion of traits moved up the Mississippi and Ohio valleys.

Each region of the Northeast, between approximately A.D. 1000–1600, witnessed gradual cultural changes that established finally the ways of life of the historic tribes that were met in the different localities by white men. The period as a whole was marked by an increase in the importance of agriculture, the growth of population, a rise in the number of settlements, the expansion of the size of the settlements, and a general advance of cultural development. In the Ohio Valley, variants of the Mississippian Culture, which had stimulated agriculture by introducing such improvements as more productive types of corn and the flint hoe, succeeded the Hopewell stage and became gradually dominant until historic times. In southern Wisconsin, the Hopewell stage turned, in time, into the Effigy Mound Culture, so named because its people built a large number of mounds in the form of animals, birds, and men. Across the northern forest zone from Minnesota and the Great Lakes to the St. Lawrence Valley and New England, a series of interrelated cultures developed into those of the ancestors of the historic tribes that spoke Siouan, Algonquian, and Iroquoian tongues. There were a few migrations into the area, and a few out of it. One Siouan group, ancestral to the Winnebago tribe of historic times, came undoubtedly from the upper Mississippi Valley to northeastern Wisconsin about A.D. 1000. After A.D. 1200, less favorable agricultural conditions in various northern parts of the area, like the Upper Great Lakes, forced some groups to rely more on hunting and on such local plants as wild rice. But where agriculture could be practiced, it flourished, continuing to spread eastward and creating the basis for a number of late prehistoric cultures, like the Fort Ancient on the upper Ohio and the Monongahela Woodland in western Pennsylvania. The people of the latter culture, with an intensive farming base, possessed palisaded villages and had connections with Algonquian bands in Virginia and with Iroquois to the north.

It was once thought that the Iroquois had been invaders, who at a late date had sliced their way from the south or west into the Northeast territory of the Algonquians and had made a home for themselves in that area by force. Today, it is known that Iroquois backgrounds are deeply rooted in the Northeast, that as a people they emerged gradually from Owascoid cultures of the Lower Great Lakes and New York, and that by about A.D. 1200 they possessed many of their traits of historic times, including the longhouse. Although some of their groups shifted on occasion with the Northeast area—various of them moving during the sixteenth century from the lower St. Lawrence to east-central New York—the cultural development that led to the Iroquois tribes, as white men found them, occurred entirely in the Northeast and was neither unique nor on a plane higher than that of other tribes in the area.

By historic times the Northeast was the home of numerous hunting, fishing, and farming tribes, the inheritors of the long sequences of development outlined above. Almost all the tribes dwelled in villages and raised corn, squash, and beans on garden plots close to their settlements. They cleared the fields by the slash-and-burn technique, cutting down the larger trees, burning over the area, and planting crops between the stumps. Hunting and fishing were also important, and among the most northerly peoples in the area, where there was no agriculture, the diet resembled that of the neighboring Subarctic hunters and fishermen. Throughout the Northeast, however, wild game, including deer, bear, and wildfowl, abounded and some of the Indians, especially in the western part of the area, hunted buffalo during certain seasons. Fish filled the streams and lakes and were taken with hook, net, or spear. Along the seacoast and certain streams shellfish were often an important element of the diet.

Several kinds of dwellings were used in the area. In large parts of the east, the villages, enclosed usually by stockades, were composed of a number of rectangular, bark-covered longhouses with barrel-shaped roofs. Wigwams, both conical and dome-shaped, formed by straight or bent poles and covered with mats, bark, or hides, were found throughout the region. Clothing was made from skins, and men wore breechcloths, shirts, leggings, and moccasins. Women's garments included a skirt and jacket, and in cold weather both sexes wore skin robes. Clothing and personal objects were ornamented with floral designs, fashioned originally with porcupine quills and later, after the white man's arrival, with trade beads as well. Indian males plucked out or shaved their hair except for a long strip that was allowed to grow and stand up from the forehead to the back of the neck. Some men also grew a "scalplock" that hung down at the back of the head to taunt an enemy.

The tribes were divided into different clans, composed of families, and tribal bonds were usually strong, especially in times of war—which were frequent. Raids were conducted for personal glory, revenge, or the seizure of property, and serious warfare was waged over territorial hunting rights. Warriors were armed with bows and arrows, spears, and various types of tomahawks, ranging from hatchet-like forms to spiked, ball-headed clubs. Special ceremonies often preceded raids, and scalp dances followed victories. The Iroquois and some other tribes were extremely cruel, torturing captives to test their courage, and indulging occasionally in cannibalism.

Various spirits were worshipped by the different tribes, but the Master of Life, or Supreme Being, was regarded as the most powerful. Unison prayers for guidance were common, and people sought contact with the supernatural through dreams. Shamans were frequently powerful personages. Quite often they were talented magicians or tricksters, able to produce spirit voices and eerie dancing lights in the darkness, or to seem to make a building shake.

The use of wampum (from the Algonquian word *wampompeag*) had become widespread through the region before the arrival of white men. Employed as mnemonic devices, as money, and as guarantees of promises or agreements in intertribal councils, wampum were bits of seashells from the Atlantic Coast, cut, drilled, and strung like beads into strands or belts. A long-stemmed pipe, later given the French name *calumet*, was also in wide use as a passport of messengers and emissaries and as an important element in councils and certain religious rites. In peace ceremonies it was passed from hand to hand and smoked by each of the participants.

Like the Algonquians who lived farther west about the Great Lakes, those along the eastern seaboard used wood and bark utensils, made finely woven mats and splint basketry, and had pipes and bowls of stone. On hunts and raids they often traveled on foot, sometimes for extremely long distances, but the more northerly peoples also moved by water in birchbark canoes. The first explorers and colonists found many of the coastal Algonquians engaged in wars with each other and with the Iroquois. For their mutual protection, loose confederacies, sometimes composed of as many as thirty villages, had been formed. Few of them, however, save for some in the southern part of the region, had developed strong leadership or organization. In lower New York, New Jersey, and Delaware, the Delaware Indians were bound together more tightly under strong headmen, as were the Powhatans of Virginia.

The Algonquians of the Atlantic Coast were generally friendly to the first settlers and helped them become established in the New World, teaching them Indian methods of hunting, fishing, farming, and canoe making. Indian foods entered the white men's diets; Indian words, such as succotash, wigwam, and moccasin, were adopted by the newcomers; and Indian customs became subtle but powerful influences on the colonists' social and political thinking. In time, conflicts arose and widened, caused frequently by the settlers' demand for Indian land and by hurts and resentments among the Indians. In ensuing wars, many of the tribes were almost wiped out. The survivors were forced to cede lands and move farther west or were allowed to remain in weak, harmless pockets where they eventually died off or left descendants who still exist and maintain their Indian identity in small communities. Among the present-day remnants of once-powerful Atlantic Coast tribes are Penobscots and Passamaquoddys in Maine; Wampanoags and Narragansets in Massachusetts and Rhode Island; Pequots and Mohegans in Connecticut; Shinnecocks on Long Island; Nanticokes in Delaware; Pamunkeys, Chickahominys, and Mattaponys (tracing ancestry to Powhatans) in Virginia; and Lumbees in North Carolina.

The northern Iroquoian-speaking tribes lived in large towns and villages, many of them protected by double or triple rings of stockades formed of upright logs. Within the palisades, houses were ranged in rows like streets. One Huron town was believed to have contained 200 large dwellings, housing between 4,000 and 6,000 people. The populous Hurons and Tobacco Hurons derived most of their food from farming. Fishing was also important, but hunting was undertaken principally to obtain hides for clothing. Hunts were usually conducted like mass roundups: deer in great numbers were surrounded and driven into corrals, or pounds, where they were slain. Huron political and social life was highly organized, the people being divided into families, clans, villages, and bands. When a person died, the Hurons believed, his soul went to a village in the sky. To assist the soul in its journey, the people participated in periodic Feasts of the Dead, in which the bones of the deceased were carried on the backs of villagers to a mass burial site. There, after elaborate ritual, the bones were buried with numerous articles, like tools, ornaments, food, fur robes, and weapons, and the souls launched properly on the journey to the distant sky village.

Legend says that a Huron refugee named Deganawidah and his disciple, a Mohawk chief or shaman named Hiawatha, founded the League of the five Iroquois tribes of New York about 1570, preaching that it would end bloodshed and wars of revenge among those tribes and would bring about a peace among all Indians based on equality and brotherhood. However it was originally achieved, the League of the Five Nations in practice rested on the organization of Iroquois political life, in which women held a special and important position. The foundation of Iroquois society was the "fireside," comprised of the mother and all her children. Each fireside, in turn, was part of a larger *ohwachira*, a group of related families in which relationships were traced through mothers. Two or more *ohwachiras* composed a clan, and the various clans within a tribe constituted the nation. All authority stemmed ultimately from the *ohwachiras* and the women who were at their heads. They named the male delegates and *ohwachira* representatives in clan and tribal councils, as well as the fifty sachems, or peace chiefs, who made up the ruling council of the Five Nations. The sachems, who were appointed from specific families, retained their positions for life, but a matriarch could depose an appointee if she found him unsatisfactory.

A second group of sachems, chosen from among famed warriors or for other special qualifications, were called Pine Tree chiefs. In effect, they constituted an additional body in tribal deliberations and could also speak in League meetings. The League usually convened each summer—although the law said it had to meet at least once every five years—

at the principal town of the Onondagas. The fifty council members voted by tribes rather than as individuals, and each tribe had one vote. Unanimous votes were required to reach decisions.

The League's council refrained from interference in the internal affairs of the member tribes, and on only rare occasions was it able to unite all the Five Nations against an external enemy. But it established agreements that ended blood feuds and serious conflicts among the members, provided them with a strong sense of unity, and in practice as well as theory was the most powerful and highly developed Indian confederation north of Mexico. Its idealistic conceptions and political structure contained elements of democracy and representative government that influenced various intellectual leaders in the Colonies.

The villages of the New York Iroquois were composed of long, bark-covered houses in which up to ten families lived side by side around their own fires. Religious life was highly organized and included a priesthood of three men and three women, "Keepers of the Faith," who supervised religious ceremonies, and various secret societies that performed curing and other ceremonies. Each society had its own officers, masks, songs, dances, and rituals. The Indians believed that all life was joined spiritually with the objects and forces of nature, and that a man's own inner spiritual power, called *orenda*, combated or resisted the powers of harm and evil. An individual's *orenda* was small, but it contributed to the combined and therefore greater *orendas* of the firesides, *ohwachiras*, and clans. A nation was made strong by the sum total of all the *orendas* within a tribe. When a man died or was killed, the loss of his *orenda* reduced those of all the different social groups of which it had been a part. To compensate for such losses and to maintain a group's total *orenda*, prisoners were often adopted into *ohwachiras* and tribes.

Despite the high ideals of the League of the Iroquois, its member tribes were almost constantly engaged in wars with Algonquians or with other Iroquoian peoples. According to Indian legends, the first wars after the establishment of the League were waged in an attempt to convert other tribes to acceptance of the code of the followers of Deganawidah and Hiawatha. But more often, those wars and the ones that were still being carried on when the white men arrived were raids for glory and prisoners. Some of the Iroquois' captives were adopted into the villages of the raiders, but others were tortured so cruelly that most of the Iroquois' neighbors feared and hated them. At the same time, the Iroquois regarded their torture of a victim as an opportunity for him to demonstrate his bravery. They often talked to the prisoner in kindly terms, encouraged him to show his courage, and honored him as a respected warrior.

In the seventeenth century, French, Dutch, and English fur traders competed for the friendship and trade of the Five Nations. The latter occupied a key geographic position in the trade and usually sided with the English, fighting not only the French but tribes that provided furs to the French. The intrigues of the trade caused a series of wars in which the Five Nations almost destroyed the other Iroquoian tribes and drove the survivors westward in great panic. Some of the remnants were adopted into the villages of the conquerors, who in the years that followed also gave haven to Algonquian refugees fleeing inland from European colonists on the Atlantic Coast. About 1715, Tuscaroras, trekking north after white settlers had forced them from their southern homeland, also joined the League, which was thereafter known as the Six Nations.

West of the Iroquoians, the Algonquian and other peoples of the Midwest and the Upper Great Lakes area supplemented their diet of agricultural products, game, and wildfowl with fish, annual harvests of wild rice, and maple sugar. In the northern areas, where agriculture was less important, the groups were mostly nomadic. Independent bands broke into smaller family units that roamed over hunting grounds in the autumn and came together with other families at fishing sites in summer. Travel was by foot or by birchbark canoe, and in winter many people used snowshoes and pulled burdens on toboggans. The nomadic groups, such as bands of Chippewas, made oval, dome-shaped wigwams that were easy and quick to construct. They were formed with saplings and were covered with birchbark strips, some twenty feet long and three feet wide, that were rolled up and carried by the women from one campsite to another. Some of the Indians around the Great Lakes wore fur mantles, painted and tattooed themselves, pierced their noses, and decorated their ears with trinkets. The Ottawas were noted wanderers who traveled long distances to hunt, trade, and make war. Although they maintained gardens of corn, they were known principally as far-ranging intertribal traders and middlemen who bought roots, tobacco, cornmeal, herbs, furs, and skins from one tribe and exchanged them with another. The name Ottawa itself meant "to trade."

Most of the Midwest groups south of the Chippewas, like the Sauk, Foxes, Miamis, Potawatomis, and others, had economies based on agriculture and were primarily sedentary peoples, although they moved about periodically to hunt or fish. Their towns, comprised frequently of long bark-covered lodges, were bordered by gardens in which the people raised corn, squash, beans, and pumpkins. During times of peace, civil chiefs and councils provided a loose form of government to the villages. In times of war and danger, influential roles were played by warriors who had gained followers by previous acts of leadership and valor. Social organization was based on relationships traced through the father, and the men in towns were divided into large general groups that competed against each other in games and in carrying out war raids. The world was believed to be filled with spirits that could give advice and help, and by fasting and solitary vigils men sought the guardianship of a spirit in a dream or vision. Sometimes, while seeking the supernatural, a song would occur to an Indian, and thereafter he might sing the song to help regain communication with his spiritual guardian. A typical Chippewa dream song went:

> In the Sky
> I am walking,
> A Bird
> I accompany.[1]

Shamans also played an important role in the people's lives. A secret group, the Midewiwin, or Grand Medicine Society, originally dedicated to healing the sick by spiritual means, had many special rituals, songs, and initiation ceremonies for a series of grades or degrees. Eventually, the society gained considerable political power and caused so much trouble that some tribes outlawed it.

The Indians of this portion of the Northeast culture area were thoroughly disrupted by the white man's fur trade. As the Indians tried to adjust to the new conditions introduced

---

[1] Frances Densmore: *Chippewa Music I*, Bureau of American Ethnology *Bulletin 45* (Washington, D.C., 1910).

by the trade, their long-established cultural traditions broke down. When the trade then moved west, beyond the area, the tribes, bereft of old standards, were faced by the on-slaught of settlers. By the end of the War of 1812, the Indians of the area had lost all independence and power. Treaties were forced upon them, making them relinquish their lands and emigrate to territory west of the Mississippi River. Many of the peoples departed for the new lands and ultimately ended up in Oklahoma. Others managed to evade the attempts to remove them, and large groups of Chippewas, Menominees, and others still reside in the states of the Upper Great Lakes, although generally in conditions of extreme poverty and neglect.

11

The Tribes of the
Southeastern
United States

THE SOUTHEASTERN PORTION OF THE PRESENT-DAY
United States, from the Atlantic Coast to the lower
Mississippi Valley, and from Tennessee to the Gulf of
Mexico, was the homeland of many populous tribes of several different language families, who lived in farming towns,
formed a number of strong confederacies—some under absolute leaders—and possessed a rich and complex culture
with roots in dynamic and accomplished mound-building
societies of the past.

A large part of the region was occupied by tribes of the
Muskogean branch of the Gulf language stock; they included
Creeks, Hitchitis, and Yamasees in Georgia, Seminoles and
Apalachees in Florida, Alabamas and Mobiles in Alabama,
and Choctaws, Chickasaws, and Houmas in Mississippi.
Other tribes, related to the Muskogeans both by language
and culture, were the Timucuas of northeastern Florida and
the Tunicas and Chitimachas of Louisiana, while still others,
who were related linguistically but were on a lower level of
culture, included the Calusas of southern Florida and the
Atakapas of Louisiana.

Large sections of the area were inhabited by members of
other language families. In North Carolina and Tennessee
were the towns of the Cherokees, a southern Iroquoian-speaking people. Caddoan speakers, including the Caddos,
Kichais, Wacos, and Tawaconis, dwelled on the cultural
area's western fringe, in eastern Texas and the Red River
Valley, where their culture contained elements of that of
the buffalo-hunting tribes of the plains. Biloxis on the Mis-

sissippi Gulf Coast and Arkansas and Quapaws in Arkansas
were Siouan-speaking peoples, and Yuchis in northern
Georgia spoke a tongue that appears to have been related
to Siouan. Finally, the Coahuiltecan language group was
represented by Tonkawas of Texas, neighbors of other speakers of the same language stock who are grouped more appro-
priately in the culture area of Northern Mexico.

While much is still to be learned about the prehistory,
migrations, and cultural sequences of the native peoples in
the Southeast before the first white men arrived there,
enough is known to indicate that the area had a very rich
and important past. The region was occupied originally by
small, nomadic bands that hunted Pleistocene animals and
fashioned fluted spear points like those used farther west.
A second stage of development, in which Plano-type points
were made, is also evident. By about 10,000 years ago, with
the disappearance of the Ice Age big game animals, an
Archaic Stage began. Hunting of smaller animals was still
important, but economies became based increasingly on
gathering activities. On the coast and along the rivers, shell
mounds, often very large, give evidence of the presence of
semisedentary peoples who lived principally by gathering
shellfish, but who also moved about in various seasons to
hunt and collect wild plant foods. In other parts of the
Southeast, campsites were left by people who lived by hunting, especially deer, and by gathering wild foods.

This way of life lasted for thousands of years, persisting
longer in some regions than in others. About 4,500 years
ago the first pottery appeared—seemingly abruptly—on the
Southeast coast. It was an undecorated fiber-tempered ware,
in which vegetable fibers or grasses were mixed with the
clay before firing. The oldest find so far, dated at approximately 2650 B.C., was of a type known as Stallings Island
and was discovered in a shell midden in the Savannah River
swamp in southeastern South Carolina. Other discoveries
of undecorated Stallings Island pottery, dated at approximately 2000 B.C., have been made elsewhere on the Savannah River and on coastal islands along the northern shore
of Georgia. Decorated types of Stallings Island ware began
appearing in this area about 1750 B.C. Undecorated fiber-
tempered pottery also appeared abruptly about 4,000 years
ago in two other areas: on Florida's St. Johns River and on
the Tennessee River in northern Alabama. In Florida, pottery decoration began about 1600 B.C., slightly later than on

the Georgia coast, but in northern Alabama the first decorated pottery did not appear until about 500 B.C.

Where this fiber-tempered pottery—the oldest in the
present-day United States—came from initially, or how it
developed, has long been a mystery. Recently, however,
archeologist James A. Ford has suggested what may be a
solution. In his opinion, Stallings Island decorated pottery
resembles, in some of its traits, Valdivia pottery, a type that
seems to have been introduced on the coast of Ecuador
about 5,000 years ago by voyagers from Japan. These traits
may have been carried, or diffused, from Ecuador to Puerto
Hormiga on Colombia's northern coast (where the oldest
pottery, with a number of similarities to Valdivia pottery,
appeared also about 5,000 years ago) and to Pacific coastal
regions of Panama, Guatemala, and Mexico. From one or
more of those areas, Ford believes, the traits made their
way to Mexico's Veracruz coast and either from there or
from Colombia's northern coast, via long-range coastwise
contact, to the Georgia coast. In Florida, meanwhile, two
types of decorated pottery emerged from the first undecorated
ware. A type known as Tick Island, dated at about 1600 B.C.,
has traits resembling those of pottery found at Barlovento on
Colombia's northern coast; that pottery, in turn, also, has
traits indicating derivation from Ecuador's Valdivia ware. A
second Florida decorated type, known as Orange Incised
and dated at about 1300 B.C., has some traits of Ecuador's
Machalilla pottery, a stage that succeeded Valdivia and is
dated as beginning at about 2000 B.C. This pottery, too,
shares motifs with ceramics found on the northern coast of
Colombia, the Pacific coast of Guatemala and Mexico, and
southern Mexico, and Ford suggests that some of these
traits were carried at about 1500 B.C. from the Veracruz coast
to Florida's St. Johns region. Both Stallings Island pottery
and the Orange ware of Florida contain traits not found in
the Ecuador pottery, but those added traits, including fiber-
tempering, are present in pottery with Ecuador traits found
in northern Colombia and Middle America. Thus, Ford
traces the derivation of the Southeast's first pottery to South
or Middle America, relying on coastwise voyages by Indians
beginning some 4,500 years ago to account for its spread.

About 1700 B.C. other migrants from Mexico appear to
have introduced a new culture in the Poverty Point region
of the lower Mississippi River in Louisiana. Huge earthworks and rich artifact remains, including skilled work in

red jasper, suggest the presence of agriculture, a large concentration of population, an advanced religious system, and a stratified society that included occupational specialists and a leadership that could organize and direct massed labor. The Poverty Point Culture seems to have reached a high point around 800 B.C.

Burial mounds first began appearing in the Southeast at approximately 1000 B.C. From then until about A.D. 700, a burial-mound period that was influenced greatly first by the Adena, and then by the Hopewell, Culture of the Northeast saw the occurrence of numerous changes, including a large increase in population, the establishment of new settlements, the growth in size of settlements, and the expansion of trade and of the interchange of ideas and material traits.

During this long period, archeologists, working largely with ceramic remains, trace the beginnings and development of several influential cultural sequences that were significant to large areas of the Southeast. One sequence, which began about 500 B.C. and became a part of the basis of what is known as the Gulf tradition, succeeded the Poverty Point Culture in the lower Mississippi Valley. Its initial cultural stage, marked by pottery of a style known as Tchefuncte—which reflected Poverty Point elements as well as influences from Florida's Orange Incised pottery—was in the Mississippi Delta and possessed a shellfish-gathering economy. A second stage, known as Marksville, beginning several centuries later and centered at the mouth of the Red River, was influenced by the Hopewell Culture and showed a greater dependence on agriculture. The rapid development there of a strong economic base and a populous society with a more sophisticated social and religious system led to a third stage, known as Troyville (for the principal site of the culture in the Red River area). Hopewellian influences and features were prominent, but by about A.D. 700 the culture was modified by the appearance of temple mounds, a manifestation of a new and important stage of development in the Southeast.

Meanwhile, a few centuries before Christ, Woodland pottery types, which had first appeared in the Northeast about 1200 B.C., entered the Southeast, and pottery spread thereafter throughout the area, developing in numerous sequences of local and regional styles and forms. Georgia and Florida, for instance, saw the development of a second important Southeastern cultural sequence. Its first stage, known as Deptford, essentially a hunting and gathering culture but with some suggestions of incipient farming, started in the Stallings Island Culture area in the vicinity of the mouth of the Savannah River, but was carried westward, both by diffusion and by migrating peoples, across Georgia and Florida. Its burial mounds, reflecting the existence of Adena-type, and then of Hopewell-type, ceremonial centers, included such artifacts as platform pipes and copper ear spools. In time, Deptford was succeeded by a second stage, termed Swift Creek, whose traits began to merge with those of Troyville. A third cultural tradition, the Appalachian, characterized by fabric-marked pottery, developed separately, split into a number of divisions, and also spread over a wide area.

About A.D. 700 a particularly influential culture began to develop—the Mississippian, or the Middle Mississippian, as it is sometimes called, because it appears to have originated along the bottomlands of the lower Ohio, Illinois, and Tennessee rivers and the middle Mississippi River. It is not known definitely how the Mississippian Culture arose; presumably it began locally with ideas and systems derived from the Hopewell Culture, then about A.D. 900 received a strong agricultural base, together with an infusion of new cultural traits, that came from the Huastec area of Mexico via the Caddoan region of eastern Texas. This culture, which spread with great intensity and vigor over much of the Southeast, especially after about A.D. 1200, was characterized by major ceremonial centers, huge and often fortified, and containing one or more temple mounds as well as ceremonial council houses that were often built partly underground. An intensified agriculture, based on new and more productive strains of corn and new implements, supported the growth of the Mississippian Culture, which was marked, also, by new ceramic forms and techniques; an increase in artistic abilities; an outpouring of beautiful objects made of many different materials decorated frequently by engraving or painting; and more tightly knit social systems organized around new religious beliefs and ceremonies.

The temple mound builders lived in villages erected around rectangular or pyramidal flat-topped earthen mounds, on the tops of which were constructed wooden temples or houses of leading men. Both the mounds and the ceremonial temples were reminiscent of those of Middle American civilizations. Within the temples, also as in regions of Middle America, the people maintained eternal fires, renewing them each year in new-fire rituals. Pottery, too, was often fashioned

in styles that were somewhat similar to certain of those in
Mexico. Some of the ceremonial centers were larger than
any of those of the Hopewell Culture and contained both
burial mounds and temple mounds. The latter were often
built in groups of four around a large central court or plaza.
As the centers increased in size, reflecting growth in population, the organization of the people must also have become
more complex. Societies undoubtedly included a division of
labor, groups of specialists, sophisticated politico-religious
systems, upper classes, and theocratic rulers who led and
directed native petty states made up of ceremonial centers
and satellites of dwelling and farming settlements around
them.

In the period soon after A.D. 700, Mississippian-influenced
temple-mound cultures began appearing in different parts
of the Southeast. In the lower Mississippi River Basin, where
the Troyville stage was followed by one known as Coles
Creek, temple mounds grew in size, number, and complexity,
and strong temple-mound cultures flourished in that region
until at least A.D. 1600. Along the Gulf Coast, from northwestern Florida to Mobile Bay, arose another temple-mound
culture, called Weeden Island. It contained elements of
Hopewellian ceremonialism, but combined both Deptford
(from Georgia) and Troyville (from the Red River) influences and, in addition, showed some influences from Middle
America. Its society seems to have been highly stratified and
theocratically oriented, and its people appear to have been
ruled by an upper class claiming relationship to a sun-god.

In southern Arkansas, northern Louisiana, eastern Texas,
and Oklahoma, meanwhile, a new Caddoan Culture had
been developing among people in that area who, up to then,
seem not to have shared the advances of the rest of the
Southeast. By A.D. 500, however, influences from the lower
Mississippi and perhaps from Mexico (coming to them, possibly, via Texas) quickened their development. With a strong
agricultural base, population grew, and major ceremonial
centers, with large temple mounds and villages of well-built
houses, appeared. Influences now ran the opposite way, and
traits from the Caddoan Culture moved eastward.

As the Mississippian Culture spread, carried into some
parts of the Southeast by what must have been large migrant
groups, it was accompanied, after about A.D. 1200, by the
diffusion of elements which, in combination, are referred to
as the Southern Cult. Symbolized by the "Long-Nosed God,"

a small mask with a long nose of copper found in various mounds, the Cult is not believed to be an indigenous phenomenon of the Mississippian Culture, but a form of ceremonialism that spread perhaps from the Caddoan Culture and became widespread during the period. The Cult seems to have had its roots in Mexico, for such elements of it as a death cult, with skulls, feathered serpents, and eagle warriors, and such customs as the torturing of war captives and the holding of dramatic sacrificial rituals, are all reminiscent of Mexican traits.

The spread of the Mississippian Culture resulted in the growth of some large metropolitan areas—satellite farming towns grouped around large ceremonial centers—held together as states by the Southern Cult. The largest Mississippian center (and the largest of all the mounds) was at Cohokia, Illinois, almost opposite present-day St. Louis, in the region in which the culture originated. In the Southeast, Mississippian reached its peak in three great temple-mound centers—Spiro, Oklahoma; Moundville, Alabama; and Etowah, in northern Georgia. Etowah was a site of what has been called the Lamar Culture. Stemming from the Southern Appalachian tradition, and combining elements of the Mississippian Culture and then of the Southern Cult, the Lamar Culture encompassed many sites and was the way of life, it is believed, of the Lower Creeks and the Cherokees at the time that white men first entered the Southeast. Members of the Moundville Culture, becoming expansionist in the late sixteenth century, spread down to and along the Gulf Coast, absorbing traits already there, expelling members of the Weeden Island Culture, and giving rise to new Pensacola and Fort Walton cultures, the latter becoming, in turn perhaps, the way of life of the Apalachees met by white men in that region.

Many variants of the Mississippian Culture appeared in different parts of the Southeast. In some localities, other cultures flourished, little marked by Mississippian traits. A Glades Culture, untouched by Mississippian influences and without agriculture, existed in southern Florida; at its remarkable Key Marco site were found beautifully painted wooden sculptures, masks, idols, bowls, furniture, and other articles, all dating from the late prehistoric period.

The Mississippian Culture reached its climax in the sixteenth century. Then there was a breakdown of the old ceremonial centers, a complete change in the religious and political structures, and a dispersal of populations to smaller towns and agricultural settlements. In some areas, the collapse resulted apparently from sudden and great population declines, caused by epidemics introduced by Europeans. Such calamities certainly occurred in the Caddoan area and in the lower Mississippi Valley.

Here and there, however, remnants of the great Mississippian stage were come upon by the first white explorers and settlers. Thanks to vivid contemporary descriptions, the best known of the surviving temple-mound cultures is that of the Natchez Indians, a group of some 4,000 people whom the French discovered living in at least nine towns along the lower Mississippi River as late as the latter part of the seventeenth century. Their society, a last relic of the old Gulf tradition, was ruled, according to the French, by a native despot who possessed absolute power. Known as the Great Sun because of the belief that he had descended from the sun-god, he was carried about on a litter and accorded slavish respect by the rest of the tribe. He also filled the role of religious leader and lived on top of one of the mounds. Surmounting another mound was a temple with a perpetual fire and the bones of the deceased members of the Sun clan. When the Great Sun died, his wife and close followers were strangled so that they might continue to serve the departed ruler in the afterlife.

Natchez society was organized tightly in classes, and the people lived according to strict codes of behavior. At the top of the social system were the Great Sun's relatives, who were known as Little Suns and comprised the membership of the Sun clan. From among this group the Great Sun chose his war chiefs, leaders of religious ceremonies, and other functionaries. Great power was also held by Female Suns who named the successors to the Great Suns when they died. Beneath the Suns were classes of Nobles, Honored Men, and Stinkards, the latter comprising the main body of the people. Custom decreed that everyone had to marry a Stinkard, the offspring of female aristocrats retaining their mother's status, but everyone else being relegated to the Stinkard class.

The Natchez and their authoritarian society disappeared under the impact of the French colonizers of the lower Mississippi. Elsewhere in the Southeast other surviving elements of mound-building cultures grew less distinct and soon vanished entirely. In southern Florida and the Keys the

Spaniards found Calusa tribes living a coastal life among large refuse shell heaps. Farther north, in Georgia and Alabama, was a confederation of many groups dominated by the Muskogis, or Creeks, as the English came to call them. The confederacy was composed of approximately fifty towns, divided into Red, or War, Towns, and White, or Peace, Towns. The former supplied the war leaders, while the White Towns, which were dedicated to pursuits of peace, controlled civil functions and gave the confederacy its principal chiefs. Other large tribes at the time of white contact, all of them in the last stages of temple mound-building cultures, were the Chickasaws, Choctaws, and Cherokees. The latter, occupying generally the hill and mountain country of western North Carolina and eastern Tennessee, was the largest tribe in the Southeast, with some 20,000 people living in sixty towns.

Villages in the historic period in the Southeast were usually stockaded and often contained more than a hundred dwellings, round an high-domed or rectangular, built on a framework of poles and covered with grass, a mud plaster, or thatch. Along the Gulf Coast and in warm areas, the buildings were little more than roofed platforms without walls, set above the ground on log pillars. Frequently a village contained a larger community house or temple, and all the buildings were erected around a central square that was kept brushed and cleaned for ceremonies and festivities. Among the more important annual events was the "green corn ceremony," or *puskita*, held after the harvest. A surviving element, perhaps, of the ceremonialism of the Southern Cult, it was a time for the renewing of life. Old fires were extinguished, worn pottery was broken, villages were cleaned, and most old feuds and animosities were ended. The "black drink" was another rite; it entailed the ceremonial drinking of a black liquid, made by boiling the roasted leaves of the cassina shrub and stirring the brew into a froth. The concoction was a strong purgative and was believed to give spiritual purification to the drinker, exhiliarating and making powerful the minds of village leaders for debate, and cleansing and strengthening the bodies of warriors for battle.

The Southeastern peoples generally had an abundance and variety of food. Villages had gardens in which the Indians raised many crops, including corn, beans, and melons, as well as tobacco. The waters and forests were filled with fish and game, the latter including bear, deer, turkeys, and wildfowl. Nuts and berries grew in profusion, and sunflowers were cultivated for their seeds. Favored dishes included bear ribs, root jelly, hominy, and corn cakes and corn soup. Dugout canoes and cane rafts were used to travel along the waterways and through the marshes of the area.

The men wore breechcloths, sleeveless shirts, leggings, moccasins, and mantles of feathers, but discarded most clothing when it was hot. In cooler weather fur or hide robes might be worn. Men's hair was sometimes drawn up into topknots that left a fringe around the head like a hat brim. Women's clothing included hide or woven grass skirts and, occasionally, loose-fitting blouses. In some areas, people were heavily tattooed. Games were popular, particularly *chenco*, or chunky, played with throwing sticks and rolling stones, and a rugged form of lacrosse, "the little brother of war," in which participants used two sticks rather than the one employed by modern players.

The coming of the white man spelled disaster to the Southeastern tribes. Many were wiped out, and the Natchez and various Gulf Coast peoples all but disappeared by the nineteenth century. In Florida, the Calusas, Timucuas, and Apalachees became extinct even earlier. After the middle of the eighteenth century, refugee Creeks and other Indians from Georgia and Alabama moved into Florida and, intermarrying with runaway Negro slaves and the last survivors of the original Florida tribes, gave rise to a new people whom the Creeks in the north called Isty-Semole, which meant "wild men" and referred to the fact that they were essentially hunters, "attending but little to agriculture." Later, as the refugees settled down in villages of their own and began gardening, their name was corrupted to Seminole, and meant simply that they were separatists or runaways from the Creeks.

With the Choctaws, Chickasaws, Creeks, and Cherokees, the Seminoles formed "The Five Civilized Tribes," a name applied to them in the nineteenth century because of their adoption—more rapidly than other tribes—of much of the white man's civilization. Many of them raised stock, tilled large farms, built European-style homes, and even owned Negro slaves like their white neighbors. They dressed like white men, learned the whites' methods, skills, and art, started small industries, and became Christians. In 1821, Sequoyah, a remarkable Cherokee, invented a syllabary for his people. The Cherokees published a newspaper, adopted a formal constitution and legislature for their nation and, like most of the other Five Tribes, put their own law codes in writing.

Despite this, calamity struck the Five Civilized Tribes. An expanding nation coveted their lands, and in the 1820's and 1830's the United States government forced their removal, one by one, to new homes west of the Mississippi River in present-day Oklahoma, which was then thought to be uninhabitable by white men. Their emigrations were cruel and bitter trials. Some, including the Seminoles, resisted, but by the mid-1840's, only relatively small pockets of Indians, including some Cherokees in the mountains of North Carolina, remained in the Southeast.

12

The Plains Indians

To MANY NON-INDIANS, THE TRIBES OF THE NORTH American plains have become the most familiar of all the Indians of the Americas, although that familiarity is generally based on a stereotype that shows little recognition of the full scope of the history or culture of the various plains peoples. In historic times, the Plains Indians, living in the broad expanse of the continent's heartland between the Mississippi River and the Rocky Mountains, and from the Saskatchewan River Basin in Canada to central Texas, were dynamic and colorful. Both their culture and history, after white contact, lent themselves to the works of writers and dramatists who so romanticized the hard-riding, war-bonneted buffalo hunters and warriors of the nineteenth century that in the minds of many persons they became the image of all American Indians. But some of their material traits of that period that seemed to make them the epitome of all Indians were not Indian at all: the horse and the gun, stock characteristics of the stereotype Plains Indian, were acquired from white men. Moreover, the flowering of the equestrian Plains life was a late and relatively short-lived phenomenon, occurring only after the arrival of white men in the New World and after the whites' destruction of most of the other Indian cultures on both continents. Actually, for more than a thousand years before the coming of whites, the dominant native peoples of the eastern plains were not nomads, but lived in semi-permanent farming villages. Although hunting contributed to their economy, agriculture was the principal source of their food.

The Plains area consists generally of two types of country, a somewhat humid region of tall-grass prairies roughly east of the hundredth meridian, where the rainfall averages from 20 to 40 inches annually, and a drier expanse of short-grass high plains, or steppes, farther west, where precipitation averages from 10 to 20 inches a year. In the past, it has been thought that, prior to the introduction of the horse that facilitated pursuit of the buffalo and the maintenance of a buffalo-based economy which the plains seemed to dictate, few Indians had occupied either part of the region, and particularly the more arid western plains.

But archeological discoveries in comparatively recent years have shown that men have dwelled on the plains, including its dry western reaches, for more than 11,000 years. In various parts of the southern and central plains have been found fluted Clovis-type spear points of men who hunted Pleistocene animals, notably mammoths, at that remote period. Folsom-type points of hunters of big bison, and other types of points of succeeding stages of big-game hunters, have also been discovered, indicating that small, nomadic bands of people were in almost all parts of the Plains area between 7,000 and 10,000 years ago. In addition to the projectile points, artifacts of these early men that have been recovered include chipped- and ground-stone cutting, chopping, and scraping tools, bolas, and bone and antler objects, including awls and simple ornaments.

From approximately 7,000 to 4,500 years ago, the plains experienced a drier and hotter period when the game animals and their hunters seem to have withdrawn from many parts of the short-grass western plains to more habitable mountain valleys farther west, or toward better watered grasslands farther north or east. (The peak of this period of extreme aridity and heat appears to have occurred from approximately 6,000 to 5,000 years ago). The Pleistocene animals had now disappeared from the region, and the remains of the period reflect the existence of gatherers and small-game hunters and trappers who, much like the inhabitants of the Great Basin, were forced to utilize all edible resources, from deer, rodents, and reptiles to seeds, roots, and wild plant foods. This economy, basically a gathering one, dominated most of the Plains area for some 2,500 years, although in some parts of the northern plains, the discovery of projectile points, skinworking tools, and the remains of bison bones, dated at about 4,500 years ago, shows the existence there of a bison-hunting economy toward the end of the dry season.

After about 2500 B.C., the relics of pedestrian hunters and gatherers suggest a renewed widespread occupation of the Plains area by many small groups. Sometime before the

beginning of the Christian era, influences from the burial-
mound cultures of the Ohio and Mississippi watersheds
extended onto the plains, and a period of Plains Woodland
cultures, characterized by pottery making, burial mounds, and
semi-permanent villages with a small amount of agriculture,
marked development in various parts of the area. Although
found most abundantly on the eastern plains, from the
Dakotas to Oklahoma, Woodland relics and small village
sites of Woodland Culture peoples, all evidencing influences
from the East, have been discovered scattered throughout
the region from the Missouri River to the Rockies.

The Plains Woodland period is dated roughly at between
500 B.C. and A.D. 1000. During that time span the Hopewellian Culture of the Ohio Valley reached its height, and
its influences also extended into parts of the plains. Fairly
advanced Hopewellian sites in the Kansas City area and in
eastern Kansas and northeastern Oklahoma, dated at approximately A.D. 200–400, indicate the presence there of a
somewhat stable village life based on an economy that combined hunting and gathering with agriculture. Remains of
corn and beans at these sites are the oldest found so far
in the Plains area. These Hopewellian sites are marked also
by numerous storage pits, small burial mounds with stone-
lined graves, and various relics, including pottery and objects
of clay, stone, bone, copper, and other materials, some of
which reflect the interconnectedness of these sites with others
in the far-flung Hopewellian-period trade network. Other
groups of sites of the Plains Woodland period have been
found in the Missouri Valley and from eastern Kansas and
Nebraska to eastern Colorado.

Beginning perhaps about A.D. 800, if not slightly earlier,
the Woodland cultures were succeeded by others of peoples
who placed more reliance on agriculture, had a much more
settled way of life, and seem to have been influenced in part
by the Mississippian Culture of the central Mississippi Valley. The new stage appears to have extended westward onto
the plains all along the front, from Minnesota to Texas,
but to have followed three principal lines of advance. In the
north, Woodland Siouan-speakers with strong Mississippian
influences moved to the middle Missouri Valley; from the
Southeast, Caddoan-speakers moved onto the central plains;
and farther south, a third stream also advanced west from
the Caddoan Culture area. For a number of centuries these
peoples, blending with the Plains Woodland groups already

in the area, developed a strong agricultural way of life, dwelling in widely separated farming communities situated along watercourses where crops could be grown and where wood was available for fuel and house-building. The villages were concentrated principally on the wooded waterways of the eastern plains, but many community sites have been found extending westward along river valleys toward the short-grass country of the high plains. Generally, the people grew corn, beans, squash, and sunflowers on the bottom-land and sent out hunting parties that perhaps roamed as far west as the Rockies, living on temporary camps during the hunts. These Plains Village Indians lived in earth-covered or mud-plastered lodges, usually square or rectangular in shape, cultivated their gardens with digging sticks and bison-scapula hoes, stored their surplus food in underground pits, and often surrounded their villages with protective stockades and ditches. Women did the farming, and men conducted the hunts.

In late prehistoric times, perhaps around A.D. 1500, many of the more westerly farming settlements were abandoned, possibly because of drought or under the pressure of enemies. People in large parts of the area returned to nomadic hunting and gathering. From the central plains, however, it appears that various groups, possibly Caddoan-speakers, moved north to the middle Missouri River territory of Siouan-speaking peoples. The contacts between them led to the development of what has been called the Coalescent tradition. Agricultural ways persisted there, and with intensive and extensive farming, communities along the middle Missouri grew bigger, increasing populations became more sedentary, and cultural advancement quickened. In this period of change, the earth-lodge dwellings became circular in shape both on the middle Missouri and in the central plains, while from central Kansas south, grass-covered lodges came into use. In the far western plains, meanwhile, where the environment had never favored the adoption of agriculture and where influences from the Woodland cultures of the East had made comparatively little impression at any time, the economy remained what it had been traditionally: a hunting, or hunting and gathering way of life, pursued by small groups of peoples who lived at relatively low levels of subsistence and cultural development.

By the time white men reached the Plains in the sixteenth century, they could observe two distinct subcultures existing in different parts of the area. The first was that of a number of semi-agricultural tribes that lived along the Plains' eastern fringe. In the prairie country of the lower Missouri River Basin were various Siouan-speaking peoples, including the Osages, Missouris, Kansas, Otos, Omahas, Iowas, and Poncas. Caddoan-speaking Arikaras and Siouan-speaking Mandans and Hidatsas were north of them on the middle Missouri. Farther west in Nebraska were the Pawnees, a confederation of Caddoan peoples who had migrated up the west side of the Mississippi and Missouri rivers, and to the south, in Kansas, were Caddoan-speaking Wichitas. All of them dwelled in villages, practiced agriculture, engaged in hunting, and possessed traits of the nomadic plains tribes farther west as well as of the Northeastern and Southeastern culture areas. North of Kansas their standard dwelling was still the circular earth-covered lodge; elsewhere they used grass, skins, or mats as covers.

The village life of these tribes was marked by many eastern influences, some of them derived originally from the ancient Hopewellian and Woodland mound builders. Pottery, often reminiscent of Northeastern Woodland types, was present. Women tended fields of corn, squash, and beans, and men sometimes raised tobacco, which was a sacred plant. Clans similar to those in the East were often a strong element of society, while the rich ceremonial life of the nomadic tribes farther west was either absent or only weakly developed. Many of the semi-agricultural tribes were divided into halves, or moieties, like the Iroquois or Creeks, and some had clans grouped into several larger units. Men sought visions from the supernatural, and shamans who had received especially strong visions were believed able to read the future, see events occurring far away, diagnose sicknesses, and perform certain acts of magic. Among the Pawnee bands, shamans composed a priesthood that possessed symbolism and ritual poetry reminiscent of that of the temple-mound cultures of the Southeast, with whom the Pawnees may have shared remote influences that had stemmed originally from Middle America and the prehistoric Caddoan Culture. Until the early nineteenth century, Pawnees also practiced sun worship, had a star cult, and observed an annual Morning Star ceremony in which a captured maiden was sacrificed and her heart cut out in a rite that suggests certain pre-Columbian rituals in Middle America.

The dress, hair styles, and decorations of the semi-agricultural tribes included elements from both the East and the plains farther west. Clothing was elaborate and fashioned from skins, usually ornamented with quills and, after white traders arrived, with beads. In some tribes the men shaved off the hair from their heads but left center strips along the crown that they heightened with the addition of a stiff, colored fringe of deer-tail hairs, called a roach, topped with feathers. In other tribes the hair was left uncut and was sometimes combed so that a straight lock fell over the forehead. Men wore feathers and showy feathered headdresses, similar to those of the plains nomads, to denote exploits in war.

It was when the semi-agricultural bands left their farming villages to hunt or engage in war excursions that the better known traits of the more westerly Plains Culture were most evident among them. Bands traveled and pursued buffalo like the nomadic tribes did, living like the nonagricultural peoples and using the products of the buffalo for food, robes, utensils, and tipi covers. Warriors raided for horses and loot and to demonstrate their daring and bravery. War dances often preceded raids, and scalp dances followed them. Boasting about courageous deeds was common, but the boaster was often permanently shamed if he exaggerated his prowess or told an untruth. An especially valiant act was to be able to "count coup"—to touch a live enemy with the hand or with a special coup stick and get away without being harmed. If the enemy was killed, honor went to the man who first counted coup on the corpse, rather than to the killer.

In the north, the palisaded farming villages of earthern mound dwellings of the Mandans, Hidatsas, and Arikaras, built along the bluffs overlooking the Missouri River, often served as trade centers. Nomadic tribes came in from the more westerly plains to exchange meat, horses, robes, and other plains articles for agricultural products and for guns that had come from Canadian and Missouri River traders. Special societies flourished in the villages, and the ceremonies and dances were colorful. One of the most dramatic rites was that of the Bull Society of the Mandan Indians, which included sequences of dances and acts to propitiate the buffalo.

Another group of semi-agricultural peoples, also showing numerous Woodland traits of the Northeast, were the Eastern, or Santee, Dakotas of Minnesota. They were a loose federation of the Mdewakanton, Sisseton, Wahpekute, and Wahpeton divisions of the Sioux that had halted their westward migration during the seventeenth century while in the general region of the Minnesota River. They did some buffalo hunting, but were more dependent on corn, wild rice, and the small game of partially wooded areas. A Yanton family of Dakotas that had ended its migration when it had reached the Missouri River in the southeastern part of present-day South Dakota had come to resemble more closely the other semi-agricultural tribes of the eastern plains. The name Sioux, given by white men to all the different Dakota tribes, was a French-Canadian abbreviation of *Nadowessioux*, from the Ojibwa term for them, *Nâdowessi*, which literally means a small snake or an enemy.

In Kansas and on the eastern edge of the southern plains were other horticultural groups, including the Wichitas who were visited by Coronado and his men in 1541. Nomadic tribes from farther west came in to trade at the Wichita settlements, much as the more northerly nomadic tribes traded at the villages of the Mandans, Hidatsas, and Arikaras.

The second large subculture of the Plains area was comprised of the tribes that dwelled west of the semi-agricultural groups and provided the typical, enduring image of the Plains Indians. They were the nomadic, horse-mounted peoples whose economy was based almost entirely on the products of the buffalo, who used berries and roots, but who practiced no agriculture and did little fishing.

Between the Saskatchewan River and the upper basin of the Missouri was the Blackfoot confederacy, composed of the Siksikas, or Blackfeet proper, the Piegans, and the Bloods, all of whom spoke the same variant of the Algonquian language. North of them in Canada were Athapascan-speaking Sarcis, who in later years allied themselves with Blackfeet. To the east were other allies, the Algonquian-speaking Atsinas, whom the French traders called Gros Ventres, or "Big Bellies," the same name they applied also to the Hidatsas of the Missouri River. Roaming southeastwardly of the Atsinas were Siouan-speaking Assiniboines, who had migrated westward from their Dakota relatives in northern Minnesota.

Between the Missouri and Yellowstone rivers were the Siouan Crows, who had separated from the Hidatsas in the eighteenth century after a fight over a buffalo. The Crows were in two divisions, referred to as the River and the Mountain Crows, the latter often being found farther south and west in the basins of the Big Horn and Wind rivers of Wyoming. In the western part of South Dakota and Nebraska, but eventually extending their movements over large parts of Montana and Wyoming, were the westernmost Sioux group, the powerful Teton Dakotas, including the Oglala, Brulé, Hunkpapa, Miniconjou, Two Kettle, Sans Arc (No Bow), and Sihasapa tribes. The Algonquian Cheyennes, who had preceded the Tetons onto the plains in a migration from Minnesota, had crossed the Missouri and after much wandering had divided into two groups, the Northern Cheyennes, roaming generally through the upper basin of the North Platte River, and the Southern Cheyennes, along the upper Arkansas River. Between them in eastern Colorado were the Arapahoes, also Algonquian-speakers, who had separated from the Atsinas and migrated south from Canada. In the southern plains, from the Arkansas River into Texas, were Comanches, Kiowas, and Kiowa-Apaches, members respectively of the Shoshonean, Kiowan, and Athapascan language families, who possessed some of the traits of the nearby Southwest cultural area. Other tribes that shared many Plains traits and who often appeared on the plains to hunt buffalo and conduct raids frequented the southern and western fringes of the region; in the south they included Lipans, and in the west the Shoshonis (whom whites sometimes referred to as Snakes); Utes; Mescalero and Jicarilla Apaches; and even Bannocks, Flatheads, and Nez Perces, who lived far to the west beyond the Continental Divide.

Before the acquisition of the horse, the various nomadic hunting peoples on the plains followed buffalo and other game on foot. As they moved from place to place in pursuit of food, they often carried their possessions on a travois, a frame consisting of two trailing poles between which was suspended a hide bag or receptacle for the load, which was dragged along by a dog. Various methods were utilized to secure game, including donning skin disguises and creeping up on the quarry, or surrounding animals and driving them into a pound, or stampeding them over cliffs. The introduction of both the horse and the gun, which reached many tribes before the actual appearance of white men, increased mobility and hunting efficiency, brought new peoples onto the plains from its fringes, and led to a richer and more flamboyant culture than had existed before.

The Spaniards were responsible for the introduction of the horse. As they moved northward through Mexico during the sixteenth century, they brought herds of livestock with them. In the various colonies they established, they tried to keep the horses out of the hands of the native peoples whom they conquered, but some Indians nevertheless learned to ride and frequently stole away with an animal to a nearby band. Indians instructed one another in how to manage the animals, and by the mid-seventeenth century Apaches and Utes were raiding Spanish settlements in the Southwest for more of them. In 1680, the Pueblo Indians of New Mexico revolted against the Spaniards, driving the whites out of that frontier province for twelve years. During the uprising large herds of horses were acquired by the Indians, and thereafter, by intertribal trade as well as raids, the animals were dispersed northward with great rapidity from one plains tribe to another. By the 1740's horses were possessed by almost every Plains tribe in both the eastern and western sections of the plains and as far north as Canada's Saskatchewan River Basin.

Possession of the animals brought great advantages to the Plains nomads, and also made long-range hunting trips easier for the sedentary tribes in farming villages on the eastern edge of the plains. The substitution of horses for dogs meant that loads lashed to travois poles could become bigger; larger supplies of dried meat could be packed from the sites of kills for use at later times; and longer lodge poles could be dragged, making possible the construction of taller and roomier tipis. Hunters gained greater mobility and freedom of movement, and with the ability to roam over larger distances for longer periods of time, their chances for successful hunts increased.

During somewhat the same time that horses were spreading north from tribe to tribe across the plains, guns and ammunition were making their appearance from the east. In the 1600's French and British fur traders had introduced firearms among the eastern tribes. With their newly acquired guns, some of these tribes attacked neighbors who had not yet acquired the weapons and drove them westward. A well-known example of this occurred in Minnesota, where Ojibwas and Crees, newly armed by the whites, pressured their enemies, the Siouan-speaking Dakotas, originally a group of Woodland tribes that farmed, used canoes, and harvested wild rice, south and west against other tribes. All moved gradually westward under the pressure and, except for the Santee branch of the Dakotas, who managed to establish new homes in another part of Minnesota, migrated in the eighteenth century onto the plains where they adopted the culture of the nomadic plains buffalo hunters.

As a result of intertribal trade and warfare, as well as of barter with the advancing whites, guns, meanwhile, moved gradually westward from one native people to another. The introduction of both guns and horses brought restlessness and change to the region. Mounted tribes that did not yet possess guns attacked those who had not yet received horses, only to be thrown back abruptly by the appearance of firearms among their enemies. The Blackfeet tribes and Atsinas of Canada, with both horses and guns, extended their hunts and raids toward the south and west, forcing the mounted Shoshonis, who had no guns, into the Rocky Mountains of Wyoming and Idaho. Farther north the Blackfeet drove the Kutenais—who had originally traded horses to them—westward across the Canadian Rockies. From the Missouri River to the mountains, intertribal trading for both horses and firearms increased, and the desire for horses led to patterns of horse raids, counterraids, and sporadic plains warfare, colored by added incentives of personal glory and booty.

In their quest for horses, some bands made permanent migrations to new areas of the plains. The Comanches separated from their fellow Shoshonis in Wyoming and traveled south, remaining permanently closer to the Spanish herds that they raided in New Mexico, Texas, and Old Mexico. Their movement forced many Plains Apaches ahead of them, out of the southern plains and into the Southwest. In the East, some of the sedentary tribes of the middle Missouri left their villages on horseback during certain seasons to hunt on the plains and trade and raid for horses. During the early part of the eighteenth century, the Crows separated entirely from the Hidatsas on the middle Missouri and, moving westward, became a nomadic people. Soon afterward the rest of the Hidatsas also began to leave their villages from time to time and appear on the plains. Some Crees and Ojibwas from Manitoba and the wooded areas in the East reached the plains, too, and stayed, adapting to the horse-using culture.

By the end of the eighteenth century, the popularly known Plains Culture of the nonagricultural tribes was in full flower. People dwelled in portable tipis, conical frames of poles covered with sewn buffalo hides that were sometimes painted with symbols, geometric designs, or pictures that had a personal meaning to the owner. Men wore breechcloths and moccasins and, in colder weather, leggings, skin shirts, and buffalo robes. Feathered adornments usually signified honors. Warriors wore eagle feathers in their hair or in horned headdresses to denote their exploits, and crowns of feathers grew into tall warbonnets, sometimes with trailing tails of feathers. Warbonnets did not necessarily indicate a chief, which was often an honorary title acquired after a certain number of exploits. Some successful war leaders trimmed their shirts or moccasins with hair. Women generally wore sleeveless leather dresses and moccasins. The clothing of both sexes was colorfully ornamented, as were almost all personal possessions, with porcupine-quill embroidery and beadwork executed by women. Shields of hardened leather and envelopes, tubes, and boxes of rawhide, called *parfleches* and used to carry dried meat and personal articles, were painted with designs and symbols and hung, as well, with bells, ribbons, and feathers. Notable occurrences or achievements were often recorded on the inner sides of buffalo hides, and members of some of the tribes painted picture calendars on the hides, signifying each year with a drawing that reminded of a single outstanding event. A year, for instance, might be recorded as one in which a certain man was killed or one in which buffalo were plentiful.

Tribes had little formal government. Most bands were autonomous under their own leaders or chiefs who, by their courageous exploits, wisdom, or other abilities and qualities, had won the respect and support of followers. But they gave advice rather than orders; councils of leading men made decisions based on unanimous agreement. Discipline was maintained by the public shaming or even ostracism of the offender. The Cheyenne Indians possessed a complicated system of laws that looked upon murder as harmful to the whole band and dealt with it sternly. Murderers were usually ousted from the band, a punishment that often meant eventual death, for lone wanderers rarely survived on the plains. Many tribes had male societies with special officers, functions, regalia, and songs. One of the best known of these was the Dog Society. Men were graded by age and would advance from one society to the next as they grew older. Some of the organizations were charged with maintaining discipline and policing villagers as well as members of war and hunting parties. Clans existed only among the Crows and a few other nomadic tribes, but most of the bands on the plains observed strict codes of rules that regulated behavior between people who were related to each other.

The nomadic bands moved frequently from one campsite to another, following the herds of buffalo. Most of them had favorite locations for hunting camps and for spending the winters. On occasion, when game was scarce, bands would split into smaller units, for there was then the chance for each group to go a different place and find enough food for its own members. The use of horses greatly facilitated the pursuit of game and permitted hunters to overtake running herds and kill animals at close range. A part of the meat was usually "jerked"—sliced thin, dried in the sun, and packed for later use. A concentrated food called pemmican was made by pounding the dried meat, mixing it with dried, crushed berries, stuffing it in an animal-membrane bag, and pouring melted fat and marrow over it to dry and harden. On the open plains, where wood was scarce, dried buffalo dung (which whites learned to use, and called buffalo chips) was employed as fuel for fires.

In camp, when many bands or tribes came together, the members of each tribe erected their tipis in a circle or semi-circle, and the villages thus formed a series of circles. On such occasions, social visits, games, gambling, and foot and horse races occurred, as did councils and ceremonies. One of the most important rituals of many of the Plains tribes was the Sun Dance, whose participants had made vows to enter the ceremony in return for supernatural assistance. Held annually in the summer, the religious event was observed in various forms. Generally, however, it included a dance conducted in an enclosed area around a painted pole that had been fashioned from a sacred tree, felled with a special ceremony. The participants, carrying out their vows in return for spiritual help, danced extremely simple steps and went without food and water—sometimes for days—until, in many cases, they dropped in a trance and had a vision. Among some tribes, the dancers had vowed to undergo ordeals of self-torture. They would stare fixedly at the sun, or suspend themselves from the sacred tree by means of skewers inserted in parallel slits in their chests. Then they would dance, or pull away from the sacred tree, until they ripped free of the skewers.

Supernatural visions, an important element in the life of

the Plains Indians, were sought by both men and women through dreams and private quests. Usually, when they were in their late teens, youths would be sent by themselves to lonely places to seek a vision. After fasting and sometimes self-torture, the youth would dream that he was visited by a supernatural being who would become his personal guardian. The spirit would teach him certain magic songs and prayers, instruct him in a personal ritual and in ways of behavior, and tell him what objects to bring together to form his own personal charm that would protect him and help him through life. Thereafter, whenever he required it, the Indian would continue to seek guidance from his special guardian, carrying the sacred objects wrapped in a skin, which white men called a "medicine bundle." Men who had strong visions often became shamans, and were believed to possess magical powers, including the important ability to heal sick persons. But special training was frequently required to conduct the various tribal rituals and carry out spiritual duties. Among some tribes, the shamans were charged with protecting their peoples' sacred objects; Blackfeet "medicine men," for instance, usually carried the bands' sacred pipes. To whites, the Hunkpapa Sitting Bull was the best-known Plains medicine man. Just prior to the Battle of the Little Bighorn in June 1876, he had participated in a Sun Dance in which he had received a vision of many white soldiers "falling into the Indian camp."

Although warfare was common on the plains, it was characterized generally by swift, short raids, sometimes with few, if any, casualties. An individual warrior, bent on acquiring personal glory, could organize a raiding party of friends or followers to steal horses, secure scalps, or try to count coup on an enemy. A successful foray, celebrated by a scalp dance, often drew a revengeful counterraid from the enemy. Among the fiercest Plains warriors were the Blackfeet, who often roamed far from their home regions to raid for horses, and the Comanches and Kiowas of the south, who terrorized white settlers in Texas for many years.

At times, tribes that had been warring with each other halted hostilities for periods of truce and trade. Often, a number of tribes, some of them enemies of one another, would come together in peaceable gatherings to trade and council. At such gatherings, speakers of as many as twenty different tongues or dialects might have been present, but all of them would have been able to converse with each other by means of the hand gestures of the sign language, a unique method of communication developed on the plains. In addition, all tribes employed smoke signals and, in later historic times, hand mirrors that reflected the sun's rays for the communication of messages across long distances.

The plains was the scene of the last major conflicts between the American Indians and the non-Indian people of the United States. The determined patriotism and fierce resistance of the nomadic Plains tribes in the U.S. gained a number of military victories for the Indians, including the defeat of Colonel George A. Custer at the Little Bighorn on June 25, 1876. But the overwhelming force and firepower brought against the tribes, together with the systematic slaughter of the buffalo herds, the Indians' source of food and the basis of their way of life, finally ended their ability to resist. With their power broken, and their food supply gone, they were gradually confined by the American government on reservations. After almost a hundred years, many of them still present the aspect of proud but conquered peoples who have not yet found a firm foundation on which to erect a satisfying and prosperous new way of life.

13

The Peoples of the Great Basin

THE GREAT BASIN OF THE NORTH AMERICAN WEST, EX-
tending across Utah and Nevada from the Rockies to
the Sierra Nevada and including fringe areas of the
southern part of Idaho, southeastern Oregon, eastern California, northwestern Arizona, and southwestern Wyoming,
is one of the hemisphere's driest and least habitable regions.
In some parts of it are low, barren, and rocky deserts and
large salt flats where human habitation is virtually impossible.
Elsewhere, limited water supplies and meager food resources
provided a poor existence for native peoples. Generally
unsuitable for agriculture, the environment inhibited the
establishment of permanent villages and restricted the growth
of population and the size and organizational complexity
of societies. As a rule, the small, scattered bands of Indians
that dwelled in the area—forced to spend most of their time
looking for food, and often living close to starvation—were
weak, timorous, and nonaggressive.

Most of the peoples of the Great Basin were Shoshonean-
speakers of the Utaztecan language family. In northern and
eastern Utah were bands of Utes. Various groups of Shoshonis lived in the north from eastern Oregon to Wyoming's
Wind River, and Northern and Southern Paiutes extended
across most of the southern and western parts of the region.
Around the westernmost shores of Great Salt Lake were
Gosiutes, and in the desert country of southern Nevada
and eastern California were Chemehuevis, Paviotsos, Monos,
Kawiisus, and Panamints, all speaking Shoshonean tongues.
Washos in western Nevada and Pit River Indians, including Achomawis and Atsugewis of northeastern California,
were of the Hokan linguistic family; although related to tribes

farther west in California, they are often grouped because of the nature of their culture with peoples of the Great Basin, rather than of California.

The environment of most of the Great Basin has been somewhat the same for the last 10,000 years (although there were, in turn, a wetter and then a hotter and more arid period), and the life of its inhabitants apparently changed but little through that long time span. What changes did take place were mostly the result of adding new cultural elements to those already possessed. Although food resources were scanty, they existed in variety and ranged from deer, antelope, mountain sheep, rabbits, rodents, reptiles, fish, and insects to various kinds of roots, berries, seeds, nuts, and greens. The maintenance of livelihood required that the people exploit all edible resources, be highly mobile, and develop efficient food-gathering techniques.

The Great Basin is sometimes included in what has been called the Intermontane, or Basin Plateau Province, a larger physiographic region that encompasses also the Columbia Plateau to the north and the Colorado Plateau to the east and southeast. Although those areas belong to the Plateau and Southwest culture areas, respectively, since their cultures eventually diverged from that of the Great Basin peoples, there were times in the prehistoric past when the culture of the entire Intermontane region—extending, in fact, southward toward the central Mexican Plateau—was similar, in part at least.

Little is known of man's earliest habitation of the Great Basin. Many archeologists believe that Krieger's Pre-Projectile Point Stage existed there, the period when men fashioned crude stone choppers and scrapers but were unable to make projectile points. During the earliest period about which anything is yet known, some 10,000 to 11,500 years ago, there is scattered evidence of man's presence in different parts of the Great Basin. The finds, showing little pattern for the area as a whole, suggest that here and there big-game hunters were present, using in some regions leaf-shaped projectile points that might have been related to, or have derived from, the Cascade points of the Old Cordilleran Culture of the Northwest and in other regions points like the Clovis and Folsom fluted points of the big-game hunters farther east. Evidence of hunters of Pleistocene animals in the Great Basin is relatively slight, however, and by about 9,000 years ago, the area as a whole was becoming characterized by what has been termed the Desert Culture—a way of life that, with only small changes, persisted into historic times. Jesse D. Jennings, one of the most respected authorities on the prehistory of the Desert West, has described this way of life as including the use of caves and rock shelters for settlements, the employment of grass or bark beds, and the possession of such items as milling stones and manos, crude scraper and chopper tools, digging sticks, fire drills, atlatls, wooden clubs, basketry (the earliest basketry known anywhere in the world, 9,000–10,000 years old, was found at Danger Cave in western Utah), netting, fur cloth, tumplines, and sandals. People were gatherers, collectors, and hunters, and—along the rivers and lake shores—fishermen. This Desert Culture had an economy based on the harvesting of small seeds and the intensive use of every other edible resource; geared to the poverty and rigors of the environment, it represented an adjustment to a difficult region and proved stable for thousands of years.

For a time, the traits of the Desert Culture, whose principal hallmarks have been described as basketry and milling stones, seem also to have spread across a large part of the western one third of the present-day United States. It is believed that, from approximately 7,000 to 4,500 years ago, much of the West experienced a hotter and drier period than had existed previously. Although this belief has recently been questioned, it appears probable that during that particular time the Desert Culture, based on a need to use all edible resources, did become dominant in much of the Columbia Plateau and Colorado Plateau, that its traits extended onto the Great Plains, and that a similar culture was present in some of Canada and in northern and central Mexico. Those who subscribe to the idea that the period was one of increased heat and aridity suggest that in various regions people moved to higher ground or to the bigger watercourses and to lake shores. During that period, some regional variations are known to have begun to occur. Agriculture was introduced into the Colorado Plateau, perhaps, about 5,000 or 6,000 years ago. In the Columbia Plateau, people were developing more of a riverine existence, turning increasingly to the use of salmon, river mussels, and other food resources of the rivers. And in southeastern Idaho, even earlier, some peoples seem to have moved northward into the higher mountain valleys, where they developed what has been termed the Bitterroot Culture.

During approximately the same period there may have been important movements of peoples through the Great Basin. Prior to 6,000 years ago, the area is believed by many persons to have been populated principally, if not wholly, by speakers of Hokaltecan languages. About 6,000 years ago, according to a theory advanced by linguistic scholar Walter W. Taylor, members of the Utaztecan language stock, including Shoshonean-speaking peoples, came south, following the western slopes of the Rockies, and spilling various of their groups into the areas, including the Great Basin, along which they passed. The offshoots who stayed in the Great Basin, it is suggested, moved southwestwardly across it, colliding with, or splitting, the Hokaltecan-speakers, whom they displaced and drove westward toward such areas as the Colorado River and California. Not everyone, it must be said, agrees with this theory; some maintain that the Utaztecan dialects actually spread through the Great Basin during a much later time (3,000–1,000 years ago) from a nuclear center in the Southwest, and a more recent theory suggests migrations of Utaztecan-speakers about 6,000–7,000 years ago down both sides of the Great Basin, with the western group spreading back, northwardly, into the Great Basin proper about a thousand years ago.

Whatever actually occurred, the Desert Culture during the period prior to about 4,500 years ago seems to have given a definite base to the Southwest, the Plateau, and other surrounding culture areas that eventually—with the addition of influences from elsewhere—developed differently from the Great Basin culture area. The latter's way of life continued in a relatively unchanged form, though with increasingly marked regional variations. Beginning about 4,000 years ago, some Basin peoples, according to finds in the Lovelock and Humboldt caves of Nevada, showed specialization in the use of lake resources; among their artifacts were nets, fishhooks and, between 3,000 and 2,000 years ago, duck decoys. Elsewhere, in many parts of the Great Basin during the passage of time, milling stones gave way to mortars and pestles; people gathered more of the larger seeds like acorns and pine nuts; and wickiups came into widespread use as dwellings. But, save for minor changes and local developments (such as the short-lived appearance of agriculture in the southeast, parts of Utah and southern Idaho, and perhaps in western regions between A.D. 400 and 1200, and the expansion of some of the Shoshonean-speaking groups northward and eastward toward the Plateau and Plains areas in the late prehistoric period), the culture remained stable. When white men first entered the Great Basin, they found most of the native peoples there living little differently from those who had occupied the area thousands of years earlier.

None of the Basin tribes practiced agriculture. Small units of people roamed on foot through limited areas, eating whatever they could gather or catch that was edible. Most groups followed a seasonal wandering routine, gathering foods that ripened or matured at different times, especially at different altitudes. After gathering greens in the lower valleys, they would make their way gradually into higher land, collecting plants, roots, seeds, berries, and nuts. Wild grass seeds and pine nuts were harvested in deep baskets, and roots were dug with digging sticks, the use of which led white men in later days to refer to the natives contemptuously, as "Digger Indians." Hunters pursued deer, antelope, and mountain sheep with bows and arrows, but often had poor results. Diets also included roasted grasshoppers, which people caught by driving them into trenches with the aid of fire; prairie dogs; lizards; mice; and birds and rabbits, which were trapped with large nets. Sometimes in the fall groups would hold communal drives for rabbits. And where there was antelope, Indians came together—usually in the spring—and, led by shamans, surrounded the animals and drove them into brush corrals where they were slain. Wherever possible, people fished. In the Snake River of southern Idaho, native groups harvested salmon in large numbers during annual runs, drying the surplus for later use.

The people were organized in small family units—usually extended families of perhaps twenty-five or thirty people—without authoritative leaders, but they were guided by the advice of their wisest members, known as "talkers." In the winter, groups of two to fifteen families might come together in winter villages, usually located in warm and sheltered locations, where they had cached surplus foods and where wood and water were available. The villages might recognize a single headman, but there was little or no formal organization. Some of the families would return to the same villages each year; others might winter one year with groups in the eastern part of their territory, and the next year with groups in the western part. The changing composition of winter villages, as well as of groups that joined for hunts, harvests, and ceremonies, created interrelationships among the different families across large parts of the area and worked against the emergence of regional variations in ways of life. Nevertheless, there was no tribal unity, and clans, too, were absent. On occasion, when families joined in the winter or on hunts, men and women, would dance and sing together, gamble, and tell stories. Group solidarity was also promoted by a sweathouse; it served as a men's club, a meeting house, and a lodging for unmarried males. Dwellings generally were wickiups, which were primitive, hastily constructed brush huts or lean-tos. The wickiups were conical in shape, made of a framework of willow or juniper poles with a covering of brush, bark strips, or grass or tule matting. In the center was a firepit, and a smokehole was in the roof above it.

The people often wore no clothing, although men sometimes used a skin breechcloth, women a fringed apron of milkweed fiber, and both sexes leggings, fiber sandals, and, when it was cold, a rabbitskin robe. Fine basketry was produced, and women wore basketry hats. Some of the baskets were watertight, and were used for cooking by being filled with water that was set to boil by the immersion of heated rocks.

The Plains institution of the vision quest was not present. But some individuals frequently attached importance to dreams, and various persons who had had powerful dreams became shamans, their principal activity being that of curing.

After about A.D. 1700, some of the easternmost bands nearest the plains acquired horses and were able to develop a richer and more abundant life. In northern parts of the Great Basin, some peoples had previously been pedestrian hunters of the buffalo. Now, the newly mounted bands were able to extend their hunts. Some groups, particularly Shoshonis, roamed far out on the Great Plains and by the time white men reached the area had taken on many of the traits of the Plains tribes. They used products of the buffalo for food, shelter, clothing, and utensils, wore plains headdresses and other regalia, and raided other tribes for horses. Some of the Shoshonis extended their raids as far as southern Alberta, before Blackfeet, armed with white men's guns, drove them back. Another group, the Northern Paiute Bannocks, migrated into Shoshoni territory in southern Idaho, where they joined Shoshoni bands and became mounted buffalo hunters. Elsewhere in the region, bands continued their traditional ways of life, even after fur trappers, miners, and settlers invaded their lands. They had numerous conflicts with the whites, for whom they were no match. Eventually, after many of the Great Basin Indians were killed, the survivors were rounded up and placed on reservations, which in the still generally unproductive environment of their original homelands, are even today among the poorest in the nation. Some of the Indians have learned to become irrigation farmers; but even they have had their difficulties with neighboring white farmers who, in many instances, have diverted water away from their lands.

14

The Indians of
the Plateau

IN THE INTERIOR OF THE NORTHWEST, BETWEEN THE
Rocky Mountains and the Cascade Mountains, a multitude of peoples speaking many dialects of several different language families dwelled in the varied country that
forms the high plateau of the basins of the Columbia and
Fraser rivers. The region is marked by forested mountains,
rushing streams, valleys, and canyons, and open, windswept,
volcanic scablands. The rivers were rich in fish resources; and
although hunting and gathering were important, the economies of the Plateau peoples were based principally on fishing. In the inland areas of present-day British Columbia were
Salishan-speaking Lilooet, Thompson, and Shuswap Indians;
Athapascan-speaking Nicolas and Chilcotins; and Kutenais,
who spoke a language of their own which is distantly related
to the Algonquian linguistic stock. In the upper portions of
the Columbia Basin were other Salish, including Kalispels
(whom French-speaking trappers called Pend d'Oreilles),
Coeur d'Alenes, Flatheads, Colvilles, Sanpoils, Okanogans,
and Spokans.

On the middle Columbia, above the present-day city of
The Dalles, and in the lower Snake River Basin were
Yakimas, Klickitats, Umatillas, Wallawallas, Palouses, and
Nez Perces, all speaking dialects of Sahaptin, a division of the
Penutian language family. The Cayuses and Molalas of the
Columbia Plateau were relatives who spoke a slightly
different tongue that had stemmed from the Penutian stock.
On the lower Columbia and inland from Puget Sound were
Chinookan-speaking groups, as well as Cowlitzes and other
members of the coastal division of the Salishan family, whose
cultural traits sometimes identify them, instead, with the

tribes of the Northwest Pacific Coast area. Finally, in south-central Oregon, Klamaths and Modocs of the Penutian language stock lived near the California border.

Since the 1950's, archeological work has proceeded at a rapid pace in the Plateau area. Although much still remains to be learned, many highlights of the region's prehistoric past have been illuminated. Widely scattered discoveries have shown that people have occupied at least parts of the Plateau area for approximately 11,000 years, and perhaps longer. From these discoveries, and from others farther north on the continent, has emerged an important theory that hunters, gatherers, and fishermen of what has been called an Old Cordilleran Culture—who possibly were speakers of a Macro-Penutian superstock, the parent of Penutian, Utaztecan, and other language families—came south from Alaska, perhaps prior to 11,000 years ago, on the western side of the Rocky Mountains. Elements of this group may have continued south, all the way to South America, for spear points and other objects resembling those of the Old Cordilleran Culture have been found in the Great Basin, southern California, Mexico, and parts of South America. Many of the Old Cordilleran relics, approximately 7,500–9,500 years old, have been found in the interior Northwest, and there archeologists have been able to trace the culture's gradual spread eastward across the Plateau area from the axis of the Cascades. By 7,500–8,000 years ago, some of the people of the culture, perhaps ancestors of the historic Sahaptin-speaking tribes, are believed to have extended into present-day Idaho. At about the same time, or slightly later, influences from the same culture seem to have spread westward also, toward Puget Sound.

The Old Cordilleran Culture, existing at about the same time as the big-game hunting cultures on the Great Plains, was characterized by a double-pointed, leaf-shaped Cascade-type spear point. It was a hunting, fishing, and gathering culture whose economy probably depended heavily on small game, particularly deer, and whose members left behind various implements of bone and antler. Near The Dalles on the Columbia, the Five Mile Rapids site, excavated by L. S. Cressman, has laid bare an almost uninterrupted sequence of habitation that goes back at least 9,500 years. The bottom, or oldest, layers show a great reliance, more than 9,000 years ago, on the taking of salmon from the river. At the same time, Pleistocene big-game hunters were also present in parts of the Plateau area. Some spear points similar to the Clovis and Folsom types have been found, although not yet in association with animal remains. But at Lind Coulee in central Washington, archeologists discovered stemmed lanceolate points and other artifacts in association with the bones of a big bison. The find has been dated at approximately 9,000 years of age, although there is reason to believe that it may be older.

In the postglacial period, as the big-game animals vanished, the region, according to a long-held premise (but one that has recently been questioned), was subjected to an increasing warmth and dryness, particularly in the south. Beginning about 7,000 to 8,000 years ago, the Desert Culture's way of life became dominant over the whole Intermontane region, including the southern part of the Plateau cultural area. People may have moved to moister and cooler areas, concentrating more in high country and along principal watercourses. The traits of the Desert Culture, identified generally with the peoples of the Great Basin, and represented by such elements as milling stones, manos, and basketry that typified a gathering economy, appeared in the Plateau, modifying and dominating the earlier hunting cultures.

After about 4,500 years ago, when some persons believe the hot, dry period gave way to a cooler one and the environment became somewhat as it is today, regional differentiations appeared in the Plateau that began to set its culture apart from that of the Great Basin in the south. Fishing became more important, and riverine settlements increased. About 3,500 to 3,000 years ago woodland-oriented migrants of what has been termed a Northern Forest Culture spread across the northern and central portions of the Plateau area. Bearing "boreal" traits that had come originally from Asia, and that were being carried to many of the northern parts of the continent, the newcomers in the Northwest, possibly ancestors of the historic Salishan-speaking tribes, seem to have introduced many new cultural items, including ground- and polished-stone implements, pipes, copper objects, stone carvings, effigy figurines, and burial mounds, that are somewhat reminiscent of contemporary relics of Northeastern Woodland Culture groups. Eventually, it is suggested, the new arrivals in the Northwest borrowed from peoples already there, and then drew together with them to form the beginnings of the Plateau Culture.

Not much is yet known of the various stages by which the Plateau Culture developed. On the whole, it appears that changes in the area were slow and gradual, marked generally by the addition of new cultural elements without the replacement or abandonment of old ones. As time passed, improvements in equipment and technologies permitted a greater utilization of available food resources, principally fish, roots, and small game, and led to the growth of populations and an increase in the size of riverine settlements. After about A.D. 1, many local variants of the culture, all based on fishing, hunting, and gathering economies, were present in the area; after about A.D. 500, new influences came inland via trade with Pacific coastal peoples; and after about A.D. 1000, social organizational patterns, different from the simpler ones in the Great Basin (and firmly established in the Plateau a millennium or two earlier, according to some), were flourishing. In the late prehistoric period, as will be noted below, additional influences, coming from the Great Plains, modified, in new ways, the culture of some of the Plateau peoples, particularly those in the eastern part of the area.

When white men reached the Plateau region in the early part of the nineteenth century, many of the native groups lived in small, semi-permanent fishing settlements along major streams and tributaries. There was little tribal identity, but bonds resulting from social and ethnic samenesses and the use of common languages existed among various villages. Each settlement was generally a politically autonomous unit with its own leading men, who were sometimes both civil and war leaders—although the people on the whole were not warlike or aggressive. In only a few groups was leadership gained through heredity. Usually, the people selected a headman for his achievements, ability, or wisdom. Unless he abdicated, he normally served for life, exercising powers that were rarely absolute but were, more often, those of a counselor and guide who advised the people, helped settle disputes, and cared for the general welfare of the group.

On occasion, villages or bands (groups of villages associated voluntarily by common bonds) of one people or of several different peoples would come together to trade, council, gather roots in a communal harvest, socialize, go on a hunt, or retaliate against a common enemy. If it were for one of the two latter purposes, the leading men of all the assembled villages might choose the best qualified person among them as a hunting or war leader to guide them all. War parties, however, were often simply small groups of warriors bent on a raid of revenge against outsiders who had entered their lands and struck at their villages.

In the winter the people lived in the warmer valleys in circular earthen-roofed houses that were built partly underground or were banked with earth against the cold. In warmer weather, rough pole dwellings were covered with mats of rushes or bark. Sometimes, especially in winter, the buildings were extended in longhouses, up to one hundred feet or more in length, that accommodated numerous families under a single roof. People slept along the inner walls of the structure, placing their family fires in a row down the center and letting the smoke escape through openings in the roofs along the ridgepoles. Lower down on the Columbia, the use of plank houses showed the influence of coastal peoples.

Salmon, which made annual runs up all the major rivers and which the Indians netted, speared, or trapped in weirs built out into the rapids, was the main element of diet. Enormous quantities of the fish were harvested in the spring and late summer, and the surplus was split and dried on racks, pounded, and stored for later use and for trade. Other types of fish, including sturgeon and eels, were also caught. In addition, camas, kouse, and several kinds of roots were dug and used in a variety of dishes; berries were harvested in season; and deer and other game were hunted. In lean times, when food surpluses ran low, moss and the inner bark of certain trees would be gathered and cooked into a gruel. There was neither agriculture nor pottery, but the Plateau peoples were highly skilled in making beautifully woven and designed grass baskets, mats, and other useful items. Cooking was done by dropping heated stones into holes or into baskets so tightly woven that they could hold water. Travel in the area, before the coming of the horse to some of the tribes, was everywhere on foot or by water. Dugouts were hollowed from fallen trees and were navigated on the rivers with poles and paddles.

Through a vision quest to a lonely place, Plateau youths sought and acquired guardian spirits. Considerable variation existed through the region, but generally people possessed one or more guardian spirits, usually of animals, natural forces, or animate or inanimate objects, through life. Those who acquired especially strong spirits might become shamans, who employed their spiritual powers as curers and healers. At the Winter Spirit Dance, an annual major religious ceremony that lasted for several days and was accompanied by feasting and social activities, opportunities were provided for dancing and spirit singing by those who had acquired guardian spirits during the preceding year.

Parts of the Plateau area were influenced by two neighboring cultural regions. In the western section, various peoples possessed certain traits of the Northwest Pacific Coast. Some of them flattened their heads, pierced their noses, dressed in shredded bark clothing, and wore slat armor like the coastal tribes. They traveled extensively by water and used canoes, which became larger and more seaworthy toward the lower Columbia and on Puget Sound. For centuries people from many sections of the region had met at central trading sites, particularly at The Dalles fishing area on the Columbia, and coastal influence had spread to a greater or lesser extent through much of the area from those trade marts.

Early in the eighteenth century, the horse reached the middle and parts of the upper Columbia Basin from some of the Great Basin and Plains peoples. Large herds were built up on the rich, natural grasses of the Plateau country, especially by the Cayuses, Nez Perces, and Yakimas, and they and neighboring peoples became mounted. Some of the members of those tribes had previously been crossing to the plains in small numbers on foot to hunt buffalo, but with horses larger groups now made regular excursions to Montana and Wyoming, remaining on the plains hunting grounds for one or two years at a time. Although the travelers continued to return to their fishing villages in the Columbia Basin, they gradually adopted many of the Plains Indians' traits, including skin clothing, leather-covered tipis, parfleches, feathered headdresses, ornamentation and decoration, and other elements that had become familiar earlier to the Kutenais and Flatheads, the easternmost tribes of the Plateau. When Lewis and Clark, the first white men known in the region, reached the Plateau area in 1805, they found sharp differences in ways of living already established between the horse-owning Indians of the middle Columbia drainage area and the canoe-using peoples in the western part of the region.

British, American, and French-Canadian fur traders introduced white men's goods in profusion through much of the

Plateau area and modified the peoples' ways of life. Further degenerations of native cultures was brought about by missionaries, miners, and settlers. In the American portion of the Plateau, the whites' pressures on the Indians led to wars that dispossessed the peoples of their ancestral fishing sites and hunting grounds and forced them onto reservations. The treaties, in many cases, gave the Indians the right to continue fishing at "usual and accustomed" fishing places under certain circumstances, but these rights have been challenged increasingly in recent years. In the Canadian portion of the Plateau, less friction developed between Indians and whites. But Indian culture degenerated also, and Indian communities there, as in other parts of Canada and the United States, have been beset by economic problems.

15

The Native Peoples
of California

THE PRESENT-DAY STATE OF CALIFORNIA WAS THE HOME-
land of one of the largest, and most varied, concentrations of Indians north of Mexico. Living principally on
the narrow coastal plain, along the lower parts of rivers, and
in the warm interior valleys, they are estimated to have
numbered more than 350,000 people when white men first
reached the area.

Access from the north and east through the mountains
and deserts to the more habitable portions of California was
generally difficult, and it appears that over a long period of
time many different groups found their way—or were forced
—into the region, settling down, developing their cultures,
and influencing, and being influenced by, their neighbors.
By historic times, the California area, as a result, possessed
a patchwork of more than one hundred and five distinct
tribes and tribelets, speaking numerous dialects of six different parent language stocks.

In the northwest corner was a concentration of Athapascan-speaking peoples, including Hupas, Tolowas, Mattoles,
and others. They possessed many traits of the Northwest
Pacific coastal tribes, who influenced them, and they are
frequently classified culturally with the people of the Northwest Coast. Among these Athapascans was an enclave of
Wiyots and Yuroks, who spoke a separate language, Ritwan,
believed to be related to the Algonquian stock of the East.
Just south of the Athapascan groups were the Yukis, speaking a language unrelated to that of any other group save the
Wappos, who lived near the headwaters of the Napa River.
In the mountain valleys of the northern interior and on various parts of the coast south of the Yukis dwelled members

of the Hokan linguistic family: Karoks, Shastas, Yanas, and others in the north; Pomos, Salinans, and Chumashes on the coast. In northeastern California, following a way of life similar to that of the peoples of the Great Basin with whom they are usually classified culturally, were the Pit River Achomawis and Atsugewis, also of the Hokan linguistic family.

In the coastal country just north of San Francisco, and extending inland along the rivers and foothills of the interior central California valleys were a number of populous groups of Penutian-speaking Indians, including Patwins, Maidus, Miwoks (living in three detached areas totaling about 11,000 people in 1770), Wintuns (about 12,000), and Yokuts (about 18,000), while another Penutian group, the Costanoans, lived on the coast south of San Francisco Bay. Shoshonean-speakers of the Utaztecan stock, many of them possessing traits received from the Southwest cultural area, and including Tübatulabals, Cahuillas, Serranos, Gabrielinos, Fernandeños, Juaneños, Nicoleños, and Luiseños (most of them named by the Spaniards), inhabited a large stretch of territory in the south and east, from the offshore coastal islands to the interior mountain valleys and deserts of southern California. Finally, peoples of the Yuman branch of Hokan extended from the Diegeños around present-day San Diego and a part of Lower California to the Colorado River and into Arizona.

Much archeological work has been done in California. Some of the discoveries, like those near La Jolla, in San Diego, and on Santa Rosa Island, indicate that hunters of a Pre-Projectile Point Stage of development may have been in parts of California as much as 30,000 years ago. Not all archeologists at this time, however, accept such a conclusion from these finds, nor do they yet agree about other discoveries that suggest the presence, at later times, of big-game hunters. Nevertheless, Clovis- and Folsom-type points have been found at some sites, and in southern California there is considerable evidence of the existence, perhaps about 9,000 years ago, of several somewhat similar big-game hunting cultures, one of which is known as the San Dieguito Culture. Its members used leaf-shaped projectile points and other chipped-stone objects, and this culture, like the others —with which it seems to be related—appears to be a blending of the Old Cordilleran Culture and an early Desert

Culture, although no evidence has yet been found of milling stones or basketry.

After that time, there is no doubt of man's presence in many parts of California. If a big-game hunting stage had ever existed in the area, it was, by about 5000 B.C., a thing of the past. The Desert Culture's milling stones finally appeared, and man's economy and way of life, some 7,000 years ago in California, particularly in the south, were similar to those of the people of the Great Basin. The Californian at that time, and for thousands of years thereafter, was essentially a seed gatherer who used food-grinding implements and supplemented his diet by hunting and fishing and, on the coast, by shellfish collecting and hunting land mammals and, eventually, sea mammals. In the interior of central California, a way of life during a stage of development termed Early Period and dated at more than 4,000 years ago may have been related to the La Jolla and other cultures farther south. All of them reflected a western extension of the Desert Culture and were marked by the gathering of wild foods and by supplemental hunting. In both areas, this way of life remained stable for several millennia. Although additional peoples seem to have entered the region from time to time, there is practically no evidence of the occurrence of warfare. Some of the newcomers, at this time or even earlier, may have been Penutian-speakers, coming from the north and intruding among Hokan-speaking groups.

Between 4,000 and approximately 1,500 years ago, the succeeding stages of development have been termed those of the Middle Period. On the southern coast, peoples progressed through a series of intermediate cultures, whose economies were based increasingly on hunting, shellfish gathering, and, in places, the catching of marine mammals (dolphins and porpoises), apparently from small boats and canoes. Settlements grew larger, people became more sedentary, and the presence of basket-mortars suggests the beginning of the use of acorns for food. This staple, which eventually became the basic food of many California tribes, required a long process of preparation (hulling, grinding, winnowing, leaching, and boiling) that may well have been developed at this time. In the coastal and valley portions of central California, people of the Middle Period became more warlike and conscious of wealth. Population built up along the central coast, and artifacts became more numerous and better made—fashioned more from bone and antler than in earlier periods. Coiled basketry, bone awls, many different abalone shell beads and ornaments, bows and arrows, atlatls, barbed harpoons, and whistles are some of the remains found from this stage. South of San Francisco Bay, where a coastal culture had developed, shell mounds have been found of people who not only fished and collected seafood, but hunted seals, sea lions, and otters. Immense shell mounds of the same period have also been found around San Francisco Bay, and evidence shows a steadily increasing population in that area and in the coastal ranges farther north.

Between A.D. 500 and 1500, or the beginning of historic times, the continuing growth of population, the accommodation to different environments, and the independence of various groups led to the emergence and establishment of a variety of somewhat differing local cultures. In the northwest, people drifting south, perhaps along the coast, brought with them traits of the more northerly coastal peoples. Pottery was introduced in the southern part of the present state, coming by diffusion across the lower Great Basin from the Southwest cultural area. Steatite and pottery vessels came into use for cooking, and objects were fashioned more abundantly than before from shells. In central California, people were influenced both from the Southwest and from the coast. Ceremonial life increased, and round council and dance houses were constructed. Acorns almost everywhere became the principal staple of diet, providing so well that agriculture was never adopted. On the coast, maritime cultures continued to develop, and in the Sierras hunting and wild-food-gathering peoples lived existences influenced greatly by the groups of the central valleys.

By about A.D. 1300 the many distinct California groups had established themselves in permanent locations where white men found them in historic times. Each group—an extended family, a "tribelet" (a number of neighboring villages joined by common language, customs, and background), or a tribe—inhabited its own land, defined by specific, recognized boundaries. The members of each group used only their own territory and refrained, save when it was unavoidable, from trespassing across boundaries into the lands of other groups. None of the peoples were warlike, but they were quick to defend the territories they owned in rare cases of intrusion by others.

The great variety and accessibility of different kinds of

food made it possible, despite the absence of agriculture, to produce food surpluses that allowed the development of a rich and complex social and ceremonial life. (If agriculture had been introduced, in fact, it would have been so unproductive in its initial stages as to have caused widespread starvation among the dense population). Oak trees grew in profusion in many areas, providing huge supplies of acorns. These were gathered in large, conical baskets, shelled, dried, and, when needed, pounded into meal from which the bitter tannic acid was leached out with water. The flour was then boiled into a gruel or baked as bread. Surplus stores of acorns and other foods were kept in big baskets and bins. In addition, the various peoples—depending on where they lived—collected and roasted numerous kinds of wild seeds; took fish from the streams and shellfish from coastal waters; utilized various fruits, nuts, roots, berries, and wild plants like yucca and sage; and hunted and caught different species of wildlife, ranging from elk, deer, and small game to birds, reptiles, rodents, and certain kinds of insects.

The mild California climate permitted simplicity in both dress and housing. Men went naked or wore skin loincloths, while women generally wore short skirts, basketry hats, and occasionally cloaks of rushes or skins. In hot weather people preferred to go barefoot, but moccasins, as well as skin robes and leggings, were generally used in cold weather, in the higher altitudes, and on journeys. Houses varied in style from group to group, usually being dome or conical in shape, and made of a framework of poles covered with earth, brush, bark, rush mats, or wooden slabs. In the Sacramento Valley, Maidu villages contained large earthen mound lodges, while the Yuroks farther north constructed square or rectangular plank houses somewhat like those of the Northwest Pacific Coast area inhabitants. In the south, Cahuillas, from the San Fernando and San Gabriel valleys eastward to the Coachella and Borrego valleys, used several types of dwellings, including the *samat*, a circular domed structure of poles covered with brush or grass, sometimes chinked and plastered with mud or adobe. These Indians, who inhabited present-day Riverside, San Bernardino, and Palm Springs, among other sites, also made houses of tule or palm fronds. In addition, many peoples, like the populous Miwoks, built large round, earth-covered lodges—frequently semi-subterranean—for dances and various social and ceremonial gatherings. Separate, smaller lodges, constructed over pits, were used for cleansing and purifying sweatbaths. Many of them were communal. The males gathered in them and steamed themselves, either by the heat of a fire or by throwing water over hot rocks.

Although there was no formal political organization among the small, extended family units, usually averaging one hundred or fewer people each, such groups possessed headmen, or leaders, who managed civil affairs but had little or no authority over the people. The larger tribelets had officers who filled several roles, including those of village crier, chief's messenger, and leader of ceremonies. All the groups followed a regular cycle of seasonal activity, moving at different periods through their own territories to secure food. Even the smallest unit had a permanent settlement; larger ones, in addition, possessed several summer or transient village sites which they occupied at various seasons. Travel was by foot, save in some areas of the coast; in the northwest, for instance, tribes plied the lower rivers in canoes hollowed from redwood logs.

The absence of a highly developed material and organizational life, despite the concentration of population and the abundance of food resources, led early white arrivals in California from the United States to circulate the contemptuous and untrue allegation that the California Indians were more primitive than others. Their development actually took different forms, and sophistication was reflected both in the excellent craftsmanship and artistry of their basketry and in the rich features of their ceremonial life. Their pottery was crudely made and not often employed, but basketry took its place; in technique and design California Indian baskets were among the finest made anywhere in the world. The Pomos of northern California, for example, weaving small, brilliantly colored feathers into many of their baskets and decorating them with shell beads, produced exquisite works of art.

The social customs and ceremonial life of the California Indians were often complex and differed even among close neighbors. In the northwest, the wealth-obsessed Yuroks had a precise system of payments by one individual to another for injuries or offenses to body, feelings, or property. Some members of that tribe were wealthier than others, and, when offended, received larger payments. In some villages throughout California, people were divided into clan groups,

which organized ceremonies and festivals and competed in
games. All the principal events of life—birth, puberty, marriage, and death—as well as the seasonal changes of nature,
were observed in ceremony and ritual, the core of which
was the dance. The latter generally occurred in the large
ceremonial round houses and sometimes lasted for two
weeks, the dancers being attired in splendid feathered headdresses and special costumes.

Several types of societies among both men and women
trained youths in religious and ceremonial lore and in relationships between the people and the supernatural. Initiation
rites were conducted for boys and girls who had reached
puberty and, later, for those who were considered ready to
enter the adult societies. In central California, societies called
Kuksu Cults, after one of the principal deities, served as
teachers of the young. The purpose of the cults was to establish contact with the spirits and thus aid in the acquisition
of supernatural power. In the ceremonies, held in winter,
masked dancers took the roles of the different deities; the
dancer impersonating Kuksu wore a magnificent feathered
headdress four feet in diameter. The rites went on for
days in the large, earth-covered lodges, while shamans
sang and demonstrated their supernatural powers with tricks
of magic, pretending to swallow live rattlesnakes and coals,
and executing other feats. In the south, another spirit gave
its name to the Chingichnich Cults, whose members did
not impersonate spirits. Initiates of these cults drank crushed
Jimson weed, a narcotic plant, to produce hallucinations that
were believed to bring them into contact with the supernatural.

Some of the rich and varied ceremonialism of the California area showed influences from other cultures. The
opulence and ostentation of the Pacific Northwest Coast
were mirrored among the Yurok, Karok, and Hupa Indians
of northern California. The rites of their annual world-
renewal ceremony included deer dances, in which participants
flaunted their wealth in rare white deerskins, dentalia shells,
scalps of redheaded woodpeckers, and other valued objects.
The Chumash of the Santa Barbara coastal area, who carved
bird effigies and fish in stone, built the only plank canoes
in North America, and venerated the large California con-
dor, may also have been influenced by the Northwest Coast
culture. In the south, ground paintings, associated with initi-

ation rites among the Luiseños and other groups, were reminiscent of the sand paintings of the Navahos and Pueblos of the Southwest cultural area.

The nonritual life of the California Indians was heightened by the possession of large funds of tales, myths, and songs. Some of the latter were strictly of the ceremonial type, but most of them were social and were associated with pleasure dances, games, or everyday activities. Musical instruments included flutes, mouth bows, rattles, whistles, and foot drums. The drums were five to ten feet long, made from sections of hollow logs, hollowed further by burning, and cut in half to form a semi-circle in cross-section. The log was placed over a pit that formed a resonance chamber, and then stamped on by the drummer to provide a rhythmic beat for the singing or dancing. Some of the songs merely recorded an incident, described a manifestation of nature, or expressed a feeling. A typical song, recorded by a Maidu woman for Dr. Frances Densmore, who collected the music of that tribe, related the simple anecdote of two boys who went to gather fresh clover for their sick grandmother. Two girls tried to go with them, but the boys drove them back, saying, in the words of the singer, "You are not going to get clover." The girls persisted, however, and the singer went on, with the girls' words, "Yes, we are."

The harmony between the California Indians and their environment, unchanged in essentials for thousands of years, ended calamitously with the coming of the white man. Beginning in 1769, Spaniards occupied the area. Priests, aided by soldiers, rounded up the coastal natives and made them live at missions, where they converted them to Christianity, taught them agriculture and mechanics' skills, and maintained strict authority over them. Many of these so-called mission Indians (in contrast to what the Spaniards called the "wild" tribes still living in freedom in the central valleys and interior hills and mountains) became, in time, mixtures of peoples who had previously been members of different tribes and tribelets that spoke different languages and dialects. For many years, under the Spanish rule, these Indians were severely regimented and sternly punished.

Nevertheless, when the United States acquired Mexico in 1848, the Indian population was still about 100,000. But the heavy influx of whites during the Gold Rush was catastrophic for the natives. Friction with the miners and settlers led to ruthless massacres of Indians, to the willful destruction of their food stores and the overrunning of their acorn-gathering grounds, and to the extermination of entire native settlements. Between 1849 and 1859, it is estimated that some 70,000 California Indians were killed or wiped out by disease. Many groups became extinct, and by the close of the nineteenth century there were probably no more than 15,000 Indians left in the state. Some had retreated to hiding places in the mountains, but even there they had mostly died away. In 1911, as recorded by Theodora Kroeber, the last "wild" Indian in the entire United States, a Yana man named Ishi from the slopes of Mount Lassen in California, gave himself up to the civilized world that had been pressing around him. Today, the California Indian population is increasing and is estimated to number about 40,000, on and off reservations. Most of them, although extremely poor and overlooked by the state's huge non-Indian population, maintain pride in the heritage of their respective tribes.

16

The Indians of the Southwest

SOME OF THE LARGEST AND BEST KNOWN TRIBES OF THE present-day United States live in the Southwest. The cultural area, comprising the state of Arizona and the western two thirds of New Mexico, as well as southeastern Utah, southwestern Colorado, and a part of western Texas, is topographically a varied one. In the north, skirting the Great Basin, is a high plateau region of canyons, mesas, and tableland, cut by the Colorado River and several of its tributaries, including the Little Colorado and the San Juan. South of the plateau, running across the middle of Arizona and western New Mexico, and bordering much of the upper Rio Grande, are mountains and narrow valleys. Farther south, extending into the northern parts of the Mexican states of Sonora and Chihuahua (sometimes included in the Southwest cultural area), are low deserts, through which run a number of rivers, including the Gila and Salt. In general, the entire region is an arid one, where water is a precious commodity. Yet agriculture, introduced in the area thousands of years ago, took hold and—nurtured carefully by prehistoric peoples who made wise use of the land and water resources— provided one of the principal bases for the development of advanced, sedentary Indian societies that almost attained an urban stage of civilization.

The tribes associated with the Southwest in historic times are, in some cases, relative newcomers and, in others, descendants of peoples long in the area. In the west, along the lower Colorado River, are Havasupais (canyon dwellers near Arizona's Grand Canyon), Walapais, Mohaves, Yumas, and Cocopas, all of the Yuman branch of the Hokan linguistic stock. The Hokan stock is one of the older ones on the continent, and Yuman speakers are ancient inhabitants of the Southwest. Chemehuevis of the Utaztecan language family also live along the lower Colorado, although they originally dwelled in the eastern Mohave Desert country of California. In addition, Yuman-speaking Yavapais live in western Arizona, and Halchidhomas of the same language group, who formerly dwelled along the Colorado, moved to the middle Gila River where they joined the Yuman-speaking Maricopas.

Occupying a large part of northeastern Arizona, as well as northwestern New Mexico and a strip of southeastern Utah, is the nation's biggest tribe (about 110,000 people), the Athapascan Navahos. The Athapascan peoples, who broke away from related groups in the northwestern part of North America and migrated south, are comparatively recent arrivals in the Southwest, some of them possibly having reached there as late as the middle of the sixteenth century, almost simultaneously with the arrival in the same area of the Spaniards. Others of these late-arriving Southwest Athapascans are the bands and groups of four divisions of the Apaches: the Jicarillas of northeastern New Mexico; the Mescaleros of the south-central part of that state; the Chiricahuas of southeastern Arizona, southwestern New Mexico, and the adjoining northern areas of Sonora and Chihuahua; and the Western Apaches of eastern Arizona. (Additional Apache divisions, the Lipans and the Kiowa-Apaches, settled farther east, on the plains, ranging from Kansas to northern Mexico, and, because they followed the life of the Plains Indians, are sometimes not included among the peoples of the Southwest cultural area.)

The rest of the tribes in the Southwest all have roots that reach far back into the area's prehistory. In southern Arizona are the homelands of two tribes of the Utaztecan linguistic family: the Pimas of the Gila and Salt rivers, and the Papagos, who live south of the Gila. The Hopis, also of the Utaztecan family, dwell in the mesa country of northeastern Arizona, while in west-central New Mexico are Zuñis, who speak their own distinctive Zuñian tongue, so far not related with certainty to any other linguistic family. Farther east, in the valley of the Rio Grande in north-central New Mexico, are Pueblos, divided into two general linguistic stocks: speaking Tewa, Tiwa, and Towa tongues of the Tanoan stock are the people of Taos, Picurís, Nambé, Jemez, and other pueblos (towns); seven additional Pueblo groups, including those of Acoma, Laguna, Cochití, and Zia speak Keresan,

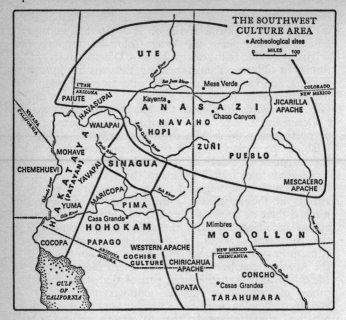

which may be related to Hokan. North of El Paso, into historic times, finally, were Tanoan-speaking Mansos. Because of their many similar traits which stem from a generally common heritage, the Hopis, Zuñis, and Pueblos are usually grouped together, the Hopis, Zuñis, and Keresan-speaking peoples of Acoma and Laguna in western New Mexico being considered western Pueblos, and the Keresan and Tanoan peoples of the Rio Grande Valley being regarded as eastern Pueblos.

For a number of reasons, the cultural history of the native peoples of the Southwest is among the best known. Because of the dry climate, numerous remains of prehistoric cultures have been excellently preserved through the centuries. Archeological work, moreover, has been facilitated by the nature of the terrain, much of it affected by erosion that has laid bare many layers of subsoil, and large parts of it also that are not obscured by heavy vegetation. In addition, white men penetrated the area in the first half of the sixteenth century, and written descriptions of the native peoples thus go back more than four hundred years. Finally, many of the tribes still retain some of their old cultural traits, which can be observed and studied, and quite often, compared with archeological findings.

There is no agreement yet on when man first entered the Southwest. Certain finds, particularly at sites in peripheral areas, like Tule Springs, Nevada, hint at the presence of inhabitants of a Pre-Projectile Point Stage, 11,000 or more years ago. In addition, big-game hunting groups left behind spear points of the Sandia, Clovis, and Folsom types that range in age from approximately 10,000 to perhaps 20,000 years old. Such relics have been found at Sandia, New Mexico, and at the Lehner, Naco, and Ventana Cave sites in southern Arizona. Most of the Southwest, however, never seems to have been as good a hunting area for Pleistocene big-game animals as were the plains that began in eastern New Mexico; and the relatively few finds of the big-game hunters in the Southwest indicate that small groups, wandering westward from the plains, may have moved only through certain limited Southwestern areas which the animals frequented.

By at least 9,000 years ago, when evidence of the region's human occupation is more abundant, the period of the Ice Age animals was on the wane, and the economy of the peoples in the Southwest had become essentially that of the Desert Culture, based on the collecting of wild foods and the trapping and hunting of small game. As in the Great Basin and its adjoining areas, the people—probably little bands of related families—roamed within limited areas, utilizing every food available. Grass seeds, mesquite beans, piñon nuts, yucca fruits, and various berries were among the wild foods that were collected, and small animals, rodents, reptiles, birds, and certain insects were all part of the diets, depending on locations. The people found shelter in caves and rock overhangs, used rabbit fur, vegetable fibers, and animal hides for blankets and articles of clothing, and fashioned such utensils and implements as milling stones and atlatls from chipped stone, wood, and bone.

A sequence of gatherers, known as people of the Cochise tradition, which archeologists divide into successive stages named for principal site locations (Sulphur Spring, Chiricahua, and San Pedro), occupied the central and southern portions of the region for thousands of years, adding to their cultural traits and changing their ways of life only slightly during that long period. They appear in general to have lived, from at least 9,000 years ago almost to the beginning of the Christian era, in temporary camps along lakes and streams that were more numerous in the area than today. They ground nuts and seeds with milling stones; dwelled in caves or in dome-shaped wickiups; did a little hunting (although remains of mammoth and other extinct animals indicate that some of the earliest Cochise, or Sulphur Spring stage, people may have killed big game on occasion); and, until the latter stage of their culture, existed without farming, permanent dwellings, or pottery.

Those three elements eventually reached first one part of the Southwest, then another, giving birth to several different cultures that progressed, stage by stage, as will be recounted below. Agriculture, pottery, and certain other traits spread northward into the area from central and northern Mexico, where more highly developed cultures already existed, coming principally by diffusion (passing from people to people), but also being brought, in some cases perhaps, by groups of migrants who entered the Southwest from farther south. Overall, therefore, the Southwest, after about 300 B.C., may be viewed as something of a far northern frontier of more advanced Middle American cultures, one in which some influences were strong and some weak, and where radiations from Middle America grew less pronounced the farther north they moved. Their initial and strongest impact in the Southwest was in southern Arizona and New Mexico; by the time the influences reached the Great Basin, their force was almost nil save in a few regions.

At least 4,500 years ago, the first of the above-mentioned elements, maize (farming), seems to have spread into the southernmost area of the Southwest from Mexico. It was too primitive a type for effective agriculture, however, and some 2,000 years passed before cultivated corn began to supplant wild foods as an important part of the diet in the Southwest, or to have any significant effect in changing ways of life or bringing about an increase in population. Beans also entered the same southern area of the Southwest from Mexico by at least 3,000 years ago, but that crop, too, had no immediate impact on the old collecting Desert Culture. Sometime during the first millennium B.C., possibly around 500 B.C., a new strain of corn, which added to the drought-resistant capability and the productivity of the crop, diffused—perhaps from an eastern source—into the moun-

tainous region along the southern part of the border between
Arizona and New Mexico, and in that high area that favored
the growing of corn, agriculture at last got a firm foothold,
spreading gradually from there to other parts of the Southwest.

At about that time, the people of that same mountainous
region—members of the last, or San Pedro, stage of the
Cochise tradition—were able also to make more intensive
use of cultivated beans and squash in their diet, and a little
later (about 300 B.C.) they were settling down near their
farming plots in permanent or semi-permanent villages. Their
homes were roundish pit houses (later, quadrangular and
other shapes), partly subterranean, with a superstructure
of beams covered with brush and earth, ramped entrance-
ways, and storage and fireplace pits dug into the floors. Two
centuries later, by about 100 B.C., these same people acquired
the ability to make pottery and were fashioning well-made
polished brownware. The source of the idea of the pit house
is not known, but it is believed to have entered the region
from California or the north rather than from Mexico. Pottery, it seems certain, came from Mexico. With its adoption
by the San Pedro people, the Mogollon Culture, one of
several new Southwest cultures that were to be built on the
base of the ancient Desert gatherers' culture, emerged in the
region.

Centered in the mountainous country of southeastern
Arizona, southwestern New Mexico, and the adjoining northern portions of Sonora and Chihuahua, the Mogollon Culture persisted with few important changes, except for those in
pottery styles, until about A.D. 1100, when it was funda-
mentally influenced by the culture of another Southwest
group, the Anasazi, who lived farther north. In the interven-
ing centuries, the culture of the Mogollon people was characterized by the retention of many of its original Desert
Culture traits—the gathering of seeds, roots, berries, nuts,
and insects, and the hunting of small game—as well as by
its newer traits—the growing of corn and beans without
irrigation, the clustering in villages of pit houses (with larger
pit houses probably for ceremonial use) by its increasing
population, and the making of coiled pottery, predominantly
plain brown at first, then decorated, red-on-brown, and,
later, red-on-white and (as a result of Anasazi influence)
black-on-white, with geometric and other designs. After
about A.D. 1100, the appearance of pueblos—above-ground,

contiguous rooms, built principally of stone—reflected the spread of Anasazi ideas across the Mogollon area. Thereafter, the Mogollon people generally adopted the Anasazi culture, and although several well-defined regional patterns emerged, Mogollon and Anasazi ways of life became essentially the same.

A second new Southwest culture, that of the Hohokam (from the Pima Indian word, meaning "those who have gone"), had arisen, meanwhile, at about the time of Christ, or a century or two earlier. It, too, developed among San Pedro Cochise people, and was centered along the middle Gila River of southern Arizona. Archeologists have divided Hohokam cultural development into four successive stages: Pioneer (c. A.D. 1–600); Colonial (c. A.D. 600–900); Sedentary (c. A.D. 900–1100); and Classic (c. A.D. 1100–1400). Some scholars use the term Hakataya (the Yuman word for the Colorado River) when referring to the Pioneer stage, indicating that during this period the people of the middle Gila and of the lower Colorado rivers possessed essentially the same culture, and that a distinctive Hohokam Culture did not arise along the middle Gila until Mexican traits were brought, or diffused, into that area on the eve of the Colonial stage. The same scholars, in addition, tend to believe that improved strains of corn first gave rise to sedentary settlements among the Hohokam, or Hakataya, of the middle Gila, and that some traits, including house forms, spread from there to the Mogollon area, and thence to the more northerly Anasazi region.

At any rate, the characteristics of the first, or Pioneer, period of the Hohokam were somewhat similar to those of the initial stage of the Mogollon Culture, and reflected the adoption of the same three basic traits—agriculture, pit houses, and pottery—that marked the close of the nomadic, collecting stage. The Hohokam people grew corn and other crops on the low land along the Gila, utilizing the river's floodwater rather than irrigation works. They built pit houses, larger and shallower than those of the Mogollon people, and made pottery that was painted red-on-buff and sometimes yellow. In addition, they worked skillfully with stone, making jars, polished, grooved axes, and other useful objects; practiced cremation rather than inhumation; and fashioned human figurines of clay, an idea that possibly came to them from western Mexico or Guatemala by way of Mexico's west coast.

The second, or Colonial, period began after the arrival
and development of many new traits that obviously originated in central and southern Mexico and that sharply differentiated the Hohokam from the other peoples in the
Southwest. It is not yet agreed how these new traits reached
the Hohokam area. In the past, it was generally believed that
they moved northward by diffusion, and that the Hohokam
of the Colonial period were the descendants of those of
the Pioneer period. More recently, many students have
tended to support another theory: that the Hohokam of the
Colonial period were colonists or invaders from Mexico,
who either overwhelmed the earlier settlers or drove them
toward the western and northern fringes of the Southwest
area. According to this theory, the older settlers had been
either relatives of Yuman-speakers who lived along the middle and lower Colorado, or a separate group referred to as
Ootams (a Pima word meaning "people"); in either case,
their Hakataya Culture, now altered by Mexican influences,
had been similar to that of the Colorado River dwellers.

With the advent of the Colonial stage (c. A.D. 600), however, the Hohokam began to build irrigation ditches, large
ball courts resembling those in Middle America, and even
truncated earthen pyramids. In time, they developed long
networks of canals that tapped the rivers and streams and
facilitated the cultivation of extensive fields of corn and cotton. Some of the irrigation works were very large—one network covered one hundred and fifty miles—and must have required a high degree of social organization. Yet, little is known
about the nature of Colonial Hohokam society, except that
it seems to have been a peaceful one and that, until later
at least, it was basically democratic rather than class structured. Population increased, and villages included huts made
essentially of posts, brush, and layers of dirt erected over
pits; flat, oval ball courts, up to two hundred feet in length,
with earthen embankments; trash mounds and occasionally
platform mounds; and cremation burial areas. The ball
games, played with a rubber ball, may have been part of a
religious system.

The Hohokam Culture, which developed through the
Colonial stage, reached a climax in the Sedentary stage, when
societies may have become class structured and been marked
by the presence of religious cults that had roots farther
south in Mexico. Arts and skills improved. Red-on-buff
pottery, decorated during the Colonial stage with repetitive

geometric or life-form designs, was painted with increasingly elaborate patterns. Carved and plain stone bowls, slate palettes, turquoise pendants, incised bone tubes, mirrors of iron pyrites set in stone disks, earplugs and nose buttons, and numerous ornaments of shell (received via trade from the Gulf of California and the Pacific) were made. After about A.D. 1000, the Hohokam developed a process of etching shells with fermented saguaro juice, making probably the first etchings in the world. The practice eventually died out, and appeared nowhere else in the hemisphere. Other notable abilities included the weaving of varied and excellent textiles and the making of clay figurines that became increasingly truer to life; later, merely heads were made, designed probably to be affixed to fiber bodies.

During the Sedentary period, the Hohokam influenced some of the peoples on the peripheral areas around them. One group of Hohokam expanded northward through Arizona's Verde Valley toward present-day Flagstaff, coming in contact with another agricultural people known as the Sinagua. Later, about A.D. 1100, Anasazi influences swept over the Sinagua, and some fifty years later the latter moved south, pushing back the Hohokam and bringing Anasazi traits into the Hohokam territory. About 1300, another Anasazi group, the Saladoans from the mountainous region of east-central Arizona, migrated into the Hohokam country of the lower Gila, where they built multistoried pueblo-like dwellings of adobe. The Sinagua and Salado invasions seem to have been peaceful; the Salado and Hohokam, for instance, appear to have existed amicably in the same villages for several generations, each group continuing in the main to follow its own way of life. Actually, the Hohokam were changing. In this period, which archeologists call the Classic, because of the arrival of Anasazi influences in the Hohokam country, the Hohokam began to build surface houses of many rooms, one story high. In addition, old traits of their culture declined, and many cultural items disappeared. The people no longer made stone vessels, pyrite mirrors, or palettes; clay figurines became rare; scant carving was done in stone, shell, or bone; and ball courts went out of use.

After 1400, the Salado, who had made beautiful polychrome pottery, moved away. Hohokam culture continued to decline. The Hohokam, most authorities believe, remained where they had been living and eventually became the Pimas and Papagos who, showing little outward reflection of the cultural high points of the Hohokam Sedentary period, were found in southern Arizona by the Spaniards. Others, however, who think that the Hohokam had originally been intruders in the region at the end of the Pioneer period (c. A.D. 600), theorize that the Hohokam migrated out of the area, possibly back to Mexico, about 1400, leaving it to the descendants of the original inhabitants, who became the modern Pimas and Papagos.

Northeast of the Hohokam country, in the plateau "four corners" area where the present states of Arizona, New Mexico, Utah, and Colorado meet, was the Anasazi Culture. The Anasazi received the stimuli to development later than the Mogollon or Hohokam peoples, and reached their cultural climax later also. At high moments in their development, however, their influences extended significantly across almost all parts of the Southwest.

The term Anasazi, a Navaho word meaning "ancient ones," and referring to remains of a people long disappeared when the Navahos first reached the area of their present home, is generally used to encompass a long sequence of developmental stages, each of which has its own name. The earliest of them, a transitional stage from the Desert Culture to an agricultural, sedentary way of life, is called Basket Maker, because of the abundance and fine quality of the basketry discovered among the remains of the period (c. A.D. 1–400). During this period, the people of the Anasazi region still followed essentially the ways of life of the Desert Culture. They were hunters of small game, using spears, nets, snares, and atlatls, and were also collectors and gatherers of wild foods. They moved about in small groups, made implements of stone, bone, and wood, and were adept at making basketry containers, sandals, and other woven goods of vegetable fibers.

Primitive forms of corn and squash were in the area (some students think the first corn reached the Anasazi region from the U. S. Southeast, rather than from Mexico), but agriculture was still in an incipient stage. By about A.D. 100, some people were beginning to live in permanent or semi-permanent habitations—domed shelters of logs and mud mortar, erected over shallow depressions. Slab-lined storage cists were also fashioned; rabbit fur was woven into robes; and dogs were domesticated—although apparently they were not used for food. Pottery, dated at about A.D. 150 and stemming perhaps from the Mogollon Culture, has been found in part of the Anasazi area; but some two hundred and fifty years elapsed before its manufacture became general among the Anasazi. Again, some students see a Southeastern source (possibly the Caddoan area) for the first widespread pottery among the Anasazi, although they recognize that later stimuli and additions came from the Mogollon area.

By about A.D. 400–500, agriculture had become more intensive and significant to the diet; increasing numbers of people were settling down in permanent dwellings, and a distinctive plain gray pottery was being made. In the so-called Modified Basket Maker stage (c. A.D. 400–700), the idea of pit houses spread across the Anasazi area, again probably from contact with the Mogollon Culture farther south. Anasazi began to live in large clusters of circular pit houses, lined with stone slabs, roofed with wood, and entered either through the roof or via an antechamber. Often the pit houses were constructed in huge caves or in rock overhangs of cliffs. During the same period, cotton and beans were added to the crops; the bow and arrow and the stone ax came into use; turkeys were domesticated; and feather cloth was made from turkey feathers. In the seventh and eighth centuries, development quickened. New varieties of corn increased the productivity of agriculture, and small gardens flourished, even along intermittent streams whose occasional floods watered the plots. Skills in basketry, sandal making, and textile production grew, and, with surplus crops (stored in mud and stone structures) and consequent leisure time, the expanding population satisfied esthetic and spiritual impulses, fashioning bracelets, beads, various ornaments of shell, wood, turquoise, lignite, seeds, and stone, and crude clay figurines, the latter possibly being effigies related to a developing religious system.

After about A.D. 700, contiguous rooms, arranged in straight lines or crescents, began to be constructed above ground, most of them made of stone mortared with adobe, others with walls of poles and adobe. The development of these above-ground structures, used at first as rooms for storage and then as dwellings, marks the end of the Basket Maker phase of the Anasazi and the beginning of the time when they are more generally referred to as Pueblos (from the Spanish word for town). As the member families of clans joined their rooms to live together, buildings became larger, and social and religious organization developed and grew gradually more complex. Pit houses were turned into round subterranean ceremonial chambers called kivas, entered by a ladder through a smoke hole in the roof, and serving also as meeting places for men.

Pueblo culture continued to develop through a sequence of stages, the first of which is known as Developmental Pueblo (c. A.D. 700–1100). That period, marked by a large and rapid population increase, was characterized also by the emergence of a definite pattern of site plan for Anasazi settlements; the development of a single large ceremonial chamber called the Great Kiva; the weaving of cotton textiles on looms; the making of more elaborate and specialized types of pottery, often indented and corrugated and usually painted with black-on-white designs; the abandonment of the dart and atlatl and the increased use of the bow and arrow; the expansion of Anasazi influences into other parts of the Southwest, particularly toward the Great Basin and into the Mogollon area in the south; and the development of an increasingly complex religious system, focused on nature and agriculture, and including special ceremonies and dances, many designed to bring rain, ensure crop fertility, and ward off natural disasters.

Pueblo culture reached a peak during what is known as the Great Pueblo period (c. A.D. 1100–1300). In that time different clan units became grouped cooperatively in numerous individual settlements of single, many-tiered communal buildings of contiguous rooms, constructed up to four stories high in the open, on the tops of mesas, or in huge, arched recesses in cliff walls. In the valleys, canyons, or open plateau country near the pueblos, the men tended gardens, practicing dry (though some irrigated) farming, and storing harvest surpluses in special rooms in the pueblos against times of drought and famine. All across the red rock canyons and juniper-covered hillsides of the high Colorado Plateau were Anasazi settlements, and particularly in localities like Mesa Verde in southwestern Colorado, Chaco Canyon in northwestern New Mexico, the Mimbres area of the old Mogollon region, the Sinagua country of Arizona's Verde Valley and Flagstaff regions, Kayenta in northeastern Arizona, and the Colorado River Basin of southeastern Utah, the Anasazi and the peoples who had adopted their culture created a classic age of colored cotton and feather cloth, beautifully painted pottery, and turquoise jewelry. Pueblo skills and artistry created many and varied household utensils and tools; necklaces, bracelets, and other decorative items, some done in beautiful mosaic work—a technique that reached them about this time from Mexico; feather robes and ornamented girdles, belts, and sandals; and, in many places, great numbers of clay figurines, probably associated with fertility cults and other spiritual activities.

During this period of increasingly complex religious and social organization, the Great Kiva went out of use among the Anasazi. Small kivas remained in use, and tower-like structures and other new architectural forms, possibly also of Mexican origin, appeared. At the same time, the gradual expansion of Anasazi influence continued southward, mostly by acculturation in the Mogollon area and possibly in the Chihuahua basin in northern Mexico, but also by migration into the Hohokam country of southern Arizona. In a reverse movement, Mexican traits, including the use of life forms in art and the mosaic work, already mentioned, together with trade items, such as copper bells and parrots, moved north into the Pueblo country.

During somewhat the same period, Anasazi influences began to decline and disappear on the northern and western frontiers, and life in those areas, north and west of the Colorado River, took on again much of the coloration of the Desert Culture. What happened is not yet known with certainty: either Great Basin peoples expanded, driving the agricultural Pueblos back toward northeastern Arizona, or the inhabitants, for some reason, reverted to the old ways of a culture that was based more on gathering and hunting than on agriculture.

This process of Anasazi withdrawal accelerated rapidly during the last quarter of the thirteenth century. For reasons that are still not definitely established, the people abandoned their dwellings in one area after the other, leaving their great centers like Mesa Verde, and moving elsewhere. Various theories ascribe the abrupt exodus to a twenty-three-year drought from 1276 to 1299; to a change in rainfall patterns and a consequent acceleration of erosion that lowered the water table and made agriculture more difficult; to an epidemic; to pressure either from hostile nomadic invaders from the Great Basin or from newly arrived Athapascan-speakers; to intrapueblo factionalism among clans; or to a depletion of wood supply. Whatever the reason—or, perhaps more likely, the succession of reasons—the Pueblos dispersed to different areas where they settled down among previously established peoples or built new towns of their own.

From approximately 1300 until the appearance of the Spaniards in 1540 (sometimes called the Regressive Pueblo period), the Pueblos experienced a "golden age" in their new locations. The areas of the heightened reflowering of their culture included the Verde Valley, the Tonto Basin, the upper Salt River Basin, southeastern Arizona, some of the Hohokam area, northwestern Chihuahua, the Hopi villages (composed of a mixture of people from different areas), the Zuñi country, Acoma, and the Rio Grande area in central New Mexico, where a very large number of the dispersed peoples settled in various scattered sites. Both the Casas Grandes Culture of Chihuahua and the well-known Casa Grande site south of present-day Phoenix date from this period. New traits also appeared: beginning in eastern Arizona and spreading to the Rio Grande, pottery was decorated with a lead glaze paint. In the Hopi country, unglazed polychrome pottery, called Sikyatki Polychrome, was introduced, and kivas were painted with murals of various life forms, masked dancers, and mythological figures, which may have resulted from an influence from Mexico and, according to some scholars, may have been associated with the source of the Pueblo Kachina cult. At this time, too, many Pueblo towns were built with one or more plazas—open spaces within the townsites—designed possibly for outdoor ceremonies and dances.

After about 1450, new large-scale withdrawals occurred. More settlements and entire districts were abandoned, as abruptly as before, and when the Spaniards reached the area, Pueblo peoples were no longer living in any part of the Southwest, save in and near the Rio Grande Valley in central New Mexico, Acoma, and the Zuñi and Hopi areas farther west. The early Spaniards apparently heard the Hopis refer to some of the abandoned settlements as those of Mokis, a Hopi word meaning "dead," and, in time, used the name Moki, or Moqui, for the Hopis themselves. Even today, many non-Indians in the Southwest refer to the prehistoric Anasazi peoples as Mokis, although it is known that those Indians were ancestors of the present-day Pueblos.

Still other prehistoric peoples in the Southwest included those of the Hakataya (sometimes also called the Patayan) Culture in the desert regions of western Arizona and along the Colorado River below the Grand Canyon. This culture, possibly related to that of the Pioneer stage of the Hohokam area in southern Arizona, emerged during the first millennium A.D., developing from a Desert Culture way of life, influenced by the Amargosa branch of the Desert Culture that had existed in southern California. The people lived in settlements of surface brush huts, rather than pit houses or pueblos; practiced farming and used floodwaters of streams and rivers to nourish their crops (but relied more on gathering and hunting than did the pueblo builders); and made a brownish pottery, sometimes painted in red. They fashioned decorations from sea shells, which they got from the Gulf of California, and which they regularly traded to the Hohokams and other peoples of the interior. Their culture persisted with little change to historic times, and they are considered to be the ancestors of the modern Mohaves and other Yuman-speaking tribes whom the Spaniards found occupying the area.

Finally, mention must be made of prehistoric nomadic or semi-nomadic groups in the Southwest. Some authorities believe that such groups were present in the area throughout the periods of the different sedentary cultures previously described. Little study has been made of them, however, and it is surmised that, in general, they must have possessed a Desert Culture-type economy, similar to that of the peoples of the Great Basin. If the evidence acquired by study of the prehistoric peoples of the southern part of the Great Basin applies also to the nomadic groups of the Southwest, it is possible that from time to time they possessed some of the traits of their more advanced neighbors. About all that seems sure, however, is that during the first millennium A.D. they substituted the bow and arrow for the atlatl and either made or possessed a little pottery. A second group of nomads (the Athapascan-speaking Apaches and Navahos) reached the Southwest sometime between A.D. 1000 and 1550. Their arrival in the area was so late, however, that they will be discussed later among the tribes known in historic times.

The white man's knowledge of the Southwestern Indians began in the early sixteenth century. Among the first tribes met by Coronado and other Spanish explorers in the region were the inheritors of the Anasazi culture. At that time, the Pueblos—from the Hopi and Zuñi settlements in the west to the eastern Pueblo groups in the Rio Grande Valley—numbered more than 16,000 people and dwelled perhaps in eighty settlements, each one politically autonomous. The

towns were compactly built, single, multistoried structures of
apartment-like rooms, often constructed, for defensive purposes, on the tops of steep-sided, rocky mesas. The buildings, made of stone or adobe, were rectangular, square, or
oval, and rose in terraced tiers overlooking plazas. In those
courts were located the kivas, the secret ceremonial chambers, frequently built partly underground, and used for
religious rites and as clubs and gathering places for the
men. Larger towns, covering as much as twelve acres, were
often long rows of contiguous rooms, sometimes two or three
stories high and facing plazas or "streets." Many ground-level
rooms had no doors but, like upper-story apartments, were
entered by ladders that led to openings in the roofs. The
largest pueblo today is that of Zuñi, a five-story communal
structure in western New Mexico, still inhabited by some
2,500 people.

The pueblo communities were closely knit units in which,
for the sake of solidarity and the welfare of all, the individual was subordinated to the group. The people were generally good-natured and peaceful (the name Hopi means
"peaceful ones"), and although they could, and did on occasion, fight fiercely for their homes and freedom, they were
not aggressive and did not wage offensive war against others.
All activity was directed by the religious societies that met
in the kivas and were responsible for separate and specific
community functions, such as the appointment of civil
officers, the carrying out of cures, hunting, or the military
defense of the town. Each society possessed its own priesthood, which contributed members to the ruling council of
the town. The council, usually made up of from ten to
thirty members, determined pueblo policies, initiated ceremonial events, and sat in judgment on persons accused of
witchcraft, disloyalty to the town, or other crimes and
offenses. Among the Hopis the town theocracies were composed of priests of four major and eight minor societies. Two
members of the councils, the civil priest and the war priest,
served as executive officers. Their orders were enforced by the
warrior society, which policed the town and was charged
with carrying on defensive action. In none of the towns were
there social classes or differences in wealth; everyone, even
members of the theocracies, worked and shared as equals.

Religion was a daily experience, permeating all of life, and
acting as a principal integrating force among the people.
Associated with all acts, it was rich in myth and symbol and

was dramatized by a year-round succession of elaborate ceremonials that utilized imaginative and beautiful costumes and paraphernalia, and included dances, songs, poetry, and rites based on mythology. None of the towns possessed powerful shamans or indulged in religious hysteria or self-torture. Religion, and the ceremonies associated with it, was orderly and meticulously prescribed by tradition to achieve results that would benefit the entire pueblo.

Observing religion occupied much of the people's time; Pueblo men, indeed, are said to have devoted at least half their time to religious activities. Many of the ceremonies lasted for nine days, and in the annual cycle of observances such ceremonies often followed one after the other. Most of them, performed to propitiate the deities so that they would bring rain, effect cures, or otherwise assist the people, commenced in the kivas where the members of the societies fasted, prepared altars, made offerings of feathered prayer sticks, and purified themselves. There were numerous deities as well as beneficent spirits, called kachinas, who visited the Pueblo peoples for six months each year as messengers of the gods. At those times, members of the societies who were properly trained donned masks that symbolically represented the different kachinas and, emerging from the kivas to participate in public ceremonies, were considered by the populace as bringing into the town the actual presence and powers of the kachinas they represented. The kachina impersonators roamed through the pueblo, taking part in dances, and giving children painted dolls that represented themselves. Some of them impersonated animal spirits. Other dancers were clowns who followed the kachinas, cavorting among the people, distracting the kachinas, and heaping ridicule and scorn upon and even whipping spectators who had misbehaved or given offense to the pueblo.

In the kivas, which were barred to women and children, the cult leaders kept their fetishes and sacred objects, including prayer sticks and painted and feathered masks and costumes for the kachina dances. At the center of the kivas were stone-lined pits looked upon as the entrance to the earth from the lower world. The pits symbolized Sipapu, a place of great mystery in the north where man had first entered the world from the underground. Between the ages of five and nine, boys were brought into the kivas for the first time to receive their preliminary initiation into the cults. At that time they were confronted by masked "scare Kachinas," who whipped them to drive the badness out of them. At adolescence, between the ages of eleven and fourteen, they were brought into the kivas again and once more given a lashing, after which the kachinas suddenly took off their masks, revealed that they were village priests who produced the presence of the kachinas by wearing the masks, and threatened severe punishment if the youths failed to guard the secret. The boys were then directed to whip the kachinas as a lesson of what some day would be expected of them. Following this often frightening experience, the boys underwent long training in the rites, obligations, and secrets of the kiva society. Once they married, they were ready to become impersonators of the kachinas themselves.

In the rigidly conformist Pueblo society, individualistic qualities, competitiveness, aggressiveness, and the ambition to lead were looked upon as offensive to the supernatural powers, and laid people open to accusations of witchcraft. The townspeople's welfare and prosperity in a land often threatened by drought and the attacks of enemies required the favor and blessings of the deities, and to maintain group harmony with the supernatural world, to bring rain, cures, and intercessions when they were needed, people were taught to value modesty, sobriety, and inoffensiveness, and to avoid conflict and violence. Parents treated children gently and permissively, but threatened them with punishment by spirits if they misbehaved. As a result, Pueblo society was among the most tranquil and cooperative in the world. But the unrelieved inhibitions and fears of the people, fed by frustrations from the suppression of aggressiveness and by the always-present threat of showing traits that would bring on accusations of being a witch (the worst thing one could be called, and resulting frequently in being hung from the ceiling by the wrists or thumbs until one confessed) led sometimes to an excess of arguing, gossip, and nonviolent discord. Such rancor would occur between large groups as well, and on at least one occasion it resulted in an entire Hopi group moving out of a town to found another one for itself.

The Pueblo people depended primarily on intensive agriculture, with corn the principal crop. In the west, where matrilineal clans were important social units, the women owned the crops, as well as the houses and furnishings. Dryland farming was practiced by the Hopis and Zuñis, with garden plots being located at the mouths of washes in order to take advantage of runoffs from rains. Along the Rio

Grande, in the east, the Pueblos planted their crops in the river bottoms near their towns and irrigated their fields. The people also raised squash, beans, cotton, tobacco, and gourds, using wooden digging sticks and hoes with which to cultivate their plots. Farm work was difficult in a country with an average of only thirteen inches of rain a year, and the men did all the labor in the fields.

Food was also provided by hunting and gathering. Members of special societies hunted antelope and deer, driving the animals into pitfalls or stockades. In some of the northern towns of the Rio Grande Valley, hunters sometimes went to the plains for buffalo. People of all the villages engaged in communal rabbit hunts, chasing the quarry into net barriers on foot and then clubbing them to death. Piñon nuts, berries, the fruits of cacti and yucca, and other wild foods were gathered by the women.

Men's clothing in pre-Spanish days consisted of a loincloth of cotton and a second piece wound around the waist to form a kilt. A rectangular piece of cotton with a hole cut in the center for the head to go through also was worn sometimes as a shirt. Women dressed in cotton garments that went beneath the left shoulder, were tied above the right shoulder, and were further secured by a belt around the waist. Most men wore their hair in bangs over their forehead with a knot in the back, which they untied during ceremonies to let the hair hang loose. Women wore a number of hair styles: unmarried Hopi and Zuñi girls coiled their hair in large whorls over each ear, symbolizing the squash blossom, while older women often let their hair hang in braids, one over each shoulder.

Cooking was done by the women, who also did a large part of the construction and all of the mud plastering on the houses and made excellent pottery and basketry. Even in modern times, Pueblo women, like the celebrated Maria Martinez of San Ildefonso, have been renowned throughout the world for the excellence of their pottery.

The Pueblos were monogamists. Marriage involved little courtship and scant display of emotion. Divorce was simple: a woman who wished to end her marriage simply placed her husband's possessions outside her door. It was a sign that she was no longer wed, and he returned thereupon to his mother's home.

The first white men to intrude among the Pueblos were advance agents of Coronado's expedition which marched north from Mexico searching for the legendary Seven Cities of Cíbola in 1540. Fifty-eight years later, Spanish colonists began a conquest of the entire area. Their stern rule led to the Pueblo Revolt of 1680, the only instance when almost all of the Pueblos of east and west united in warfare against a common enemy. The Spaniards were ejected from the region, but returned twelve years later, re-establishing their rule and causing some of the Pueblos of the Rio Grande Valley to flee to some of the westernmost towns and other Indian groups, where they successfully warded off Spanish dominion. All the Pueblos were able, with greater or lesser success, to cling to their ancient beliefs and customs, despite pressure from Spaniards, periods of severe drought, and disrupting aggressions by Apaches. Eventually, the Pueblos acquired sheep and goats from the Spaniards and added pastoral activities to their daily life. During the Mexican War, United States troops arrived in the Pueblo country. A brief but bloody uprising at Taos, inspired by the Mexicans against the Americans in 1847, was put down with stern reprisals, and in 1848 the United States acquired the region from Mexico.

Since then, the Rio Grande Pueblos, Hopis, and Zuñis, by passive resistance and the deliberate policy of trying to exclude outside influences that might destroy their way of life, have managed to retain many of the traits of their original culture. But changes and new traits have appeared among them also (the Hopis have become expert silver-smiths); and the forces and products of the outside world, including the white man's schools, forms of government, and manufactured goods, have had an effect in the pueblos, lead-ing to schisms in some towns between traditionalists who want to continue life as it has always been lived and pro-gressives who wish to adopt some of the aspects of the white man's modern culture. In general, the traditionalists have retained the upper hand. Ancient ceremonials are still observed; one of them, for instance, the Hopi Rain Dance, in which members of one of the religious societies dance with live rattlesnakes in their mouths, is held every other year in August. Like other Pueblo ceremonies that may be viewed by outsiders, it regularly attracts many non-Indian visitors, but it is felt by the Indians that anyone who watches with sympathy and respect is also a participant and contributes to the efficacy of the rite. The strong attachment to such established rituals, together with the maintenance of personal responsibility to the group, the security afforded by the close-knit relationships and society of the pueblo, and the continued observance of personal and group conduct designed to ensure harmony between the people and the supernatural world, still protect the towns, to a remarkable degree, from the disintegrating influences of the surrounding non-Indian culture. To many persons, the continuance of these traditional Indian societies in such strong form is underscored by the fact that two of the Pueblos' towns, Acoma and the Hopis' Old Oraibi, the latter being one of twelve Hopi towns that exist today on three mesas in Arizona, date back to at least A.D. 1150 and are the oldest continuously occupied towns in the United States. Significantly, also, an increasing number of non-Indians, concerned and confused by the egocentric materialism of the white man's world, have turned in recent years to an examination of the Hopis' way of life, with its rich spiritual beauty, democratic group orientation, and peace.

Much more recent residents of the Southwest are the Athapascan-speaking Apaches and Navahos, who broke away from their Athapascan relatives in the far northwestern part of the North American continent and migrated south. Neither the time of their arrival in the Southwest, nor the route, or routes, they followed in getting there are yet established with certainty. Some of them may have reached the Southwest from northwestern Canada as early as A.D. 1000; groups of them were almost surely there by 1550. It is generally believed that they came south on the eastern side of the Rocky Mountains, moving down the western Great Plains, and then spreading westward to the San Juan River Valley. But some or all of them may have migrated southward on the western side of the Continental Divide, through the Great Basin.

The Apaches, whose name derives from a Zuñi word meaning "enemy," were hardy nomads with a fearsome reputation as raiders who conducted their sorties, sometimes far from their home territories, primarily to steal horses, cattle, mules, and other booty. There were six tribes, or large divisions, of Apaches, as enumerated at the beginning of this chapter, but none of them had a semblance of political unity. The usual basic organized unit of the Apaches was what can be called a local group, made up of a number of matrilocal-extended families who were united by kinship and common place of residence. Each one of these local groups enjoyed autonomy, and, with their own leaders, they were the largest cohesive Apache social and economic units. A number of local groups, by loose association within defined territorial limits, composed a band or semiband; at various times, usually for military action, the local groups within such a band would work together, even under a single war leader. In turn, those bands that considered themselves one people as distinct from all others constituted a tribe, although the term had no political significance. None of the tribes—the Kiowa-Apaches and Lipans on the plains in the east, the Jicarillas and Mescaleros of New Mexico, or the Western Apaches and Chiricahuas who were farther west in New Mexico and Arizona—had any sort of tribal government or officers.

The many individual local groups, often conducting their affairs independently of each other, possessed several types of leaders, although the details of leadership differed from tribe to tribe. Usually each local group had a head chief who made decisions for the families within the group, directing their movements from place to place, sending out raiding parties, and announcing the time for hunts, ceremonies, and other activities. His authority was limited, was essentially that of an adviser, and rested on his influence among the people and his effectiveness. At any time, a family dissatisfied with his leadership could leave his group and join another one, but a chief with a good reputation might attract the following of families from other groups. Among some groups, the position of head chief was a hereditary one and passed to members of the same clan. Elsewhere, chieftainship was generally given to the son of a dead leader or to a member of a wealthy and influential family, but the recipient had to possess qualities as a hunter, warrior, speaker, or counselor.

Beneath the head chief were usually subchiefs who were influential and respected heads of families within the local groups. They organized and directed the activities of their own families and were men who had proven themselves as hunters or warriors or who were looked up to for their wisdom, generosity, or oratorical power. They were known as rich men, or strong men, and their wives, known sometimes as rich or strong women, were often regarded as women chiefs, with the duties of organizing and directing the activities of the women in the group. The best warriors in each group were also recognized as war chiefs and, with the other subchiefs, gave leadership to the families, especially in the organizing of ceremonies connected with war or raids.

Often, a number of local groups, to conduct raids or fight an enemy, would come together in bands or semi-bands of up to several hundred persons. The various head chiefs and strong subchiefs would then compose a council. Usually, one man, whose fighting and leadership abilities were recognized by all the groups, would be accepted as war leader. Sometimes, individual groups preferred to follow their own war leader, and a band might go into war under two war chiefs. At times, the band's council would also select a civil leader or outstanding speaker, but often he would be the same person as the war chief. Major war actions generally required the approval of the councils and band leaders, but individuals could organize raids on their own and enlist followers to accompany them. Prior to raids and war missions, special dances and ceremonies were held to enlist the support of the supernatural. Successful war or raiding parties would be hailed, on their return, with other ceremonies, including a scalp dance, in which everyone participated.

To varying degrees all the Apache groups possessed cultural traits received in, or influenced by, the different areas in which they had lived, or from the peoples with whom they had had contacts. Their religion, which showed strong similarities to that of their Athapascan relatives in the Far Northwest, included the use of shamans, powerful personages in the groups, who were usually older men—and sometimes women—and whose principal functions were to intercede with the supernatural to effect cures, prophesy the future, ward off illness and evil, and ensure success in raids, hunts, and amorous affairs. Most bands possessed a rich store of sacred mythology, part of it a blending of their original northern Athapascan lore with the legends and tales of some of the peoples of the Plains, Great Basin, and the Southwest. Ceremonies, too, showed such a blending; one of them, a Jicarilla ritual, combined an Athapascan night ceremony around fires in a green wood enclosure; a Pueblo-influenced masked dance; a Great-Basin-type dance of the two sexes; and the use of Navaho-Pueblo sand paintings. A large store of myths of some of the Apache bands concerned the Mountain Spirits, supernatural beings who were thought to dwell within certain mountains. The Mountain Spirits, known as *Gans*, were believed to possess great power, for good or evil, over the people, and in various ceremonies, including an important four-day puberty rite that was both sacred and social, painted dancers in black masks and high wooden-slat head-dresses represented the Mountain Spirits. Some of those dances, still held today, are incorrectly referred to by non-Indian visitors as "Devil Dances," the Mountain Spirits being equated thoughtlessly by whites with devils. At the same time, the Apaches had a great fear of witches and of the dead, whose ghosts, they thought, could visit the living. The homes and possessions of deceased persons were burned to prevent contamination from them, and the site of a death was abandoned.

The diet of the various Apache tribes differed. The Kiowa-Apaches—Apaches who joined the Kiowas of the southern plains but kept their own language—and Lipans—who may have been an offshoot of the Jicarillas and are now almost extinct—ranged the plains in the east, engaged in gathering wild foods, but also hunted buffalo and acquired many elements of the Plains culture. The Jicarillas also hunted buffalo and possessed influences of the Plains in their culture, but, in addition, farmed rather extensively and, in their ceremonies, displayed influences from the Pueblos. The Mescaleros, principally hunters and gatherers, also had some Plains elements in their culture; they got their name, however, from the Apache custom of gathering and roasting the heads of mescal, or agave, plants. In the west, the major bands of Chiricahuas, the Eastern, Central, and Southern, were primarily hunters and gatherers, engaging in little agriculture, while the Western Apaches, who at one time may have separated from the Navahos, were the most agricultural of all the Apache tribes. The Western Apaches, whose many local groups were subdivided among bands of White Mountain, San Carlos, Cibecue, and Northern and Southern Tonto Apaches, derived about one fourth of their food from domesticated plants, including corn, beans, and squash; about 35 per cent from wild plants; and the rest from hunting. Both irrigation and dry-farming methods were used, and men and women alike tilled the plots. The men hunted, usually in groups, killing deer antelope, rabbits, small game, and occasionally elk and mountain sheep, and the women gathered such wild foods as piñon nuts, juniper berries, mesquite beans, wild onions, mescal heads, and acorns.

Most Apaches, like the people of the Great Basin, lived in thatched wickiups, which were circular, conical, or dome-

shaped, and were constructed—usually by the women—of
mesquite, cottonwood, or willow poles, bound with yucca
fiber, and covered with brush and bear grass. Some wickiups
were large and roomy, others little more than temporary
brush shelters. In cold weather, the wickiups might be
covered tightly with skins which, in warm weather, were
rolled up or removed. When it was hot, the people spent
much of their time in the shade of remadas, open-air
shelters of brush and grass roofs set upon poles near the
wickiups. Clothing was made of skin, and included long-
sleeved shirts and breechcloths for the men, two-piece
dresses for the women, and, for both sexes, high moccasins
with soles that projected and turned up in front. Men wore
their hair long and unbraided, usually bound at the forehead with a strip of buckskin (later, cloth) to keep it out
of their eyes. Both men and women wore decorative earrings,
necklaces, pendants, and bracelets, usually acquired from the
Pueblos, but—except for the sacred objects and hats of the
shamans—only occasionally used feathers for ornamentation.

Household utensils and implements included wooden fire
drills, stone manos and metates, gourd cups and dishes, skin
bags, pottery, and various kinds of baskets. Apache women
generally were adept at basketry, fashioning useful and beautifully woven and designed carrying baskets, storage baskets,
bowls, trays, and watertight jars sealed with pitch. Some of
the Apache coiled basketry, distinguished by its black and
brown colors and geometric and animal and human forms
woven into the designs, is among the finest made anywhere
by American Indians.

Although Apache raiders struck terror in hearts for generations throughout the Southwest, they were not essentially
horsemen, as were the Plains Indians. Apache raids were
usually conducted for loot, and the animals seized during
them served principally as meat. When the Apache bands
first appeared in the Southwest from the north, the Spaniards
with their horses and cattle were apparently not yet on
the scene. Many of the Apache newcomers spread across the
Pueblo country, raided the rich Pueblo towns for slaves and
booty, and engendered consternation and fear among the
Pueblo peoples. Soon after their own arrival among the
Pueblos, the Spaniards noted the presence of these fierce
nomadic raiders in the countryside. Various bands of Apaches
continued their strikes, hitting both Pueblos and Spaniards.
But there were also periods of peace when the Apaches

would come into Pueblo towns to trade amicably. In this long process of contact, the Apaches, as well as the Navahos —who may be considered as originally an Apache group— borrowed many traits from the Pueblos. Apaches learned to ride, but preferred eating the horses and raiding for more animals when they needed them. Many raids, and most fights, were conducted on foot.

Apache hostility to the white man was heightened by the latter's harsh treatment of these Indians. The Spanish policies of catching Apaches to make them slaves and of offering bounties for their scalps were adopted by the Mexicans. A constant turmoil in the Southwest, abetted by these cruel tactics, was inherited by the Americans, who did little to assuage the Apaches' fear of the whites. Guerrilla warfare between United States troops and Apache groups, under such leaders as Mangas Coloradas, Cochise, and Victorio, often resulted from injustices of the Americans, and dragged on for many years. It was finally ended in 1886 with the surrender of Geronimo, leader of a group of Chiricahuas, who had maintained a raiding-and-fighting last stand in the mountainous border country of Arizona and Mexico. Today there are some 10,000 Apaches living in southwestern Oklahoma and on reservations in Arizona and New Mexico.

The Navahos are sometimes referred to as a seventh Apache tribe, which is not correct today, although at one time the Apaches and Navahos were probably a single ethnic group. The ancestors of both peoples were Athapascan-speakers who migrated to the Southwest, possibly (although it is not yet proven) at the same time and over the same routes. Both had simple hunting and gathering cultures, and in 1630 the Navahos were still so like the Apaches that Spaniards alluded to them as *Apaches de Navajo*, for an abandoned Pueblo site known as Navajo in northern Arizona, which they occupied. By that time, however, the Navahos were spread principally across northern New Mexico (calling the heart of the region *Dinetkah*, meaning "Home of the People"), and soon afterward they were absorbing people and cultural elements of older groups in the area. Some of the latter were from the Great Basin, but most of them were Pueblos who had fled the Rio Grande to escape Spanish retribution after the Pueblo Revolt of 1680. The Pueblos taught the Navahos to farm and weave and through the years influenced significantly the Navaho religious and ceremonial systems. With the passage of time, the Navaho tribe of today developed from many ethnic elements and from cultural traits derived from the newcomers, as well as from the Spaniards and Americans; but, despite the people's heterogeneous composition and backgrounds, members of the tribe still speak an Athapascan language of remarkable purity. Navahos of today can still understand some of the words used by Athapascans in northwestern Canada.

Navahos live on the largest reservation in the United States, about 24,000 square miles, or close to 16 million acres, mostly in Arizona and New Mexico but also in southeastern Utah. (Others reside in neighboring areas off the reservations and in three small nonreservation colonies in New Mexico.) The vast reservation is desiccated and badly eroded, and so much of it is barren and unproductive, even for grazing, that it has been estimated that it can support no more than 35,000 people. Yet the Navaho population is increasing at an estimated rate of 2.25 per cent per year, and is already at about 110,000 (up from about 15,000 in 1868). Despite the development of new sources of tribal income, including uranium, natural gas, and tourism facilities, many Navahos are still among the poorest Indians in the United States.

Navahos do not dwell in towns or compact villages but are spread across different areas of the large reservation in dispersed settlements of scattered hogans. The basic social unit is the nuclear family. Society is matrilineal, and the position of women is very strong and influential in all phases of life, social, economic, political, and religious. Married couples usually (though not always) build their hogan near that of the wife's mother, but a married man keeps strong ties to his own mother's family. Extended families, composed of husband and wife and unmarried children, together with married daughters and their husbands and children, all usually living near one another, form a cooperative unit whose members work together in farming, herding, and housebuilding. Two or more extended families, bound together by marriage ties and identified with a specific area, may also live near each other, joining in economic and ceremonial activities. Called today an "outfit," this circle of relatives, numbering from fifty to more than two hundred persons, may acknowledge the informal leadership of the male head of the most prominent family. In turn, a number of "outfits," occupying the same general area, compose a local group, called a "community." Such groups, although often not well-knit, and based only on common area of residence, may elect a headman, who has administrative functions but no policy powers. Decisions bearing on policy are arrived at by unanimous agreement in public meetings, attended by both men and women.

In the past, Navaho political organization was somewhat similar to that of the Apaches. There was no tribal council or executive; each local band, occupying a definite territory, was autonomous. By 1846, band unity seems to have been achieved to the point where each band possessed a single peace *natani*, or leader, inducted into office with a ceremony and serving for life, as well as one or more war chiefs. In addition, an overall *natani* may also have exercised chieftainship for limited periods over the headmen of two or more cooperating bands. In the 1920's, tribal organization came to the Navahos for the first time: in order principally to conduct affairs with the United States government and deal with economic matters affecting all of the people, the Navahos set up a General Council, which in time has become a Tribal Council of seventy-five elected members who make policy decisions and handle tribal assets. But "home rule" is still strong, and the local group, or "community," is still the largest effective unit concerned with the day-to-day affairs of the people.

Navahos are also divided into some sixty or more large matrilineal clans, which in the past exercised strong social control over their members. Clans generally are named for specific localities, but some bear the name of a tribe or group (Ute, Zuñi) from which the ancestors of the clan's members came originally. Clan members feel a strong attachment to each other despite the fact that, because of distance, they may rarely if ever see one another. Today one of the principal functions of the clans is to regulate marriage; a man may not marry into the clan of his mother or father, such conduct being viewed with repulsion as incest. Many kinship obligations, some connected with the clan system, are observed. Brothers and sisters avoid physical contact and are restricted in their speech to each other. Men may not converse, or even be in the same room, with their mothers-in-law.

At the heart of Navaho existence is the desire to keep one's life in harmony with the supernatural and with the universe. The Navahos acquired many ritual elements from the Pueblos, but fitted them to their own cultural requirements and their own basic religious ideas. The universe, according to the Navahos, contains mortals, called the Earth Surface People, and supernatural beings, the Holy People, who possess power that can help or harm a mortal. The latter, it is believed, can bring about or restore harmony in the universe—that is, between the Holy People and the Earth Surface People, or the individual man—by the performance of ceremonies and rituals, meticulously prescribed and carried out. Illness is considered a sign of the disruption of harmony, and curing ceremonies, accompanied by curing chants, are carried out not only to end the sickness but to put the universe back into harmony and balance. The ceremonies, conducted by shamans, show Pueblo influence, but they possess notable differences. Although the shaman is well trained in sacred prayers, rituals, and chants, and exercises his powers for society generally, he acts as an individual. There are no organized priesthoods or religious societies, as among the Pueblos. The Navaho ceremonies are long, well prepared, and expensive, and relatives of the patient usually contribute to the cost of holding them. The shamans, known as chanters, sing the sacred songs, manipulate holy objects, and make symbolic paintings of colored sand, pollen, crushed flowers and minerals, and other dry pigments. All the ceremonies follow a prescribed sequence and must be word-perfect. A mistake loses control over the supernatural power, and evil may result. Ceremonies can extend over several days, and if they are successful they will restore a contented feeling of unity between the people and the supernatural world. Navaho curing ceremonies have had an increasing interest for many non-Indians, for, as in psychosomatic medicine, the mental and physical are viewed as interrelated, and, to cure an illness, the whole man is treated.

The basis of Navaho economy is agriculture, which was also learned from the Pueblos. The Navahos engage principally in dry farming, but in some areas they can practice limited irrigation. The principal crops are corn, beans, and squash. Fruit trees, particularly peaches, and oats and wheat were acquired from the Spaniards and are raised on some parts of the reservation. Sheep, goats, horses, and a few cattle, all obtained from the Spaniards, have been important. In the late nineteenth century, the Navahos ruined large parts of their reservation by building up too large flocks that overgrazed the land. A livestock reduction program, enforced by the Bureau of Indian Affairs in the 1930's, was unpopular with the Indians, although it was undoubtedly necessary to halt the disastrous loss of grass covering and the consequent erosion of the land.

Navahos do little hunting or gathering of wild foods today. Formerly, their hunting methods resembled those of the people of the Great Basin; they used disguises, stalked the game, drove it into ambushes, encircled it, and employed pitfalls. The wild foods they gathered included greens, nuts, and cactus fruits; piñon nuts are still collected occasionally but are generally sold to non-Indians.

The typical Navaho dwelling, the hogan, is a low, dome-shaped structure of logs and mud, covered with earth, with an opening in the center of the roof for a smoke hole. In the past, a conical "forked-stick" type of dwelling was used; it had a foundation of three upright poles, locked together at the apex. Additional logs were leaned against the foundation and were covered with mud and earth. Other structures, some built at a distance from the hogan, were sweat lodges, constructed like "forked-stick" hogans but without the smoke hole; storage dugouts; open remadas like those of the Apaches; and brush corrals. Families often possessed several hogans, built in different areas, to which they would move at various seasons. Today some hogans are built of stone and have glass windows. When an occupant dies, homes are frequently abandoned. Many Navahos still fear the dead and will not touch a corpse.

Clothing originally seems to have resembled that of the Great Basin Indians. What little the people wore was made generally of fibers, twisted together. Men wore breechcloths, and women employed skirts and sandals. Rabbit skins were made into cloaks and blankets for cold weather. Later, clothing was made out of buckskin and cotton. The Pueblos taught weaving to the Navahos, and after the Spaniards introduced sheep to the area, Navaho woolen rugs and blankets, woven by the women, became celebrated as the finest made by any North American Indians. Clothing styles also changed. Navaho dress and hair styles were increasingly influenced by the Pueblos, although Navaho women wove more brilliant garments. After the middle of the nineteenth century, the women adopted their own distinctive garb of velveteen blouses and full calico skirts, which they still wear. In the nineteenth century, also, the Navahos learned silversmithing, probably from Mexicans, and were soon creating beautiful silver and turquoise jewelry.

During the Spanish reign in the Southwest, Navahos, like the Apaches, consistently raided the white men's ranches for horses and other loot. Depredations continued for generations and were stopped by the Navahos only after the acquisition of the region by the United States. In 1864, Kit Carson and American troops decisively defeated the Navahos, rounded up the whole tribe, and moved the people to temporary exile on the Bosque Redondo in New Mexico. In 1868 the government established a reservation in Arizona for the tribe. The people, now crushed, settled down there peaceably. Their lot since then has been a hard one, for despite several enlargements having been made in their reservation, they have not yet been able to share the fullness of the economic life enjoyed by the rest of American society. Today, outside pressures are becoming stronger on the tribe. Schooling, the search for economic improvement, and various intrusive forces of the white man's world are changing the people. But the changes are causing confusion and personal anxiety among some of the Indians, whose ancient beliefs and ways of life are being questioned. The Navahos, in some ways, in short, are in transition, torn between faith in what has been and the promise of something new.

On western Arizona's desert plateaus and along the lower Colorado River, from the Grand Canyon to the Gulf of California, were a number of Yuman-speaking tribes. Three of them, the Havasupais, the Walapais, and the Yavapais, all sometimes called the Upland Yumans, lived in an especially harsh, arid environment and showed relatively little development from the ways of life of the Desert Culture people of thousands of years before. Essentially hunters and gatherers, they possessed traits of the Great Basin area and were characterized by great simplicity in their social organization, ritual, and material culture. The Havasupais, who still live along lovely Cataract Creek deep in the bottom of a side canyon of Arizona's Grand Canyon, and are known as People of the Blue Green Water, were somewhat distinct from the other two tribes in that they adopted certain farming methods and some religious ceremonies and rituals from the Hopis. They irrigated crops, including cotton and tobacco, with the waters of Cataract Creek, used prayer sticks, and performed rain and other dances borrowed from the Hopis.

Man's antiquity in the Western Hemisphere was first established by this find, near Folsom, New Mexico, in 1927, of a spearpoint between the ribs of an extinct bison of the Ice Age. The fluted point, about two inches long, was fashioned by a big-game hunter some 10,000 years ago.

A PICTURE PORTFOLIO

This duck decoy, looking still serviceable, was made from 2,000–3,000 years ago by a waterfowl hunter, living the existence of the Desert Culture at Lovelock Cave in the Humboldt Basin in west-central Nevada.

A Middle American Indian, whose people practiced agriculture and lived in villages, modeled this naturalistic pottery figurine at Tlatilco in the Valley of Mexico about 1,000 years before Christ.

The Castillo, or Temple of Kukulkan (below), a pyramid with steps on all four sides and a temple on top, was built at Chichén Itzá by Mayas. But it, like the Chac Mool (the statue of the reclining figure with a basin in its stomach, in foreground), shows similarities to the style of the Toltecs, who may have invaded the Mayan Yucatán country about A.D. 1000.

Tlaloc, the rain god, pictured above holding a stalk of corn by an Aztec artist, was an important deity to many farming peoples of Middle America.

The Mayan pottery figure of a woman with her child and dog, at left, is from the Late Classic Period (c. A.D. 600–900).

Mayan writing: a surviving leaf from an ancient book of glyphs and picture symbols records principally astronomical calculations and ritual material.

The visages of men of the powerful militaristic Mochica state on Peru's northern coast (above, left) were modeled on ceramic pitchers more than 1,500 years ago.

The knots made in the quipu, or counting string, seen at the right above, served as memory aids to pre-Columbian peoples in Peru.

Textiles that are among the finest ever produced anywhere in the world were turned out, beginning some 2,000 years ago, by Peruvian weavers, particularly at Nazca and Paracas on the southern coast. The pre-Columbian Peruvian fringed tapestry shown below depicts men in boats.

The Inca fortress-city of Machu Picchu, its magnificent stonework buildings and agricultural terraces crowning an 8,400-foot-high ridge in the Peruvian Andes, was only discovered by white men in 1911.

Excavated some 25 miles southwest of Phoenix, Arizona, this ball court was used about A.D. 700 by Hohokam people of the Colonial period. Such courts, up to 200 feet in length and with earthen walls as high as 20 feet, were the scenes of ball games that were introduced from Mexico.

A member of the Mogollon Culture at Casas Grandes in present-day Chihuahua, Mexico, fashioned the delightful effigy vessel seen at left.

Bowls made by the Mogollon Culture's Mimbres people (tenth–twelfth centuries A.D.) in New Mexico were broken, or "killed" (below), when the owner died and placed in the dead man's grave.

The Inca fortress-city of Machu Picchu, its magnificent stonework buildings and agricultural terraces crowning an 8,400-foot-high ridge in the Peruvian Andes, was only discovered by white men in 1911.

Excavated some 25 miles southwest of Phoenix, Arizona, this ball court was used about A.D. 700 by Hohokam people of the Colonial period. Such courts, up to 200 feet in length and with earthen walls as high as 20 feet, were the scenes of ball games that were introduced from Mexico.

A member of the Mogollon Culture at Casas Grandes in present-day Chihuahua, Mexico, fashioned the delightful effigy vessel seen at left.

Bowls made by the Mogollon Culture's Mimbres people (tenth–twelfth centuries A.D.) in New Mexico were broken, or "killed" (below), when the owner died and placed in the dead man's grave.

This figure of a mother and child was found in a burial mound of the Hopewell Culture in Illinois (c. 300 B.C.–A.D. 700).

A late Mississippian Culture temple-mound village at Ocmulgee in present-day Georgia is depicted in this modern drawing. The scene shows a cornfield in the river bottom (foreground) and a file of people ascending one of the temple mounds that loom above the thatch-roofed houses.

Two men of the Temple-Mound Culture were pictured by lines incised on the shell gorget, or neck ornament, above, about 600–700 years ago at Spiro Mound, a center of the Southern Cult in Oklahoma. Temple-Mound centers still existed when the first whites reached the U.S. Southeast.

This wooden deer's head was carved and painted by a Calusa Indian on Key Marco, southern Florida, in the fifteenth century only a short time before Columbus "discovered" America.

Many groups of native Americans were given their historic names by white men who either contrived descriptive terms of their own for them (Creeks) or adopted expressions by which they were known to other tribes (Iroquois). Often, groups referred to themselves only with words that meant "The People," or the people who live at a certain place. Thus, Eskimos called themselves the race of Inuit, "The People." But white men heard Crees refer to them as Eskimos, meaning "Eaters of Raw Meat," and they adopted that word. Above: an Eskimo of the Canadian Arctic uses a bow drill.

Right: A bewhiskered Tsimshian displayed his genealogy
(and his status as a man of
wealth) on his resplendent
coat which was woven from
mountain goat hair on a
cedar-bark base. The home
of this Northwest Coast Indian was on British Columbia's Skeena River.

Glenbow Foundation, Calgary

Below: Kwakiutls of the Northwest Coast used these big seagoing
canoes to trade, raid, and hunt.

Edward L. Curtis photo; courtesy Provincial Archives, Victoria, British Columbia

The domestic scene above, inside a Micmac lodge in Nova Scotia, was drawn in the 1830's by Lieutenant Robert Petley, a British officer based at Halifax. The Micmacs, Algonquian-speakers of the Northeast, were principally hunters and fishermen who lived too far north to base their economy on agriculture.

A chief of the Timucua Indians, left, was pictured by Jacques Lemoyne de Morgues, an artist at an abortive French colony on the northeastern Florida coast in 1564-65. Victims of white men's imperialistic wars, the Timucuas were extinct within two centuries.

An 1887 photograph shows a Blood Indian in Canada undergoing self-torture in the Sun Dance ritual. Thongs from the pole in the center of the lodge are attached to the dancer by skewers inserted in the flesh of his chest. He will pull back until they rip out. Plains Indians vowed to endure such ordeals during the dance in return for supernatural aid.

A Paiute woman of the Great Basin posed with her seed-gathering baskets in this photograph of 1872. It was made in southeastern Nevada by John K. Hillers, who accompanied an exploring expedition headed by Major John Wesley Powell. These Indians, inhabiting generally arid country, were among the poorest in the hemisphere, following a Desert Culture way of life that changed little during 10,000 years. Their economy was based on gathering or catching anything that was edible.

Above: Soon after their return from exile at Fort Sumner, New Mexico, in 1868, these Navahos were photographed on their new reservation in Arizona. Navaho women were already noted for the blankets they wove. Below: Objects of wealth, including white deerskins, were flaunted by Hupas of the northern California coast during the White Deerskin Dance.

The drawing of the Indian below, probably an Arawak or Carib from the Caribbean islands, was made from life in 1529 by a German artist, Christopher Weiditz, who saw the Indian in Spain where Cortez had just brought him from America. Some years earlier, Amerigo Vespucci had written of these Indians: "Wealth such as we use in our Europe or other parts, like gold, jewels, pearls, and other treasures, they hold in no esteem." Instead, he noted, the Indians' riches consisted of cloaks of multicolored birds' feathers, necklaces of bone, and green and white stones that they inserted in their cheeks, foreheads, lips, and ears. A man with such primitive tastes seemed little more than an animal to some Spaniards of the day.

United Fruit Company

A Lacandón man of Mexico's Mayan lowlands regards a likeness of a Mayan carved more than a thousand years ago on a stela at Bonampak.

Courtesy Clifford Clifford Evans and Betty J. Meggers Smithsonian Institution

Strings of the white man's beads, worn as armbands and necklaces, adorn a Wai Wai Indian, a tropical forest villager of the Guiana area of the Amazon River Basin. Dwelling in small settlements along waterways in the humid rain forest, such South American villagers exploited riverine resources and cleared patches in the jungle to grow crops. The wearing out of the soil under the leaching rains prevented the raising of surplus foods and forced groups to change their locations frequently.

Inhabitants of the arid, windy steppes of Patagonia in southern Argentina, these Tehuelches were photographed in 1898. Originally foot nomads who lived a marginal existence stalking guanaco, rhea, and small animals, the Tehuelches wore mantles of guanaco skins and lived in skin windbreaks supported by poles. After the arrival of the Spaniards, the northernmost Tehuelches adopted the horse and trapped game in large surrounds.

This Yahgan shaman, a member of the southernmost people on earth who lived by gathering shellfish along the cold, rocky shores of Tierra del Fuego and neighboring islands south of the Strait of Magellan, was painted by Charles W. Furlong during an exploration of the region in 1907–8. Today the Yahgans, who were also known as Canoe Indians because of their use of bark boats, are virtually extinct.

Smithsonian Institution, Office of Anthropology

Smithsonian Institution, Office of Anthropology

The whites' discovery of the New World was also a discovery of peoples with cultures totally different from those of Europeans. Published accounts of what the newcomers saw often carried crude woodcuts like this German print of 1505 that tried to depict the practice of cannibalism by South American coastal Indians, as described by Amerigo Vespucci.

An Indian invention, new to whites, was the hammock. The illustration at left of a Brazilian Indian woman in a hammock "attached to two trees" appeared in a French book of 1625.

The Indian canoe, propelled by paddlers, was depicted in an Indian book published in Venice in 1572. This type of large, somewhat square-prowed craft, steered by a sternsman, was common in the Caribbean.

Everywhere the Europeans went, conquest followed discovery. The illustration below of Aztec warriors attacking Cortez's lieutenant, Alvarado, during the Conquest of Mexico appeared in a manuscript of 1579–81 by Fray Diego Durán. The Indian warriors include elite eagle and jaguar "knights," distinguished by their animal dress.

Spanish rule of conquered Indians could be harsh. At left is an illustrated petition from Mexican Indians to the Spanish government in 1570, listing their grievances and asking for better treatment.

The imaginative view at right, based on a sixteenth-century engraving, shows Pizarro's conquistadors capturing the Inca ruler, Atahualpa, during the Conquest of Peru in 1532.

A painting by Franklin Arbuckle for the Hudson's Bay Company

For many years in large parts of North America almost the only whites known to Indians were French and British fur men who were usually interested only in peaceful trade. In this modern painting, a Hudson Bay's Company trader (left) is seen witnessing a confrontation in 1715 in the Far North between Athapascan Chipewyans and their enemies, Algonquian Crees, to whom the British had already traded guns.

Above: Conflict between expansive whites and resisting Indians was a constant theme in U.S. history. This early nineteenth-century print depicts a 1763 incident in which whites from Paxton, Pennsylvania, angered by Indian attacks, massacred some peaceful, Christianized Indians at Lancaster. The atrocity incurred the wrath of responsible Colonial leaders.

Below: The Treaty of Greenville in 1795 that followed Anthony Wayne's victory over Ohio Valley Indians at Fallen Timbers was the first of many treaties that wrung large land cessions from defeated Indians. The cessions of the Miami leader Little Turtle and his allies, shown negotiating with Wayne, opened most of Ohio and part of Indiana to white settlers.

Red Cloud, a war leader of the Oglala Sioux, led his people in a temporarily successful resistance to the white man's invasion of Indian hunting grounds in central Wyoming and Montana during the 1860's.

W. H. Jackson photograph;
State Historical Society of Wisconsin

Smithsonian Institution, Office of Anthropology

Set-Tainte (Satanta), a Kiowa patriot of the southern plains, fought hard to keep his country free of whites. When he was captured, he committed suicide by jumping from a prison hospital window in 1878.

W. H. Jackson photograph;
State Historical Society of Wisconsin

Chief Joseph and his Nez Perces, ousted from their Oregon homeland in 1877, tried to reach sanctuary in Canada. They retreated more than 1,000 miles, outfighting pursuing troops, until they were forced to surrender in Montana.

Geronimo, leader of a small group of Chiricahua Apaches, resisted being penned on a reservation. He evaded soldiers in the wild country of the Arizona—Mexico border, but finally gave himself up in 1886.

The ferocity of the American military's attempt to secure the plains for white travelers, miners, and settlers was illustrated in this 1868 Harper's Weekly engraving. It shows Lieutenant Colonel George A. Custer leading his Seventh Cavalry in a surprise attack on the unsuspecting village of Black Kettle's Cheyenne Indians on the Washita River in Oklahoma. Indian men, women, and children were slaughtered indiscriminately.

H. B. Alexander, "Sioux Indian Painting" courtesy Yale University Library

The painting above by Sioux artist Amos Bad Heart Bull shows the Oglala hero Crazy Horse, mounted on a white steed, charging in among Custer's disorganized troopers at the dramatic Battle of the Little Bighorn, June 25, 1876. The Indian triumph was short-lived. Within a year the army had crushed forever the power of the Plains Indians.

The end of freedom: a wire fence on the Pine Ridge Sioux reserva-tion in South Dakota in the late nineteenth century.

National Film Board of Canada

Enveloped by the whites, most Indians, like this Canadian Indian woman in Manitoba, have adopted clothing and whatever other material possessions of the dominant culture they find useful and can afford. But the aged still possess Indian riches: stories and values and memories they would like to pass onto the next generation if it will listen to them.

Poverty, lack of motivation, and indifference or misunderstanding by the whites who dispossessed them are the lot of young Indians almost everywhere. The King Island Eskimo boy below has little opportunity among the shanties of "Eskimo Village," Nome, Alaska, where his family moved when the federal government closed the King Island school.

Association on American Indian Affairs, Inc.

Violent Indian resistance to white dispossessors is generally a thing of the past, and the present resistance, fought in law courts, makes little noise. But the long, defensive struggle over rights to ancestral homelands and the use of natural resources, including water, still continues. The Nevada Paiutes below, fishing like their forebears in Pyramid Lake, which is gradually drying up, are among Indian groups in various parts of the United States that are fighting neighboring white irrigation farmers or other seekers after land or natural resources which, by solemn treaty guarantees from the federal government, the Indians deem their own.

Photo: Gus Bundy

Above: The fight for survival of identity as Indians in the dominant non-Indian environment has led to different tribes adopting some similar traits that mark them readily as Indians rather than as members of a particular tribe. These Six Nations Iroquois at Brantford, Ontario, are dancing in headdresses of a type never worn by their own ancestors, but copied from the well-known warbonnets of the Plains Indians.

Below: On South Dakota's Rosebud Sioux reservation, self-torture, once banned by the government, is again a part of the Sun Dance. The man at left, blowing an eagle-bone whistle, is attached by a skewer in his chest to a rope tied to the center pole, from which he will pull away until the skewer rips free. The Indian at right endures the pain of barbed feathers stuck in his arm and shoulder. The respectful presence of spectators does not interfere with the rite's spiritual integrity.

Photo: Richard Erdoes

Photo: Alvin M. Josephy, Jr.

A mass of problems, including cultural differences, language barriers, and neglect, inefficiency, and lack of understanding have thwarted Indian education in the past, but today many tribes assign highest priority to the education of their young who, in their opinion, must also be taught to have pride in their own Indian heritage. These children, descendants of members of Chief Joseph's band of Nez Perces, are seen attending an integrated public school of Indians and non-Indians at Nespelem, Washington.

Most tribes in the U.S. today have organized their political structure after the fashion of the white man. In their Chickee Chobee (Big House), right, Miccosukees, one of Florida's Seminole groups that finally ended their state of hostility to the United States in 1962, are seen holding a meeting of their tribal council, elected according to a constitution written under the white man's influence.

Association on American Indian Affairs, Inc.

Although it represents a treasure for all the world, Indian creative expression in all its forms was long ignored and, at times, even officially stifled in the United States. Today, it is receiving new encouragement, notably at the Bureau of Indian Affairs' Institute of American Indian Arts at Santa Fe, New Mexico. This concrete mosaic with volcanic stones is the work of a young Santa Clara Pueblo student at the Institute.

Photo: K. Wiest, Institute of American Indian Arts.

United Fruit Company

Mayan farmers, at work in a field near a pyramid (background) of the old Mayan ceremonial center of Zaculeu in the Guatemalan Highlands, use the same primitive methods as their ancestors.

An Arawakan-speaking Campa Indian woman below, member of a tropical forest village group in the area of the headwaters of the Amazon River in eastern Peru, displays her weaving.

Museum of the American Indian, Heye Foundation

Photo: J. W. Manson

Painted designs adorn the face of this Seri Indian girl, whose people live along the coast of the Gulf of California in Sonora, Mexico, and possess an economy still based to a large extent on fishing.

Self-confidence: like an increasing number of Indians, the Crows of Montana, still expert horsemen, are working for a future in which their people will feel equally capable and at ease on their reservation and in the non-Indian society off the reservation.

Pride: a Cree man of today.

In the winter they ascended to the plateau to gather piñon nuts and to hunt.

Save in what they learned from the Hopis, however, they were like their Walapai neighbors and the Yavapais. All lived in small family groups or bands, usually under headmen of little authority who acquired their position through oratorical ability, skill in warfare, or force of personality. The tribes were loosely organized and had no overall leaders. People dwelled in dome-shaped huts of poles, branches, and thatch, or in brush wickiups like those of the Great Basin. The women gathered desert fruits, seeds, nuts, and berries, and the men stalked deer, antelope, rabbits, and other game. Both the Walapais and Yavapais were principally nonagricultural but some of the people cultivated small plots wherever water was available. Clothing was simple and made of buckskin or bark fiber. Men wore shorts and breechcloths, and women wore skirts or front and back aprons. Rabbit skins were made into blankets that were worn as robes in cold weather. The bands possessed shamans who received their powers in dreams and functioned principally as curers, singing, shaking gourd rattles, and pretending to suck out the agent of illness from the body of a sick person. The Walapais (Pine Tree People) adopted a few traits, including a war club and certain ceremonies, from their more aggressive neighbors, the Mohaves. The Yavapais (People of the Sun), whose local bands were grouped in three divisions, or subtribes—the Northeastern, Southeastern, and Western —sometimes joined forces with groups of Western Apaches in raids on the Walapais and Havasupais, as well as on the Maricopas and Pimas of southern Arizona. The Southeastern Yavapais, particularly, adopted some of the traits of the Western Apaches, with whom they intermarried at times, and were called confusedly by white men "Mohave-Apaches" or "Yuma-Apaches." The Western Yavapais, who did have close relationships with the Yumas and Mohaves, adopted some traits from the Yumas, including river bottom farming methods and a style of house.

The Yuman-speaking Mohaves, Halchidhomas, Maricopas, Yumas, and Cocopas, together with the Chemehuevis of the Utaztecan language family, all lived, at one time or another, along the lower Colorado River. The Chemehuevis came originally from the eastern Mohave Desert of California; the Maricopas migrated from the Colorado to the middle Gila River in the early nineteenth century; and the Halchidhomas nomadic people, many of them being forced to move, from season to season, to wherever water was available. Large numbers of them therefore had several residences. Pima villages were bigger than those of the Papagos, and Pima planting and harvesting were done on a cooperative basis. Both tribes lived in round, flat-topped houses, thatched with grass and covered with earth, and employed little clothing. The men wore breechcloths, and the women wore wrap-around skirts. Hide sandals were used on journeys to protect the feet from cactus. The Papago men did the farming and let the water from flash floods irrigate their crops; their women gathered cactus fruits, grass seeds, mesquite beans, and other wild foods. The tribe got its name apparently from its reliance on cultivated beans and, in time of scanty crops, on its use of mesquite beans.

Tribal organization was strong among the Pimas, who had a single tribal leader elected by the headmen of the different villages. The organization of the Papagos was looser and was centered in autonomous units of related villages. The latter were governed by headmen, selected for their personal qualities, and by councils composed of all the adult males. The elders in the council dominated meetings; young men were expected to maintain respectful silence, and decisions were made only by unanimous agreement. Individual striving for personal prestige or power was frowned upon.

With the arrival of the Spaniards in their country, the Pimas added wheat and alfalfa to the crops they raised. The more barren Papago land proved better suited for grazing, and the Papagos in time became cattle raisers. Americans were less considerate of both peoples than the Spaniards or Mexicans had been. After the United States acquired the region, American settlers diverted water cruelly from the Pima fields to their own settlements. Dams and storage reservoirs limited further the Indian water supply, and the helpless Pimas were reduced to poverty and starvation. The Papagos suffered even more in their unproductive desert home. For many years, with an increasing population, and without adequate resources with which to support themselves, they have been among the poorest Indians in the Southwest. Recently, however, government assistance in the form of economic development programs has been offered both tribes, and conditions have begun to improve.

17

The Indians of
Northern Mexico

THAT PART OF MEXICO STRETCHING SOUTH FROM THE
United States border to about the Tropic of Cancer,
and from the Gulf of Mexico to the Pacific (thus including the long peninsula of Baja California), is usually considered a separate cultural area. Its northern and southern
boundaries, however, are somewhat arbitrarily drawn because
a large part of its northern region was in many ways merely
an extension of the Southwest cultural area (the international boundary being only a political, and not a cultural,
demarcation line between native peoples); and in the
regions's southern part—often regarded as a frontier, or
periphery, of the highly developed cultures of Middle America—some peoples possessed characteristics that linked them
to the great civilizations of the Valley of Mexico and of other
regions farther south.

The northern Mexico area, nevertheless, was not simply
a transitional zone between the Southwest and Middle
America. From time to time, the agents of contact and
cultural traits moved across it from Middle America to both
the Southwest and Southeast in what is now the United
States; but northern Mexico had a cultural complexion and
importance all its own—not the least of which was the fact
that, according to present archeological knowledge, it encompassed what seems to have been the earliest birthplace of
agriculture in the New World.

To a large extent, the area is a stern and arid one, containing broad deserts, rugged gorges, and formidable mountain ranges. Much of this harsh country was inhabited by
poverty-stricken, nomadic peoples who pursued a primitive
existence much like that of the Great Basin tribes. But there

were also more hospitable valleys, plateaus, river flood plains, and fertile foothills where larger numbers of people could engage in farming and build permanent settlements. On the whole, the area had a great many tribes. Along the Gulf Coast in the east were Coahuiltecan-speakers: Karankawas (who actually lived on the coast of what is now Texas, but are included in this cultural area), Coahuiltecs, and Tamaulipecs. Farther west, across northern Mexico to the Gulf of California, were members of the Utaztecan language family, including Jumanos, Conchos, Tarahumaras, Opatas, Pima Bajos, Acaxees, Tepehuans, Tepecanos, Huichols, Cahitas, Yaquis, Mayos, and Coras, as well as Tobosos, whom some believe were Athapascan-speakers, like the Apaches and Navahos. Finally, in Baja California and along the west coast of mainland Mexico were Hokan-speaking tribes, including Cochimis, Waicuris, Pericus, and Seris.

The area has been inhabited for at least 12,000 years, for Clovis and other type spear points have been found, indicating the presence of hunters of late Pleistocene big game. How much earlier man may have been there is not known, but there may have been a lengthy Pre-Projectile Point stage in northern Mexico. Much of the region was a physiographic extension of the Great Basin and Southwest, and life throughout all those areas must have been marked by the same characteristics, with early inhabitants hunting, gathering, and—where feasible—fishing for their sustenance. About 8,000 to 10,000 years ago, as the Ice Age animals disappeared from the area, the gathering of wild foods became more important, and northern Mexico, all the way down to the Valley of Mexico, was characterized by the same Desert Culture that existed farther north. Small nomadic groups occupied various parts of the region, gathering wild plants and hunting small game, living in caves, rock shelters, or in the open, making basketry, netting, fur cloth, sandals, and atlatls, and grinding the wild plant foods with milling stones. In many of the stern sections of the area, this simple desert economy continued, almost unchanged, for millennia, from about 8,000 years ago until the arrival of the Spaniards in historic times.

Elsewhere in the region, agriculture appeared and brought changes. The oldest agricultural finds, discovered in recent years by Richard MacNeish in caves of the Sierra Madre Oriental and Sierra de Tamaulipas regions of the northeast Mexican state of Tamaulipas, are of cultivated pumpkins, chili peppers, bottle gourds, and a sort of runner bean, between 7,500 and 9,500 years old. This was tentative, incipient agriculture; the people who engaged in it were still almost entirely gatherers of wild foods, who also hunted and trapped animals. As gatherers, who relied heavily on wild grasses and other plants, they had somehow acquired the knowledge of making certain of the plants reproduce. Cultivation increased very slowly, however, and domesticated plants only gradually became an important element in the economy. In the Ocampo district of Tamaulipas, it took apparently 2,500 to 3,500 years before common beans were grown; another 500 to 1,500 years passed before a pod-pop type of corn appeared; still more time was required for squash and cotton to become part of the inventory; and it was only about 3,000 years ago—perhaps 4,500 to 6,500 years after the beginnings of agricultural knowledge—that farming, with fully developed corn, finally became the principal means of providing food in that locality.

Meanwhile, agriculture had appeared elsewhere—some of it undoubtedly diffused from Tamaulipas. After about 1000 B.C., it became increasingly important to a number of different peoples in various parts of northern Mexico, but only to those who lived in the lush river valleys or in other localities suitable for growing crops. Everywhere, its establishment took a long time, while many northern Mexico groups never did adopt it.

Among those who became farmers, pit houses, storage bins, and pottery all appeared during the last thousand years before the time of Christ. The art of pottery came north to them from Middle America, where the stronger and more widespread establishment of agriculture was furnishing a base for the growth of larger populations and advanced cultures. At the same time, northern Mexico itself was beginning to transmit influences farther north. The area was already providing routes of travel for the spread of agriculture and other traits to less developed northern peoples: to the Southwest area of the Mogollon, Hohokam, and Anasazi cultures and to the Southeast area where the Caddoan Culture would arise. In the southern part of the northern Mexico region, closest to the developing ceremonial centers of Middle America, small nuclear villages began to appear, and about 300 B.C. small ceremonial mounds, like those farther south, were built in the eastern part of northern Mexico.

During the first millennium A.D., the region as a whole

was marked by a division between peoples who were still nomads with a simple Desert Culture and those who, as village farmers, were increasing in population, developing regional and local cultural variations, and making different kinds of decorated pottery. In Chihuahua, the culture was developing like that of the Mogollons of the Southwest. In the Casas Grandes area south of present-day New Mexico, people drew together to live in villages built on high terraces, but without defensive works, near their agricultural fields. The east and large parts of the center and west were still populated by many groups of nomads.

Between A.D. 900 and 1200, urban and ceremonial centers developed in agricultural areas along the eastern and western sides of the large western mountain range, the Sierra Madre Occidental. Population there had increased, and, in various places, the appearance of cultural items and traits like copper bells, ball courts, shell trumpets, and new calendar and religious systems, including new gods, reflected influences from the Toltecs' culture farther south. Some of those characteristics, probably brought north by traders or groups of merchants from Middle America, spread beyond northern Mexico into the Southwest, moving undoubtedly along established coastal and inland routes that linked populated centers from Middle America to the present-day U.S. Southwest. Farther east, other Middle American influences seem to have followed a similar overland route—as well, perhaps, as sea routes by watercraft across the Gulf of Mexico—from the Huastec and other regions of eastern Mexico to the Texas coast, the Mississippi River Basin, and the Southeast. At the same time, the bow and arrow, making its way down from the north, came into use in many parts of northern Mexico.

A great stirring of peoples, generally in a southward direction, appears to have begun in the twelfth century. As in the case of the Anasazis of the Southwest, it may have resulted from a widespread and long-lasting drought. Various farm areas were abandoned by highly developed peoples, but nomadic groups too were involved in migrations and changes of residence. The pressures were felt all the way to the Valley of Mexico, into which flowed waves of "barbarians" from the north, groups of marauding newcomers, who were mostly farmers from the southern part of the northern Mexico cultural area, but also nomads, and whom the Middle Americans referred to collectively as Chichimecs (Dog

People). Including in their ranks the ancestors of the Aztec empire-builders, they overran and destroyed the Toltec civilization.

After about 1200, the northern Mexico cultural area developed a pattern that existed into historic times. Farming continued to thrive in certain areas, and some urban centers were reconsolidated. Casas Grandes in Chihuahua, like the Pueblos of New Mexico at their height, approached the threshold of civilization. The agricultural settlements and towns, particularly in the more westerly portions of northern Mexico, were like oases, situated along rivers and streams in an otherwise arid and unworked land. Irrigation was used, and the people whom the fields supported lived in towns that differed from those of the Pueblos farther north in that they were not single, apartment-like clusters, but contained individual houses, spread out, with land between them. Some of the towns had at least several hundred buildings and several thousand inhabitants. Each urban center possessed its own government, headed by an influential man who usually inherited his position but had to display ability. Among the Acaxees and Cahitas life was also directed by a number of men's and women's religious societies, reminiscent of the societies of the Pueblos.

Many of the northern Mexico sedentary groups were more aggressive than the Pueblos of the Southwest area. Some possessed large armies, divided into different battle units, each with its own leader. On the march, as well as in combat, they seem to have maintained disciplined order. The warriors carried maces, bows and arrows, feathered staves, and round hide shields. Scalps and whole heads were taken as war prizes and the skulls and bones of vanquished enemies were preserved in special buildings or displayed on poles in the town centers. Triumphs were followed by scalp dances, and the victors sometimes engaged in cannibalism, eating the flesh of dead enemies probably to acquire their supernatural power.

In the southern part of the region, where contact with the Middle American cultures was stronger, and where farming was more feasible and efficient, towns were generally larger and were often busy trade centers. Social classes, including a nobility, were present; markets thrived; individuals followed special skills in a limited division of labor; and people used an abundance of specialized and sophisticated utensils and implements, either traded or copied from the south. Arts and crafts were developed, and wealth was greater than in most parts of the north. Many of the stronger southern towns exacted tribute from the weaker ones.

Throughout the cultural area, the sedentary peoples fashioned houses mostly of wattle and daub and made clothing from cotton. The Yaquis, Mayos, and others who lived in the lower river valleys of streams in northwestern Mexico practiced floodwater farming in the rich bottomlands along the watercourses. Some tribes, like the Tepecanos and Coras, who inhabited the mountainous terrain of the Sierra Madres, could engage in only simple and limited agriculture; their economy had many traits of the Desert Culture, but they possessed rich ceremonials and handicrafts. The Tarahumaras, in a rugged area that was hostile to agriculture, developed a way of life much like that of the early Basket Makers of the Four Corners country of the Southwest. Along the Gulf of California the Seris, who occupied desert areas unsuited for farming, depended for their food upon fish and shellfish, as well as on gathering and hunting.

Spaniards, moving north from the Valley of Mexico after their conquest of the Aztecs, gradually extended dominion over the northern peoples. Following generally the ancient Indian trade routes, they established missions, mines, ranches, presidios, and towns. In the process, large numbers of Indians died of diseases or were enslaved or killed. The white aggressors exterminated some native groups, dislocated others, and sent many Indians fleeing to hiding places in the mountains. Priests gathered other Indians around missions, and more of them died there of sickness and malnutrition. Still others managed to retain their strength and old ways for long periods, however, and even in recent times some of them had a reputation for fierce resistance to white men. The Yaquis fought a series of desperate wars against the Mexicans that lasted until 1920. Some of the Yaquis, escaping from time to time, crossed the international border from Sonora and found sanctuary in southern Arizona, where groups of them still reside. No longer under political pressure, they live in six communities near Tucson and Phoenix, with a culture that blends their own traditional Yaqui ways with traits of the sixteenth century Spanish conquerors who first made inroads upon them. The Tarahumaras have also experienced hardships: living a somewhat isolated existence in mountainous country of northern Mexico, they have been beset by poverty and near-starvation.

18

Indian Civilizations
of Middle America

S OME OF THE SOLDIERS AMONG US WHO HAVE BEEN IN many parts of the world, in Constantinople, and all over Italy, and in Rome, said that so large a market place and so full of people, and so well regulated and arranged, they had never beheld before."

In words of wonderment and awe, like these, Bernal Díaz del Castillo, soldier of Hernán Cortés, described the white men's first view in 1519 of the city of Tenochtitlán (modern Mexico City), the busy and radiant center of the civilization of the Aztecs. It is curious that ever since then some persons have regarded the great pre-Columbian civilizations of the Aztecs, Mayas, and other advanced peoples of Middle America—as well as those of South America's Central Andes—in a way that disassociates them from the cultures of the less developed native peoples of the New World. It is as if they were the work of non-Indians, or of people who were no longer Indian. They were on a level of development so far above that of more primitive peoples elsewhere in the hemisphere, the reasoning goes, that a relationship should not be drawn between them. It would be, in short, like discussing the ancient Greeks and the barbarians of northern Europe in the same context.

That point of view is specious. The culture history of Middle America is one of nomadic hunters and gatherers who, like many Indians elsewhere, became farmers and villagers. In time, as population increased, societies became more complex and sophisticated; arts, skills, and crafts flourished; and gradually true civilizations arose. Radiations traveled to other cultural areas from Middle America, and, in turn, influences and traits entered Middle America from

the north and south. The peoples of Middle America were
Indian, and a full understanding and appreciation of their
accomplishments can only be gained by recognizing them
as a part of the full panorama of Indian culture and history
throughout the Western Hemisphere.

Middle America—or Mesoamerica, as some students call
it—encompasses central and southern Mexico (including
Yucatán); Guatemala; British Honduras; Honduras; El Salvador; and a part of Nicaragua. Archeologists and others sometimes divide that large area into smaller geographical subregions (the Valley of Mexico; the Oaxaca area; the Huastec
region of the Gulf Coast; the Southern Gulf Coast, including Veracruz and Tabasco; western Mexico; the Mayan
Highlands; the Southern and Western Lowlands; Chiapas
and the Guatemalan Pacific Coast; northern Yucatán, etc.),
each of which was marked in large measure by a unity of
development and by many common traits. But numerous
interrelations existed, also, among the subregions, and many
elements gave a cultural unity to the area as a whole.

Within Middle America were many different tribes, speaking a large number of languages and dialects. The linguistic
relationships among the tribes were complex, and scholars
have not yet arranged the languages into a system of classification on which all can agree. Studies, now underway, are
providing new insights into the derivations of the various
tongues, as well as the ancient relationships and movements
of the ancestors of the historic tribes. While the results of
these studies are still theoretical, and are subject to argument
and change, tentative tribal-language groupings can be made.
Among the best-known Middle American peoples were the
following:

Deriving from what some authorities term a Macro-
Penutian superstock (and thus related to Penutian- and
Utaztecan-speakers in the present-day United States), were
Totonacan-speaking Totonacs in northern Veracruz; Mixes,
Zoques, and Huaves of a Mizocuavean language group,
mostly in southern Mexico; members of the Utaztecan
Nahuatl family group, including Aztecs, Tlascalans, and
others in central Mexico; and tribes of a widespread Mayan
language stock, including Huastecs in northern Veracruz;
Chontals, Lacandóns, Tzeltals, Chortis, and others of a Chol-
Tzeltal division in the south of Mexico, Yucatán, and north-
ern and eastern Guatemala; people of a Chu-Kanhobalan
division in southern Mexico and western Guatemala; Mams,
Motozintlecs, and others of a Moto-Mamean division in

PRECOLUMBIAN MIDDLE AMERICA
c. 1500 B.C.-A.D. 1500
• Archeological sites

western Guatemala; Quiches, Kekchis, Pokanchis, and others of a Quiche-Kekchi division in central Guatemala and El Salvador; and others of a division known simply as Mayan in Yucatán, British Honduras, and northern Guatemala's Peten district.

Speaking languages that stemmed from a parent Macro-Otomangean superstock were Otomís and Pames in central Mexico, north of present-day Mexico City, and Zapotecs, Mixtecs, Chinantecs, Popolocas, Mazatecs, Triques, and Chiapanecs, all south of the Valley of Mexico, generally in Oaxaca and neighboring regions. Tarascans, not yet identified definitely with any other linguistic group, inhabited Michoacán in west-central Mexico, and a third superstock, Hokan-Coahuiltecan, included Tequistlatecs (often called Chontals, but not to be confused with the Mayan Chontals) on the Pacific coast of Oaxaca and, possibly, Tlapanecs of southern Mexico and Subtiabas in Nicaragua (although the latter two are usually grouped, linguistically, by themselves).

For many generations after Cortés's conquest of Mexico, whites assumed that the Aztecs had been the greatest and most accomplished native peoples in Middle America, and that no culture as impressive had preceded theirs. Gradually, archeological studies placed the Aztecs in a more accurate perspective, and it is now known that they were, in fact, the inheritors of a sequence of brilliant Indian cultures that had risen, fallen, and disappeared, but had bequeathed to the Aztecs many of their skills, ideas, and institutions. The lure of learning more about these vanished cultures that white men never saw still draws scores of archeologists to Middle America, and each year new knowledge—some of it demanding new interpretations of pre-Columbian history in the area—is acquired. Already, however, much is known of the major stages of more than 10,000 years of human habitation in the region.

Who the first people were in Middle America is not known. Bands of hunters, foragers, and fishermen may have traveled through the area, moving on toward South America, and leaving behind them no descendants. The oldest remains found so far are of hunters of Ice Age animals, people who were probably also gatherers of wild foods. At Tequixquiác northwest of Mexico City and Valsequillo south of Puebla City crude stone and bone relics suggest the existence of a Pre-Projectile Point stage that might date back some 30,000 years. Finds of a more certain time period have been made at Santa Isabel Iztápan, Tepexán, and Los Reyes Acozac, all in the Valley of Mexico, and at Valsequillo, showing that men hunted mammoths in those localities toward the end of the Ice Age, about 10,000 years ago, using projectile points similar to the Scottsbluff and Angostura types of the so-called Plano Culture hunters farther north. Near Guatemala City has been found a Clovis-type point of what may be an earlier time period. Elsewhere, there is little evidence yet of the presence of Pleistocene hunters; the widespread jungle terrain and a lack of interest by archeologists in that phase of prehistory in the area have left much knowledge still to be acquired concerning earliest man in Middle America.

As the Ice Age ended and the glaciers in the north withdrew, the climate in Middle America warmed. Grasslands dried up, and the big-game animals retreated toward the north or died. The small bands of people in the area turned increasingly to hunting and trapping deer, rabbits, and other small animals, birds, rodents, and turtles, and collecting wild plant foods. In recent years, a team of almost fifty scientists in different fields, working with archeologist Richard Mac-Neish, laid bare in dramatic fashion the stages of development of peoples who occupied one Middle American locality, the valley of Tehuacán in the central Mexican state of

Puebla, during an almost uninterrupted span of 12,000 years. The archeological digging downward into layers of occupation, one beneath another, in caves and rock shelters in that vicinity revealed the following sequence of development:

Prior to about 9,000 years ago, during what MacNeish termed the Ajuereado phase, small bands of people roamed the valley from season to season, hunting small animals, killing infrequently the remaining species of Pleistocene antelope and horses, and collecting various wild plant foods. They used flaked-stone implements and possessed only the simplest social organization. Between approximately 8,700 and 7,000 years ago, during an El Riego phase (for the name of one of the caves), the people shifted gradually from being predominantly hunters and trappers to being gatherers. More use was made of wild foods, including wild varieties of beans, chili peppers, and amaranth. But, somehow, the people learned to cultivate some products, and during this stage they first domesticated squashes and avocados. Temporary settlements seem to have been used by some families during the growing season; various stone implements, including grinders, mortars, and pestles, came into use; and certain burials suggest that shamans or religious curers directed ceremonies connected with the dead.

By about 7,000 years ago, a new phase, known as the Coxcatlán culture (also named for a site), was underway. Some 90 per cent of the people's diet still came from hunting, trapping, and collecting wild foods, but during this period the number of plants which the people learned to domesticate increased. By at least 6,000 years ago, they were cultivating corn with small cobs. In addition, they grew gourds, chili peppers, tepary, jack, and possibly common beans, zapotes, amaranth, and two species of squash. Polished-stone implements, including forerunners of the mano and metate, also came into use. By about 5,400 years ago, in the next, or Abejas stage, people derived some 30 per cent of their food from agriculture. The first fixed settlements—small pit-house villages—appeared during this stage, and dogs were domesticated. During the Purrón stage, commencing about 4,300 years ago, more productive hybridized types of corn were cultivated, giving bigger crops and larger ears; and pottery, fashioned in the same forms of bowls and ollas that had previously been made of stone, was produced for the first time.

With a larger and more secure foundation of agriculture, population increased and became more concentrated, and after about 3,500 years ago, with the rise of a culture called Ajalpán, a complex village life flourished in the valley. Pottery was marked by certain refinements, and a developing religious system included ceremonies and a figurine cult. A more sophisticated culture, known as Santa María, began about 850 B.C., characterized by the use of irrigation to grow hybrid corn, a sharp increase in population, the building of temple mounds, and strong influences from the Olmec Culture in Veracruz. Thereafter, the people of the area moved steadily toward civilization. By about 200 B.C., they possessed large irrigation works and hilltop ceremonial structures; some occupations became specialized; and many new domesticated food products appeared. In succession, the people were influenced by Oaxaca's Monte Albán Culture and the Mixtecs, and after about A.D. 700 true cities arose in the valley. By then, agriculture provided about 85 per cent of the food; trade and commerce were flourishing; and the people possessed a complex religious system. A standing army also came into existence, and during a militaristic period, prior to Cortés's arrival, the area fell under the domination of the Aztecs.

Many aspects of this sequence were duplicated in the Oaxaca Valley, where archeologists laid bare the evidence of a somewhat similar cultural development, and undoubtedly elsewhere in Middle America, although the timing of parallel stages may have differed from region to region. The investigations in the Tehuacán Valley reveal, among other significant things, the earliest agriculture yet found in the Middle American area, and the first cultivated corn discovered anywhere so far. The extremely early dates for the first fixed settlements and the first appearance of pottery are also significant. The pottery, dating from the Purrón stage (4,300–3,500 years ago), is similar to a so-called Pox ware, discovered recently in shell middens on the Pacific coast of Guerrero in western Mexico and dated at about 4,440 years old. The oldest pottery yet found in Middle America, the "Pox ware" may have reached the Guerrero coast from South America or elsewhere and its idea been carried inland.

Generally, the discoveries of pottery in Guerrero and the Tehuacán Valley and of fixed settlements in the latter region precede what is yet known for the rest of Middle America. But in many parts of the area, prior to about 1500 B.C., the development of agriculture, including the growing of hybridized corn that provided food surpluses and permitted the increase and concentration of populations, set the stage for the establishment of fixed settlements and the growth of villages. At the same time, two points must be noted. First, recent archeological studies in different parts of the world indicate that agriculture may not necessarily have been a precondition for the establishment of fixed settlements. Village sites, probably temporary, of pre-agricultural peoples have been found in many areas, indicating that some hunting and gathering groups occupied settlements of constructed dwellings for certain periods of the year near good hunting grounds or supplies of shellfish or wild foods. This may have been the case with various Middle American peoples before they had learned to cultivate crops. Secondly, even after the spread of agricultural knowledge, development was uneven. Nomadic and semi-nomadic hunting and gathering peoples existed simultaneously with agricultural peoples, and Middle America has been likened to a mosaic or patchwork, in which high cultures arose in various localities, while in between them, at the same time, some peoples progressed to a lesser degree, depending on the adaptability of the terrain to agriculture and other circumstances.

It is believed by some authorities that the development of the more productive types of corn (with stronger stalks and larger ears) occurred in the central Mexican highlands as a result of the repeated crossing of maize with Tripsacum grass and teosinte (*Euchlaena Mexicana*), and that the resulting varieties were diffused down river valleys to the lowlands, where they thrived and provided the basis for the first strong development of village farming as a way of life. Outside of the Tehuacán Valley, however, the oldest known sites of village cultures, arising after about 1700–1600 B.C., include Yarumela in Honduras; El Arbolillo, Zacatenco, and (somewhat later) Tlatilco in the Valley of Mexico; and settlements in the Río Panuco area of northern Veracruz, at La Venta and San Lorenzo in the southern Veracruz-Tabasco region, in the Oaxaca Valley of central Mexico and Chiapas in southern Mexico, on the Guatemalan Pacific coast near La Victoria, and—starting perhaps about 1100 B.C. —at Kaminaljuyú in the Mayan highlands near modern-day Guatemala City. Strangely, at this early period, between approximately 1500 and 1200 B.C., there is strong evidence that peoples of the Pacific coasts of Ecuador and Guatemala or southern Mexico were in direct contact, and via long-distance sea voyages were exchanging ideas and material traits. Middle American voyagers are thought to have introduced the cultivation of corn to South Americans at this time, and types of pottery decorations as well as of pottery forms are similar in both coastal regions.

The earlier phases of village life in Middle America were characterized by people who lived together, with simple social organization, in small settlements whose houses were constructed of poles, mud, and thatch. Diets were based principally on cultivated corn, but also on the gathering of wild foods and the hunting and trapping of small game. Gardens of corn, beans, squash, and perhaps of cotton and manioc were planted along rivers, lakes, and coastal inlets, and were watered by rainfall and by natural flooding. The people wore little or no clothing, but made various types of excellent pottery as well as ceramic figurines. As population increased, villages grew in size; organizations became more complex; communities were probably ruled by councils of elders or shamans or by chiefs; and fertility and rain cults became more influential and important. Lowland forested areas, cleared by slash and burn, were opened up to agriculture. More and better products were made; trade developed between settlements and between regions; and ideas, products, and skills were diffused from one district to another.

Prior to 1200 B.C. a strong, influential culture began to develop on the Mexican Gulf Coast in the present states of Veracruz and Tabasco. Known as the Olmec (for later people who lived in the same area) Culture, it presents numerous mysteries, for little is yet known of its beginnings and growth or of its content or history. Presumably, it developed from simple lowland farming villages like La Venta, which eventually became one of its great ceremonial centers, but some persons believe that the culture—or a large part of its content—may have been received from peoples or influences that had come from another region, possibly the Pacific Coast where contact had existed with even more distant peoples, including those of the coast of Ecuador. In any case, by 1200 B.C., at least one great ceremonial center, San Lorenzo, had arisen amid surrounding farming villages that supported it and had given birth to a pattern of civilization that was to spread from the Olmec region to many other areas of Middle America.

The Olmec Culture is known principally from the remains

of the period during which it was at its height (approximately 1200–400 B.C.) and from its profound and widespread influence on the rise and development of other Middle American cultures. Those influences were so fundamental, in fact, that the Olmec Culture is characterized by many students as the mother culture of all Middle America. The building of earthen temple mounds may have occurred earlier in villages elsewhere, but the Olmec sites at San Lorenzo, La Venta, and Tres Zapotes are the first known large, planned religious centers, reflecting the existence of primitive states, or chiefdoms, with a political or religious leadership possessing the authority to direct the work of massed labor and skilled artisans. The centers were not cities but religious capitals and abodes of elite groups that presided over surrounding farming populations. The sites include temple mounds, monumental stone carvings, colossal sacrificial altars, and vertical stone slabs—or stelae—sculptured in relief with images of chiefs, priests, or warriors. A strong religious cult, encompassing a jaguar deity of fertility, was present, and a constant motif in Olmec art is a snarling, baby-faced figure, half feline and half human. The most popularized among their works are huge heads, modeled in the round from basalt, eight feet high and weighing up to twenty tons; found resting in the jungle, they have long been objects of mystery. Their carved headdresses, likened to present-day football helmets, probably indicate that the sculptures are those of priests or chieftains. The Olmecs, whose artwork shows that they practiced head shaving, tattooing, and face and body painting, left, in addition, exquisite sculptures in the round, decorated pottery, terra-cotta figurines, and magnificent jade statuettes, masks, and other objects, and there is evidence that they were the first Middle Americans to devise glyph writing and, perhaps, to develop calendrical systems.

Their culture, including the possession of a feline deity, is reminiscent, in some aspects, of that of the Chavín Culture of Peru, which flourished at about the same time, and it is possible that a connection, via long-range diffusion or through a common inheritance of some traits from a same parent area, existed between the two. The many innovations of the Olmec Culture, however, together with the Olmec art style—which some authorities characterize as the most impressive that ever appeared in Middle America—diffused, or were carried by traders, missionaries, and warriors across

much of the area, influencing other peoples and contributing
to the development of additional cultures and civilizations.
In the Valley of Mexico and the central Mexican plateau,
the Olmec Culture met and intermixed with a separate developing inland plateau culture and left its imprint on the
life of the peoples of Tlaltilco, Tlapacoya, Cuicuilco, Monte
Albán, and Monte Negro. Its stimulation was felt, also, by
rising cultures in Chiapas in southern Mexico, on Guatemala's Pacific coast, at Altar de Sacrificios and Uaxactún in
the Guatemalan lowlands, and at Kaminaljuyú in the Guatemalan highlands. Olmec Culture was spread both by diffusion and by actual invasions of regions as far away as El
Salvador, and the ideas and techniques its people exported
before the culture's decline in its Gulf Coast homeland during the centuries immediately after 400 B.C. provided a
foundation for the advancement of other peoples.

Throughout Middle America, the period from about
1100 B.C. to about 300 B.C., during which the Olmec Culture
was at its height, is termed by some scholars the Middle
Preclassic (following a previous Early Preclassic Period). It is
also called, by others, the Middle Formative; but since the
Olmec Culture was certainly a golden one, such labels—generally used in relation to the Mayan cultures—have little
meaning when applied to Middle America as a whole. Nevertheless, within that time span, temple mounds made their
appearance in various centers of population, and a number
of important cultures, most of them reflecting knowledge
and traits derived from the Olmecs, arose. At Tlapacoya,
about 500 B.C., people built the earliest purely religious structure found so far in the Valley of Mexico, a mud-plastered,
stepped platform. Soon afterward, at Cuicuilco, near modern-
day Mexico City, monumental edifices, including a sixty-
seven-foot-high truncated conical mound of earth faced with
stones, were erected. Other large religious buildings were
raised near present-day Puebla City at about the same time,
and at approximately 500 B.C., also, in locations about
Oaxaca, where an early phase of the Monte Albán Culture
was beginning to receive Olmec influences, stone religious
structures were built, with carved designs, glyph inscriptions,
calendrical symbols, and representations of deities. Ceremonial mounds also appeared in the Huastec area of northern Veracruz; and in the Mayan country during the same
period stepped pyramids, with staircases, terraces, tombs
of important persons within the mounds, and religious

superstructures of wood, were erected at Altar de Sacrificios, Uaxactún, and Tikal in the lowlands, and at Kaminaljuyú in the highlands. The oldest known Mayan corbeled vault, found at Altar de Sacrificios, dates from this period.

These many structures, combining skills in architecture, engineering, painting, and sculpturing, reflect, in sum, American Indian societies that were becoming increasingly sophisticated and complex. In general, the populated centers, like those of the contemporary Olmec Culture, from which many of them were drawing inspiration, were characterized by the production of large food surpluses based on a more intensive and efficient agriculture that included the use of hillside terracing to prevent erosion; a growing social organization marked by an increase in the division of labor, a developing specialization in arts and crafts, a growing social differentiation among the people, and the rise of a class of religious leaders or priests who acquired authority over political and economic as well as spiritual affairs; an increase in the number of deities and their functions; and the formalization of religious systems. During the same period, some towns became merely ceremonial centers for large rural populations, living in houses of poles and thatch with mud-daubed walls in the surrounding countryside. A few centers, with numerous mounds, streets, and plazas, became true metropolises. In addition, as we have seen, glyph writing appeared; astronomy and the calendar began to develop; regional varieties of pottery and the products of artisans and craftsmen multiplied; architectural and engineering skills were achieved; high art itself was born; and trade relations, including a sea commerce between coastal settlements and distant peoples in the hemisphere, increased.

In what has been called the Late Preclassic or Late Formative Period (about 300 B.C.–A.D. 300), two great Mexican centers, Teotihuacán in the Valley of Mexico and Monte Albán at Oaxaca, developed into true urban metropolises, each one a strong political entity, and each supported by, and serving, large surrounding suburban and rural populations. In time, Monte Albán, with an early sculptural and ceramic style influenced by the Olmec Culture, spread its own influences from Puebla to Chiapas; but Teotihuacán, by diffusion, as well apparently as by political domination in at least one direction, became one of the most influential of all Middle American civilizations, exporting features of its culture in all directions, from the Southwest curtural area in the north to Honduras' Copán in the south, and from the Gulf Coast to the Pacific.

The growth of both centers may have resulted from the steady intensification of agriculture (utilizing at Teotihuacán *chinampas*, or "floating gardens"—artificially made islands in lakes—and possibly irrigation works) that led to bigger surpluses and large populations; the increase of control by religious leaders over complex ceremonial systems; and the heightening of commerce and trade among different regions. From its beginnings, presently estimated to have been about 300 B.C., Teotihuacán, which became a true Indian city, is traced by its pottery and art styles through three initial phases (Tzacualli, Miccaotli, and Xolalpan). By the start of the Christian Era, during the Miccaotli phase, the growing city had established its urban pattern, and in the third century A.D., during the Xolalpan stage, it entered its period of greatest brilliance and influence.

At its height, Teotihuacán, about thirty miles northeast of present-day Mexico City (and called "the place where the gods reside" by the Aztecs, who arrived in the region long after the city's demise and knew less about it than do modern-day archeologists), covered more than eight square miles and had an estimated population of about sixty thousand, including some ten thousand in the suburbs and surrounding small communities. The city was dominated by a huge stepped pyramid (called the Sun Temple by the Aztecs), about 200 feet high with a base more than 650 feet long on each side, and a smaller pyramid (called by the Aztecs the Moon Temple), and included concourses, avenues, and plazas, lined by a vast array of other temples, palaces, public buildings, and great blocks of one-storied, multi-roomed residential units, with lime-plastered walls and floors, terrace roofs, and mural paintings in some rooms. The streets and plazas were paved with cement that covered underground drain conduits. Who lived in some of the city's dwellings is not yet confirmed; the heart of the city was essentially a ceremonial center, and its buildings almost certainly housed the religious and secular leaders and their retinues, together with skilled artisans, intellectuals, and merchants. Other buildings, however, may have been occupied by craftsmen (grouped by trades in separate quarters, or attached to individual religious or secular complexes). Whether members of the farming population also lived within the city is not yet established, but most farming families dwelled in clusters of small villages, some with their own pyramid temples, in the surrounding countryside, occupying flat-roofed masonry houses.

Society was stratified, and the demands and needs of the elite urban class for functional and luxury goods led to an outpouring of works by full-time specialists, including craftsmen, painters, sculptors, masons, and artisans. A wealth of jewelry and decorative garb and ornamentation was produced, as were utensils, implements, ceramic objects, carvings, murals, and thin orange-ware pottery. Calendar systems were in use, and cycles of fifty-two years were observed by the populace. At the end of each cycle, fires were extinguished and new ones lit, temples were enlarged or reconstructed, and the world's rebirth was celebrated. A major deity was the Plumed Serpent, Quetzalcoatl, the bringer of civilization and good ways of life, who was frequently locked in conflict with gods of evil. Rounds of ceremonies and rituals, presided over by the priest class, included sacrifices of birds, flowers, dogs, and other animals, as well as humans, to feed hungry gods, whose strength, it was believed, was required to continue life and keep the world in harmony.

Monte Albán, inhabited by Zapotecs, was located atop a large hill overlooking a valley, and is thought to have been so placed because of defense needs. There is some evidence, in fact, that during this period (about 300 B.C. to A.D. 300), when the site was becoming urbanized, its leaders maintained military forces. Not as large as Teotihuacán, Monte Albán nevertheless contained many temples, palaces, residential quarters, and other structures, built principally in a planned arrangement on a large rectangle leveled atop the mountain. Some residences lined one of the slopes and overflowed to neighboring ridges. Although Monte Albán too was supported by a large surrounding rural population, it is believed that a deep division existed between the cultures of the urban dwellers and those on the farms until later times, when the growth of new sites throughout Oaxaca indicated an extension of the city's influence. In its earliest phases, as already stated, Monte Albán received Olmec stylistic influences. By the third century of the Christian Era there were stylistic links between Monte Albán and Teotihuacán.

Centers in other areas were also developing. At Izapa on the Pacific coast of Chiapas near the Guatemalan border, people of a culture that showed many Olmec influences raised large temple mounds faced with boulders and pro-

duced carved monuments in a style which they seem to have
passed on to Mayan peoples in both the highlands and
lowlands of Guatemala. The Izapa Culture, in fact, is viewed
by some authorities as an intermediary one between the
Olmec civilization and that of the Classic Maya. At
Kaminaljuyú, in the Guatemalan highlands, Izapa's culture
appears to have influenced a Miraflores Culture of this
period that had succeeded earlier Arevalo and Las Charcas
cultures. During the Miraflores phase, Kaminaljuyú became
a large sacred metropolis, with rich tombs, monumental
sculptures, and fine work done in marble, jade, and ceramics.
Around Kaminaljuyú, the growth of villages was attended by
the establishment of lesser Mayan ceremonial centers, many
of them with monuments carved with glyphs. In the Mayan
lowland areas, at the same time, a Chicanel phase (named
for a pottery type) followed earlier Xe and Mamom phases.
Regional variations occurred, as population increased in different parts of the area, and in Guatemala's Petén district
the growth of two large centers, Uaxactún and Tikal, began
to foreshadow the great Mayan civilization that still lay
ahead. In the northern Yucatán, Dzibilchaltún, with a large
population—composed, possibly, of a non-Mayan people in
its earliest stages (prior to about 300 B.C.)—received Mayan
influences from the Petén as well as from Chiapas. Various
parts of northern Yucatán seem to have been populated at
an early period, but the flowering of that region, which had
no running streams and few natural resources other than
stone, wood, and wild game, was, also, still in the distant
future. In some sites (lowland Guatemala's Holmul, Zacualpa
in the highlands, Monte Albán, and locations in Chiapas and
present-day British Honduras), the presence of certain traits,
including Mayan polychrome pottery, rudimentary corbeled
vaults, and new ceramic forms, some of which appear to have
come from southern sources, has led various students to
designate the period from about A.D. 100 to 300 tentatively a
Protoclassic one, or the eve of the Early Classic Period.

Such terms, again, have little meaning for areas in which
great cultures had already been flourishing. Indeed, some
authorities regard the traits that gave rise to the identification
of a Protoclassic period as merely those of a burial cult or
complex that existed in certain localities. Nevertheless, the
time span from about A.D. 300 to 600 is generally referred
to as the Early Classic throughout Middle America, and the
period from about A.D. 600 to 900 as the Late Classic.

During the first period Teotihuacán and Monte Albán reached the heights of their growth and influence. Teotihuacán, especially, extended many of its cultural traits over long distances in many directions. In the east, it exerted a strong influence on the Totonac people at Cerro de las Mesas in Veracruz. In the south it affected Mayan centers in British Honduras, the Petén lowlands, and the Guatemalan highlands. At Kaminaljuyú, it seems probable, in fact, that persons of Teotihuacán origin acquired leadership over the city and dominated the native population about A.D. 500. From Kaminaljuyú, under such leadership, Teotihuacán influences were radiated elsewhere through the highlands, along the Pacific slope, and southward to Copán in Honduras. Finally, toward the end of the Early Classic Period, traits of the Teotihuacán civilization were carried northward with significant force by traders and others over large parts of the Mexican plateau. As new centers appeared in the north, the focus of civilization edged gradually in that direction, and one important spearhead of Teotihuacán traits moved up the Sierra Madre Occidental toward the peoples of southern New Mexico and Arizona.

About A.D. 600–650, Teotihuacán was destroyed, burned apparently by a hostile force. It was never rebuilt to its former greatness; but, although its power had thus suddenly ended, its cultural traditions lived on, transmitted to succeeding civilizations along the Gulf Coast and in the Valley of Mexico. At about the same time, or soon afterward, Monte Albán began to decline. By A.D. 900 it was being abandoned. Decay set in, many of the monuments of its great period were allowed to collapse and crumble, and the site itself became a burial place. With the end of these two metropolises as capitals of central Mexico's population, other centers assumed importance. At Cholula, in Puebla, a city had been rising with what is termed the Mixteca-Puebla style, an art style that eventually would pervade much of Middle America. About A.D. 700, an Olmec-Xicalanca dynasty began, apparently, some five hundred years of rule in the Puebla area. The one great monument known so far of the period of Cholula's hegemony is a great pyramid built on top of earlier and smaller structures. Approximately 186 feet high and more than 900 feet long on each side of its base, it exceeds the volume of Teotihuacán's Sun pyramid, and is the largest structure ever built by American Indians.

In the same post-Teotihuacán period, a large fortified
city developed on a hilltop at Xochicalco in the valley of
Morelos. The major structures around a plaza included a
temple pyramid of the Feathered Serpent, with façades decorated with stone carvings. The buildings of the city were
surrounded by ramparts and moats, all of which were
overlooked by a citadel on a slightly higher ridge. Another
hilltop city, Cacaxtla, overlooking the Puebla plain, may
date from about the same time and would indicate a period
of military ferment. At El Tajín on the Gulf Coast in
Veracruz, meanwhile, Totonacs reared another city dominated by an impressive seven-tiered pyramid and including
a compact group of temples and palaces. El Tajín shows
influences both from Teotihuacán and Oaxaca (pillars used
as interior supports) and from the Mayas in the south (two-
storied buildings with interior stairways, the corbeled arch,
and the use of poured concrete for structural work). But its
civilization, with an art style usually called Classic Veracruz,
included innovations like an elaborate ornamental sculptured
design of interlocked scrolls and the production of variously
shaped stones—yokes, palmate forms, and thin slabs—carved
with figures in profile or with symbolic or decorative abstract
designs. The functions of these stones (the yokes and palmate forms may be representations of paraphernalia worn in
sacred ball games) are still a subject of inquiry, but they are
considered some of the finest sculptures of pre-Columbian
America. From the same area, at the same time, came
distinctive terra-cotta figurines with smiling faces and great
expressiveness of life, as well as various paraphernalia for
the playing of games of ball that had ceremonial or ritual
attributes.

In central Mexico, the Late Classic Period closed with the
rise to dominance of a mixture of many peoples of the northern agricultural frontier—Nahuas, Otomís, and Nonoalcas—
ruled by a leadership composed primarily of Nahua-speakers.
Called Toltecs (from the name of the capital city they
built, Tollan, near present-day Tula, about fifty miles north
of Mexico City), their crystallization into a large political
unit reflected the growth of civilization, with Teotihuacán
influences, among northern farming peoples in such areas
as the modern states of Querétaro, Guanajuato, San Luis
Potosí, Jalisco, and Zacatecas. The ascendance to power of
the multi-ethnic Toltecs is shrouded in legends, but there is
reason to believe that they are founded on historical occur-

rences and point to the appearance, sometime between A.D. 800 and 900, of Mixcoatl, a conqueror from the Jalisco-Zacatecas region, and a rude following of frontier peoples. Assimilating the cultural traits of the groups they overran, they built their own city of Tollan (or Tula) and gradually created a powerful and refined culture of their own that spread its influences across a large part of Middle America.

The Toltecs became master architects and builders who erected palatial structures with pillared halls, profusely ornamented pyramids, and masonry courts on which were played ceremonial ball games. Pillars and walls were decorated with carved and polychromed figures of warriors and representations of various aspects of the many Toltec deities. From the south (presumably from Peru and Ecuador by way of the west coast of Mexico), metallurgy was first introduced into Middle America during this period, and the Toltecs were among the first Middle Americans (along with the Tarascans, farther west) to do fine work in gold and copper. Although artistic, they were also severe, austere, and disciplined, and apparently practiced human sacrifice, to feed hungry gods, on a much larger scale than ever before. Rule came to be divided between a civil and a religious leader, and a growing religious strife between militaristic and theocratic elements for control eventually weakened the state. Exactly what happened is not known, but legends indicate that followers of the cult of the warlike, angry god Tezcatlipoca, deity of the night in one of his many forms, were more powerful than partisans of the benign Quetzalcoatl, who were overthrown and forced to leave Tula. The internal conflict, coupled with plague and the pressure of new groups of primitive migrants from the north, sapped the strength of the Toltecs, and about A.D. 1200 Tula finally fell to a horde of plundering northern invaders, known collectively as Chichimecs (Dog People).

Finally, during the later stages of this same period, the Mixteca-Puebla style, noted earlier in connection with the rise of Cholula, spread throughout Middle America—and beyond, extending into Central America, and reaching far north to influence the Mississippian cultures of the present-day United States. At the same time, in Oaxaca, Monte Albán was succeeded by rising new centers of population, including Mitla, which, according to native histories, was at first the residence of the Zapotecs' religious leaders. In time, Mixtecs expanded into the area, taking over the ruins of

Monte Albán as well as Mitla, and turning the latter site into their own religious and political center. At its height, Mitla represented a mixture of Zapotec and Mixteca-Puebla influences. Its majestic buildings and monuments were decorated in relief with angular mosaics of protruding stones set in rhythmic repetitions of geometric designs, but on interior walls were beautifully painted frescoes that contrasted sharply with the exterior rigid mosaic patterns and were reminiscent of the Mixteca-Puebla style at Cholula.

In the meantime, important developments had been occurring farther south. There, a great civilization had been flourishing in numerous large and small centers of different Mayan peoples, from Yucatán and Chiapas to Guatemala, Honduras, and El Salvador, attaining peaks of beauty and intellect never again reached by American Indian cultures. In most respects, the Mayas were inheritors of the inventions and ideas of previous Middle American cultures rather than innovators themselves; but they elaborated on their legacy, developing to a remarkable degree hieroglyphic writing, astronomy, mathematical knowledge, and calendrical systems, and creating more realistic art styles in painting and bas-reliefs, as well as certain distinctive architectural traits, including the corbeled vault and towering roof combs atop pyramid temples.

In some ways, the Mayas were intellectually ahead of their Old World contemporaries. At least 1,200 years before Europe adopted the Gregorian calendar, which with its need for an adjusting leap year is still in use today, Maya astronomers and mathematicians employed more precise, accurate, and intricate calendrical systems and recorded them on carved stelae. These large slabs, up to thirty feet tall, were raised in Mayan centers at specific intervals to commemorate certain dates and events; they were usually covered with human figures in complex poses and relief sculptures of glyphs that conveyed calendrical and astronomical computations. A thousand years before the Hindus, Mayas also used a zero for which they possessed a glyph sign; and their astronomers, painstakingly studying the heavens, worked out the movements of celestial bodies and the recurrences of eclipses.

A mystery concerning the Mayas is how they reared such an impressive civilization in so forbidding and inhospitable an environment. Much of the Mayan country is a thick tropical rain forest, difficult to clear for agriculture, and

just as difficult to keep cleared of weeds and new jungle
growth. In many parts of the area, there are few, or no,
running rivers, and a water supply is uncertain, resting on
the ability of people to catch and store rain water in reservoirs. At the Mayan center of Tikal, for instance, where rain
water was stored in numerous reservoirs, modern drillers
probed 320 feet deep without reaching subterranean water.
Other than wood, stone, and wild game, there were few
natural resources: the Mayas had no metal and little or
none of the most sought after commodities, including obsidian, jade, vanilla, cacao, salt, and rubber. Trade was pursued vigorously with many near and far peoples, but travel,
too, was difficult requiring passage through jungles and
swamps that often necessitated the building of earthen or
masonry causeways.

Nevertheless in just such a hostile environment in the lowland regions of the Mayan country arose the first Classic
Maya centers, including places like Uaxactún, Altar de
Sacrificios, Tikal, Bonampak, Piedras Negras, and Copán,
excavated chiefly so far in the Usumacinta River Valley, the
Petén district of northern Guatemala, and parts of Honduras
and British Honduras. None of them were true cities with
suburbs, like Teotihuacán, but rather religious capitals inhabited by relatively small numbers of theocratic rulers and their
retainers, including intellectuals and artisans. The bulk of the
people were farmers, living in hamlets of wattle and daub,
pole and thatch, and masonry and pole houses scattered
across the agricultural lands surrounding the ceremonial
centers; using slash-and-burn methods to clear fields from
the jungle; and cultivating an evergrowing list of agricultural
crops. The fertility of the tropical forest soil was short-lived,
and plots could only be used for a few years. When their
productivity declined, they were abandoned for a while.
Farmers cleared new plots, let the old ones go back to wild
growth, and then eventually returned to them.

The ceremonial centers themselves often extended over
large areas, encompassing, as time passed, an increasing number of complexes of courts and plazas surrounded by masonry
buildings, frequently constructed on eminences and connected by causeways. The buildings—temple-pyramids, pal-
ace-like structures, monasteries, sanctuaries, baths, platforms,
terraces, astronomical observatories, and, in time courts for
ceremonial ball games—were massive-walled and impressive.
By modern standards however, the interiors were peculiarly

inefficient; because of their use of the corbeled vault, or arch (overlapping stones built inward from opposite walls until they could be bridged by a capstone), the Mayan architects were forced to construct rooms that were narrow and unable to hold more than a few dozen people. The pyramids and the temples atop them reflected many changing and regional styles; generally, the pyramids were mounds of earth and rubble faced with stone and with steep flights of steps, and the temples (one or more) on top were of stone slabs with towering roof combs. The latter, as well as parts of the façades of the temples and of the various other structures of the centers, were often elaborately ornamented with abstract geometric designs and with naturalistic and stylized masks and figures of birds, animals, and humans, carved in stone or stucco. Many pyramids had a shaft leading down from the temple to a burial chamber of an important person within the pyramid mound.

Mayan life seems to have been guided and dominated by religious systems, presided over by large priesthoods, and based on dictates resulting from calendrical studies and astronomical knowledge. Most learning, architecture, and artistic expression had a religious motive, and great and colorful ceremonies, following exact lore and ritual, were held in the ceremonial centers to the rain, sun, moon, and other deities. But Mayan astronomers, studying the heavens, worked out complicated and interlocked systems of calendars that prescribed daily, seasonal, and annual activities which the people followed faithfully in economic, social, and political affairs. Much of this information was recorded in carved glyphs on the periodically raised stelae and on other monuments. The Mayas had no alphabet, but the glyphs represented words, ideas, concepts, dates, and numbers, as well as pictures or symbols of things whose spoken names resembled the sounds of what was meant.

Little is known of Mayan social or political organization during either the Early or Late Classic periods, but the different centers can be likened, perhaps, to city-state capitals from which the elite castes of priests and nobles ruled the surrounding countryside in feudal manner. Some of the districts may have been joined in loose federations. Until a later period, warfare was apparently infrequent and on a small scale, although the murals and carvings of warriors indicate that the Mayas were by no means pacifists. From the evidence of its architectural achievements, Mayan society must have been disciplined and authoritatively directed; but the elite groups must have been deeply religious, meditative, and appreciative of beauty and learning. Many of the centers had full-time craftsmen and laborers. The craftsmen were skilled artists with a sensitive feel for esthetic values: the architects, sculptors, painters, and artisans in ceramics, jade, and wood left works that bear comparison with those of any ancient Old World civilization except perhaps Greece. Their artistic objects include stone mosaics, painted scenes on many different kinds of pottery, done in various regional and temporal styles; carvings in jade and other precious stones; and almanacs, or codices (only three remain), with picture symbols of religious lore and rituals painted on folding screens of paper.

In other aspects, Mayan civilization was also advanced. People wove cloth from cotton, and while the basic dress for men included little more than a woven breechcloth, the upper classes garbed themselves with richness and elegance. Priests and members of the nobility wore mantles and headdresses, and ornamented themselves with lip, ear, and nose plugs made of precious stones. Warriors had their own costumes that included mantles made from the skins of jaguars and helmets of carved animal heads. Trade was widespread, and regular markets were held in the centers. Commerce was controlled by the nobility, but there were apparently special classes of itinerant merchants or professional traders, some of whom engaged in a sea trade, transporting their products through the Gulf of Mexico in large dugout canoes.

There is considerable evidence that persons and ideas from Teotihuacán regularly entered the Mayan lowlands to influence the rising civilizations in the various centers. Trade diffused many products and traits, and at Tikal, for example, stone monuments of the Early Classic Period are carved with faces of Tlaloc, the rain god, in Teotihuacán style. The principal influences from Teotihuacán during the Early Classic Period, however, are found in the Mayan highlands of Guatemala, where Kaminaljuyú, as previously mentioned, seems actually to have come under the rule of people from central Mexico and to have become, prior to A.D. 600, an outpost of Teotihuacán culture. From Kaminaljuyú, in turn, Teotihuacán traits, as also stated, spread farther south among Mayan peoples.

The period known as the Late Classic, approximately A.D. 600–900, was, for the lowland Maya, the era of their greatest development of architecture, sculpture, painting, and other artistic achievements. Wall paintings at Bonampak and masks, jewelry, and other objects found in many tombs at Palenque are among the finest creative works of American Indian cultures. In the Mayan highlands, where many old centers had been abandoned, new ones, including Nebaj, Zaculeu, and Zacualpa, influenced during the Early Classic Period by Teotihuacán (as well as by Puebla, the Mexican Gulf Coast, Izapa, and the southern lowlands), continued to show strong influences from Mexico, suggesting to some authorities that that part of the Mayan area was never without Mexican or Mexican-influenced rulers. During the Late Classic Period, ball courts and various traits from the Mexican Gulf Coast proliferated in the Mayan highlands. In that period, it is possible that migrants from the destroyed city of Teotihuacán, or other Mexicans (and, perhaps, at a later date, groups from the Toltecs' Tula), established new dynasties over Mayan highland centers, being absorbed, in time, by the Mayan groups whom they ruled. Elsewhere, civilizations flourished at such places as Tonala on the Chiapas Pacific coast, in the district of Cotzumalhuapa on the Pacific slope, in Honduras, El Salvador, and on the island of Jaina off the Campeche coast. In the northern Yucatán, toward the end of the period, a so-called Florescent Period saw the rise of splendid Mayan centers at Uxmal, Kabah, Labná, Sayil, and other places. Famous ruins at those sites, characterized by a style known as Puuc, are of palatial, multi-storied monumental buildings, steep pyramids, columned structures, and ceremonial courts, many of them beautifully ornamented with carved stone mosaics.

Beginning about A.D. 900, Mayan lowland civilization went into a gradual decline from which it never recovered. The cause is not known; one theory suggests that the increase in population and overuse of the poor soil brought about an agricultural crisis which led to revolts by farming populations against the ruling priests. Evidence for this, and for all other suggestions, is scanty, however, and all that is known is that a general cultural deterioration set in. The monumental centers decayed, and, as their inhabitants dispersed, the buildings slowly became ruins. The people in the country-side, ruled perhaps by local headmen, seem to have continued their daily existence, eventually coming under the sway of conquering highland dynasties. Central Mexican products and traits reached them, and by the time the

Spaniards arrived in the lowland regions, many of the more populated areas were interwoven in a network of Indian trade and commerce that extended from central Mexico to Guatemala.

In the Guatemala highlands, almost continually under strong Mexican influences, Mayan culture continued to flourish for a considerable time after A.D. 900. New architectural forms, new ceramics, metallurgy, including the making of objects of gold or copper and of alloys of these with silver, zinc, and tin, as well as various other innovations, came in, and merchant guilds arose. Gradually, still influenced by events in central Mexico, a militaristic period began: the people became grouped in small warlike kingdoms, centered in walled fortress towns surrounded by agricultural hamlets and villages. Mayan chronicles like the *Popol Vuh* and the *Annals of the Cakchiquels* relate the history of successive rulers and constant wars between such towns as Utatlan of the Quiches, Iximché of the Cakchiquels, and Chuitinamit of the Zutuhils. When the Spaniards reached the region in the early sixteenth century, petty conflict was still common, and the glories of the great age of the highland Mayas had disappeared.

In the northern Yucatán for a while history ran a different course. Sometime around A.D. 1000 the brilliant Mayan cities of the Florescent Period seem to have lured the Toltecs who, from their capital at Tula, had become masters of much of central Mexico. Toltec warrior groups—possibly ousted followers of the Quetzalcoatl faction—invaded Yucatán and established temporary rule over that region, setting up the seat of their power at Chichén Itzá, and introducing Toltec political ideas, Toltec religion, and Toltec styles in architecture and art. It has recently been suggested that the invaders actually introduced little but their sociopolitical ideas and religion to Yucatán and, instead, sent back to Tula most of the art styles and architectural features that link the two places. Archeologists have not yet reached unanimous agreement on which way the flow went; but to most students it still seems probable that such traits as colonnaded patios, Chac-Mools (reclining stone figures with heads turned to one side and knees drawn up toward basins in the stomachs), warrior orders like the Eagles and the Jaguars, and round towers were all introduced to the Yucatán Mayas from Tula, and not vice versa. As Toltec power increased, the old centers of Uxmal, Kabah, and Labná were gradually abandoned, and Chichén Itzá became a great capital. The cult of the Toltecs' Quetzalcoatl, reappearing with the Mayan name Kukulcán, became dominant, and religious ceremonies took on Mexican coloration, including an increase in the sacrificing of humans. Mayas traveled to Chichén Itzá from all over Yucatán to visit a celebrated *cenote*, or natural well, believed to be the home of the rain gods, and in times of drought they threw gold-laden victims into the *cenote* as sacrifices to those gods.

By about A.D. 1200, the area witnessed a renewal of Mayan traditions. Tula was overthrown in central Mexico, and the Toltec conquest in Yucatán gradually withered. A final militaristic phrase, sometimes called a Decadent Period, began in Yucatán. Chichén Itzá lost its importance, and population, still dense, became concentrated in and around new walled cities, notably Mayapán and Tulum, the first truly urban localities in a Mayan country. The Yucatán Mayas of this period were more warlike than before, and revolts and conflicts brought chaos to the region. Control passed to warrior overlords who ruled as despots, seizing local headmen as hostages for tribute. While art and intellectual pursuits declined, the area was ruled for a while by three great, precariously allied families: the Itzás, the Xius, and the Cocoms. Gradually the Cocoms of Mayapán forced their domination over the others until about 1450, when they were overthrown and individual Yucatán localities became independent under local chieftains. Petty warfare went on; the culture continued to decay; and the big centers fell to ruins. The Spaniards, arriving in the sixteenth century, were able to find Maya allies who helped them win easy conquests.

To the north, in central Mexico, the overthrow of the Toltecs' capital city of Tula, about A.D. 1200, had been followed, there also, by a period of turmoil and conflict. The Chichimecs—the various new migrant groups that conquered Tula and overran the civilized areas of central Mexico—were made up, it is believed, of mixtures of northern peoples, including hunting and gathering tribes pushing south from drought-ridden areas, rude farming groups from the northern agricultural frontier where civilization was less advanced, and descendants of colonists who had earlier moved north from the central Mexican populated areas. The arrival of the newcomers is associated with many political and cultural changes: the warlike Mixtecs, during this period, for instance, seem to have expanded determinedly into the old Zapotec country of Oaxaca, where, at Mitla, they created beautiful turquoise mosaics, stylized miniature-painting codices, and fine and delicate gold work; the Tarascans appear to have established dominance over a large agricultural population in Michoacán and set up capitals at Tzintzuntzan and Ihuatzio; and in the Valley of Mexico several city-states arose, competing for hegemoney.

Although the new arrivals are usually regarded, in a relative sense, as "barbarians," comprising a variety of cultures and shades of cultures of their own, they rapidly became assimilated into the ways of life of the civilizations they overran. Tula was dead; but the legacy of Toltec civilization, and of all that the Toltecs had inherited, lived on in populated centers, and the newcomers, becoming quickly acculturated, soon reared new civilizations based in large measure on the old ones. Some of the new peoples, like the Toltecs before them, spoke Nahuatl dialects of the Utaztecan stock. Others, who became Tepanecs, were a combination of Otomí, Matlatzinca, and Mazahua. Eventually, various of these groups became established in the Valley of Mexico and built or expanded a number of competing city-states around the shores of Lake Texcoco. One weak and relatively primitive Nahuatl-speaking tribe that had entered the region during the thirteenth century was forced to settle on islands in the marshes on the western side of the lake, where they founded two settlements, Tlatelolco and Tenochtitlán (Place of the Cactus in the Rock). Their tribal name was Mexica, but in time they took the name Aztecs for the area from which they had started their migration, Aztlán, which was somewhere vaguely to the northwest and may even have been in the present-day U.S. Southwest. The traditional date for the founding of Tenochtitlán (present-day Mexico City) is 1325, but it may have been earlier. At any rate, from Tenochtitlán, which eventually conquered and absorbed Tlatelolco, the Aztecs rose in power. Prior to 1427, hegemony over the valley was won by the Tepanecs of the city-state of Azcapotzalco. Under their conquering ruler, Tezozomoc (1363–1427), the Tepanecs defeated the competing city-states and managed to unify control of a large economic area of central Mexico, thus setting the stage for the creation of a true empire, with centralized authority over tribute-paying vassals and widespread producers of raw materials and foods. In the struggle for power that followed Tezozomoc's death, the

Aztecs formed a triple alliance with two other cities and fought and conspired their way to leadership. They soon dominated the alliance, and under strong and able rulers subjugated most of the peoples of central Mexico, being rebuffed principally by the Tarascans and the people of Tlaxcala. By the time the Spaniards under Cortés arrived in 1519, the Aztec Empire was flourishing under Moctezuma II.

The Aztecs' culture in general reflected inheritances from the Middle American high civilizations that had preceded it. But the growth and organization of urban life in Tenochtitlán, with an estimated metropolitan population of more than 60,000 at its pre-Spanish peak, and the political rule and administration of the empire, comprising more than 5 million people, were achievements that belonged to the Aztecs alone. The cohesion of the empire was actually a loose one: most subjugated regions were not absorbed into the Aztec state but were left alone as long as they recognized the Aztecs' superiority. The Aztecs' principal interests were to dominate trade and markets and receive tribute and unending streams of defeated peoples whose hearts could be cut out on the altars of the Aztecs' own god, Huitzilopochtli (Hummingbird Wizard), to feed the sun-god and keep him strong. Aztec oppression and the exaction of tribute often caused restlessness and resistance, and some conquered groups were strong enough to maintain varying degrees of self-government, management of their own affairs, and even exemption from the payment of tribute. In many areas, the Aztecs exerted tighter control and administration, utilizing vassal rulers, overseeing affairs and relations by the employment of ambassadors, tax collectors, spies, merchants, and bureaucrats, and stationing military garrisons where they were needed. But most bonds were tenuous, and the power and extent of the empire rested on the ability of the Aztecs to enforce obedience.

An intensive, integrated agricultural economy, employing large irrigation systems, artificial islands in the lakes (*chinampas*), and hillside terraces, permitted the growth of the big population of Tenochtitlán and the other cities in the Valley of Mexico. The main crop was corn, but farmers raised a great variety of other products, including beans, squash, tomatoes, potatoes, chili, and (in lower altitudes) cotton, and made use of many fruits, including mangoes, papayas, avocados, and cacao beans. Wild plants, game, and domesticated dogs and turkeys were also eaten. The produce from the different agricultural areas, like the regional products secured in trade from peoples far and near, were brought across Lake Texcoco in canoes, or over causeways, and were sold (using cacao beans, jade, turquoise, gold quills, or copper knives as mediums of exchange) in huge, bustling markets in the capital.

The political and social organizations in Tenochtitlán were complex and advanced. The city was divided, largely by geography, into twenty *calpullis*, or clans, composed of groups of families. Each *calpulli*, occupying a different section of the capital, managed its own governmental affairs and possessed its own set of elected officials, priests, schools, and temples. The schools, called "houses of youth," trained children in farming, arts and crafts, warfare, history, citizenship, and religious lore and observances. Special schools prepared youths for the priesthood, and boarding schools existed for girls who planned to become priestesses. The leaders of the nation received the education of priests, and in their persons Aztec religious and civil authority merged at the top. Elevation to leadership stemmed from the clans. One of the three principal officers of each clan, known as a speaker, represented his clan on a council of state which, in turn, chose four of its members as executive officers of the nation. Each of the four men represented a different quarter of the city. This group selected and advised the ruler of the empire, who was known as the Chief of Men. In practice, he was usually selected from a single lineage. The Chiefs of Men, of whom Moctezuma II is the best known to history, headed both the civil and religious hierarchies of the empire and were regarded almost as deities themselves. They were borne about on litters under rich and brilliant canopies of feathers ornamented with gold, silver, pearls, and jade, housed in a splendid palace of one hundred rooms, shielded from view during their meals, and approached only in the most reverent manner—barefoot, in the clothes of a commoner, and with downcast eyes.

The Chiefs of Men were at the pinnacle of a stratified society dominated by rank. There were numerous subdivisions, but the major classes were the members of royalty; a nobility that included priests, civil officers, wealthy merchants, and war chiefs; commoners who formed the most numerous class; a propertyless group comprising certain unskilled laborers, minor craftsmen, and the shiftless; and slaves. Skilled artisans plied numerous specialized crafts, working with wood, feathers, cloth, gold and other metals, jade, and various precious stones, and a busy trade in their products and in the goods of the various regions extended among towns and markets throughout the empire. The state encouraged commerce, and insults to itinerant Aztec merchants by other peoples were sometimes the cause of wars. Writing was developed in the form of hieroglyphics supplementing pictorial representations of history, religious lore, geography, tribute rolls, and other matters, and some codices contained phonetic syllables based on rebuses.

Religion permeated Aztec life. The Aztec pantheon was a large one, containing more than sixty major deities and numerous lesser ones. The old central Mexican gods Quetzalcoatl and Tezcatlipoca were revered, but the principal deity was Huitzilopochtli, the war god, who supposedly had guided the Aztecs during their migration from Aztlán. The gods were ranked in importance, and each one had its own cult and special hierarchies of priests. The year was divided into two hundred and sixty days, and a sacred calendar, used also for divination, called for an annual cycle of religious ceremonies and festivals, each one dedicated to a deity. Many of the rituals required the sacrificing of thousands of human victims to the gods, whose strength needed perpetual renewal with the most spiritually powerful of all foods: human hearts and blood. Victims were led up the steep steps of pyramids to temples on top, where their hearts were cut out and their heads impaled on skull racks. Other victims were flayed, and their skins worn by priests, who themselves often practiced rituals of self-sacrifice, drawing blood from their tongues, ears, and other parts of their body. The grim sacrifices, carried to an extreme unequaled by previous Middle American societies, shocked the Spaniards, but the rites were so clothed with religious zeal that frequently even those who were sacrificed were eager to serve as offerings to the deities.

Most of the Aztecs' victims were captives taken in wars, some of which were bloodless, ceremonial combats, called "Wars of the Flowers," fought only to secure prisoners for sacrifice. Aztec armies, reflecting the evolution of militaristic bodies during the long period of conflicts that had wracked central Mexico in previous centuries, were organized efficiently into units from brigade size down to squads of a few men, led by war chiefs and various ranks of lesser officers.

All able-bodied males over fifteen, except priests and civil officials, were subject to serve in the armed forces. The soldiers were members of military orders, also, and wore helmets carved to represent jaguars, wolves, and other animals for whom the orders were named; officers added brilliant plumage to their helmets. The warriors were armed with bows and arrows, darts and dart throwers, maces, clubs, and swords edged with volcanic glass. Shields were made of quilted cotton soaked in brine and then stretched over round frames; tunics worn as light armor were also of quilted cotton. Although the military apparatus was a formidable one in numbers and organization, its function was principally to take prisoners rather than to fight pitched battles and slay opposing troops.

With the Spanish conquest of Mexico, beginning in 1519, the long, independent Indian development in Middle America came to an end. One can only speculate on what heights Indians might have reached had there been no European invasion. But Cortés's intrusion was complete, and the Aztec Empire, together with its capital city, was destroyed. Despite the small size of Cortés's army (some 400 men), several factors aided the conquerors. Their guns and horses at first frightened many of the Indians, who were further confused by the belief that the strangers were the white gods of their myths. Moctezuma had been a stern diplomat and a courageous warrior; but in the face of the mysterious Spaniards he turned fearful and vacillating, looking for omens to guide him, misreading Spanish motives, and placing trust in the newcomers until it was too late. The authoritarian Aztec system of government was unable to provide effective leadership after the death of Moctezuma and the other principal leaders; and the slaughter that resulted from the fierce, determined nature of Spanish warfare was new to the Indians. The combination of the well-trained Spanish army, with a long tradition of fighting behind it, and various Indian allies anxious to help overthrow Aztec domination and oppression, was more than a match for the bravely resisting Aztecs. Following the capture of Tenochtitlán, the Spaniards leveled the pyramids and temples, ended the native priesthoods, burned their books, and obliterated as much of the Indians' civilization as possible. But many Aztec ways of life, rooted in previous Middle American cultures and civilizations, continued and still exist today in Mexico, mostly in modified forms. Many Indian languages also still persist, including Nahuatl, Mixtec, Zapotec, Huastec, Otomi, and still others. And in the Mayan lands, Chontals, Lacandóns, and other native groups still speak Mayan tongues.

Final mention should be made of the pivotal position occupied by Middle American native cultures in the hemisphere as a whole. Archeologists are almost agreed that in the earliest times all of the hemisphere possessed somewhat similar basic hunting and gathering cultures. Owing principally to its invention of agriculture (although other causes must also be considered), Middle America witnessed the development of cultures that elevated most of its peoples above all others—except those in the Central Andes, where agriculture also spurred development—and added layers of complexity and refinement above the basic hunting and gathering culture. From time to time, in the long history of the area, radiations went out from Middle America, diffusing ideas as well as goods beyond its borders. In that sense, Middle America was a hearth, spreading such things as agriculture, types of pottery, religious forms, architecture, systems of organization, and arts and crafts toward Central and South America, the Caribbean, and the present-day United States. But there were also interrelations, and Middle America also received traits from the outside. The bow and arrow entered the area from more primitive peoples in the north. Metallurgy came to Middle Americans from South America. Not everything traveled; the complex calendar systems of Middle America, for instance, never reached the Andes. But, in general, it is becoming established to an increasing degree that, by commerce, trade, and deliberate and errant movements of peoples, more frequent contacts than have previously been suspected occurred at various times between Middle Americans and certain other peoples in the hemisphere. Periodic contacts, via long-range sea voyages, now seem to have occurred between the Ecuador coast and Pacific coastal areas of Middle America; the same sort of contacts may have taken Mexican traits to the Mississippi Valley and the U. S. Southeast. And ruled out no longer as fantasy are the glimmerings of hints, which may soon be substantiated, that various Asiatic traits, carried across the Pacific by people in seagoing craft, reached the southwestern coast of Mexico beginning about A.D. 700 and went on to influence the cultures of the Toltecs of Tula and the Mayas of Chichén Itzá.

19

Indians of Central America and the Caribbean Area

THE INDIANS OF NICARAGUA, COSTA RICA, PANAMA,
Colombia, the northern part of Venezuela, and the
West Indies are usually grouped in a single cultural
area known as the Circum-Caribbean, which refers to their
geographical location about the Caribbean Sea. Frequently
(especially when discussing their cultural history), they are
also divided into two subregions. Those in Central America,
Colombia, and western Venezuela are described as occupying
an Intermediate Area that lay between the high civilizations
of Middle America and the Central Andes and received influences from both of those advanced areas. The Indians
farther east, along the northern South American coast, as
well as those in the West Indies, constitute the second
group, which received influences principally from the Intermediate Area and from the interior of Venezuela.

Much less is known about the prehistoric development of
cultures in the Circum-Caribbean area than in neighboring
Middle America or Ecuador and the Central Andes. Archeologists have revealed sequences of styles and cultures in a
a number of scattered sites and regions, but too little is still
known to provide more than a sketchy synopsis of the pre-
Columbian history of the area. On the other hand, Spanish
explorers and conquerors left many accounts of what Indian
life was like when white men first reached the region, and
although they are full of distortions, misunderstandings,
and omissions, they nevertheless provide an idea of Indian
cultures in the area in the early part of the sixteenth century.
From those accounts it is clear that the Circum-Caribbean

lands were characterized at that time by a great number of different chiefdoms—somewhat autonomous communities and groups that had become federated or united into larger political and religious units under despotic supreme chiefs.

The chiefdoms, many of which practiced cannibalism, were generally of two types. The first, found by the Spaniards mostly in Central America and Colombia, were intensely militaristic petty states of various sizes and degrees of power that waged constant warfare for territory and tribute, but especially for victims for temple sacrifices to gods—as in Mexico—as well as for human flesh to eat and human trophies for personal prestige and social status. Some of these chiefdoms displayed technological and artistic achievements second only to those of Middle America and Peru, and all of them possessed stratified class structures, a leadership with power to direct the activities of the mass of people, and a religious system that required human sacrifice. The second type of chiefdom, existing principally—but not entirely—in eastern Venezuela and the Greater Antilles, possessed many of the traits of the first type, but had religions in which human sacrifice played only a minor, or no, role. Although less militant than the first group, they, too, were bellicose; but captives were taken more often for human trophies or for food than for sacrifice on altars to gods. In the Circum-Caribbean area, also, were enclaves of less advanced peoples—groups of tropical forest village farmers and even nomadic hunters and gatherers. But some parts of the area had enabled intensive agriculture which, with plentiful fish, game, and wild plants, had led to food surpluses and population density. With these preconditions as a base, social stratification, religion, and military activities had then given rise to the chiefdoms.

The area, by the early sixteenth century, was a kaleidoscope of many tribes, reflecting prehistoric migrations of different groups, a mosaic of diffused traits, and the intermixing of speakers of numerous languages that stemmed principally from three large linguistic superstocks: Macro-Chibchan, Andean-Equatorial, and Ge-Pano-Carib. Speaking various tongues that had derived from Macro-Chibchan were most of the tribes of Central America, including the Lencas of Nicaragua and the Guaymís and Cunas of Panama. Colombian tribes included speakers of all three language superstocks. Some of the important ones were the Gorróns, Liles, Armas, Quimbayas, and Catíos of the western part of the

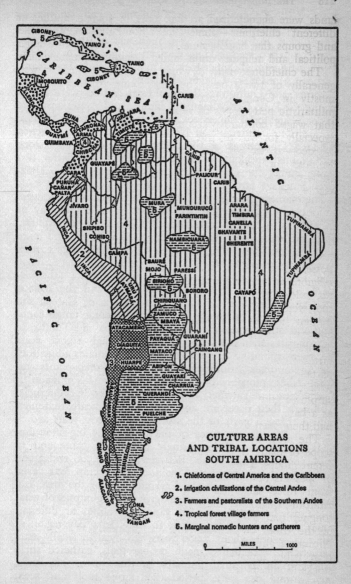

CULTURE AREAS
AND TRIBAL LOCATIONS
SOUTH AMERICA

1. Chiefdoms of Central America and the Caribbean

2. Irrigation civilizations of the Central Andes

3. Farmers and pastoralists of the Southern Andes

4. Tropical forest village farmers

5. Marginal nomadic hunters and gatherers

0   MILES   1000

country; the Calamaris, Cenús, Mompoxes, and Taironas of the north; and the Chibchas of the central highlands. Many Venezuelan Indian tribes were members of the Ge-Pano-Carib superstock, speaking Cariban languages, or of the Andean-Equatorial superstock. They included Timoteans, Laches, Motilones, Chakés, Jirajaras, Caracas, Palenques, Goajiros, and Quiriquires. In the Lesser Antilles were Caribs of the Ge-Pano-Carib linguistic family, and Arawaks of the Andean-Equatorial superstock were in the Greater Antilles. In addition, immigrants in Nicaragua from Middle America included Chorotegas of the Macro-Otomangean superstock and Nahuatl-speaking Nicaraos and Siguas, the latter two being among the southernmost of all peoples of the Utaztecan language family.

The earliest people in the Circum-Caribbean area were undoubtedly hunters and foragers with a nomadic way of life similar to that of early man throughout the hemisphere. Finds still undated with certainty, but believed to be more than 10,000 years old, are grouped by archeologist Alex Krieger as belonging to a Pre-Projectile Point stage. They have been discovered in northwestern Venezuela (the Camare and Manzanillo complexes of finds and the Muaco site) and in western Colombia (the Tumba de Garzón site and in the Department of Chocó) and include crude chopping and other types of tools. At the Muaco and Tumba de Garzón sites man's relics, possibly more than 16,000 years old, were found in association with the remains of extinct Ice Age animals. Additional discoveries of fluted points and other relics, probably of later periods, have been made in Costa Rica and Panama, as well as at El Jobo in Venezuela. Although their dates are uncertain, they indicate that men moved through parts of the area at least 7,000 years ago.

With the disappearance of the Pleistocene big-game animals, people turned increasingly to smaller game and to gathering wild plant foods. Between about 7,000 and 3,000 years ago, the cultivation of manioc, a root crop, was developed, spreading through the lowland parts of the area. Isolated archeological investigations give a few glimpses of what life must have been like in various localities at different times during that early period. In the Parita Bay region of Panama, people about 7,000 years ago lived in small, semipermanent settlements, made pebble tools, gathered shellfish, and hunted small animals. In the Guiana highlands, men during the same period used stone tools and seem essentially to have been hunters. About 5,000 years ago, pottery and agriculture began to enter people's lives in several regions. Some of the oldest pottery found so far anywhere in the Americas (dated at about 4,875 years old) was discovered at Puerto Hormiga, near Cartagena on the northern coast of Colombia. This pottery has resemblances to the Valdivia pottery that is believed to have been introduced on the coast of Ecuador by Japanese voyagers about 5,000 years ago, and it may have spread from Ecuador to Puerto Hormiga. Other pottery of somewhat later dates was found at Rancho Peludo in northwestern Venezuela (about 4,700 years old); at Monagrillo on Parita Bay, Panama (about 4,090 years old); and at Barlovento near Cartagena (about 3,470 years old). The Monagrillo and Barlovento wares, particularly, also show influences from the Ecuadorean Valdivia pottery. Evidence of the use of manioc was also discovered at Rancho Peludo, and some authorities believe that root agriculture began at all those sites at approximately the same time (between 4,000 and 5,000 years ago).

At this early time, however, the cultivation of crops was still in its incipient stage. People at Puerto Hormiga, Barlovento, and Parita Bay still relied principally on fish, shellfish, wild seeds, and game, and the inhabitants of the Rancho Peludo area, who may have been descendants of the big-game hunters of the northwestern Venezuelan Ice Age sites, mentioned above, still hunted and gathered wild fruits and vegetables. Nevertheless, agriculture had begun, and in the ensuing millennia it spread across much of the area and became increasingly important as a source of food. Pottery, consisting at first of simple bowls, jars, and burial urns, coarse, thick, and crudely decorated, spread, also, proliferating rapidly in a variety of regional styles that changed from time to time. These styles both regional and temporal, serve in many cases to mark succeeding phases of the development of individual peoples. At Parita Bay in Panama, for instance, a Sarigua phase (about 3,000 years ago), characterized principally by different pottery styles, followed the earlier Monagrillo phase of about 4,100 years ago, when pottery had first appeared in that region. In the Puerto Hormiga and Barlovento areas, new ceramic objects and styles characterized the succeeding San Jacinto and Malambo phases. During the latter phase (approximately 3,000 years ago), people in this northern Colombian area were living in permanent settlements, relying to a greater degree on the

cultivation of manioc and probably other crops, and still
hunting and fishing. In northwestern Venezuela's Rancho
Peludo area, about the same time, agriculture and village
life had also developed, setting the stage for the growth of
more complex societies.

On the central and northeastern coast of Venezuela, excavations show the presence, meanwhile, of nonagricultural
peoples whose lives were oriented toward the sea. Near
Tucacas on the central coast have been found stone implements, some of them dating back almost 6,000 years ago.
On Cubagua Island off Venezuela's northeastern coast were
discovered bone points and implements about 4,150 years
old, while nearby, at Manicuare on the mainland, were shell
middens of people who made shell points, gouges, beads,
and pendants, as well as celts, about 3,570 years ago. The
inhabitants of Cubagua and Manicuare gathered shellfish,
caught fish with nets, hunted game, and collected wild
plants. Their island settlement sites, together with their
possession of implements with which they would have been
able to make watercraft, suggest that they traveled out into
the Caribbean and had a rudimentary knowledge of navigation.

Man seems, also, to have been on at least some of the
islands of the West Indies this early, although his place—
or places—of origin is still in doubt. At the Marban site in
the Dominican Republic have been found relics, about
4,170 years old, of nonagricultural peoples, referred to by
archeologists in the Circum-Caribbean area as Meso-Indians.
This is the oldest site yet found in the West Indies. Another
Meso-Indian site, at Krum Bay in the Virgin Islands, disclosed relics that seemed affiliated with pre-pottery cultures
in Panama. In Cuba, however, traits have been found similar to those of the people of Manicuare on the Venezuelan
mainland, mentioned above, while Tucacas-like artifacts have
been found on Puerto Rico. Other early Indians, unrelated to
any group known so far in Venezuela, left remains in Trinidad. The pattern in the islands appears to suggest that from
time to time, prior to the first century of the Christian Era,
nonfarming peoples arrived on various islands from different
starting points in the areas bounding the Caribbean, including the Venezuelan coast, Central America, and perhaps
Middle America, northern Mexico, and Florida. Some may
have been blown accidentally to the islands, while others
made deliberate voyages.

After about 1000 B.C., development in parts of Colombia quickened, being influenced in lowland areas by the introduction of traits from Middle America, including the cultivation of corn. In the Andean highlands parallels with developments occurring both in the Central Andes and in Middle America appeared. During this period, the cult of the jaguar god, common to the Olmec Culture (flourishing at that time in Mexico) and the Chavín Culture of Peru, was diffused over large areas, reaching highland Colombia as well. There, sometime prior to 550 B.C., a San Agustín Culture arose, showing definite influences, including that of the feline cult, from both the north and the south. There is evidence that Middle American seafarers reached the Colombian coast about 500 B.C., and their traits and influences probably diffused to the highlands, giving added stimuli to the San Agustín and other highland areas. The San Augstín Culture, representing successive stages of development between approximately 555 B.C. and A.D. 1180, has been identified in a complex of more than thirty small scattered areas in a region of several hundred square miles. The sites contain many low earthern mounds, some used as shrines, and some for burials; numerous monumental stone carvings and sculptures, some of them bas-relief carvings of animals, humans, and fanged anthropomorphic figures on slabs, and others sculptures in the round; and various structures including subterranean stonelined galleries and crypts. The bulk of the population, living in small clusters of circular houses, engaged in agriculture, but social organization must have been advanced. Although there were no large temple centers, with major buildings, the remains indicate the presence of authority, an organized religious system, ceremonialism, social stratification, and artisans of outstanding workmanship. Pottery forms increased, the styles became more artistic, and a little work was done in gold. With the passage of time, elements of the San Agustín Culture were paralleled elsewhere in the highlands, and cultures became increasingly sophisticated.

Farther east, on the middle and lower Orinoco River in Venezuela, people of a Saladero Culture (named for the principal site) were living in villages by about 1000 B.C., cultivating manioc, making pottery of their own, and acquiring the beginnings of social stratification and occupational specialization. Sometime about 900 B.C. members of a new culture, the Barrancas, which may have derived originally from northern Colombia or Panama, entered the area, co-existing for a while with the Saladero people, then forcing some of them toward the coast and onto Trinidad. As time went on, people of the Saladero Culture spread west along the Venezuelan coast, coming into contact with earlier groups of sea-oriented shellfish gatherers. The two cultures intermixed about the beginning of the Christian Era, and until the arrival of white men the economy of that coastal region, based on both seafood and agriculture, remained essentially the same. At the same time, the newly arrived Saladero peoples learned navigation, and about A.D. 1–300 some of them pushed northward through the West Indies, populating the islands and introducing pottery and agricul-ture to the fishing settlements of the earlier Meso-Indian inhabitants. In general, the pattern of Saladero expansion was one of conquest; in most places, these Indians, who may have been Arawakan-speakers, overran the earlier island settlers or shoved them back. By the time of Columbus, the remnants of the more primitive original peoples, without pottery or agriculture (and known as Ciboneys), occupied only the southwestern tip of Haiti and the swampy coast and islands of southern and western Cuba.

Elsewhere in the area, knowledge of the development of peoples during the first millennium A.D. is still relatively meager. In Central America, where groups were influenced by trade and traders from both the north and south, agri-culture was the principal source of food, but fishing and hunting were also important. By A.D. 500, peoples in Costa Rica and Panama had cultures that included earth mounds, some social stratification and religious ceremonialism, and diversified pottery styles. Technical advances, the working of jade, the appearance of specialized artisans and merchants, and an increase in interregional trade marked the period from A.D. 600 to 800 in Nicaragua and Costa Rica. In Panama, during the same time, beautiful work was done in precious and semi-precious stones; metallurgy was practiced at Parita Bay; and burials at Venado Beach indicate the existence of a class-structured society ruled by chiefs or priests whose deaths occasioned the forced or voluntary suicide or sacrifices of certain subjects. Between A.D. 900 and the arrival of the Spaniards in the early sixteenth century, devel-opment accelerated throughout Central America. Villages and towns increased in number and size; population in some areas became dense; monumental structures and sculpture appeared in many places; earth and stone mounds, often raised around plazas, attested to growing authority, social stratification, and the specialization of labor; and carvings and ceremonialism reflected the importance of religion. Art reached a climax. Noteworthy sculptures in the round, tall statues, and low relief carvings were produced in different regions. Multicolored painted pottery with various geometric and naturalistic styles, many mirroring religious inspirations, were fashioned in Costa Rica and Panama. Metates were richly carved, and numerous decorative articles for the nobility and religious leaders were made of jade and precious stones. In Panama, especially, exquisite work was done in gold and tumbaga, an alloy of gold and copper. Many of the cultural elements, particularly in the northern part of Central America, came from Middle America; migrations of Chorotegas (c. A.D. 800), Nicaraos (c. A.D. 1100), and others brought in Middle American traits not already introduced by trade or diffusion. One way or the other, ball courts, markets, domesticated turkeys, Chac-Mool stone statues like those of the Toltecs, and other elements spread south.

In many areas of Colombia, meanwhile, corn had become the principal crop. In the lowlands of the north, the density of population increased, and cultures became varied in details in different regions. Hillsides were terraced for planting; buildings were constructed in the round or on platforms; and pottery forms and styles grew in number. Between A.D. 1000 and 1500 many of the traits that were later described by the Spaniards—including palisaded villages, the taking of slaves and human trophies, the practice of cannibalism, and the production of numerous objects of gold and copper—became common. A Tairona Culture, centered on the slopes of the Sierra Nevada de Santa Marta, was characterized by a distinctive ceramic style and by achievements in architecture and engineering on the difficult terrain: people of the Tairona Culture, seemingly regimented under authoritative leadership, built paved roads, stone bridges, stairways, terraces, porticoes, columns, tombs, and irrigation canals. In the towns, which were large urban centers, religious leaders ruled over militaristic societies that were characterized by a division of labor, social stratification into classes, and the presence of specialists. Metallurgy was advanced, and trade between regions was well developed.

The Andean highlands of Colombia also became densely

populated. Between A.D. 500 and 1000 the area witnessed the flourishing of the Quimbaya Culture—a federation of six subgroups, headed by a supreme chief, noted especially for their goldwork—followed eventually by the ascendance of the Chibcha Culture. The date of the rise of the Chibchas has not been established with certainty; it may have begun about A.D. 1200. Lacking monumental stone architecture and an advanced degree of urbanism, the Chibchas nevertheless achieved a high political and social level of development, whose details—outlined below—were recorded by their Spanish conquerors.

Still another region of significant development after A.D. 1000 was central Venezuela, where different ceramic styles characterized individual phases of sequences of cultures in various districts. In the Lake Valencia Basin in the north, cultural traditions, including ceramic styles, from the middle and lower Orinoco River and from western Venezuela became intermixed, helping to stimulate cultural growth in that area. By A.D. 1500, the region had a large agricultural population organized in chiefdoms, displaying in their towns the beginnings of urban life, social stratification, and formal religion. To the east and north, further diffusions and movements of groups of people continued to bring new influences to the West Indies. Between approximately A.D. 1000 and 1500, the islands acquired various traits, including ball courts, carved stone collars possibly used in ball games, and the inlaying of shell and gold in wood carvings, that had probably originated in Middle America. Beginning about a century before the arrival of Columbus, Caribs from South America invaded the Lesser Antilles, driving the less warlike Arawaks to islands farther north.

As a whole, the Circum-Caribbean area never progressed as far as the areas to its north and south. While parts of it received traits from both directions, none of its people ever acquired the intricate calendar systems, the knowledge of mathematics and writing, or other major cultural achievements of the Middle Americans, nor did they equal the political organization, military ability, construction, or metallurgy of the Central Andes civilizations.

At the time of the arrival of the Spaniards an enormous variety of foods was in use in the area. The Indians' diets differed, according to the altitude at which they lived. Manioc was the staple of the lowlands. Tropical fruits in profusion, wild plants, yams, sweet potatoes, beans, peanuts, and corn were basic foods in various lowland districts as well as in the middle altitudes. In the highlands, the people raised white and sweet potatoes, quinoa (a small plant whose seeds were made into gruel and whose leaves were cooked), sweet manioc, squash, beans, corn, and tobacco. The farming was often done by men; sometimes they only cleared the land, and the women worked the fields. Among some peoples, the slash-and-burn technique, like that of the Mayas, was used; elsewhere crops were watered by irrigation canals or by flooding, and terracing was employed on hillsides. Fishing and hunting were still important in many areas, and all kinds of wildlife, including rabbits, iguanas, tapirs, deer, peccaries, turtles, caymans, anteaters, rats, and birds, were hunted with nets, bows and arrows, and spears. Domestic animals—Muscovy ducks, dogs, turkeys, and guinea pigs in the northern Andes—were also eaten. A native beer called *chicha* was made from fermented fruits and vegetables.

The people's clothing also varied according to region. Most of the Indians wove cotton, and in the highlands and middle altitudes of Colombia, where tribes traded farther south for articles of llama wool, people supplemented their cotton breechcloths and wrap-arounds with sleeveless tunics, capes, and blankets. Weaving was less developed in northern Venezuela, and in the West Indies Arawaks probably did no weaving at all, but netted or twined cotton and wild fibers into bags, hammocks, and other objects. In Central America, Indians made a thin cloth from the inner bark of certain trees. In the lowlands, little or no clothing was used. People in the mountains of the northern Andes generally lived dispersed in small villages or in scattered houses of stone or of wattle and daub walls and thatched roofs. The villagers were affiliated with nearby political or religious centers, and when warfare threatened, they gathered in special hilltop forts. In the lower country, people lived closer together, working jointly on the construction of irrigation works and often clustering in palisaded villages of 1,000 to 3,000 inhabitants. The lowland houses, which sometimes accommodated several related families, were made of poles and thatch, and in watery areas and lagoons were frequently built on piles above the water. (Seeing such villages on the northern coast of South America induced Amerigo Vespucci to name the area Venezuela, or Little Venice). Elsewhere, houses were usually arranged around a central plaza containing a temple and the homes of the chiefs and nobles.

Furnishings of the homes included carved wooden stools, hammocks, and platforms used as beds.

Arts and technologies were highly developed, although they were generally inferior to those of Middle America and the Central Andes. In Panama, the Cuna Indians produced beautiful pottery in various shapes, painted with geometric and animal designs in three or four colors. In the northern Andes of Colombia and in Panama, gold and copper, mined in different regions by full-time laborers, were fashioned by professional artisans into effigies, containers, idols, paraphernalia for warriors and temples, and brilliant articles of personal decoration and ornamentation, including nose and lip plugs, necklaces, masks, beads, crowns, and chest plates, for chiefs and religious leaders. Outstanding lapidary work was done with precious stones, especially emeralds from Colombia, and in many areas colored stones, used as decoration, were inserted into incisions in the face. Feather mosaics and other featherwork were produced, and fine products were turned out in copper, tumbaga, shell, bone, and teeth. Markets were numerous, and many parts of the area were linked in trade and communication. Roads ran through the mountains, spanned gorges by suspension bridges, and stretched from village to village in the lowlands. A sea trade, plied by dugout canoes of different sizes, existed among the islands of the west Indies and between the islands and the northern coast of South America, as well as along the eastern coast of Central America and Mexico.

The chiefdoms—the dominant type of society throughout the area—differed in many particulars, but in general they were characterized by some kind of class structure, priests, state gods, and the organization of at least several communities into small states or federations. Many of them were composed of four social classes. At the top were the rulers, whom the Spaniards called by the Arawak word *caciques*. Below the rulers was a class of nobles, who included lesser chiefs or rulers of villages or territories within the chiefdom, religious functionaries, noted warriors, and probably artisans. Then came commoners, the largest class, made up of the basic farming groups, and, finally, came the slaves. The rulers possessed great authority. They were often considered semidivine, and usually had power of life and death over all their subjects. They lived lives of luxury, wore fine garments and jewelry, presided in state on beautifully carved wooden stools, and could have many wives. When they died, their wives and retainers—stupefied by drugs or poisoned—and their rich possessions were usually buried with them. Chieftainship was hereditary only in the more highly organized regions. Among the nobles, there was movement upward by men who acquired wealth or military fame. Commoners supported the nobility with economic services or with tribute; however, commoners were often related to members of the noble class, and the gulf between the two groups was not always great. Slaves were usually captives, and were not generally used as laborers. Most of the males were displayed as a form of wealth, or were ultimately sacrificed, while women were kept as concubines.

Many of the chiefdoms, particularly in Central America and Colombia, embraced a priest-temple-idol complex. The classes of priests, who were sometimes hereditary, conducted public ceremonials, usually accompanied by human sacrifices and bloody rites, in state temples that housed the idols of the gods. Many of the temples were large structures raised on mounds, but in some localities the idols, made of wood, stone, or gold, were kept in the homes of the chiefs. The most common local deities were those of the sun, moon, and jaguar. In some areas, natural objects and sites, like mountains and lakes, were considered sacred and were even deified. Many chiefdoms possessed both shamans and priests, or only shamans. The latter, unlike the state priests, usually served individuals, interceding with the supernatural, effecting cures, and foretelling the future.

The largest and most highly organized chiefdom in the area was that of the Chibchas in the highlands of central Colombia. Its people, numbering about 300,000, were spread over a large territory, but were divided into five political units, each one ruled by an authoritative chief. The largest unit, Zipa, the area of present-day Bogotá, maintained a precarious rule over the whole, but the different divisions sometimes raided each other for tribute or otherwise contended for power. The Chibcha chiefs were accorded great respect. They were borne in gold-covered litters, preceded by attendants who threw flowers in their pathways, and were approached with bowed head and face averted. They lived sumptuously in wooden "palaces," wore ornate dress and jewelry, and were supported by taxes in labor, cloth, and other commodities levied on the commoners. Succession was through the female line, and the son of a ruler's sister inherited the position. But inheritance of property was through the male line, going from a ruler to his own son. Each political division of the Chibcha realm had its own temples and hereditary priesthoods, and ceremonies were accompanied by the sacrifice of victims, who were often small children purchased by traders from non-Chibcha tribes. Before their sacrifice, the children were housed in the temples where they were regarded as sacred. At puberty they were taken to the Temple of the Sun and, in rites reminiscent of those of the Aztecs, had their hearts cut out in offering to the gods. Not all sacrifices were of humans: parrots were often taught to speak and were then killed. Handsome textiles and glittering goldwork were also used as offerings, particularly in the state temples.

Agriculture was carried on intensively, and Chibcha farmers raised corn, quinoa, white and sweet potatoes, beans, squash, sweet manioc, and tobacco. Trade was conducted with lowland chiefdoms for tropical fruits, salt, cotton, precious stones, and metal. The Chibchas fought political wars among themselves, and also raided non-Chibcha peoples for human trophies. The warriors carried lances, spears and spear throwers, clubs, slings, and wooden shields.

Elsewhere in the Circum-Caribbean area, traits varied. Many native armies, according to the Spaniards, were accompanied by women who participated in the fighting. Cannibalism and grisly treatment of the bodies of captives were widespread. Some groups ate their captives to acquire valor, others simply because they relished human flesh above animal meat. In northern Venezuela, individual warriors and chiefs gained status from the possession of human heads, teeth, hands, entrails, and even the entire skins of enemies, stuffed and displayed as trophies on special benches in the house.

In contrast to most other groups, the Arawaks of the Greater Antilles were relatively peaceful. Human sacrifice played no role in their religion, which took a form different from that of other chiefdoms. The Arawaks possessed personal guardian spirits, whose powers increased according to the status of their human protégés. The spirits of the chief were the gods of the tribe. The spirits were represented by a hierarchy of idols, called zemis, which were believed to possess the supernatural powers of the spirits and were symbolized by three-pointed stones carved with elaborate designs. Some of the zemis were human, and others animal. The Indians housed the figures of zemis in temples, but brought them out at times of worship and ceremony, which occurred on slab-lined ceremonial ball courts and dance plazas and in caves.

In the eastern Bolivian lowlands and the nearby Mato Grosso, farther south in the South American continent, it is interesting that there were also a few chiefdoms—those of the Majos, Baures, Manasís, and Paressís—whose essentially tropical forest way of life contained elements similar to those of the Indians of the Circum-Caribbean area. Many of those southern communities were autonomous, ruled by hereditary leaders of authority; but some of them became integrated with others in federations. Intensive agriculture, village deities represented by idols, shamans who served as priests as well as oracular functionaries, and the use of the chief's house as the center of a village's religious activities were all somewhat like the characteristics of the chiefdoms of the Circum-Caribbean area. Whether early connections had existed between the peoples of the two regions, however, is not known.

The Spanish conquest of the Circum-Caribbean area, commencing with Columbus's discovery of the New World in 1492, destroyed the Indians' culture and institutions. Whole groups of Indians were killed or swept away by disease. As the chiefdoms disintegrated, survivors melted into the new European-dominated life, or disappeared into relatively inaccessible regions, reverting to more primitive levels of existence. Within a century after the arrival of the Spaniards, the chiefdoms, with their social classes, religions, and skills, were gone. Even the Indians who continued to dwell in the same geographic locations had deteriorated to the level of tropical forest village farmers or nomadic hunters and gatherers. Some of them have existed on that level until today.

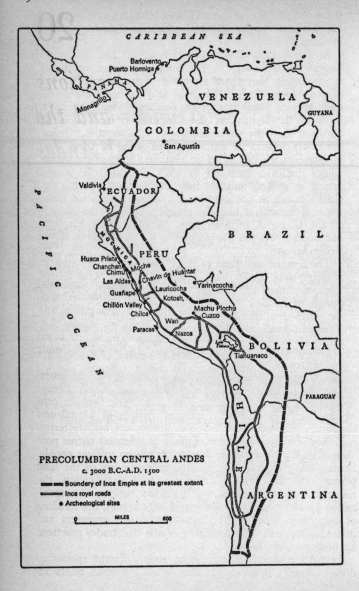

PRECOLUMBIAN CENTRAL ANDES
c. 3000 B.C.-A.D. 1500

━━━ Boundary of Inca Empire at its greatest extent
═══ Inca royal roads
● Archeological sites

MILES
0 ———————————— 600

20

Indian Civilizations of Ecuador and the Central Andes

ALONG THE ECUADOREAN AND PERUVIAN COAST OF WEST
South America and in the cool, rainy highland basins
of the Andes, in Ecuador, Peru, and Bolivia, there
flourished Indian civilizations rivaled only by those of Middle America. The Inca Empire, found and destroyed by the
Spaniards, was the last of them. Rich, accomplished, and
highly militaristic—one of the most tightly regimented societies the world has ever known—the Inca civilization was,
in fact, the final sunburst of some 6,000 years of development, during which a succession of regional states, based
upon intensive agriculture, arose from a beginning of simple
and scattered farm villages.

The area is seemingly inhospitable, characterized by coastal
deserts from which the high, rugged Andes chain sweeps
precipitously upward. Indians could farm only two per cent
of the land, yet by highly efficient systems of coastal and
highland agriculture, employing irrigation and hillside terracing, they made it support eventually the densest native population in the hemisphere, approximately 10 million people.
During the millennia, as well, the intensive use of the land
permitted—as in Middle America—social stratification; the
rise of complex religious and political institutions; the organization of widespread commerce and large armies; the building
of huge and varied public works by skilled engineers and
massed labor; and the flourishing of arts and trades practiced
by numerous specialists.

The Andeans raised more than sixty different species of
domesticated plants. In addition, coastal peoples made in-

tensive use of rich sea resources, and on the coast and in the altiplano—the high plateaus and valleys among the towering Andes—the Indians herded llamas and alpacas, which they used as sacrificial animals and beasts of burden as well as sources of meat and wool. Domesticated dogs, ducks, and guinea pigs were also eaten, while trade with the tropical forest peoples of the interior provided additional foods native to that eastern lowland region.

The mountains supplied a wealth of metals—gold, silver, copper, and tin—which the Andeans utilized in developing an early and highly skilled metallurgy. The weaving and use of wool was unique among pre-Columbian American Indians. Barter trade was well organized, linking together from at least 500 B.C. various regions of the coast, the highlands, and the interior tropical lowlands, and making many regional raw materials and products, as well as foods, available to different parts of the area. Engineering and basic building technologies were developed by comparatively early peoples, but were brought to a climax by the Incas. Stonework was spectacular. As many as 30,000 people at a time labored on forts and other public works, constructing them of massive stones, which they often moved for many miles on rollers from their places of origin, and then edged and fitted together so perfectly that a knife blade cannot be inserted between them today. Roads, extending for hundreds of miles, were graded, paved, and bridged, and whole mountainsides were faced almost from top to bottom with rows of stone-lined terraces on which crops were planted. The Central Andeans fell short of the Middle Americans in some intellectual accomplishments; they had no system of writing, for instance, nor did they possess complex calendars. During one period, however, the people of the Mochica Culture drew patterns on beans that may have had symbolic significance, and at a later time the Peruvians developed the use of knotted strings called *quipus* to make simple arithmetical tallies.

The principal tribes in the area included the Caras, Paltas, Puruhás, and Cañars of the Ecuadorean highlands; the Esmeraldas and Mantas of the Ecuadorean coast; and the Chancas, Urus, Huancas, and Collas of Peru and Bolivia. The languages they spoke were principally Quechua, Aymara, and Uru of the Andean-Equatorial superstock.

For many years, the area has attracted archeologists. New and important discoveries are frequently made, and it is evident that the region's pre-Columbian history, still far from thoroughly known, will require periodic reevaluations. Until recently, little, especially, was known of the area's earliest inhabitants, although it seemed apparent that they must have been nomadic hunters, gatherers, and fishermen who moved from the north into both the coastal and highland areas. Recent discoveries in the Chillón Valley on the central coast of Peru, north of Lima, have laid bare a sequence of cultures, the earliest of which may be from 12,500 to 14,000 years old. Its people fashioned small quartzite tools—scrapers, perforators, and burins, sharpened by percussion. (Burins of a somewhat similar age have been found, also, in other parts of Peru, in Chile, and, of a somewhat later age, in Ecuador.) Beginning about 11,500 years ago, or slightly earlier, people in the Chillón Valley seem to have made thick, pointed, bifacial tools, large scrapers, and percussion-flaked spearpoints. Similar artifacts, notably chopping tools and spearpoints that were coarsely flaked on both sides by percussion, have been found in northwestern Venezuela, elsewhere in Peru, in Ecuador, in the desert of northern Chile, and in the Andes of northwestern Argentina, and have led some archeologists to believe that they were fashioned by people of a single widespread cultural stage that existed between approximately 11,500 and 9,000 years ago (although not necessarily at the same time everywhere) throughout the Andes. This stage has been termed the Andean Biface Horizon.

After 9,000 years ago, hunters in Peru's Chillón Valley region seem to have established camps during the winter in fog-shrouded patches of vegetation, called *lomas*, near the coast. In these areas each winter, when the *lomas* were greenest, they lived existences based on the gathering of seeds, wild grasses, wild potatoes, snails, and lizards, and hunted deer and guanaco. Archeologist Edward P. Lanning has traced a development through a sequence of cultures for some 4,500 years in this area, during which the people continued as hunter-gatherers, living each winter in the *lomas*. By about 4,500 years ago, agriculture had appeared in the region, and the people were growing cotton and making twined cotton textiles.

Nearby, meanwhile, on a beachsite known as Pampa, a new group of people seem to have intruded in the area sometime between 5,600 and 4,500 years ago. They hunted birds and sea lions, fished, gathered mussels, clams, and wild plants, and cultivated two species of squash. By 4,500 years ago, the first permanent villages appear to have been established in the region; after that, agricultural products increased, surplus food provided a base for an increase in population and for an organization of society that enabled the rearing of public works in the area, and a major ceremonial center rose at Chuquitanta.

Elsewhere in the Central Andes, archeological discoveries are beginning to throw more light on the earliest history of the region as a whole. At the Lauricocha caves in the northern Peruvian highlands archeologists have found percussion-chipped artifacts made by hunters 9,500 years ago, and projectile points, scrapers, and other artifacts made about 8,000 years ago. In Peru's southern highlands, caves and shelter sites near Toquepala have given evidence that suggests that hunters were present there, also, about 9,500 years ago. Additional finds of projectile points and other relics have been made at the Ichuna rock shelter in Peru, as well as at Viscachani in Bolivia. These discoveries, together with a few others, including one of projectile points and other obsidian objects of an age estimated variously at between 5,000 and 10,000 years, found at the El Inga site in the Ecuadorean highlands near present-day Quito, suggest a pattern of early nomadic habitation somewhat similar to that of the rest of the hemisphere.

In the highlands, after about 9,500 years ago, people turned increasingly to the gathering of wild plant foods and the hunting of small game. As in Middle America, incipient agriculture at last began. A somewhat similar development occurred in regions along the Ecuadorean and Peruvian coasts. There, people at first were hunters, fishermen, and gatherers of shellfish and wild plants. At length, they learned agriculture and began to settle down in permanent and semi-permanent villages. A number of early agricultural sites have been found, including those at Chilca, Asia, and San Nicolás on the central and southern Peruvian coast, showing evidence of the cultivation of bottle gourds and lima beans, and ranging in age from 6,700 to 5,000 years ago, thus indicating the start of agriculture at a somewhat later time than in Middle America. By 5,000 years ago, various discoveries reveal that the inventory of food crops was increasing, and that the growing of cotton had begun. The introduction of cotton is a mystery. A common belief is that linted cotton reached the Andean coast in some way from Asia about 3000 B.C. and hybridized with the wild, unlinted cotton of the area to produce the distinctive Peruvian cotton which is still grown today.

At any rate, by about 4,500 years ago, sites like those of Huaca Prieta on the northern Peruvian coast and Paracas, San Nicolás, Asia, Pampa, and Chilca on the southern and central coast show a pattern of farming village life in which people grew domesticated gourds, squash, jack beans, chili peppers, and cotton on the watered plains bordering streams. Corn and pottery were still unknown on the Peruvian coast; irrigation was not yet practiced; and sea fishing with nets close to shore, as well as the gathering of shellfish and wild plant foods, were still important. Cotton was twined into textiles with the fingers and was woven with simple, rudimentary weaves; bark cloth was produced; and baskets and mats were made of reeds. People lived in houses of cane poles and grass, some above ground, others semi-subterranean. On the south coast, projectile points and atlatls show that land hunting was practiced. There, too, have been found shellfish hooks, bone tools, and grinding stones.

On the Ecuadorean coast, recent dramatic discoveries have been made by archeologists Emilio Estrada, Clifford Evans, and Betty J. Meggers. In that region, about 5,000 years ago, a highly developed pottery appeared abruptly among a people who subsisted on fishing, the gathering of shellfish and wild plants, a little hunting, and possibly the meager results of incipient agriculture. Numerous and detailed stylistic similarities between this pottery and that of the Jomon Culture, which existed in Japan at the same time, seem to indicate that, somehow, transpacific voyagers, possibly from the southern part of the island of Kyushu, introduced the pottery to Ecuador about 3000 B.C. Estrada, Evans, and Meggers have called the newly revealed Ecuadorean ceramic culture the Valdivia (for the site), noting that it was characterized also by the making of small stone figurines, which were unrelated to the Japanese Jomon Culture, and which were eventually superseded by the making of female figures of clay. Archeologists have long suspected that Asiatic fishermen or seamen made landfalls in the Americas from time to time, introducing transpacific cultural elements to local or regional groups of Indians. Once Asiatic peoples had learned how to build and navigate craft capable of making long distance voyages, such landfalls in the Western Hemisphere, whether deliberate or accidental, could have resulted. The recent discoveries by Estrada, Evans, and Meggers in Ecuador appear to come closest so far to providing proof that contact from Asia did occur.

The making of the so-called Valdivia style of pottery, the oldest yet known in the Americas, took hold on the coast of Ecuador, and soon afterward other pottery, with Valdivia-like traits that suggest its spread from Ecuador, appeared on the northern coast of Colombia (Puerto Hormiga, about 4,875 years ago), the northern Peruvian coast (Guañape, about 4,300 years ago), and Panama (Monagrillo, about 4,090 years ago). Between approximately 4,000 and 3,500 years ago, a new culture, the Machalilla, with a new style of pottery appeared on the Ecuadorean coast. Its place of origin is uncertain, though the people who introduced it may have come from the Pacific coast of Central or Middle America. (On the coast of Guerrero in western Mexico, for instance, archeologists recently discovered the so-called Pox pottery, dated at 4,440 years of age, and seemingly ancestral to pottery in interior Mexico.) At any rate, the people of the newly arrived Machalilla Culture coexisted on the coast of Ecuador with those of the Valdivia Culture until about 3,500 years ago, when the Machalilla group suddenly expanded southward, and the Valdivia people retreated and disappeared. The Machalilla Culture was characterized by higher-quality pottery, including bowls and stirrup-spouted jars. If it did not originate farther north, it soon became linked with Middle American cultures, for almost simultaneously with the disappearance of the Valdivia Culture, certain Middle American elements, including possibly corn, were introduced into the Machalilla Culture, which, with these new elements, is thereafter (1500 B.C.) called the Chorrera Culture. The new traits, principally ceramic forms, obsidian blades, and ear spools in the shape of napkin rings, did not diffuse to the Andean area via Central America, but came by way of long distance sea voyages from the west coast of Middle America. In the Ocós and Conchas phases at La Victoria on the Guatemalan coast, archeologist Michael D. Coe has revealed evidence that the peoples of that area and of the coast of Ecuador were in touch with each other, and apparently exchanging traits, beginning about 1500 B.C., and it now seems probable that the Chorrera Culture of Ecuador resulted from a mating of the earlier Machalilla Culture with elements from Guatemala.

Development in Ecuador accelerated after 1500 B.C. The Chorrera Culture spread over much of the coast and into the

highlands. Population increased, probably as a result of the
introduction of corn, and settlements extended inland, up
fertile river valleys where corn could be planted. A remarkable pottery with thin walls and mirrorlike polished surfaces
—so excellent that archeologists Estrada and Evans pronounced it as having no equal in later Indian cultures—was
produced. Its high quality indicates that craft specialists must
have existed, a premise that, in turn, suggests the presence
also of organized religious systems, and possibly of certain
religious buildings. In succeeding centuries, these developments continued in various parts of Ecuador, leading to the
rise of highly advanced regional cultures after about 500 B.C.

In Peru, meanwhile, the oldest pottery—possibly derived
from Valdivia—has been found, as stated, at Guañape on the
northern coast and dated at 4,300 years old. In Peru's central highlands, the lowest of six levels containing ceramic
relics, dug at Kotosh ("heap of stones" in the Quechua
language), disclosed pottery 3,800 years old, the oldest yet
found in the high country. The pottery's derivation is still
in doubt, but it may reflect a mixture of influences from
Ecuador's Machalilla Culture and from Barlovento on the
northern Colombian coast, where the pottery, in turn, had
been influenced by Ecuadorean Valdivian ware.

Corn, which had reached Ecuador about 1500 B.C., was
present farther south, in villages on the Peruvian central
coast, about a century later and—strangely—at Huaca Prieta
on Peru's northern coast slightly later. For a time, the cultivation of corn gave little impetus to Peruvian development;
then gradually, as population increased, changes occurred.
Villages became larger; house walls were built up of cylindrical or conical lumps of adobe; the loom was invented; small
irrigation works were built by cooperative effort; and many
new crops—some of them, like peanuts, sweet manioc, and
avocados, coming originally by trade with the tropical forest
people of the interior—were introduced. The increasing
dependence on agriculture, stimulated about 900–800 B.C.
by the appearance of a new and improved strain of corn,
resulted in population becoming more concentrated in arable
areas and, at the same time, spreading up fertile river valleys
and across highland farming basins. The establishment of
communities quickened the organization of social and religious systems and gave rise, between approximately 800 B.C.
and 300 B.C., to a period known as that of the Cultist Temple Centers. Culture elements that had a wide inter-Ameri-

can distribution at the time (trade contact, broken apparently after 1200 B.C., seems to have begun again between Middle America and Ecuador after 500 B.C.), including temples, mounds, priests, and the cult of a feline god like that of the Mexican Olmecs, appeared in different regions of the Andean area. The temple mounds became the centers of small theocratic states in which priestly classes presided over religious ceremonies, directed specialists and massed labor, and probably exerted authority over scattered agricultural communities. The temples, built of adobe or stone, were sometimes small platforms and sometimes more elaborate stepped pyramids; they often contained many rooms with ramps, steps, airshafts, passages, clay columns, and carved or painted walls. One of the oldest temple sites, containing a long platform and mounds, is that of Las Aldas on the central coast. Perhaps the best known site of the period, however, is that of Chavín de Huántar in the northern Peruvian highlands. It appears to have been an important ceremonial center to which pilgrims came from other parts of the region to receive inspiration from the cat-god, possibly a puma. The location contains a number of impressive structures, including a large temple of stone masonry 250 feet square at the base and more than 45 feet high, with numerous rooms and interior passages and external walls decorated with carved stone heads.

The flowering of what is known as the Chavín style may owe a debt, in part at least, to the arrival in northern Peru at a somewhat earlier period of certain Olmec influences from Middle America. Olmec elements have been discerned by some archeologists on pre-Chavín pottery and other objects found at sites both on the northern coast and in the central highlands of Peru, and in decoration and shapes of pottery at Chavín itself. At any rate, arts and skills, typified by a Chavín style, now flourished in the Central Andes. Textiles were woven; gold was fashioned into objects of ornamentation; carved earplugs were made; and work was done in bone and stone. Chavín influences spread south through the highlands and to the southern coast at Paracas. Farther south, in the Cuzco and Titicaca basins of the highlands, where Chavín influences apparently did not reach, the people possessed local styles of pottery that have been dated as far back as approximately 1000 B.C.

The period from about 300 B.C. to A.D. 600 witnessed the formation and cultural flowering of a number of regional states whose brilliance produced a truly Classic period in the Central Andes. Technological knowledge increased everywhere, but different regions began to develop their own local art styles and cultural forms. Pottery flourished in the north, with jars modeled in many shapes taken from forms in nature and decorated with white paint. Sometimes figures were mounted on the jar and joined to the spout. In the south, weaving reached a high stage of development. At Cavernas on the Paracas Peninsula on the southern Peruvian coast, and elsewhere in that part of the area, weavers began to use wool, human hair, and maguey fiber. In all sections of the Central Andes, daily life was enriched. Metal workers employed newly invented casting, gilding, and engraving techniques to produce many objects of pure copper or a gold-copper alloy. Silver came into use, and was soon being alloyed with the other metals. More emphasis was placed on clothing, and weavers turned out shirts, shawls, knee-length skirts, belts, turbans, and various kinds of headgear. Flutes and clay panpipes were made to provide music.

Agriculture grew more intensified and diversified, as many new crops appeared. A native beer, *chicha*, was made, and coca leaves, which contain cocaine, were chewed for their narcotic effect. Irrigation works were expanded and became more complex, and, in the highlands, stone-faced farming terraces were constructed on the mountainsides. The population soared in numbers, and new settlements continued to be built. Some of them became towns of a thousand or more houses. Social control, probably theocratic in nature, grew stronger, and huge stepped platforms and round temple substructures with encircling ramps were erected by massed labor. Sometimes each settlement had its own temple; sometimes a single temple mound served a group of settlements. Remains of the temple cults give only scant evidence of the nature of the deities of the time, but in the south the cat-god—a jaguar or puma—seems to have persisted and to have been joined by a "Weeping God," indicated in art styles by a human face with tear streaks extending down the cheeks.

Between 200 B.C. and A.D. 450 the various states increased in number, matured, and flourished, attaining a golden age whose material arts were the finest ever produced in the area and which often equaled, if not surpassed, those of any ancient civilization in the Old World. Agriculture reached its peak of efficiency: almost all arable or irrigable land was brought into production by immense systems of canals, ditches, terraces, and aqueducts and by guano fertilizer, which Indians brought back in balsa rafts from offshore islands. Farmers experimented with hundreds of species of plants and domesticated many new crops, including white potatoes and scores of tropical fruits and vegetables. Population became dense in some areas, and social stratification increased. The huge irrigation systems and immense public works of the period were made possible by centralized state authorities who planned and controlled construction and directed large labor forces. The people did not equal the Middle Americans in pure intellectual achievements, but they attained great practical skills. Peruvian physicians and surgeons at this time were notable herbalists and setters of bones, and they practiced trepanning—successfully removing sections of the skull—on an extensive scale, possibly to cure headaches or disease.

Militarism became strong in the large states of the north, where wars were fought at first for sacrificial victims, human trophies, and the capture of loot, and then increasingly for conquest and expansion of power and influence. Uniformed warriors, accompanied by war dogs and by trumpeters blowing conch shells, went into battle equipped with spears, spear throwers, maces, semi-circular knives, helmets, and shields. A powerful militaristic state of the northern coast was that of the Mochicas who expanded south along the coast. Much can be learned of Mochica daily life from the vast outpouring of Mochica painted and modeled pottery, whose uninhibited, realistic pictures and ceramic figures and scenes show almost every aspect of human life, no matter how intimate. The Mochicas were ruled by warrior priests, who were often depicted in the guise of deities. Beneath them were social and occupational classes of war leaders, state officials, lesser priests, architects, artisans, dancers, musicians, doctors, and various attendants, messengers, and servants. The bulk of the population produced the food, served in the army, and provided labor for the building of state public works.

On the arid southern coast, organized social, political, and religious systems were less developed than in the north. Population was less dense, and there were no large state centers. Religion appears to have been centered on a cult of the dead rather than on a militaristic state cult, and great attention was paid to the elaborate wrapping and burying of mummies. The supreme achievement of the southern coast was the weaving of textiles. Those of Nazca and Paracas are perhaps unsurpassed anywhere in the world. Wool from llamas, alpacas, and possibly vicuñas, along with cotton, was employed in the production of brocades, laces, tapestries, embroidery, and braided work. The textiles were ornamented with polychrome designs, sometimes showing as many as one hundred ninety different hues in a single fabric. Textiles were used for elaborate turbans, togas, and other articles of clothing, and for the wrapping of corpses in mummy bundles.

In Ecuador, during the same period, extreme differences in material culture and in levels of social development existed in various regions. In some places, culture remained relatively simple, still based largely on fishing, gathering, and hunting, and perhaps on limited agriculture. On the other hand, the Bahía Culture (or phase of development), which arose on the coast of Manabí Province, attained a florescent stage, like that of the Classic regional states of Peru. Bahía social and religious systems, technological abilities, and arts, suggested by remains that include large sites with stone-faced platforms, mounds, and water storage reservoirs, place its culture, also, on a level comparable to some of those achieved about the same time by various Classic civilizations in Middle America. Regular contact by sea, in fact, seems to have linked those civilizations with the Ecuadorean coast. The Bahía people, apparently unmilitaristic, were artful navigators and busy traders, and their remains display evidence of many Middle American elements and traits. In addition, about 200 B.C., new objects, including figurines with one leg folded above the other, pottery neck rests, stone and pottery pendants in the shape of tusks, pottery house models with columns and saddle roofs, and other distinctive articles common in eastern Asia at the time, appeared on the Ecuador coast and suggest strongly that transpacific voyagers, once again, arrived there. The objects did not spread far, and it does not seem that the Asiatic influences, if such they were, had a deep or lasting effect on the region's culture.

The concentration of administrative, religious, and military controls in regional states in different parts of the Central Andes area led, after A.D. 600, to further changes. The states had reached limits of growth and exploitation in their own areas, and could expand only at the expense of their neighbors. At the same time, as the more aggressive states conquered others, and extended their influence over wider areas, local styles and free, vigorous artistic expression were replaced by standardized, mass-produced designs and forms. Between approximately A.D. 600 and 1000, a unifying influence extended across large parts of the Central Andes, bringing into existence the first Pan-Andean empire. Created by military conquests of a strong and aggressive cult, this empire seems to have had a base and originating point at Wari, a great walled center in the Ayacucho region of the southern Peruvian highlands. Wari itself appears to have developed through several phases in which it received a succession of influences from elsewhere, including most notably the Nazca region on the south coast and Tiahuanaco, a large town or city in the Titicaca Basin of the southern highlands. Tiahuanaco influences had affected Wari strongly. The former site reached a Classic stage of its own as early as A.D. 600, embracing vast architectural works, including platforms, courts, stairways, stone seats and other forms carved from rock; a large mound surmounted by house sites; a reservoir; a monolithic Gateway of the Sun, hewn from a single stone ten feet high; flat stone carvings of friezes; human statues, generally of men standing rigidly with hands on their stomachs; and other achievements through which ran the theme or motif of the "Weeping God." The Wari conquests spread elements of this style across much of the highlands, including the Cuzco Basin, and northward along the coast, obliterating the styles of the Mochica and other regional states. Pure Tiahuanaco styles, meanwhile, spread southward.

During this period, many roads seem to have been built (presumably for military movements), and much of the population became urbanized. In the Cuzco region and on the central and northern coasts, people moved into big, high-walled cities containing hundreds of homes. The concentrations may have been for defensive purposes, to free more land for cultivation, or to bring labor together where it could be controlled and directed more easily. Wari hegemony, however, was relatively short-lived. The cause of the dissolution of its power and of the loss of favor of the dominant Tiahuanaco elements in its culture is not known. But by approximately A.D. 1000 the use of Tiahuanaco styles and themes had ended, and a number of strong regional kingdoms, headed by powerful local rulers, were arising in the wake of the vanished empire.

The most vigorous state in the north was the Chimu kingdom, a resurgence of the old Mochica state. Chanchan, its major administrative and ceremonial center, covered about six square miles and had a population of about 50,000. Elsewhere along the coast, including Ecuador, the rulers of lesser kingdoms exerted power from urban centers over many river valleys or large areas. In the highlands, local chiefdoms, less highly organized than the coastal kingdoms, were established and, in places, were linked in regional alliances. Although the period was marked generally by new building, resting on the increased organization and control of labor, there were few new inventions save in metallurgy. True bronze was discovered and widely used, and in Ecuador's Esmeraldas Province platinum was fashioned into miniature jewelry. The working of platinum in Ecuador was unique among American Indians.

One of the small regional chiefdoms was that of a group of *ayllus*, or family lineages, of Quechua-speaking Indians in the Cuzco Basin of the southern highlands. Their ruler was called the Inca, and the people are known today as Incas from the title of their kings. Tracing their descent from the semi-mythical Manco Capac, who supposedly ruled about A.D. 1200, the Incas began gradually to dominate the peoples around them. By 1438, under the leadership of the Inca Viracocha, they had established rule over a large area surrounding Cuzco. During the next half century the military and political genius of three successive Incas was visited on all parts of the Central Andes. In a series of rapid conquests the Inca Pachacuti and his son, Topa Inca Yupanqui, extended Inca rule from Ecuador to Chile and into portions of Bolivia and Argentina. By 1525, a third conqueror, Huayna Capac, had consolidated the Inca Empire of approximately 7 million people in an area of some two thousand miles from north to south, and from the Pacific coast to the edge of the interior Montaña, the jungle foothills east of the Andes. The conquests were most successful where established states and regimented societies, with strong central authority and class structures, had already existed. There, the conquered peoples more readily accepted a new set of rulers for an old one. But in less developed regions, the simple villagers of the Montaña and the relatively unorganized farmers and herders in Chile would have required large Inca garrisons. These were not worth the effort, and the Incas never succeeded in enrolling them fully in their empire.

The Inca conquests were high points of American generalship and statesmanship. Persuasion was mixed with military threat and action and with the use of diplomacy, intrigue, and alliances with peoples already subjugated. As soon as conquest was accomplished, dictatorial methods were employed to consolidate gains. The Incas forcibly moved troublesome populations to safer areas, and settled loyal peoples among the disaffected. Former rulers, permitted to retain symbols of status and wealth but not of independence, were appointed as regional and local administrators if they were loyal. The adoption of the Inca language, Quechua, of the Inca cult of the sun, and of Inca customs was forced on the entire empire, and all classes were strictly regimented. Even history was retold; although the Incas had no written language by which to record history, they submerged and obliterated the lore of earlier peoples and enforced the adoption of their own version of the past.

Absolutism also characterized the Inca economy. The government owned and controlled the entire means of production and distribution. Individuals could own neither private property nor productive capital. The Inca emperor held title to all land and allotted it among the religious institutions, the state, and the commoners. The latter worked all three types of allotments: the head of a family, assisted by his wife and children, labored first on a temple plot, then on a government plot, and finally on his own. State officials maintained a census and a careful accounting of the situation of each family. The sick, crippled, needy, and victims of famines were fed from public granaries, which stored surpluses from the government plots. Government officials also supervised the movement of crops from region to region so that various foods reached all parts of the empire. In addition to their work for the temples and the government, commoners were subject to *mita* assignments, or drafts of their labor, for military service, or for work on state construction projects.

The Inca emperor, his royal family, and their descendants were at the summit of political and religious life. The emperor, possessing absolute power, was worshipped as the direct descendant of the sun and was so exalted that only his full sister could marry him. Members of the royal family headed a huge hierarchy of officials and bureaucrats, who controlled the army, the economic system, and the religious institutions. The empire was divided into four quarters, and each quarter, in turn, was divided into provinces that conformed roughly to previous states or cultural regions.

Each province had its own capital and was further split into two or three political divisions made up of a number of *ayllus*, as the local communities of related lineages were known. Most of them were scattered farm settlements, but some *ayllus* were gathered into single towns or within compounds in walled cities.

The noble class, including the military leaders, priests, and civil administrators who ran the empire for the Inca, lived in pomp and splendor. Their homes and personal possessions were incredibly luxurious, and food, services, and a wealth of goods were supplied to them by artisans and commoners. They possessed several wives, as well as concubines; they dressed in fine clothes of alpaca and vicuña wool; and the emperor permitted many of them to ornament themselves with gold and silver, including large cylindrical earplugs. They were borne in litters, sat in state on carved stools, and hunted in royal preserves. When they died, they were buried with their wives and retainers, who were given a stupefying potion and then strangled.

There were almost no technological inventions or improvements from previous times. Agriculture was intensified, if possible, but the same domesticated plants and systems of irrigation and terracing were used. Tools, weapons, and utensils were those developed in earlier periods. Magnificent palaces, temples, forts, and other public works were built, the stonework perhaps being better than ever before. Many roads and bridges were also constructed; but humans and llamas still carried burdens, and the wheel remained unknown.

Religious life was centered on the worship of the god Viracocha, the supreme deity, believed to be a bearded, white-skinned man who had created other gods, as well as men and animals, and who had given the people their possessions and knowledge. The sun-god, Inti, who was the direct ancestor of the emperors, was the second most important deity. Others were the thunder- and moon-gods. In addition, certain stars, animals, lakes, mountains, and caves were worshipped as containing supernatural power, and hundreds of objects and places were regarded as *huacas*, or sacred shrines. The principal temples were used for ceremonies to the imperial gods, although temples generally were not employed for public worship but were the residences of priests and noble virgins, as well as repositories for images of the deities.

The totalitarian nature of the Inca Empire, with all power at its head, was an important contributing factor to its sudden end. In 1532, Francisco Pizarro landed on the coast with a small army of Spaniards, whom many of the Indians regarded at first as supernatural beings. After marching inland, the white invaders treacherously seized the emperor Atahualpa, used him to force the payment of a vast ransom in gold, and then murdered him. With the fountainhead of its entire political and religious system suddenly gone, the Indian empire was helpless before the newcomers. There was no clear rule concerning the emperor's successor, and three years passed before the Incas could organize an effective opposition. By that time it was too late, and the entrenched Spaniards suppressed the revolt. A large part of the population retreated to less accessible regions in the interior and founded a Neo-Inca Empire that lasted for several decades. But in 1572 it too was destroyed, and Indian power was at an end everywhere in the area.

21

The Indians of the
Southern Andes

I N THE AREA SOUTH OF THE CENTRAL ANDES, INCLUDING
northern and central Chile and northwestern Argentina,
lived Indian tribes whose cultures, varying regionally, contained mixtures of elements and influences that had come to
them from both the Central Andes and the tropical forests
east of the Andes. Largely because of terrain obstacles, the
peoples of the Southern Andes fell short of attaining the
organizational or technological levels of the Central Andeans.
In places, population became fairly large; but the ability to
develop intensive agriculture was more limited by nature
than farther north, and towns remained relatively small,
never achieving the status of urban centers. Similarly, political, social, and religious systems were generally less developed
than those of the Central Andeans; architecture and building
was less impressive; and specialized skills and arts, while
notable in some regions, were as a whole on a lower plane.

Immediately south of the Central Andes were Atacameño
Indians of the Macro-Chibchan linguistic superstock. They
lived in small, isolated groups along a narrow strip on the
coast and in a few watered oases in a broad belt of one of
the world's most formidable deserts, the Atacama, extending
from southern Peru and northern Chile across the mountains
and into northwestern Argentina. To their south, inhabiting
the steppes east and west of the Andes, were Diaguitas,
farmers and llama herders whose town dwellings resembled
those of the Pueblo Indians of the U. S. Southwest. South of
the Argentina Diaguitas were Huarpes, principally hunters
and gatherers, while the mild valleys of central Chile were
occupied by a large population of Araucanians, farmers and
herders of the Andean-Equatorial language superstock. In

most parts of the area, people grew the same crops as those in the Central Andes, and they domesticated llamas. They constructed houses, public buildings, and ceremonial structures of stone; did fine work in pottery, wood, and metals; and carried on a widespread trade. But they lacked even the priest-temple-idol cults, the hereditary classes, and the drive to federation and conquest that were present among the chiefdoms of the Circum-Carribbean region north of the Central Andes.

Archeological work has revealed that very early hunters, gatherers, and fishermen were present in the area and left remains—some of which may be 12,000 or more years old— of percussion chipped tools of a Pre-Projectile Point Stage at Ghatchi in northern Chile and in the Ampajango area of northwestern Argentina. Lanceolate projectile points, dated at about 8,000 years of age, have been found at Inti-huasi Cave and at the Ayampitín site, both in Argentina; at Ghatchi and Zuniquena in Chile; and elsewhere. Of the same age are manos and milling stones, discovered also at Intihuasi and Ayampitín, and indicating a reliance on the gathering of wild plants. With the passing of time, collecting became more important throughout the area, although hunting of small game continued. Triangular points, making their earliest appearance about 5,000 to 6,000 years ago, have been found in many places, associated with grinding implements connected with the gathering of plants and possibly with the beginnings of agriculture.

When the domestication of plants actually began in the area is not known. Sometime between 500 B.C. and the start of the Christian Era, influences that probably originated in the Central Andean highlands diffused into northwestern Argentina, introducing types of pottery, rudimentary metallurgy, the domesticated llama, and possibly the cultivation of crops, including potatoes, quinoa, and perhaps corn. The development of regional cultures thereafter is imperfectly known. During what is called the Early Ceramic Period, from the first introduction of pottery to about A.D. 700, a number of ceramic styles reflected the existence of a succession of different cultures, some of them containing traits and influences from southern Bolivia, some from the river valleys and tropical forests on the eastern side of the Andes, and some from coastal Peru (by direct sea contact between the Peruvian and Chilean coasts). In some places, the various components—including stone sculpture, ceremonial platforms and terraces, settlement patterns of small houses around a patio, grooved axes, a feline cult, pipes, burial urns, egg-shaped slingstones, and polychrome pottery—met and mixed.

In the Middle Ceramic Period (A.D. 700–1000), influences from the Tiahuanaco area of the Central Andean highlands became pronounced in parts of northern Chile and northwestern Argentina. Pottery, metallurgy, and woodwork in one Chilean region so closely resembled Tiahuanaco production that some archeologists suspect the presence there of a colony from the Central Andes. In Argentina, this period saw also the flowering and decline of the Aguada Culture, characterized by styles in art using motifs of the cat cult as well as representations of human beings in large headdresses; the employment of bronze; the making of polychrome pottery and mosaics of stone on wood and stone on stone; and the presence of many elements from Tiahuanaco or other Central Andean sources.

The Late Ceramic Period (A.D. 1000–1450) witnessed the arrival in northwestern Argentina of strong influences from the tropical forest area that seem to have overwhelmed and obliterated many of the earlier elements that had come from the Central Andes, including the cat cult and types of pottery. For a time, communal pit houses, like those in forest dwelling areas, became common. The bow and arrow was widely used, replacing the atlatl, or spear thrower, in many regions. Metallurgy became more advanced, and pottery styles changed. Gradually, communal pit houses were replaced by small stone buildings. Warfare appears to have spread, and fortresses were built in almost every region. After 1450, the Incas conquered some parts of the area and spread new traits to many of the existing cultures. When the Spaniards arrived, they found several different ways of Indian life present there.

In the north, the Atacameños dwelled in widely separated and autonomous villages located wherever there was water. Along the Chilean coast, small groups pursued a precarious existence by fishing and gathering shellfish. In the inland desert, other groups farmed at oases, using irrigation ditches and implements similar to those employed in the Central Andes and raising the same crops, although in less variety. Agriculture was supplemented by hunting, llama herding, and wild-food gathering. The Atacameños maintained extensive trade across desert routes with the Incas and the Diaguita Indians, and they probably copied technical and artistic styles of both peoples in producing their own out-standing arts and crafts.

Settlements were generally small, and each village was composed of a group of related families. The construction of walls and fortifications and the presence of leather armor and weapons in archeological finds indicates that warfare, probably defensive in character, was fairly common. In the western section, the wealthier Atacameño towns might have drawn attacks by Diaguitas and Aymaras from the Bolivian highlands, and the Incas occupied part of the Atacameño territory for a time. There is no evidence of an organized religious system that included temples or idols, but burial remains suggest that important religious observances and rites centered around the dead.

The Diaguitas, who lived south of the Atacameños, are best known through study of one of their subgroups, the Calchaquis, who inhabited northwestern Argentina. They were a warlike people who dwelled in two kinds of villages: unprotected clusters of houses arranged in streets along streams, protected by a separate fortified retreat on a nearby hill; and walled, fortified settlements that did not require a separate fortress. Most of the structures were built of stone, and each village was autonomous, although military coopera-tion often existed between the settlements. The Diaguitas' villages of stonewalled houses with adjoining rooms, as well as their ceramics and other traits that were reminiscent of the Pueblo culture of the U. S. Southwest, showed strong influences from the Central Andes. They built agricultural terraces but practiced little or no irrigation. They raised llamas and perhaps vicuñas, and wove wool into superb tex-tiles of many colors. Their pottery, often influenced by Peruvian forms, was outstanding and original in design, and they were accomplished metallurgists, who cast copper and bronze crescent-shaped knives, star-headed clubs, chisels, and tweezers, and made bells of gold and silver. Like the Pueblos, they feared witchcraft, were quick to charge sorcery, and engaged in interfamily feuds.

Warfare seems to have been frequent in pre-Columbian times, and early white chroniclers reported that the Diaguitas accorded prestige to outstanding warriors, tortured captives, and cut off enemy heads as trophies. They fought bravely for a long time against the Spaniards and were not fully conquered until the second half of the seventeenth century. Several of their groups were deported to mines in the

Peruvian highlands, and others were resettled in Buenos Aires. As a result of these actions of the white man, the tribe today is extinct.

Chile's best-known tribe, the Araucanians of the central part of the country, occupied territory more favorable for farming, and their agriculture supported a denser population, estimated to have been between 500,000 and 1,500,000 at the time of the arrival of the Spaniards. Nevertheless, they did not possess the advanced social, political, or religious institutions of the Central Andes, which had failed to spread to them across the desert to their north. They had no large towns but lived in small, autonomous hamlets composed of several family lineages and located near cultivated fields, which in a country of adequate rainfall required little or no irrigation.

The Araucanians comprised three divisions: the Picunches, Mapuches, and Huilliches, who occupied the northern, central, and southern zones of their territory, respectively. The Picunches lived along river valleys in small clusters of thatch-roofed houses built of stones and adobe or of mud-plastered wickerwork. Agricultural work was done by large, cooperative groups. Each settlement was autonomous, under a single hereditary chief, but in wartime neighboring settlements sometimes joined under the most powerful leader. Shamans and certain persons who had acquired surplus wealth were accorded prestige in something of the beginnings of a status system. The Incas conquered the Picunches easily, but maintained only a brief rule over them. After the Spanish conquest, the Picunches managed for a short time to unite in armies of several thousand men under a single leadership. They raided Spanish garrisons but were soon forced to capitulate.

The population of the Mapuches and Huilliches was much larger than that of the Picunches. They practiced a slash-and-burn agriculture and raised a large variety of crops. In the colder areas of the south, potatoes grew better than corn and were more important in the people's diet. The Indians who lived along the coast hunted, fished, and trapped, and most of the people kept huge herds of llamas. Baskets, nets, and cordage were made; excellent colored blankets were produced; and fine work was done in stone, pottery, and woodwork. Dugouts, reed balsa rafts, and planked canoes, which may have been acquired in relatively recent times from contacts with Polynesian peoples, were used along the coast. House styles varied from one region to another, but dwellings were usually made of pole and thatch and were similar to those of tropical forest village farmers, whom the Araucanians also resembled in their family system and in their possession of such items as wooden mortars and pestles. Households generally sheltered families related through the male line, and each large family group, whether living in one house or divided among many, was autonomous. Kinship heads, called *lonkos,* were accorded respect and authority; they initiated the agricultural and cooperative projects. Feuding and intersettlement raids were frequent, usually occurring over murder, trespass, or other incitements. Captives were sometimes adopted into settlements or employed as laborers, but more often they were slain, and their leg and arm bones were made into flutes.

The Araucanians prayed in public ceremonies and private rites to a supreme deity, or creator god, as well as to a number of lesser spirits. Shamans, who were often women, appealed to supernatural helpers to assist them in curing and warding off death. Certain shamanistic practices, unknown elsewhere in South America, were similar to those of Siberia and the Arctic: they included drumming on a tambourine, wearing the clothing of the opposite sex, and practicing ventriloquism and sleight of hand during curing rites.

The southern Araucanians were never completely conquered by the Spaniards. They adopted the horse soon after the whites introduced the animal in the region, and under powerful war leaders fought the Spaniards and Chileans on almost equal terms from 1541 to 1883. Their courage and tactical skill were celebrated in an epic poem, *La Araucana,* written by a Spanish soldier named Alonso de Ercilla y Zúñiga who had fought against them. The Chilean government subjugated them finally toward the end of the nineteenth century and placed them on reservations. About 200,000 Araucanians live in Chile today.

22

The South American Tropical Forest Tribes

From the Colombian and Venezuelan coasts of northern South America to Paraguay and northeastern Argentina, and from the Atlantic coast of Brazil westward to the eastern slopes of the Andes, were a multitude of tribes that lived in small villages in the humid, tropical forests and existed principally by growing various crops and by exploiting resources of the rivers. Many features of their culture, including pole and thatch houses, palisaded villages, types of basketry and pottery, hammocks, loom weaving, bark cloth, dugout canoes, and certain staple foods like manioc, were shared with more advanced peoples of the Circum-Caribbean cultural area, some of whom, in the north, were their close neighbors. In the Montaña on the eastern flank of the Andes, as well as in parts of Bolivia, moreover, several tropical forest tribes possessed a few material culture elements, including platform beds and the belt loom, that were derived from the high civilizations of the Central Andes. But the relatively small amount of arable land and the rapid decline of soil fertility under leaching rains in the forest tribes' jungle environment prevented the production of surpluses and the growth of dense populations. With a way of life in which villages remained small, and were moved frequently to new plots of farming land, the people did not develop the social, religious, and political institutions, the class differentiations, or the occupational specialist groups that arose in the Circum-Caribbean and Central Andes areas.

The culture of the tropical forest tribes was characterized generally by simple village societies of small kinship and community groups that lived mainly along rivers and coasts, cultivated tropical roots and plants, fished and hunted, and in many cases were warlike and cannibalistic. They included members of many different linguistic families. In Colombia, Venezuela, and the Guianas (sometimes not far distant from better situated farming groups that were able to develop chiefdoms characteristic of the Circum-Caribbean area) were Arawakans and Caribans, including Camaracotós, Palicurs, and Guayapés. Arawakan tribes were also in eastern Peru and southwestern Brazil, and Columbus found tropical forest Caribs in the Lesser Antilles, which those Indians had invaded from northern South America beginning about a century before the arrival of the Spaniards. Tupian-speakers of the Andean-Equatorial language superstock included Mundurucús, Parintintins, and others on the lower Amazon; Tupinambás in a long narrow area along the Brazilian coast; Guaranís and Chiriguanos in Paraguay; and others on the eastern side of the Bolivian Andes. Ge tribes lived in interior Brazil; Jívaroans, Panoans, and others were in the Montaña; a patchwork of different language groups occupied the upper tributaries of the northwest and southwest portions of the vast Amazon Basin and were in eastern Bolivia; and Chibchan-speaking Mosquito Indians and other forest tribes inhabited lowland regions of Central America.

The history of the Indians' cultural development in this huge area is still poorly known. Some archeologists have done considerable work in the South American tropical forests, but they have been few in number. Moreover, they have been handicapped by the formidable rain-forest terrain and by the fact that many prehistoric relics of wood and other materials have perished in the wet climate. Although finds so far have been, in general, in widely separated areas, some information has been gathered, and more is being acquired each year. Many parts of the area appear, initially, to have been inhabited by small groups of hunters, fishermen, and gatherers. Evidence of the presence of early people too primitive to fashion thin projectile points is scant, although archeologist Alex Krieger assigns some finds of crudely made tools at various sites in southern Brazil, Uruguay, and northeastern Argentina to a Pre-Projectile Point Stage of development. Finds of projectile points, blades, and choppers fashioned by early hunters have been made at a number of scattered sites in savannas near rivers in eastern Venezuela and the Guianas, but the oldest relics dated so far come from caves and rock shelters near Lagoa Santa in eastern Brazil and in various *sambaquís*, or shell mounds, along the continent's eastern coast, especially between Rio de Janeiro and Buenos Aires. At Lagoa Santa, where archeologists have found human skeletal remains, artifacts, and the bones of extinct animals, the age of the human remains and artifacts has long been in dispute. Recent dating with carbon-14, however, indicates an age of about 10,000 years for the human remains. Artifacts found in the shell middens show a sequence of cultural stages, ranging from approximately 7,500 to 1,500 years in age. The oldest relics are crudely chipped artifacts; those of the more recent time periods include bone tools, polished stone axes, and shell ornaments. Finally, in the interior of southern Brazil, archeologists have found stone arrow points, axes, scrapers, and bone awls and needles of primitive hunters and gatherers who seem to have been in that area as early as 6,500 years ago.

For millennia, development was probably slow. Then, from time to time, different regions were invaded by newcomers with new ideas and traits that led to changes. In the Amazon and Orinoco basins, where prehistoric developments are best known, the Indians' cultural growth—following the period of the hunters and gatherers—has been divided by archeologist Clifford Evans into three general stages. The first one, which he terms the incipient agricultural stage, was characterized by the appearance of small villages of people who farmed a little, but still placed their main dependence for food on hunting, fishing, and gathering. During this stage, also, people made their first pottery. Some progress has been made in discerning the way in which agriculture spread through at least a part of the area. Similar pottery of a so-called Zoned Hachure Horizon Style (for a way of decoration of the pottery), found in eastern Peru, on the middle Amazon, and on Marajó Island on the lower Amazon, indicates a movement down the Amazon, from west to east, of peoples or influences that spread the ideas of pottery and probably of agriculture from the Andean area. Elements of this pottery style, or culture, seem to have been at Yarinacocha in what is called the Early Tutishcainyo phase on the eastern side of the Peruvian Andes about 1000 B.C. and, also at an early date, at Yasuní in eastern Ecuador. The origin of the pottery at both of these sites on upper tributaries of the Amazon is uncertain. Guesses have been made that knowledge of pottery was diffused, or carried, from

Valdivia on the Ecuador coast (c. 3000 B.C.) to the northern Colombia coast and from there, with knowledge of agriculture, inland to Yasuní and, via Kotosh in the central Peruvian highlands (c. 1800 B.C.), to Yarinacocha. At any rate, by about 1000 B.C., the pottery style, having moved down the Amazon, had reached Marajó Island, where it gave rise to the Ananatuba Culture whose pottery-making people lived in villages of single communal dwellings large enough to house up to one hundred and fifty persons. The people made dugout canoes and probably relied mainly on fishing and hunting, although they also practiced agriculture. Elsewhere through the tropical forest areas it is presumed that both farming and the making of pottery were spread in somewhat similar fashion, either by migrations or diffusion.

During the second stage of development, defined by Evans as the tropical forest slash-and-burn agricultural stage, people came to rely on root and seed crops for the main portion of their food supply, although they continued also to hunt and fish. In the tropical forests, the slash-and-burn method was used to clear farming plots, but the soil was too poor to support a strong agriculture, and it wore out quickly. Villages remained small and were moved frequently, as new fields were cleared. People lived in different types of houses, ranging from large communal dwellings to single-family thatch and pole structures. Some social stratification may have appeared, but complex social or religious systems did not develop. Arts and crafts, particularly in basketry, featherwork, pottery, textiles, and the making of stone axes, often reached a high degree of ability. Archeologists have identified a number of cultures of this stage, grouping them, once again, by similarities in their ceramic styles. Cultures of an Incised Rim Horizon Style of pottery decoration included one known as the Mangueiras, a people who intruded on and assimilated the earlier Ananatuba people of Marajó Island in the lower Amazon. Others were those of several groups along the Amazon, as well as the Nericagua and other cultures in the Orinoco Basin. The Incised Rim Horizon Style is dated by some authorities at about A.D. 100–800, and various of its traits, particularly along the Orinoco, seem to have originated in the Colombian highlands.

Additional cultures evidencing traits of the same slash-and-burn agricultural stage of development are grouped by similarities in another pottery decoration style known as that of the Incised and Punctate Horizon, dated generally at about

A.D. 1000–1500. This style too seems to have originated in the Colombian highlands and to have spread along the Orinoco, across to the Amazon, and down that river. The pottery style has been found at sites in both watersheds and in present-day Guyana, including locations of the Mazagão Culture north of the mouth of the Amazon, Guyana's Mabaruma Culture (which may have been introduced about A.D. 500 from the Orinoco delta), and the widespread Santarem Culture along the Amazon and on the lower portions of many of the Amazon's tributaries. Villages of those cultures were still small ones and were frequently moved to new farming sites. Griddles, used in the making of cassava bread from bitter manioc, appeared in the Mazagão villages, while the Santarem peoples made distinctive pottery, decorated with ornately modeled animals, birds, and human figures. Other tropical forest cultures of the same developmental stage existed in late prehistoric, and even historic, times. One of them, the Corobal on the upper headwaters of the Orinoco, possessed traits derived from the Andes and appears related to cultures of people who had pushed out into the Antilles. Other cultures, discovered in the interior of Guyana, were of tribes that had migrated from the Amazon after the start of historic times, probably seeking refuge as a result of the internal pressures of tribe against tribe that followed the arrival of the white man in Brazil.

The third, and ultimate, prehistoric development level in the Amazon and Orinoco basins is termed the sub-Andean agricultural stage and was characterized by a temporary ability to engage in a more intensive agriculture that permitted, for a time, greater permanency of habitation; a larger production of food; the growth and concentration of population; the organization of social systems with stratification, an occupational division of labor, and specialized artisans of outstanding ability; and the building of mounds, large villages, and burial sites that required an authority capable of directing massed labor. In the tropical forest environment, these cultures could not endure and continue their development to higher levels; inevitably, agricultural yields declined, villages were forced to move or revert to slash-and-burn techniques, and advanced cultures collapsed. In the Amazon drainage, the stage is identified with a Polychrome Painting style of pottery decoration, found at sites from eastern Ecuador to Marajó Island at the Amazon's mouth. Marked by habitation and burial mounds, by burial patterns that sug-

gest social stratification and elaborate ceremonials, and by
excellent pottery that indicates specialized craftsmen, the
culture seems to have spread down the Amazon from eastern
Ecuador, where it is dated at about A.D. 1000. Carriers
of its traits appear to have reached the mouth of the Amazon
about A.D. 1200. It flourished there for about a century, but
eventually declined in the tropical forest environment and
disappeared by the time of the arrival of white men.

Other archeological work has been done farther south in
the drainage of the Paraná River in southern Brazil, Paraguay, Uruguay, and northeastern Argentina. Andean influences do not seem to have played a role in this region, and
tribes progressed only from a level of incipient agriculture to
one of slash-and-burn technique. Pottery found in shell middens and other sites is classified generally so far as that of
either Tupí-Guaraní peoples or their predecessors in the
region. The Tupí-Guaranís, described below, appear to have
spread from south of the Amazon River to the Paraná water-
shed, down that river to its delta, and then north and south
along the coast. Their arrival in southern Brazil is estimated
to have occurred around A.D. 800.

In historic times, the cultures of tribes met by white men
throughout the tropical forest area were generally those of
the slash-and-burn agricultural stage of development. People
throughout the area also depended on hunting and fishing,
and villages—whose sizes were generally dictated by the
amount of nearby arable land—were concentrated along the
rivers and coasts. The principal crops were corn, beans,
sweet and bitter manioc, sweet potatoes, yams, squash, peanuts, and several kinds of palms. Bitter manioc contains
hydrocyanic acid, a deadly poison, but the Indians removed
it by shredding the root into a pulp, putting the pulp into
a long basketry cylinder called a *tipití*, and pulling the *tipití*
into a narrow, elongated shape, which compressed the pulp
and squeezed the juices from it. The dried pulp was then
baked into cakes or dried into a flour known as *farinha*.
White men adopted manioc as a staple, deriving both tapioca
and *farinha* from it. In addition, the tropical forest peoples
grew many useful plants, including cotton, calabashes, and
arrow reeds, and gathered wild fruits and nuts. They took
numerous species of fish, caught caymans and turtles, and
collected turtle eggs. More than one hundred drugs, made
from wild and cultivated plants, were used to throw into
streams and pools to stupefy fish and make them float help-

lessly to the surface, where they could be easily taken. Fishing was also done with nets, weirs, hooks, traps, and tri-pronged arrows. The game of hunters in the forests included peccaries, deer, monkeys, tapirs, armadillos, anteaters, birds, and numerous other creatures. Traps, spears, spear throwers, blowguns, and bows and arrows were used in hunting. The long blowgun was employed with darts tipped with poison made from certain vines, particularly one that supplied the paralyzing curare. The bows and arrows were very large, the arrows sometimes being five feet long and the bows having a proportionate length.

Settlements in the forest were often comprised of only one huge thatched building, which housed a single lineage of less than one hundred people. Elsewhere, communities were larger and consisted of clusters of houses of several lineages, the houses often being crowded together within defensive palisades. In some regions the multifamily houses surrounded the home of the village headman as well as a central men's house in which the males ate, slept, and spent much of their time. The houses, which varied in size from huge loaflike structures up to two hundred feet long and sixty feet high to small lean-tos, were usually made of a framework of poles covered with thatch. Some of the villages along the larger rivers were semi-permanent, but most of the others throughout the area were frequently moved. The wearing out of agricultural plots was the principal cause for the shifts, but the death of an inhabitant, especially the headman, might also cause the villagers to change their site.

Political development was slight. The smaller settlements were led by the elders of kin groups. In the larger villages, headmen were frequently also shamans who received respect because of their supernatural powers, and were looked upon to give leadership and perform rites. The kin group was usually a patrilineal lineage, but in the Guianas and in parts of Venezuela, Colombia, and the Antilles relationships were quite often traced through the female line. There was no class stratification; but here and there serflike groups of captives and slight tendencies toward status differences existed.

Religion was unsystematized. There were few priests or special religious leaders, and none of them were hereditary or possessed a superior status. The people believed in magic and in many spirits, some of which like those of the bush and the rivers were thought to be evil and were shunned in fear.

Other spirits were celestial beings, identified with the sky, clouds, sun, moon, and stars, but they were wrapped in myth and were considered generally to have little connection with daily life. The Tupians possessed a "grandfather" culture hero, sometimes associated with thunder. A Grandfather Cult promised the Tupians a happier existence in another country, the Land of the Grandfathers, and led various of their groups to make protracted migrations in search of that mythical country. The tropical forest peoples in general, also, had many ceremonies, including group harvest and fertility rites. Special rituals, accompanied by sacred musical instruments taboo to women and children, conducted boys into men's societies and ancestor cults. At the age of puberty, boys and girls of most tribes were subjected to ordeals. Boys were circumcised, had their noses pierced, or were required to prove their courage by such trials as being tied to a bed of biting ants. Girls were scarified, whipped, drugged, or were required to have their hair cut or perform certain dances. Musical instruments, including gourd rattles, long trumpets, stamping tubes, panpipes, jingles, and different types of clarinets, oboes, and flutes, were used in ceremonies as well as in festivals, and drums were employed effectively also to send messages and signals over long distances.

A widespread practice was that of couvade at the time of birth. It was thought that a newborn infant had a stronger supernatural bond with his father than with his mother. To avoid doing anything that might adversely affect the baby, the father took to his hammock at the time of the child's birth and carefully avoided all activities for a certain length of time. Usually he remained in his hammock long after the mother had arisen from childbed and resumed her own activities.

Many of the tribes engaged in constant warfare, raiding their neighbors either for revenge or to take human trophies and captives. The male prisoners were used for cannibalistic rites, and the women were taken as wives. Fierce cannibalism existed among some of the tribes, particularly certain of the Caribs and Tupians who relished human flesh and ate it in preference to other food. Tribes in the Guianas took scalps as trophies; in the Montaña on the eastern side of the Andes, the Jívaros shrank the entire heads of their victims; and in the lower Amazon Basin, the Araras flayed and preserved the complete skin of their enemies. Prior to the arrival of the whites, some tribes used captives as slaves, but generally allowed them to marry into the tribe and become free. With the coming of the Europeans, however, Portuguese slave traders encouraged tribes to make war against each other to obtain captives to sell to the whites as slaves.

In the hot, dank climate, tropical forest peoples needed, or wore, little clothing. Many Indians went entirely naked, painting and tattooing their bodies and wearing numerous ornaments in their ears, nose, lips, and cheeks. Sometimes they wore breechcloths, waistbands, arm and leg bands, and ornamental headdresses of feathers of tropical birds. Feathers of desired colors were obtained by a process known as tapirage: after removing the feathers of a live bird, usually a parrot, the Indians rubbed the bird with certain irritants that induced the growth of new feathers of desired colors. Many tribes wove upon a heddle loom, using domesticated or wild cotton to produce hammocks, bands, and other objects, some with interwoven stripes of different colors. In less developed regions where looms were absent, tribes produced bark cloth by a method similar to that used in southeast Asia and on islands in the Pacific: the bark was stripped from trees, softened, and separated into layers, after which the layers were placed crosswise on each other, moistened, and pounded until they became joined. Then the cloth was usually painted and used for masks or clothing. Some of the tribes also made use of the sap of rubber trees, fashioning figurines, rings, balls, and hollow syringes from the substance. The tropical forest peoples may have been the first to use the rubber tree's sap, although Middle American groups produced a kind of rubber, also, from latex-yielding plants in their homelands. For transportation along the rivers, most of the tribes made dugout canoes, but they also employed hollow logs and bark canoes, especially on the smaller headwaters. Coastal peoples, particularly around the Caribbean, were excellent navigators and built large ornamented seagoing canoes with built-up sides in which they traveled long distances.

In various regions, distinctive traits and differences characterized the tribal groups. Among the villages in the Guiana lowlands, where matrilineal societies were strongest, prospective bridegrooms lived with and served their future fathers-in-law for a number of years prior to marriage. Sometimes, especially among some Carib groups in the region, the sons-in-law, as well as male captives from outside groups, constituted a kind of serf class under the fathers-in-law. Religion in the Guianas centered on the shaman, who administered as a curer and seer to individuals, and only served the group by practicing magic to promote the growth of crops. In their elaborate curing rites, shamans sat on special carved benches, shook rattles, smoked cigarettes, blew upon patients, and then pretended to suck out the disease-producing objects. Warfare was constant in the Guiana region, particularly among the Caribs, whose name gave the word cannibal to European languages. The Caribs were spread through the Guianas, parts of Venezuela, and the islands of the Lesser Antilles, which they had reached via Trinidad. Arawaks, who had come to those islands earlier, were no match for the aggressive Caribs, and when the Spaniards arrived in the West Indies, they found the Caribs still expanding, raiding Arawak settlements farther north in Jamaica.

The Caribs of the islands were essentially a maritime people who made some of the best canoes in the New World. Many of their craft, hollowed from a log and with built-up sides, could carry as many as fifty people and had two or three masts and sails of reed matting or woven cotton. The Caribs warred incessantly for prestige and to capture male prisoners for cannibalism and females for additional wives. On each island, the warriors were headed by a war chief, who, to be eligible for the position, had to have inherited an ornament called a caracoli, made of a gold-copper alloy and traded originally from Colombia. Before setting out on raids, warriors aroused a war spirit by eating preserved human flesh and drinking chicha. Attacks on enemy villages were made with fire arrows and poisoned arrows and with javelins and clubs. The bodies of slain enemies were butchered and eaten at once, and male prisoners were taken home to be subjected to grisly torture before being cut up and roasted or boiled. The female captives became wives of the warriors, but were treated subserviently, although their children were born free. Frequently, captured Arawak women outnumbered the Carib women in a village, and all the women came to speak Arawak, while the men spoke only Carib. This linguistic division was furthered by the fact that the men lived in special houses, segregated from the women. The latter, including the Carib women, generally occupied a slavelike status. They fed and tended to the dressing of their husbands, did the farming, and cleaned the men's houses.

The Montaña on the eastern side of the Andes was characterized by other regional traits. That area was the home of numerous tropical forest tribes and language groups, including the Panoan Shipibos and Conibos, the Jívaros, and Arawakan-speaking Campas. Certain culture elements had been carried into the region from the nearby civilizations of the Central Andes, and had been adopted by some of the Montaña's villagers. In the higher country, people possessed llamas, alpacas, and guinea pigs, and some wore long, flowing robes called *cushmas*, like those of the Andean peoples, and employed platform beds, using hammocks only as cradles. Excellent pottery, decorated with bold lines, was made; white potatoes were grown; and the Muscovy duck (which received its name after it had been introduced to Russia) was probably domesticated in this region. Some of the tribes were able hunters and warriors, and the area may have been the birthplace of the blowgun in South America. The Jívaros believed that ownership of an enemy's head gave them supernatural power, but this power soon weakened and had to be renewed by the taking of more heads. After decapitating an enemy, the Jívaros removed the skin from the skull and shrank the skin by boiling it and filling it with hot sand and pebbles. They then sewed the lips of the trophy with long pendant strings.

After the Spanish conquest, missionaries entered the Montaña, introducing the Incas' Quechua language—which became a lingua franca—and many white customs to the tribes they could reach. In the eighteenth century, the Indians began a series of revolts against whites in the region. Intertribal warfare was encouraged by the intrigues of slave traders, and chaos ruled until the nineteenth century. In the early twentieth century, a rubber boom stirred the Montaña and destroyed much of what still remained of original Indian life. In some remote areas, however, the tropical forest culture still exists.

After Arawakan-speakers, the most widely spread language group in South America were the many Tupian peoples. Although they began to disperse in pre-Columbian times from a central region south of the Amazon, their migrations received a new stimulus after the white men had commenced to disrupt Indian life. Their wanderings in quest of the better existence promised in the mythical Land of the Grandfather ultimately spread them in a great arc along the lower Amazon and its southern tributaries, down the coast of Brazil, and back inland across Paraguay to the flank of the Bolivian Andes.

The largest number of Tupian-speaking Indians still dwell in their original homeland south of the Amazon; but, with the exception of a few tribes, including the Mundurucús who became rubber hunters for the white man, comparatively little is known about them. Another of their groups, the Tupinambás, was found by explorers occupying a 2,000-mile-long stretch of the Brazilian coast, and was well known to the early Europeans on that part of the continent.

Living in settlements of up to 1,500 people, the Tupinambás were an aggressive, cannibalistic people, who also practiced agriculture and engaged in offshore fishing. Their villages, among the largest of any of the tropical forest tribes, were enclosed by double palisades and contained from four to eight large houses, each of which held from thirty to sixty families related through the male line. The fierce Tupinambás made constant warfare on neighbors. They ate many of their captives immediately, but brought others back to their villages and, for a while, treated them well. Eventually, however, they slew them too and ate their flesh in drunken feasts. In their relations with each other, the Tupinambás were generally mild and restained, and frowned on quarrels. Warfare and cannibalism provided the principal outlets for suppressed feelings, and as a result frustrated and emotionally upset villagers sometimes went berserk, burning down their own houses and committing suicide by eating handfuls of dirt.

Another group of Tupians who migrated to Paraguay became known as the Guaranís, and their descendants comprise the major part of the country's present population. Maté, the South American tea, was first cultivated by them, and it is one of Paraguay's principal exports today. Beginning in 1471, some of the Guaranís, known as Chiriguanos, migrated from Paraguay to the Bolivian Andes, possibly still searching for the Grandfather Land. During their wanderings, they came on mild Arawakan-speaking Chanés, who offered no defense against them. In an unparalleled example of pacifism carried to the extreme, some 60,000 Chanés let themselves be slain, many by the bows and arrows of Chiriguano children. The migrants absorbed other Chanés, continued on to the Andes, and during the early part of the sixteenth century even raided the frontiers of the powerful Inca Empire.

The vast highlands south of the Amazon River, an area of extreme contrasts that includes both arid uplands and jungle-bound streams, were—and still are—populated by numerous other tribes, principally of the Ge language family. The Ge Indians differ in three respects from most of the other tropical forest peoples. First, since their unproductive land supports only small-scale agriculture, they are as much hunters and gatherers as farmers. It is probable, in fact, that they are fairly recent converts to agriculture, and some persons class them with the marginal nomadic tribes of South America rather than with the tropical forest villagers. Second, although they have access to rivers, they are essentially landsmen. Some are good fishermen, but they make little or no use of the canoe and fail to exploit the resources of the rivers as well as the Tupian Indians who dwell along stretches of the waterways in their midst. Finally, Ge settlements are divided into a large number of kinship groups, age-grades, occupational associations, and moieties, each with its own special ceremonies and rules of behavior.

The eastern Ges include the Timbiras, Cayapós, and Suyás. Farther south, on the plains and in the forests of southeastern Brazil, are Caingangs, who comprise a number of separate peoples. On the headwaters of the Paraguay River are tall Bororos, who speak a language distantly related to Ge, but are classified in the same group. The Ge tribes maintain only small settlements, often abandoning them temporarily at flood times or to go on hunts. An unusual feature associated with the more eastern Ges is their construction of roadways, ten miles or more in length, that extend in straight lines across the plains. The shorter ones lead to agricultural plots or hunting grounds; the longer ones are used for their favorite sport—relay racing, in which teams representing the various moieties race with heavy logs on their shoulders.

Ge material possessions, in prehistoric times, were fewer and simpler than those of other tropical forest tribes. Some Ges had no pottery. In contrast to the many musical instruments possessed by some other forest peoples, the Cayapós had only rattles. But they were good singers, and enjoyed singing in groups. The Ges waged war for vengeance in continuing, traditional blood feuds, rather than for human trophies, victims for cannibalism, or territorial conquest. Since the arrival of white men, some Ge tribes have become extinct. Several of the surviving groups, notably certain of the Shavantes and Cayapós, are still unconquered, and are hostile to intruders who, on occasion, have hunted them down with modern weapons and murdered them.

23

The Marginal
Nomadic Indians of
South America

THE NONAGRICULTURAL INDIANS OF SOUTH AMERICA are usually classified in a single cultural group referred to as the Marginal tribes. They did not occupy any one area, but were scattered in various localities and regions from western Cuba to the southern tip of the continent. Although they had little in common, their manner of subsistence— nomadic hunting, gathering, and fishing—was the same. Some of them appear to have changed scarcely at all during prehistoric times, while it is probable that at different times others possessed higher cultures that later degenerated, possibly when stronger peoples forced them into less favorable environments.

The tribes that most fully deserved the name Marginal lived in the southern part of the continent—in almost all of Argentina and Uruguay and in the western part of Paraguay and the southern third of Chile. Dwelling in generally unproductive lands distant from the centers of advanced Indian cultures, they included shellfish gatherers of the coast and offshore islands; nomadic hunters of the steppes and pampas; and tribes of the Gran Chaco, the plain in northern Argentina and Paraguay between Brazil's Mato Grosso and the Andes. The introduction of the horse by white men led to the emergence of still another type: the mounted nomad. Other Marginal tribes north of those areas lived in small, scattered enclaves among tropical forest and Circum-Caribbean tribal groups in swamps, plains, and scrub areas that did not support farming.

In some of the regions inhabited by Marginal tribes

archeologists have found relics of nomadic hunters and gatherers of great antiquity. Krieger assigns various finds of crudely made artifacts in different parts of Patagonia and Tierra del Fuego at the continent's southern tip to an early Pre-Projectile Point Stage of development, although none of the relics have been dated with certainty, and some, if not all of them, may be of simple nomadic cultures of comparatively recent times. However, discoveries have been made of peoples of a very great age who made projectile points and, thus, being at a more advanced stage of development, would seem also to have lived at a later time. Finds at Palli Aike and Fell's caves near the Strait of Magellan, both of which contained human remains as well as those of extinct giant ground sloths and horses, were dated at around 9,000 and 11,000 years old, respectively. There may be some doubt concerning the 11,000-year age for the human relics at Fell's Cave, but none at all for the 9,000-year date at Palli Aike Cave. Other discoveries have been made in regions occupied by Marginal tribes, showing (by more skillfully made types of projectile points and other artifacts) advancing stages of development of later peoples—but always of nomadic hunters and gatherers who did not progress to a sedentary, agricultural way of life. By historic times, the tribes were still following essentially the same patterns of existence as peoples of thousands of years before them.

From north to south along the bleak, rugged coast and offshore islands of southern Chile were small, wretchedly poor groups of shellfish gatherers—the Chonos, Alacalufs, and Yahgans. Charles Darwin, who studied their life at first-hand, considered them the most miserable humans he had ever seen. The land they occupied is almost similar to that of the Indians of the Northwest Pacific Coast. But since the Chilean waters have virtually no fish and cannot provide an economic basis for a great population or even permanent settlements, the South Americans lacked the resources with which to match the development that occurred on the northern continent. The Chilean shellfish gatherers were divided into wandering families—husband, wife, and children—who erected temporary huts of brush framework covered with skins. The Chonos in the north raised a few potatoes, and all the groups ate some wild plant foods and land game, which they hunted. But shellfish was their principal diet.

Women usually secured the food. They gathered the shellfish on the beaches or went out in boats with shellfish spears, often six feet long. When the water was too deep for spearing from the boats, they dove to the beds of mollusks and sea urchins. Although the water ranged from 40 to 50 degrees Fahrenheit, the Indians had a body tolerance for cold that was a marvel of physical adaptation. In addition, the men hunted sea birds and mammals—cormorants, penguins, ducks, seals, and sea otters—although the results of such hunts were usually meager. Occasional dead, beached whales provided feasts.

To safeguard their source of food, the Indians practiced conservation, moving from the different shellfish beds before the yields dropped too low. They traveled by water, and because their subsistence and transportation depended so thoroughly on the use of boats, they are often called Canoe Indians. The best craft were made by the Chonos, whose sturdy dugouts had built-up plank sides. The Yahgans fashioned only flimsy, leaky bark boats until a stray Indian from Brazil happened among them and taught them how to make dugouts.

The inhospitable region had no attraction for white men, and the wandering groups of shellfish eaters were generally ignored until the nineteenth century. In 1829, an English ship took aboard three Yahgan youths and returned with them to England. The older boy and girl were given the names of York Minster and Fuegia Basket, and the youngest, who had a winning personality, was named Jeremy Button. They were taught the English language, converted to Christianity, educated as young Britons, and returned to their homeland two years later on the ship that took Darwin to Tierra del Fuego. York Minster was eventually killed in a fight; the engaging Jeremy Button led a massacre on a settlement of missionaries; and Fuegia Basket lived to an unhappy old age in which she forgot the entire English interlude in her life. Civilization and white men's diseases eventually came to the area. The Chonos became extinct; and by the middle of the twentieth century the Alacalufs numbered but a few hundred and the Yahgans only nine.

On the plains of Argentina, east and north of the shellfish gatherers, were bands of foot nomads who hunted small- and medium-sized land game, principally the guanaco, a relative of the llama, and the tuco-tuco, a burrowing rodent. The tribes included Onas, Tehuelches, Puelches, and several others. After the white man introduced the horse, most of these peoples were transformed into mounted nomads. The only group whose original pedestrian culture has been studied are the Onas, who lived inland in Tierra del Fuego; presumably the others lived a somewhat similar life.

Ona bands—larger than the simple family units of the shellfish gatherers along the coast—were composed of several families related through the male line. Comprising from fifty to one hundred persons and led by the oldest man, they wandered after game over small, restricted areas, perhaps no more than twenty miles square. Territorial rights were jealously guarded; an invasion of another band's hunting grounds was an invitation to war.

The Onas wore mantles fashioned from guanaco skins and lived in simple windbreaks made of skins held up by a few poles. They were easily portable, but provided scant protection against the blustery weather. Occasionally Ona bands came together to celebrate marriages or to hold important rites that initiated youths into manhood. Their religion included belief in a supreme being, who was occasionally worshipped, but was generally considered remote from human affairs. Shamans relied on supernatural assistance from the spirits of dead ancestors, not on aid from the supreme being. Diseases and a white policy of extermination almost wiped out the Onas during the nineteenth and early twentieth centuries. Only seven Onas were known to be alive in 1960.

The nomad tribes in the Gran Chaco—Zamucoans, Matacoans, Guaycuruans, and others—were almost entirely fishermen and gatherers. The name Chaco actually means "hunting grounds," but it had only relative meaning, since it was bestowed on the area by Andean Indians who had almost no game animals of their own. Hunting was significant only in the eastern and southern parts of the Chaco, and even there it was less important than fishing and gathering. Some farming was done, but it, too, was supplementary and did not tie people to permanent settlements. Despite the importance of fish to the economy, few of the Chaco peoples employed any form of water transport save the simplest rafts or skin tubs. One tribe that did have canoes, the Payaguás of the Paraguay River, became feared river pirates. After the horse was introduced, some of the Chaco Indians became mounted. The Zamucoans, Matacoans, and several others remained pedestrian tribes and kept to their old ways, but most of the Guaycuruans adopted the life of horse nomads.

The European conquest scarcely touched the various

groups of nomadic hunters and gatherers of southern South America. Their population density was so low, their land so poor, and the bands so impoverished that the Spaniards had little interest in them. But the Spaniards did bring them the horse. As in North America, the white men tried to keep the animals out of Indian hands, but had the same ill success. By the 1700's, many of the nomadic tribes had become mounted and were raiding Spanish settlements from the Chaco to Patagonia. There were many parallels between the horse culture that emerged in this part of the hemisphere and the culture of the Plains Indians of North America. The terrain of the two areas was somewhat similar—the cool, windy steppe of Patagonia, the long grass plains of the pampas, and the open scrub forest of the Chaco are reminiscent of parts of the central plains of the northern continent. The two cultures also developed at about the same time period, and fell almost simultaneously before the advance of civilization.

Both North and South American horse nomads invented and used pemmican, the highly nutritious mixture of pounded dried meat and dried fat. Individuals in both areas sought guidance from the supernatural in dreams and visions, and indulged in self-mutilation during times of mourning. The development of these and other similarities between the two cultures is somewhat puzzling, since they cannot be accounted for fully by the resemblance of their environments. Nor is it possible that diffusion could have carried the traits of one horse culture across thousands of miles of dense jungles to another. There were marked differences among them, however. The South American Indians adopted the Spanish horse paraphernalia, including the saddle, bridle, stirrup, and lariat, and also invented a type of toe stirrup of their own. In addition, they preferred the use of their own bola to the white man's lasso. In the absence of huge herds of game animals, like the buffalo, they subsisted mainly on cattle stolen from the Spaniards, and did not possess the material traits of the northerners' famed "buffalo economy." Finally, the Chaco Indians never built up large herds of their own horses, but made continuous raids on the Spaniards for animals. A single Chaco Indian might escape with as many as five hundred horses, while his pursuers floundered in the swamps trying to catch him.

The most southerly of the South American horse nomads

were the tallest Indians in the Americas, the six-foot-tall Tehuelches of south central Argentina. The Spaniards called them Patagones, "big feet," and Patagonia derived its name from them. Puelches and Querandís lived farther north on Argentina's long-grass pampas, while across the Plata River on the Uruguayan pampas were Charruas. In the Chaco were many Guaycuruan tribes—the Abipóns, Mbayás, and others. In addition, a number of Araucanian bands that had fled across the Andes from Spanish oppression in Chile allied themselves with the Puelches and also adopted the horse nomad existence.

The horse culture radically changed the Indians' ways of life. Warfare, usually over hunting territory, increased. The use of the long lance, especially effective in charges against the Spaniards, largely replaced the bow and arrow. Nomadic bands in Patagonia and on the pampas became bigger. Small groups of single family lineage grew to become multilineage bands of many hundreds of persons not restricted to any one area; and men who proved themselves to be persuasive leaders or outstanding warriors tended to acquire the authority that had formally been exercised by kinship elders. In time, after their subjugation and partial assimilation, many of the horse nomads became the celebrated Gauchos, the cowboys of the pampas.

The Chaco tribes developed a few new traits of their own. One group, the Mbayás, settled in permanent villages and built up a strong class structure somewhat similar to that of the Circum-Caribbean chiefdoms. Prior to the introduction of the horse, these nomadic hunters and gatherers had conquered a sedentary tribe of farmers, the Arawakan-speaking Guanás, and had kept them as serfs. When they got the horse, the Mbayás developed their class structure to include six classes and subclasses: chiefs; lesser hereditary nobles; nonhereditary, lifetime nobles; warriors; serfs made up of the Guanás; and a hereditary class of captured or purchased slaves. While the serfs and slaves farmed and cared for the villages, the Mbayá nobles and warriors rode off on far-ranging raids.

The Mbayás were unusually indulgent toward their children, sometimes even moving camp or selling prized horses at a child's whim. This pampered upbringing, coupled with the caste system and the Mbayás' ability in war, led the Mbayá adult to regard himself as superior to all other Indians and to the neighboring white men. One wife of a petty Mbayá chieftain even refused to attend church with the wife of the governor of Corumba, asserting that only the Queen of Portugal was her equal.

In more northerly parts of the continent, numerous Marginal tribes were scattered in pockets across large areas that were otherwise occupied by tropical forest and Circum-Caribbean Indians. Generally, they lived in inhospitable regions of swamps or arid lands—along the headwaters of the Orinoco and Amazon rivers and their tributaries, in the almost impenetrable jungles between rivers, and in a coastal strip of Brazil extending north from Rio de Janeiro. They were of two types: foot nomads, who wandered in medium-sized bands, and canoe nomads, who traveled the waterways in family groups.

The best known of the foot nomads are the Tupian Sirionós, who lived an exceedingly primitive existence in the forests of eastern Bolivia. Pushed into this region at a remote date, they even forgot how to make fire, and had to carry burning brands wherever they went. They were small-time farmers, and at the beginning of the dry season, cleared small patches and planted a few crops. Then they moved on, returning from time to time to care for the plantings and to harvest the crops. Most of the year they gathered wild plant foods and hunted game, using bows up to eight feet in length and arrows as long as ten feet. A Sirionó hunter did not eat the game he himself had killed, but gave it to the other members of his band; his abstention, he believed, would preserve the supply of game. There was no warfare among Sirionó bands, but members within a group often became involved in fights with each other during drinking bouts, which were one of their few means of relaxation. They had no shamans, but feared the spirits of the dead. In recent years, the Sirionós were converted by missionaries and taken out of the jungle. Some 90 per cent of them contracted tuberculosis, and many went insane from an inability to cope with civilization. Their number dwindled from 1,000 to 600, and it is feared that they will soon be extinct. Other foot nomads include the Guayakís of eastern Paraguay and the Nambicuaras of the southern Mato Grosso. The language of the latter Indians, according to linguistic scholar Morris Swadesh, may be one of the oldest still-surviving tongues of any native group in the hemisphere, suggesting that their ancestors were among the earliest arrivals in the Americas and were pushed into undesirable country by stronger groups who arrived at a later time.

The farthest north of the forest nomads were the Ciboneys of the western shores of Haiti and Cuba. They were descendants of the earliest known inhabitants of the West Indies, the nonagricultural Meso-Indians, but were dispossessed from the other islands by the agricultural Arawaks. There are similarities between Ciboney artifacts and remains found in southern Florida, but not enough is known about the Ciboneys to permit more than speculation regarding possible connections between the two areas. After the discovery of America, the Spaniards quickly exterminated or absorbed the Ciboneys.

Mura Indians, excellent rivermen who lived and slept in their canoes much of the year, lived on the Madeira and Purús rivers of western Brazil. They plied their canoes across great stretches of inundated land during flood season, and at other times occupied small riverbank settlements. With harpoons or bows and arrows they took fish, turtles, otters, and other aquatic game from the rivers, and for other food often raided the garden plots of their more settled tropical forest neighbors. In the eighteenth century, the Muras began to extend the sphere of their raiding; but they aroused the enmity of both the Brazilians and the strong Tupian Mundurucús and were forced to seek peace. They are now on the verge of extinction as a separate group.

24

The Impact of the White Man on Indians

FROM THE PERSPECTIVE OF A LONG-RANGE POINT OF view, the white men came as the last of many migrants to the Western Hemisphere, but their effect as conquerors of all the peoples living there was final and, with minor exceptions so far, total. The European conquest of the Americas had been termed one of the darkest chapters of human history, for the conquerors demanded and won authority over the lives, territories, religious beliefs, ways of life, and means of existence of every native group with which they came in contact. No one will ever know how many Indians of how many tribes were enslaved, tortured, debauched, and killed. No one can ever reckon the dimensions of the human tragedy that cost, in addition to lives, the loss of homes, dignity, cultural institutions, standards of security, material and intellectual accomplishments, and liberty and freedom to millions upon millions of people. The stain is made all the darker by the realization that the conflict was forced upon those who suffered; the aggressors were the whites, the scenes of tragedy the very homelands of the victims.

In the bitter narrative of man's suppression and extermination of his fellow man in the Americas, no single European nation or special group of whites was more—or less—blameworthy than others. The long conflict that followed Columbus's arrival in America and that successively embroiled one part of the New World after another, as the white man spread through the continents, was essentially part of a worldwide expansionism. The people of western Europe, armed with superior firepower and supported by advanced technological civilizations, sailed out of their ports to conquer or dominate "inferior" men of color everywhere in the world. The Indian peoples of the Americas, like peoples in Africa and Asia, fell victim to conquerors who conceived of themselves as a superior race. In the Western Hemisphere, Indians, to the whites, were all the same, and the newcomers disagreed among themselves only over the extent to which the native populations differed from, or seemed to be inferior to, Europeans. On their part, the Indians, with rare exceptions, had no such unifying influence nor any conception of being involved in a total conflict of one race against another. Their own centuries-old differences, rivalries, feuds, and jealousies were readily discernible to the white men, who facilitated their own conquests by pitting one native group against another. The "divide-and-conquer" policy never worked better than in the Western Hemisphere, from the time of Columbus in the West Indies, Cortés in Mexico, and Pizarro in Peru to the period when the United States Army employed subjugated tribesmen as scouts and auxiliaries against undefeated Indians on the western plains and in the Southwest.

In justice to the whites, there is another side of the story. From time to time, there were many individuals, groups, and even governments that spoke out loudly or labored earnestly in efforts to place white relations with the Indians on foundations of fairness. In the earliest period, religious leaders in New Spain and New France, like Friar Bartolomé de las Casas in the West Indies, fought courageously in the Indians' behalf (though denying the Indians the right to their own religions), and the Spanish court itself took many steps designed to protect the natives. The enforcement of royal measures—as well as of papal bulls, like that of Pope Paul III in 1537, which tried to halt the alienation of natives from the desire to be converted by threatening excommunication to any whites who enslaved Indians or deprived them of their possessions—was, however, often impossible. Later, in the English colonies, the British Crown and its provincial officials sometimes attempted to interpose themselves as protectors between the Indians and the expanding settlers. It rarely worked and, in fact, turned many colonists against the royal government. After the formation of the United States, Thomas Jefferson, John Marshall, and many other leaders in and out of government tried to inject morality, justice, and strict legal procedures in the headlong dispossession of the Indians. Almost without exception, however, their decrees, pronouncements, and pleadings were nullified by events on the frontier and by champions of the anti-Indian elements.

The Indians themselves were not wholly innocent in the complex and intense struggle. Although the conflict would not have occurred without the intrusion of whites into countries the Indians already occupied—a fundamental cause of every manifestation of friction that bears reiteration because it is so often overlooked—the warlike nature and bold provocations of some tribes or groups of warriors led to violence and injustices that might not otherwise have taken place. Many Indians, for various motives, even welcomed white newcomers and brought eventual ruin on themselves by the use they made of the whites. In repeated instances native leaders who were unable to foresee the ultimate consequences appealed for white help against rival chiefs and bands; others became slave catchers, tribute collectors, fur traders, petty administrators, overseers over other Indians, and mercenary fighters in the employ of whites, and in intertribal wars for monopoly positions in the traffic of European arms and manufactured goods they destroyed other Indian groups with relish.

It was unfortunate for the Indians that the white engulfment of the Western Hemisphere commenced when it did. In the sixteenth century, Western civilization was emerging from long centuries of feudalism, and competitive new nations were forming. Merchant classes were on the rise, and trade, including overseas commerce, was expanding. At the same time, the dedicated struggle against Islam was being replaced by fierce religious wars between Christians. The combination of aggressive nationalism, lust for wealth, and crusading religious zeal struck with full force against the Indians and was made even harsher by the brutality and other vestiges of medieval conduct among Europeans, including torture, dismemberment, and punishment by burning, which the Age of Enlightenment would later moderate. Today, with much of mankind's moral force arrayed in the United Nations against colonialism and aggression, the conquest of the Americas is a symbol of what man is capable of doing, but, hopefully, will never repeat.

The Europeans' principal motives for expansion and aggression differed in various parts of the New World. In the beginning, national policy was served by seizing sources of new wealth. Conquistador armies, composed of adventurers and restless veterans of European wars, ravaged for gold, silver, pearls, precious stones, and other loot for themselves. Their governments supported and encouraged them—even to the extent of inspiring them to raids and piratical attacks upon each other—and took a large share of the treasures of their conquests to finance their courts and European wars. Indian slaves, too, were a source of weath, as miners and laborers in the treasure-producing countries of the New World, as cheap labor in Europe, and as objects of sale in the mushrooming slave markets in the world. Columbus himself initiated and encouraged the enslavement of Indians; but no nation or colony was entirely guiltless of following suit, and private fortunes based at least partly on Indian slavery were made even in New England and New York.

Conflicts among the white men often arose over whether Indians were more valuable free and alive, or enslaved, or dead. Looters, exploiters, and adventurers argued in an attempt to prove that since Indians were not acquisitive, did not hunt gold for themselves, and resisted doing more work than was necessary to feed themselves, they therefore were not normal people but rather members of a subhuman or animal species, lacking souls. Others maintained that Indians were savages, unworthy of freedom, the right of ownership, or even life itself. Against these arguments, religious leaders and missionaries, supported by the Pope and home churches, insisted that the Indians had souls that could be saved; with some success they extended their protection to large parts of the native populations, converting them to Christianity and organizing them into labor forces under their own comparatively benign direction and control. If they saved the Indians from death, however, their efforts had destructive effects often as ruinous as the aggressions of those from whom they were trying to protect the Indians. For they, too, destroyed the Indians' societies, institutions, and cultures, undermined the Indians' ability to cope with hostile white men, and, in the end, left most of the peoples they had saved weak, disorganized, and helpless in the midst of whites who had already overrun their lands.

At the same time, governments, as well as the European merchant classes and their representatives in the New World, recognized the huge dimensions of the Indian market for manufactured goods. Gradually, trade with the native populations became a significant source of weath for

Europeans. In Spanish America, satisfying the needs and wants of the Indians worked to keep them in slavery or peonage, for they could be kept perpetually in debt. Where tribes were still unconquered, joint-stock companies, formed by private merchants and royal investors, and given charters, patents, and various forms of monopolistic rights by the governments, discovered that it was profitable to maintain good relations with the Indians. In the present-day United States and Canada, especially, manufactured goods were traded to the natives at prices that represented huge profits, and the Indians paid the whites with furs and other valuable commodities which were much in demand in Europe and parts of Asia. The joint-stock companies, often establishing permanent settlements and posts in tribal · territories, led directly to the introduction of what became the greatest acquisitive drive of all among white men in the New World —the greed for land. Settlers were sent over to establish colonies around the trading posts, and as new forces arose to induce others to emigrate to America, and the tide of colonists swelled, the Indians were pushed back or wiped out. Once started, the invasion of homeseekers never fully halted.

Every means and method was utilized in the long effort to dispossess the Indian. In some areas, land was bought or traded fairly; elsewhere intrigue, deception, legal chicanery, or outright confiscation were the rule. If the Indians resisted, militias with superior arms or organized troop units of the governments involved usually came to the assistance of the settlers. Treaties of peace invariably wrung from the defeated Indians the land the settlers had wanted. The pattern had variations, and on occasion the Indians won temporarily or were able to compromise or restrain white aggression long enough to bargain for retention of part of their homelands as preserves. In the United States, troops were sometimes able for brief periods of time to interpose themselves as police against the expanding whites; eventually, in each case, their protection of the Indians collapsed, and they were soon attacking the Indians whom initially they had been ordered to protect. Canada was more successful in giving its Indians a long-continued protection, and many of the native groups were settled on guaranteed lands of their own before the most rapacious, land-hunting whites could reach their countries. In time, however, even many of those groups felt the pressures of white inroads. Elsewhere, tribes and remnants of defeated peoples withdrew into jungles, swamps, mountainous areas, deserts, and other relatively inaccessible or unwanted regions, where their descendants either died off or managed to continue an isolated existence.

Most white men, as related earlier, viewed Indian life and institutions from their own familiar points of reference; they either did not grasp Indian fundamentals which differed from their own, or they were uninterested in seeing Indian customs continued and did their best to modify or eradicate them. Few whites could comprehend the Indian's common ownership of land, and they failed to realize that most Indians, in turn, could not grasp the white man's concept of private ownership of pieces of the earth. A man, said the Shawnee chief Tecumseh, could not sell the land any more than he could sell the sea or the air he breathed. The Indians usually did not realize that when they accepted gifts for granting the right to use part of their tribal domain, they also gave up their own right to use it.

At the same time, white men often failed to recognize some of the cultural essentials of various Indian societies they met. Their own intrusions into Indian homelands inevitably exposed them to practices such as horse thefts, raids for personal prestige, torture, and even cannibalism and human sacrifice and trophy-taking that repelled and angered them. Although these practices were accepted traits in native religious, political, and social systems, they outraged the intruders' sense of morality and were opposed and ended by force and violence. In the areas of chiefdoms and authoritarian Indian states, Europeans generally replaced one form of absolutism with another. But elsewhere, white men could rarely perceive democratic, group-oriented elements where they existed in Indian societies. This oversight led to numerous episodes of capricious behavior by the whites, who arbitrarily selected friendly or venal Indians as chiefs and leaders and endowed them with power and prestige over tribes that possessed long-established methods of their own for choosing their leaders and spokesmen. The habit was prevalent in the United States but occurred in other parts of the hemisphere as well: settlers, government agents, and military officers all failed to recognize such traditional Indian customs and institutions as the autonomy of the individual and of the group within a tribe; the frequent absence of leaders who could speak and act for entire tribes; leadership by merit; councils of elected spokesmen and civil chiefs with limited or little authority; decision by unanimous agreement; devotion to the group and antipathy to individual ambition or status-seeking; and other elements of native societies.

Despite resistance and conflicts, however, the Indian almost everywhere was changed by the white man's presence. Firearms, steel, and manufactured goods for a while made life easier and richer for many tribes, and the horse was a significant new element in the existence of nomadic peoples. Wherever traders appeared, Indians bartered eagerly for white men's goods, substituting them for their own more primitive weapons, utensils, and implements. Missionaries were often a principal influence in persuading Indians to wear white men's clothes, to learn farming and mechanical skills, to study reading, writing, and numbers, to cut their hair, to give up all their wives save one, and to adapt in many other ways to the white man's customs and ways of living.

The cost to the Indian was usually high. The newcomers introduced diseases to which the Indians had low resistance, and many more natives died from sicknesses than from warfare against the whites. On both continents, epidemics of smallpox, measles, dysentery, typhoid, tuberculosis, and other diseases wiped out whole peoples and decimated others. By the early seventeenth century, for instance, it is estimated that Indian population losses in the highland areas of Spanish America were as high as 90 per cent in many localities. Wars between white traders as well as between the imperial powers of Europe, in addition, enmeshed Indians who had become dependent on white men's goods, and tribes took sides with white men and warred upon each other to the ultimate benefit of the whites. Slave catchers and fur traders, offering whisky and other goods, encouraged activities that disrupted and eventually destroyed Indian societies. And, finally, when Indians had lost their strength and freedom, they were often left in a powerless and demoralized condition. Alcohol and drugs provided means of escape from the degradation and hopelessness of life until the arrival of death.

The remnants of some tribes on both continents dragged on in poverty and finally became extinct. Among other peoples, flickers of hope were raised from time to time by the emergence of native religious leaders and movements that promised disaster to the whites and a miraculous return to the happy life. The prophets or messiahs, who often mixed various elements of native and Christian beliefs and rituals with shamanistic magic, arose in different parts of the hemisphere at times of Indian crisis. After their subjugation, the Tupinambás of Brazil stopped their daily work and sought to reach the promised Land of the Grandfather by dancing. In the United States in the early years of the nineteenth century, the Shawnee Prophet helped rally Great Lakes Indians to the cause of his brother, Tecumseh. Another religious leader, Smohalla, a Sahaptin of the middle Columbia River, aroused dejected Plateau tribes to the promise of a brighter future after their military defeat in the 1850's. And Wovoka, a Paiute of Nevada, inspired the so-called Ghost Dance religion in the late 1880's, principally among the Plains tribes whom the U. S. Army had crushed. Wovoka's followers did a prescribed dance, accompanied by certain songs, which the prophet claimed would eventually cause the disappearance of the whites, bring back the dead Indian peoples, and restore the buffalo and old ways of life on the Plains. The dance was broken up by the Army, which feared its influence; many of Wovoka's followers among the Sioux were wiped out at Wounded Knee, South Dakota, in December 1890 and the movement disintegrated.

Although Indians suffered tremendously and their cultures experienced great changes, the white man's impact, with all its technological superiority, aggressiveness, and zeal to conquer and refashion Indians in the European image, did not fully end Indian life. Many tribes disappeared; many became more or less assimilated in the white society around them; and most adopted various material traits of white culture. But large numbers of Indians on both continents have continued to maintain some of their native beliefs and customs, and a few, in the most remote parts of the hemisphere, are to this day almost completely untouched by civilization.

25

The White Man's Conquest
of the Indians:
Latin America

IN A PATTERN THAT WAS TO BE REPEATED ALMOST EVERY-where in the Western Hemisphere, Christopher Colum-bus and the first Europeans in the New World received welcome and hospitality each time they met Indians who had never before seen white men. The gentle and unwarlike Arawaks of the Greater Antilles were described by Columbus as showing "as much lovingness as though they would give their hearts . . . they remained so much our friends that it was a marvel." Six years later, in another region of the Caribbean, Amerigo Vespucci described Indian receptions with lavish meals, dances, singing, and other festivities for the whites. "Many of them carried presents they had given us in their sleeping nets: rich feathers, bows and arrows, innu-merable parrots of many colors. . . ."

Yet Columbus had scarcely drawn back the curtain on the New World, when he was writing back to Spain: "From here, in the name of the Blessed Trinity, we can send all the slaves that can be sold. Four thousand, which, at the lowest figure, will bring twenty contos."

The Spaniards who poured into the Americas in the wake of Columbus were bent on riches and glory. They were tough, rapacious plunderers, who used the aid of Indians when they needed it, and then horrified the natives by their cruelty and lust. The West Indies was the first region to feel their tyranny, and the outraged Spanish Dominican mis-sionary, Bartolomé de las Casas, trying to interpose some protection for the Indians, provided a graphic account of the conquest of the Arawaks and Caribs in his *Brief Relation of the Destruction of the Indies*:

> They [the Spaniards] came with their Horsemen well armed with Sword and Launce, making most cruel havocks and slaughters.... Overrunning Cities and Villages, where they spared no sex nor age; neither would their cruelty pity Women with childe, whose bellies they would rip up, taking out the Infant to hew it in pieces. They would often lay wagers who should with most dexterity either cleave or cut a man in the middle.... The children they would take by the feet and dash their innocent heads against the rocks, and when they were fallen into the water, with a strange and cruel derision they would call on them to swim.... They erected certain Gallowses ... upon every one of which they would hang thirteen persons, blasphemously affirming that they did it in honour of our Redeemer and his Apostles, and then putting fire under them, they burnt the poor wretches alive. Those whom their pity did think to spare, they would send away with their hands cut off, and so hanging by the skin.

The Indians were bewildered by the ferocious hostility of a people to whom they had done nothing but, on the contrary, had welcomed with delight. Las Casas related the story of one chief named Hathvey who fled to Cuba from another island and told the Indians there that the Spaniards seemed to worship gold as a supernatural power; perhaps if they appealed to the same spirit, they could get it to appease the Spaniards' wrath. But despite the natives' prayers to a chestful of gold, the Spaniards came to Cuba in 1511, captured Hathvey, and burned him alive. In the Indian's last moments, when a monk tried to tell him of the glories of the Spaniards' Heaven, the chief replied, "Let me go to Hell that I may not come where they are."

Although it is not known how many Arawaks, Caribs, and Ciboneys the Spaniards slaughtered before they finally overran all the islands, estimates of Indian deaths, from one cause or another, have ranged up to six million and more. Many of the natives were forced to work as slaves in the Spanish mines, and their women, when not raped and killed, were impressed as domestic and estate workers. The Indians of the West Indies did not become extinct, as has sometimes been said, but they died off in great numbers, and the survivors eventually became mixed with their Spanish conquerors and with Negro slaves imported from Africa.

As Spanish gropings continued to new lands, rumors of riches greater than any yet found drew the conquerors to the mainland and Mexico. In 1519, Hernán Cortés landed near present-day Veracruz. Through a combination of many factors, including diplomatic and military skill, unprecedented ferocity and determination, the possession of horses and guns that struck fear among the Indians, advice from his valuable Indian mistress and interpreter, Doña Marina (also called La Malinche or Malintzin), the aid of Indian allies who hated the Aztecs, and indecision and confusion on the part of the Aztec leaders who thought the Spaniards might be white gods, Cortés moved inland and entered Tenochtitlán, the Aztec capital of Moctezuma II. However, while Cortés was away settling difficulties with his coastal rear guard, the cruelty of his lieutenant, Pedro de Alvarado, resulted in an Aztec uprising that led to the death of Moctezuma, but also drove the Spaniards out of the capital. In 1521, Cortés was back; with a huge army of Indian allies he defeated Cuauhtémoc, Moctezuma's nephew and successor, and in an eighty-five-day battle conquered and virtually destroyed the city.

The overthrow of the Aztec regime was an almost incredible event, but the conquest of Peru in 1532 was accomplished with even greater speed. Francisco Pizarro, also aided by Indian allies as well as by a schism in the Inca leadership, simply seized the leading claimant to Inca rule, Atahualpa, during a meeting and with that act of treachery tumbled an empire. The daring stroke could have worked so successfully only in such a top-heavy, regimented state as that of the Incas. Although a splinter Neo-Inca state resisted until 1572, most of the Indians quietly accepted the change in rulers. The wealth of Peru was awesome: Atahualpa's ransom—consisting of nearly enough gold and silver to fill a large room—amounted in value to more than $150,000,000.

Rumors of riches north of Peru, particularly of the existence of El Hombre Dorado, "The Golden Man," drew Spaniards to the realm of the Chibchas in present-day Colombia. Possibly the report stemmed from a Chibchan custom of covering a chieftain with gold dust at the time of his accession. The tale soon developed into the legend of El Dorado, a land whose riches would surpass anything yet found. It was to be a constant lure to Spanish exploration and conquest, a golden myth never fulfilled but always just over the horizon. While it was no El Dorado, the Chibchan realm was rich enough. It was conquered by Jiménez de Quesada in 1537, falling as easily as Peru, without large battles. The divided political structure of the chiefdom was as ruinous to effective opposition to the Spaniards as the one-man rule of the Incas and the Chibchans were overcome in less than a year.

There were other conquests and lootings of native peoples in Panama, Guatemala, Venezuela, and elsewhere, but there were no more Mexicos and Perus. One of Pizarro's lieutenants, Diego de Almagro, conquered Chile but found no gold there. Francisco de Coronado in 1540 marched north from Mexico in search of the wealth of the Seven Cities of Cíbola, reported by the wanderer Cabeza de Vaca and the priest Fray Marcos de Niza. Cíbola proved to be the mud-walled Zuñi pueblos whose only wealth was corn and turquoise jewelry; but an Indian assured Coronado that great riches lay in the land of Quivira farther to the northeast. Coronado pursued his second will-o'-wisp to the grass huts of the Wichita Indians on the plains of Kansas, then unhappily turned back. The Southwest after that was abandoned until near the turn of the century.

As the wealth of the Indians was seized, their cultures destroyed, and their lands enfolded in the white man's new provinces, a Spanish colonial pattern gradually emerged. It differed from that which was later established by the French and English in North America. There, the natives were either enrolled in a somewhat free trade with the whites, or were displaced by settlers who worked the land themselves and raised cash crops for the world market. In the Spanish colonies, the Spaniards established themselves as rulers of the Indians whose enforced labor they employed to extract raw materials and produce commodities for the conquerors. The Spanish colonial empire was essentially parasitic. It consumed everything and manufactured nothing. By the time the sources of wealth dried up and other countries became industrialized, Spain was a shell and a second-class power.

The principal Spanish device for the administration of the Indians was a system of indirect rule called the *encomienda*, a grant made to a favored individual for the right to the land and labor of the natives in a given area. In theory, the *encomiendero*, or grantee, did not acquire ownership of the land or the right to interfere in native affairs; he had to work through local Indian leaders known as *caciques* (the West Indian Arawak word for "chieftains"), who were given special favors to act as puppet bosses over the other Indians. In return, the *encomiendero* was given responsibility for the physical and spiritual well-being of his charges. The system was designed to channel Indian labor to productive use and to facilitate the Indians' conversion to Christianity, two motives that were frustrated by the unbridled savagery of many of the Spaniards in the colonies. The device therefore was meant to give the Indians a degree of protection for ends deemed purposeful by Church and State, but it was abused almost everywhere. Despite efforts in Spain to reform the system and make it work, there was little enforcement of court orders in the colonies. In practice, the *encomienda* system merely quickened the enslavement of the Indian population.

From time to time native revolts shook different parts of the empire. At the same time, the native population declined drastically, principally as a result of epidemics. Finally, the *encomienda* system was replaced with direct rule over the Indians by Crown representatives. Indian labor in many areas was allotted by the political authorities to individual Spanish landowners, miners, or other colonists under an institution known as *repartimiento*. The Indians' lot improved only slightly; their labor was still compulsory, and although they received wages, they continued to pay tribute in money or in kind to the representatives of the Crown. *Repartimiento*, in time, ended also. The shrinking Indian population and the rising demand for their labor led to competition for workers. For a time, Indians were allowed to contract freely for their labor. Eventually, most of them ended in a state of peonage, hopelessly in debt to their employers. The debts were inherited, generation after generation, and peonage continued for large numbers of Indians in Latin America until well into the twentieth century.

In Peru, the spread of livestock and the new crops introduced by the Spaniards, as well as the growth of the tribute economy, gradually reduced the capacity of the land to support the people. Some Indians abandoned the land to work in the mines, along with those who had been taken from their home settlements for forced labor. Other natives moved to the colonial cities where they were employed as servants and public workers and were eventually absorbed into a growing, part-white mestizo class. In some cases, the Spaniards moved whole communities to new locations where the people were impressed into a labor pool. For a while outright slavery was legal. Members of a native class called *yanaconas* were bound in serflike conditions to individual landowners. Much of the new order was an adaptation of traditional Inca institutions, including draft labor, the relocation of unreliable villages, and a class system, but it was administered in a way that was calamitous for the Indians. The natives were no longer ruled by a relatively small nobility which, in turn, was careful to protect the welfare of the people. They were the serfs of a nation that used them as a labor force with little concern for their condition. The heavy burdens on the Indians, and the corruption of the administrators resulted in a series of uprisings in Peru from 1779 to 1783 led by Tupac Amaru II, who claimed to be a descendant of the royal Incas.

Although these, and other native revolts, were put down, Spain's weakness made possible, by the early part of the nineteenth century, the overthrow of its colonial rule and the establishment of independent republics. In Peru, the mines were played out, but the landowners were now free to produce crops for world markets. Huge estates, called *haciendas*, were worked by Indian sharecroppers and peons; elsewhere many Indian groups withdrew into closed, self-sufficient, stable peasant communities—in effect, self-imposed reservations that grew apart from the white and mestizo political, economic, and social life of the country.

The Spanish colonial tribute state, in regions from Mexico to Peru, had rested on the presence of productive land and a large, docile population to work it. In other Latin American regions, the combination of these conditions had been generally absent. In Chile, where the land was good and the native population large, the Araucanians had never known the rule of the Incas or of powerful chieftains, and they were not willing to accept it from the white men. The Spaniards subdued a northern group of Araucanians rather quickly, but the more populous Indian groups in the south resisted the Spaniards throughout the colonial period and continued their hostility to the Chilean republic until near the end of the nineteenth century. The interior areas of the tropical forest tribes, at the same time, possessed both poorer land and a sparse, scattered population. When Pizarro killed Atahualpa, the entire Inca empire fell; but when the Spaniards captured a tropical forest headman, they won command over a single settlement of a few hundred people who owned little or nothing of value to the conquerors.

When the tropical forest tribesmen were attacked, more-over, they could simply withdraw farther into the jungle, from where they could—if they were so disposed—strike back at the white men at will. After their conquest of Peru, the Spaniards established several communities, totaling 20,000 people, on the borders of the Montaña country of the Jívaros, but in 1599 the Jívaros wiped them out. In the process, the Jívaros carried off many white women, and even today the features of some of their people show evidence of these white female ancestors.

The tropical forest tribes that lived along the coasts and main waterways, principally in Brazil, were less successful in their resistance. The Portuguese at first attempted colonization only halfheartedly, using Brazil mainly as a source of Brazil wood, which provided a red dye, and as a way station for the East India trade. But colonization was accelerated in the mid-sixteenth century, the Tupinambá settlements were overcome, one by one, and the Indians were put to work as slaves on the coastal plantations. The Portuguese slave trade soon depopulated much of the area, as Indians died off or faded into the interior country.

Along the middle reaches of the Amazon and its tribu-taries, tribes were undisturbed for a longer period, but eventu-ally the inroads of trade and commerce reached many of them, bringing changes to their lives. The Tupian Mundu-rucús, for example, were attracted to the rubber boom of the middle of the nineteenth century. As they sold their services as rubber tappers in exchange for food, trade goods, and luxury items, they gradually lost knowledge of native manu-factures. Today Mundurucú villages of rubber tappers trade raw latex for goods and credit at interior posts run by traders who act as patriarchal leaders and patrons of the Indians.

Throughout the period of conquest and colonialism, the emissaries of the Catholic Church were almost a separate Europeanizing force, sometimes working with the soldiers and administrators, but often against them, or in areas where their influence did not reach. Franciscan, Dominican, and Augustinian friars went out, barefoot and unarmed, to Indian settlements, where, aided by native interpreters, they learned the language, performed baptisms, smashed idols and tem-ples, and sought to convert the chief and principal people. Frequently the friars and priests were intolerant destroyers of Indian culture who condoned and cooperated in the ravages of the conquistadors; but at other times they were the best friends, and the only protectors, of the Indians. In most cases, they sincerely believed that they were acting for the natives' best interests—although the Indians themselves would not always have agreed—and this was a motive to which few conquistadors or colonists could even pretend. The activities of two well-known religious leaders, both of them at one time bishops in territory of the Mayas, demonstrate the extreme points of view that existed among the Catholic missionaries in the New World. The Dominican friar Bartolomé de las Casas, already mentioned, accompanied the conquistador Diego Velásquez to Cuba in 1511. Appalled by Spanish cruelty to the Indians, he devoted his life to fighting the barbarism of the conquests and the evils of the *encomienda* system. He even carried his struggle to the Spanish court and eventually obtained a royal decree that outlawed slavery in Peru. In 1544, he was appointed bishop of Chiapas in southern Mexico, but a hostile administration and a disloyal clergy forced him to leave after a few years. On the other hand, Diego de Landa, a Franciscan friar who became bishop of Yucatán, was an intolerant and uncompromising zealot who stamped out Mayan spiritual beliefs as "idolatry," destroyed Mayan writings, and ruthlessly punished any attempt to cling to native teachings. Yet once he had burned the Indian books, destroying all the valuable information of the past that they contained, he spent much of his time writing down Mayan history, preserving the meaning of the date-glyphs carved on stone, and recording the details of Mayan culture. His work bequeathed to the future, however, only a part of what he had destroyed, for the information he left related principally to the late prehistoric period.

Of all the missionaries, the most influential were probably the Jesuits, who established missions in many parts of Latin America, even where colonists had barely appeared. These became in practice miniature theocratic states, and some of them played important roles in the history of South America. In Brazil, Jesuits were strong defenders of the Indians under their care, and mission Indians played a significant part in helping the Portuguese eject the Dutch from that colony during the imperial struggles of the seventeenth century. The Jesuits were especially active on the northern frontier of Mexico and in southwest Brazil and most of Paraguay. In the latter area, they helped Indians evade "Paulista" slave-catchers from the São Paulo region of Brazil, withdrawing and concentrating the Guaraní population into Jesuit "reductions," tightly disciplined missions that eventually came to comprise what was practically an Indian state ruled by the Jesuits. The regime was severely criticized by whites, who accused the Jesuits of enslaving the Guaranís, profiting from their labor, and defying the Crown. In time, Jesuit political activities in both Europe and America angered the national monarchies, and in 1767 the Jesuits were expelled from the New World.

On the whole, the Church played an important role in the degeneration of Indian culture. Conversion was often only superficial; many lesser Indian gods and spirits simply became merged with Christian saints, and some peoples retained parts of their earlier beliefs and mixed them with Christianity. In regions of Guatemala even today, for example, the results of such blendings can be seen in the religious practices of some of the peoples in the Mayan highlands. But mission life broke down native political institutions, brought together tribes that had previously been scarcely aware of each other's existence but now proceeded to wage war against one another, and served unwittingly as centers from which many of the devastating epidemics of European diseases spread through the Indian populations.

26

The White Man's Conquest
of the Indians: The United
States and Canada

IN A.D. 1006, ACCORDING TO A NORSE SAGA, LEIF ERIKSSON'S
brother, Thorwald, exploring somewhere along the northeast coast of North America, seized and killed eight Indians, whom he and his men called Skrellings. This is the
oldest known account of contact between peoples of the Old
World and the New. Viking explorers and colonists, thereafter, certainly did get to know Eskimos in Greenland. In
addition, Viking sites have been positively identified on the
Newfoundland coast. But by 1492 whatever settlements the
Norsemen established on the North American continent had
disappeared, and so, apparently, had all European knowledge
of the native inhabitants of that part of the earth.

The accepted history of relations between Europeans and
Indians north of Mexico begins, instead, in Florida, with the
discovery of that peninsula in 1513 by Juan Ponce de León,
who had sailed north from Puerto Rico. Eight years later, Ponce
de León returned to Florida, planning to found a settlement.
Instead, he offended the local Calusa Indians, who inflicted a
mortal wound on him and drove away his expedition. Subse-
quently, Spanish slave-catchers ravaged the Florida coast, out-
raging the Calusas who, in turn, looted Spanish treasure ships
driven ashore during storms in the Florida straits. To secure
the area against the French, who were exploring farther
north, the Spaniards made another attempt at colonization
in 1526; but a settlement of some five hundred men, women,
and children under Lucas Vásquez de Ayllón, planted somewhere on the Carolina coast, vanished without a trace. Two

years later, Pánfilo de Narváez landed an expedition of conquest, this time on the Gulf Coast near Tampa Bay. Coun-
tering the attacks of Indians who had been made hostile by
the raids of Spanish slavers, he moved north, exploring and
searching for wealth. A series of disasters, including attacks
by Apalachee Indians who resented his cruelties, depleted
his ranks. The survivors circled the Gulf, trying to return to
Mexico, but only a handful got as far as the Texas coast.

Four of them, including Álvar Núñez Cabeza de Vaca and
a Moorish slave named Estevanico, wandered inland across
the Southwest (1535–6), until they were found by Spanish
slave hunters in northwestern Mexico. During their long trek,
they met many Indian bands in present-day Texas and New
Mexico, who treated them with friendship as powerful spiritual men, and told them of fabulously rich Indians farther
north. These stories, related by the survivors when they
reached Mexico, induced the Spaniards to send Estevanico
back north on a reconnaissance trip with a Franciscan priest,
Fray Marcos de Niza. Estevanico reached the Zuñi pueblo of
Hawikuh, where he incurred the anger of the Indians, who
killed him. Returning safely to Mexico, Fray Marcos, however, confirmed the original stories of rich Indian cities in
the north, and his exaggerations led to the expeditions of
Francisco Vásquez de Coronado and Hernando de Soto.

Thinking he would find the mythical Seven Cities of
Cíbola, Coronado followed false leads (1540–2) that led him
not to treasure but to the Southwest adobe towns of the
Zuñis and Pueblos and the grass-thatched huts of the
Wichitas in Kansas. De Soto, with a rival expedition of some
five hundred men, landed on the west coast of Florida on
May 30, 1539, and struck off for Cíbola. Lured in an errant
fashion by constant rumors of great riches just ahead, the
expedition members wandered for three years through the
Southeast, meeting Creeks, Cherokees, Chickasaws, Mobiles,
and numerous other Indian groups, and leaving behind them
a crimson trail of cruelty and pillage. They impressed Indians
as guides; seized others as servants and dragged them along in
chains with collars around their necks; looted and burned
villages; tortured and murdered native leaders; and massacred thousands of people. After circling through parts of
what are now Georgia, South and North Carolina, Tennessee,
Alabama, and Mississippi, the expedition crossed the Mississippi River, wandered through present-day Arkansas, and
returned to the lower Mississippi, where de Soto died. In

1542, the survivors managed to make their way through Texas to Mexico.

Other Spaniards continued to try to colonize the eastern coast of Florida but without success until 1565 when they founded St. Augustine among the Timucua Indians. Three years earlier, Frenchmen had built a settlement (Charlesfort) on the South Carolina coast, but had abandoned it, and in 1564, had constructed Fort Caroline at the mouth of the St. Johns River in Florida, where they had become embroiled in intertribal wars of the Timucuas. Now, the newly arrived Spaniards overwhelmed and massacred the French, and from then on exerted complete control over the region. Jesuit priests established a few Spanish missions along the coast as far north as Chesapeake Bay and began to convert the Indians. The latter turned on the priests, however, and the Spaniards abandoned all the missions except those in Florida, where they were gradually able to pacify and convert the Timucuas, Apalachees, and Calusas.

Coronado's frustrations in the Southwest, meanwhile, caused the Spaniards in Mexico to lose interest temporarily in that area. After 1580, however, a few abortive attempts were made to take possession of the region, and in 1598 a large colonizing expedition of settlers, soldiers, and priests under Don Juan de Oñate finally set out to establish control over the Pueblo country. Arriving among the eastern Pueblos on the Rio Grande, Oñate evicted the Indians from one of their towns and declared it the capital of his new colony. Some of the pueblos resisted, but they were sacked and their inhabitants killed, tortured, or enslaved. The Spanish *encomienda* system, binding the Indians as serfs to their lands, was imposed. Franciscan friars were installed in the pueblos; and churches were built. A permanent Spanish capital was established at Santa Fe in 1610, and the frontier province of New Spain seemed under control. But many of the Indians clung secretly to their own customs and beliefs, and continued to carry out their ceremonies in the underground kivas. Serious conflict between civil and religious officials weakened Spanish authority over the Indians, and after 1660 a series of droughts and raids by Apaches so worsened the Pueblos' lot that they turned back increasingly to their own native religion.

One of the leaders of the religious revival was Popé, a "medicine doctor," or priest, from San Juan pueblo. He soon began to preach resistance to the Spaniards, sending messages to the other pueblos and holding secret meetings to unify the Indians. In 1680, the Pueblos staged a concerted uprising, killed more than four hundred Spaniards, and drove the rest completely out of the Pueblo country. Popé's success turned his head, however; he became a tyrant and killed all Indians who opposed him. Without the protection of Spanish soldiers, the Pueblos were unable to ward off Apache raiders, who made away with tribute, Pueblo women, and horses. The Spaniards had been fairly successful in keeping horses out of the hands of the nomadic, raiding Indians; now the animals began to spread north in large numbers to Utes, Shoshonis, and tribes of the Plateau and the Plains. A few years after the revolt, Popé died, but Pueblo difficulties increased. A plague swept the towns, and the Spaniards —regrouped in El Paso, where they had fled with a few Pueblo Indians—began to make attempts to reconquer the province. Many of the Pueblo people moved out of danger, some to the Hopis in the west, some to the Navahos, and some to join groups of Apaches and Utes. Both the Hopis and Zuñis, in addition, moved their own towns to mesa tops. Finally, in 1692, the Spaniards reentered Santa Fe and after four years of fighting repossessed the province.

Spanish rule, however, never extended thereafter much beyond the Rio Grande area. In the west, the Hopis were never reconquered. Spanish missions were founded eventually by Padre Eusebio Kino among the Pimas of southern Arizona, but beyond them, the Yumas, Apaches, and Navahos were too warlike for the establishment of small Spanish settlements among them, or too remote, nomadic, or few in number to make a large settlement economically feasible. New Mexico, for generations, remained essentially a frontier colony, surrounded by bands of Indians that alternately raided and traded with the Spaniards. The latter, in turn, let the hostile Indians relatively alone, occasionally sending out punitive expeditions when Apache or Navaho raids increased, and buying slaves from, and trading with, Comanches and other Plains tribes on the east and northeast whom they looked upon as something of a defensive buffer between their New Mexican settlements and the French who were expanding westward.

Much earlier, the French had entrenched themselves on the continent's northeast coast. From the time of the Cabots, the explorers who had reached that part of the New World had reported the presence of rich fishing banks and Indians who would trade furs for trinkets. European fishermen flocked to the Gulf of St. Lawrence and confirmed the stories, and in 1534, when Jacques Cartier reached the area, he found Algonquian-speaking tribesmen trading furs to fishermen who came ashore to dry their catches. Shortly afterward, French hatters began to make a cheap, fine-quality, and almost-inde-structible felt from the beaver furs coming from this part of the New World, and the demand for beaver suddenly increased. The new market stimulated trade with the Indian tribes, and the natives, in turn, began to war against each other for exclusive rights to barter furs to the Europeans for the goods the whites gave them. It was the start of a pattern of savage rivalry for monopoly trade privileges that spread disastrously, from tribe to tribe, across the continent during the next three hundred years. To each native group the acquisition of guns, powder, steel, kettles, and other European goods meant new power and prestige and an enriched existence which they wanted for themselves and tried to keep from their rivals and enemies. Sometimes tribes interposed themselves between white traders and enemy groups; often it led to violence against the traders or between tribes. In 1608, for example, Samuel de Champlain found the Hurons and some of the Algonquian-speaking tribes of the St. Lawrence Valley at war with the Iroquois of New York. The following year, Champlain and some of his men explored southward with Hurons, coming on the lake that now bears Champlain's name. At the south end of the lake, on July 29, 1609, the party ran into Mohawks, and Champlain used his muskets to aid the Hurons against the Iroquois band. The action incurred a long-lasting resentment against the French by the Mohawks and other Iroquois of New York, who had no guns with which to oppose their enemies and did not acquire them until the Dutch began trading with them in the region of present-day Albany after 1624.

By that time, Frenchmen were exploring far into the interior of the continent. Going up the St. Lawrence and other waterways, they reached the Great Lakes, arriving by 1623 at the eastern end of Lake Superior in the homeland of midwestern Algonquian-speaking tribes. Licensed traders, missionaries, and soldiers followed the explorers, building posts and missions, enrolling Ottawas, Ojibwas, Foxes, and other tribes in the fur trade, and winning them to alliances with the French. Unlicensed traders also appeared in the interior. Known as *coureurs de bois* (runners of the woods), they were generally restless adventurers who defied the laws designed to protect the fur monopolies and stole away from the St. Lawrence settlements to make their way into the newly discovered regions and gather furs for themselves. Many of them took to wilderness existence, married Indian women, and adopted native ways of life. In time, their half-blood children comprised a large element of the personnel of the fur trade, working as free trappers and hunters for themselves or as engagés and voyageurs for others.

To the south, along the Atlantic coast, other Europeans had begun meanwhile to compete with the French and Spanish exploiters of the New World. British mariners, returning from coastal surveys, had excited wealthy merchants and prominent patrons in England with the potentialities of permanent trading posts, secured by colonists, in unoccupied regions of the North American coast. In 1584, Sir Walter Raleigh dispatched an expedition that explored the outer islands of North Carolina. The next year a Raleigh-backed colony was established on Roanoke Island. Friction developed with the Indians, however, and the colonists returned to England in 1586. The following year, a new colony of ninety-one men, seventeen women, and nine children was settled on the same site under Governor John White. Returning to England for supplies, White was held up by the approach of the Spanish Armada, and when he finally got back to Roanoke Island, all the members of the colony, including his granddaughter, Virginia Dare, the first child born of English parents in the New World, had vanished. Although Indians may have wiped out the settlement, there is more reason to believe that the colonists had moved elsewhere, possibly among friendlier Indians. At any rate, the fate of the "Lost Colony" has never been solved.

Another group, including many gentlemen adventurers who hoped to realize profits from their undertaking, finally established the first permanent English settlement in America at Jamestown, Virginia, north of Roanoke Island in 1607. The region was ruled by Powhatan, the strongest chief of a confederacy of some two hundred villages of approximately thirty Algonquian-speaking groups spread across most of tidewater Virginia from the Potomac River almost as far south as Albemarle Sound. Many of the settlers, ill-suited to the hardships and labor of the new life, died of disease, while the rest stayed alive by seizing or buying corn from the Indians. There were sporadic clashes, and in later years John

Smith related how, on one occasion, he was captured and saved from death only when Pocahontas, Powhatan's daughter, threw herself on top of him. The story may or may not be true, but at one time Governor Thomas Dale staved off a war with the Indians by kidnapping Pocahontas and holding her as a hostage. Later, converted to Christianity and baptized Rebecca, Pocahontas married John Rolfe, one of the colony's leading men, and accompanied him to England, where she died of smallpox in 1617.

For several years, an uneasy peace, sometimes interrupted by clashes between the colonists and individual native villages, existed around the new settlement. Powhatan, who was probably more than sixty years old, came to recognize the benefits of peaceful trade with the English, and the colony's backers in London encouraged the settlers to conciliate the Indians rather than get into a war with them that might be ruinous to the venture. By the time that Powhatan died in 1618, however, relationships between the whites and Indians had become seriously strained. A rich market had developed in England for the tobacco that the colonists were planting, and the settlers were pressing the natives for more land on which to grow the crop. Friction increased, and in 1622 Powhatan's brother, an elderly man named Opechancanough, led the Indians in a sudden attack on the colony. In a few hours, three hundred and fifty whites were slain and several settlements were destroyed. A long war followed, during which the whites, aided by Christianized natives, gradually crushed the warring Indians and killed Opechancanough. When hostilities ended in 1644, the Powhatan confederacy had been smashed. Remnant Indian groups took refuge on the eastern shore of Chesapeake Bay or elsewhere; a few powerless elements were allowed to remain in Virginia where their descendants, known as Pamunkeys, Mattaponys, and Chickahominys, still reside in little communities.

In other parts of the Atlantic coast, the train of events was somewhat the same. Indians greeted with friendship the first whites they saw, and lived to regret it. In New York, the Indians were friendly to the Dutch, who founded their colony of New Amsterdam in 1609, and brought the settlers food and other gifts and traded furs to them. Part of the area (Staten Island and Long Island) was the home of Canarsies and other members of the Delaware confederacy and part (Manhattan, Bronx, and the lower Hudson River

Valley) was occupied by members of the Wappinger confederacy, relatives of the Mahicans, or River Indians, who
lived farther up the Hudson River. One of the Wappinger
tribes, the Manhattes, made the famous trade of Manhattan
Island to the Dutch for goods that supposedly had a value of
twenty-four dollars at the time. Inevitably, conflicts arose
between the newcomers and the Indians, and by 1643 the
settlers and the Wappingers were at war. When hostilities
ceased, hundred of natives had been killed, and the power
of the confederacy had been broken.

In New England, similarly, coastal explorers and traders
were greeted by the Indians with warm friendship until one
of the sea captains treacherously seized some natives to sell
in the Mediterranean slave markets. Resentments arose along
the coast and were felt by the Pilgrims in 1620 when they
came ashore tentatively on Cape Cod. Moving on to
Plymouth, they established themselves in an area almost
entirely depopulated by an epidemic that had been introduced by white sea traders and had caused the deaths of
great numbers of Indians. Nevertheless, in March 1621, a
few months after the Pilgrims' landing, an Indian named
Samoset appeared at Plymouth and in friendly fashion
greeted the colonists with English words that he had
learned from coastal traders. Soon afterward, he brought to
Plymouth the grand sachem of the Wampanoag Indians,
Massasoit. The latter, like Powhatan in Virginia, quickly
learned the value of peaceful trade with the newcomers whose
friendship and goods would give him prestige and power
over leaders of rival tribes. Peace was also desired by the
Pilgrims, and during Massasoit's lifetime the whites and
Indians lived in friendship and maintained a trade that was
beneficial to both sides. In the first years of their settlement,
the Pilgrims were aided by an Indian named Squanto, who
instructed them in wilderness living. Prior to the Pilgrims'
arrival, Squanto had been kidnapped by a trader and taken
to Europe for sale as a slave. Ransomed by an Englishman,
he had been taken to England and taught to speak English.
Eventually, a ship had returned him to Massachusetts. Without his aid, it is possible that the new colony would not
have survived the long bitter winter of 1621–2.

In time, the colonists pushed inland, buying and trading
property from the Indians. Immigration swelled, and new
settlements were established from Maine to Connecticut.
The newcomers included many who treated the Indians

high-handedly, and native resentments flared. The first violence erupted in the southern Connecticut homeland of the Pequots, a division of the Mohegans who were a separate branch of the Hudson River Mahicans (both names meant "wolves," and both groups were sometimes called Mohicans). The Pequots and Mohegans had engaged in intertribal warfare, but in 1636 Massachusetts Bay Puritans, who were comparative newcomers to the New World, became angered by an alleged Pequot attack on some white men. Their destruction of a Pequot town led to a brief but savage war in which the whites were aided by Mohegans and by Narraganset Indians of Rhode Island. Encouraged by their clergymen who regarded the Pequots as agents of Satan, the Puritans crushed those Indians, firing their principal town near the Mystic River in Connecticut and roasting to death or shooting more than six hundred of its inhabitants.

After that, anti-Indian feeling increased everywhere, and following Massasoit's death in 1661, the era of good relations between the Massachusetts settlers and the Wampanoags ended. Numerous injustices were visited upon the Indians, who smarted with resentments. Brooding on the Indians' difficulties, Massasoit's son Metacom, known to the colonists as King Philip, tried to form an alliance among the New England tribes, and even the Mohawks of New York, to oust the whites from the country. Philip was twenty-four years old when he assumed leadership of the Wampanoags in 1662. He was proud and statesmanlike, and his able oratory and agility at outwitting the whites with whom he treated in council infuriated the English. For many years he threatened war, while he labored without success to create an Indian alliance. Old rivalries among the tribes, as well as distrust by other chiefs of his motives and youthful capabilities, frustrated him; but in 1675 war erupted anyway. Philip had initial successes against the colonists, and their dramatic impact induced some of the tribes, including the Nipmucs of Massachusetts and the Narragansets, to join him. More Indian successes followed, as the natives, warring in relatively small bands, assaulted one town after another from the Connecticut River to Massachusetts and Narragansett Bay. Fifty-two of the ninety white settlements in New England were attacked at one time or another, twelve were completely destroyed, and at one point the colonies seemed in danger of total defeat. Early in 1676, however, the Indians began to run out of food, and Philip suffered serious

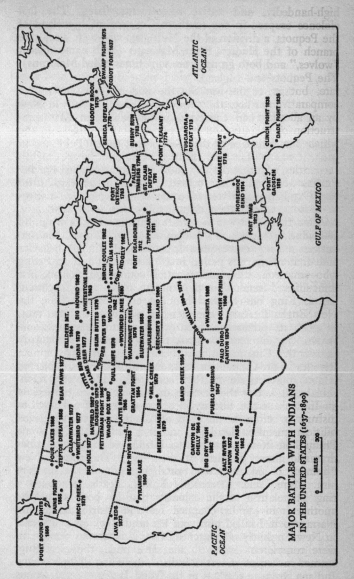

MAJOR BATTLES WITH INDIANS
IN THE UNITED STATES (1637–1890)

defections. The colonists, at the same time, began to employ friendly Indians to help run down hostile groups, and the tide of war changed quickly. With the help of an Indian informer, Philip was killed on August 12. The individual bands were wiped out, one by one, and Indian power came to an end in New England.

One result of the war was the undoing of much of the work of John Eliot, the "Apostle of the Indians" in New England, who had converted many natives in Massachusetts to Christianity and had translated the Bible into the Algonquian language of the Massachuset tribe. (Published in 1663, it was the first Bible printed in America by the English authorities.) During the war, most of Eliot's so-called Praying Indians were loyal to the colonists; but the latter were fearful of all Indians, and treated some of the converted natives as enemies, turning them against the whites and Christianity. Another byproduct was the creation in the white man's mind of enduring images of "Indian savagery." From then on, settlers moving ever-westward equated all Indian behavior with that of the war period in New England and, expecting the worst from every Indian, often committed violence first and suffered retaliation that might never have occurred. Scalping was one of the vivid images to emerge from the war. Settlers thereafter considered it a universal Indian trait, although its origin has recently come into question. Some Indians in different parts of the hemisphere, particularly among the Circum-Caribbean chiefdoms, did take human trophies in pre-Columbian days; and the Spaniards, subjected to such practices during their conquests, undoubtedly retaliated in kind. But the practice of scalping, or customs close to it—such as the cutting off of ears—was not unknown to Europeans before the discovery of America. Poachers received such treatment in England, and it is certain that, in some parts of the New World, whites introduced scalping to tribes that had never practiced it themselves. The war in New England, at any rate, was brutal; but not all the savagery was on one side. After King Philip's death, it seemed a matter of course to the colonists that his body should be quartered, his limbs chopped off and distributed among those who had killed him, and his head stuck on a pole and displayed publicly. Of interest, also, is what was done with live Indians; not averse to the slave trade, the New Englanders packed off defeated Indians, including Philip's widow and son, to slave markets in the West Indies.

Indians in the Middle Atlantic colonies fared little better than those in Virginia, New York, and New England. Maryland settlers, showing little patience with the Nanticokes, rapidly rid them from that colony, killing many of them and forcing the rest to take refuge with other tribes farther inland. Swedish settlers in Delaware got along better with the members of the Delaware confederation, and most of those Indians were tolerated by the whites in a general state of amity, buttressed by a peaceful trade, for more than a century. It was the Delawares' good fortune, temporarily, to have their country settled upon by William Penn and his Quakers, for the latter showed more concern for Indian rights than most settlers elsewhere. Several Delawares, including the leader Tamanend, whom the English called Tammany, made the celebrated treaty with Penn in 1682. The goodwill lasted for about fifty years. Then whites began crowding the Indians out of eastern Pennsylvania, and by 1751 the Delawares, together with remnants of the Mahicans who had been forced out of the Hudson River Valley, were looking for new homes for themselves on the western side of the Alleghenies near the Shawnees.

The ardent competition for profits from the fur trade, meanwhile, had affected many tribes from upper New York to beyond the Mississippi River. By 1624, the Dutch, who had built a post near the present site of Albany, were supplying guns to the Iroquois for furs. Almost at once the Iroquois turned their new weapons against the French and their Huron and Algonquian allies farther north. A crisis arose for the Iroquois, however, when their country began to be depleted of furs. In order to secure beaver Iroquois hunters had to invade the lands of other tribes farther north and west. Quarrels ensued, and the Iroquois, in some measure of desperation, tried to arrange a peace with the Hurons and secure the furs those people were getting from Canadian hunting grounds in order to trade them with the Dutch. The French resisted this diversion of beaver pelts from their own depots at Montreal and Quebec, and for some years the Iroquois tribes and the French, with their native allies and suppliers, struck back and forth at each other. During the same period, Jesuit missionaries moved through the troubled fur country, residing in native villages, suffering privations, torture, and death, but laboring steadfastly to convert the Indians to the Catholicism of France.

The intrigues and machinations of the Dutch and French

kept the Indians stirred up against each other until 1649. In that year, after numerous frustrations, a war party of at least a thousand Senecas and Mohawks made their way, undetected, into the Huron country of Georgian Bay north of present-day Toronto and with extreme savagery shattered the Huron nation almost overnight. With their principal towns burned and great numbers of their people slain, the Huron survivors fled in fear, heading westward and spreading panic before them. Some of them managed to recombine in new locations where, in time, they came to be known as Wendats, or Wyandots, their name for the Huron confederacy that no longer existed.

The Iroquois, in the meanwhile, launched a series of wars of annihilation against various neighbors of the Hurons. Just west of the former Huron homeland, they fell on the Tionontatis, or Tobacco People, crushing them utterly in December 1649. In the early 1650's, they destroyed a confederacy of peoples north of Lake Erie, known as the Neutrals because they had tried to avoid involvement in the Iroquois-Huron struggle. The Eries of western Pennsylvania fell victim next in a four-year conflict, and in the mid-1670's the Iroquois vanquished the Susquehannocks, or Conestogas, of central Pennsylvania. The three decades of fighting tired and weakened the Iroquois, but they adopted large numbers of the defeated peoples into their own towns, and with the loyalty of the newcomers soon regained their vigor. In their wars up to this time, the separate tribes that comprised the Five Nations had generally made policy for themselves and fought alone or in combination with one or two of the other tribes. Now they began acting in concert, and the full strength of the League was made apparent. During the 1680's and 1690's, the French, with Indian allies, struck repeatedly at the Iroquois, but without effect. After that, the Iroquois position hardened into one of independence. Occupying a central location between the English—who had succeeded the Dutch in New York—and the French, they continued in general to be more friendly to the English, but maintained a watchful neutrality and exercised a balance of power between traders and authorities of both sides.

The Iroquois had begun their wars with the aim of seizing control of the huge traffic in furs that came down from the Great Lakes in canoes to the French on the St. Lawrence. With the abrupt elimination of the Hurons as middlemen suppliers of furs to the French, the trade had been seriously disrupted. Moreover, Iroquois war parties had roamed westward after fleeing enemies, and the Great Lakes tribes, in whose lands most of the furs were harvested, had become fearful and moved farther west themselves. Ottawas, Potawatomis, Sauks, Foxes, Illinois tribes, and others had all shifted their locations, and the pressures of tribe against tribe had been felt as far west as the villages of the Dakotas, or Sioux, in Minnesota. Eventually, the French reorganized the trade; furs were again gathered, and the Ottawas replaced the Hurons as middlemen and began bringing furs out of the western country by way of the Ottawa River, which was north of the St. Lawrence and beyond the reach of the Iroquois. With the trade's revival, the French continued pushing westward, rebuilding old alliances and seeking new tribes to turn into fur gatherers.

In 1659–60, two French traders, Pierre Esprit Radisson and the Sieur des Groseilliers, traveled from the western end of Lake Superior into Canadian fur country inhabited by the Crees. They recognized that northward-flowing rivers in that region would provide an easier exit for the furs, via Hudson Bay, than the long canoe routes, often threatened by the Iroquois, that led back to Montreal. Although they failed to persuade the French fur merchants in Montreal to shift their operations to Hudson Bay, they found an attentive audience in England. In 1668, with British partners, they began trading at Hudson Bay with Indians who brought their furs out of central Canada, and in 1670 the partnership received a royal charter as the Hudson's Bay Company. In Montreal, the French realized that furs were being diverted from them, and for years the French and British fought for Hudson Bay. In the end, the British were left in control, and the French were forced to step up their activities in the interior and try to prevent furs from moving to York Fort and other English posts on the bay.

In their movements westward, French traders continued to meet new tribes. They put guns in the hands of the Ojibwas who, joined by Crees, used them against their enemies, the Sioux. As those people came under pressure, their relatives, the Assiniboines, broke away from them, moving to the Lake Winnipeg region and effecting enough of a peace with the Crees and Ojibwas to venture sending ambassadors to Upper Michigan to meet Frenchmen and suggest the opening of trade that would give them guns. In more southerly regions, French priests, traders, and soldiers,

bent on exploration, the enlisting of new tribes in the fur
trade, the conversion of natives, and the making of alliances
of friendship, entered the Illinois country and the Mississippi
Valley. Moving past the mouths of the Wisconsin, Missouri,
and Ohio rivers, they opened trade with prairie tribes and
in time—as the result of the labors of men like Marquette,
Jolliet, and La Salle—established dominion for France over a
vast heartland area from Minnesota to the Gulf of Mexico.
Erecting forts at strategic locations, they named the country
Louisiana in honor of Louis XIV.

The arrival of the French so far west alarmed the Spaniards, who hurried to establish forts and missions in the
countries of the Caddos and other tribes in Texas and Louisiana. In 1720, after the French had also begun to probe
across Texas, a Spanish expedition with Pueblo Indian
auxiliaries marched onto the plains from Santa Fe to recon-
noiter the situation, but on the Platte River in present-day
Nebraska it ran into a force of Frenchmen with Pawnee and
Oto allies who almost wiped it out. Thereafter, the Spaniards
watched defensively from their New Mexico and Texas
settlements, warding off Apache and Comanche raiders and
keeping an eye out for French intruders. The latter showed
little sustained interest in moving across the southwest
plains, however; they, too, would have had trouble with
the Comanches, and beaver was not believed to be plentiful
in that direction. Instead, they pressed their explorations
farther up the Missouri and its tributaries, into the countries
of the Missouris, Osages, Kansas, Otos, Omahas, Poncas, and
Pawnees, where fur was more abundant. Gradually, the Indian lands along the Mississippi and in the lower Missouri
valley became familiar to Frenchmen from Canada and from
a new settlement at New Orleans. Many of them lived and
traded with the Indians, introducing the white men's goods
and ways to native peoples from the Chitimachas, Natchez,
and Quapaws of the lower Mississippi to the Miamis and
Peorias in the Illinois country and the Arikaras in present-
day South Dakota. Other Frenchmen, including retired fur
men, clustered around the new posts and forts, settling
down on small farms and establishing permanent settlements
along the rivers. Sometimes there were serious conflicts with
the Indians; after the Natchez sacked a French post on the
lower Mississippi in 1729, Frenchmen, aided by Choctaws
and other native allies, practically exterminated the Natchez,

sending survivors fleeing for sanctuary with the Chickasaws, Creeks, and Cherokees.

In Canada, meanwhile, other French traders continued to push west. A family of explorers, the Vérendryes, traveled to lakes Winnipeg and Winnipegosis in the 1730's and 1740's and erected posts on the Red and Assiniboine rivers. The Vérendryes also crossed the plains to the Missouri River in present-day North Dakota, visiting the earthen mound villages of the Mandans and Hidatsas who both farmed and hunted. Those two agricultural tribes were just beginning to acquire horses in trade from nomadic plains tribes, including the Cheyennes, who had recently been pushed west of the Missouri River by some of the Sioux—themselves coming westward at this time from Minnesota under pressure from the Ojibwas. Continuing their explorations farther west on the plains, the Vérendryes met Crows, who had separated from the Hidatsas on the Missouri after a quarrel over a buffalo, and possibly Shoshonis, who already possessed large numbers of horses. The explorers probably reached the Black Hills before they turned north and discovered the lower Saskatchewan River. That ended their travels, but the French traders who followed their route from Lake Superior to Lake Winnipeg discovered that they were now among Crees and Assiniboines who were sending their furs via northern waterways to the British at Hudson Bay. The French hurried to build posts at strategic sites along the main routes to the bay and soon were able to intercept much of the British trade and divert furs to their own storehouses.

Rumors of the new French posts reached the British, and in 1754 they sent inland one of their men, Anthony Henday, to investigate and, if possible, to find new tribes beyond the French reach. Henday traveled far west through Canada to the vicinity of present-day Calgary, meeting bands of Atsinas as well as Blackfeet, Bloods, and Piegans of the Blackfoot confederacy. Shoshonis, who had horses and roamed almost at will across a huge plains area between the Wyoming Rockies and the South Saskatchewan River, had been attacking the Blackfeet. But sometime about 1740 the latter had begun to acquire horses too—possibly in trade from the Kutenais and Flatheads farther west—and they were now beginning to hold their own against the Shoshonis. Henday appears to have given some of the Blackfeet their first guns; soon afterward they acquired more of them from traders and Cree middlemen. Eventually, they were able to drive the

Shoshonis, as well as the Flatheads and Kutenais, none of whom possessed guns, into hiding places in the Rocky Mountains.

Henday failed to interest the Blackfeet in the fur trade. They told him they were more interested in hunting buffalo than in traveling in canoes through fish-eating country to bring furs to Hudson Bay. But the explorer's report aroused an interest among his superiors in the Hudson's Bay Company in going after the trade of Indians like the Blackfeet by building inland posts in their own countries. Before the company could move, however, plans were interrupted by the outbreak of the French and Indian War in 1754.

That conflict, the American phase of the Seven Years' War in Europe, brought to a climax the intermittent struggles that had been fought between England and France for possession of North America. In the wars of the late seventeenth and early eighteenth centuries English settlers on the New York and New England frontiers had borne the brunt of attacks by Frenchmen and their Indian allies from Canada. Schenectady, on the Mohawk River in New York, had been raided and destroyed in 1690, and fourteen years later settlers at Deerfield, Massachusetts, had been surprised in their sleep and either massacred or taken captive. From time to time, one or more of the Iroquois tribes had sided with the British, but in the main they had stayed at peace, declaring themselves neutral in the quarrels of the white men and maintaining for themselves a strong bargaining position with both sides. Using skillful diplomacy, they had asserted their own power and achieved their own ends, extending their claim to large areas in Pennsylvania and Ohio, and resettling on those lands under their own protection the dispersed remnants of various tribes that had been defeated by the colonists. The frontier wars and the intertribal conflicts over the fur trade had filled the interior country with displaced Indians, wandering bands of many tribes who were looking for new homes. At the same time, the destruction of the Susquehannocks had left unoccupied a portion of Pennsylvania south of the Iroquois. To keep this vacuum from filling with whites, the Iroquois had settled it with Mohicans, Nanticokes, Tutelos, Shawnees, and other landless groups. They had also proclaimed sovereignty over the Delawares, who were being pushed out of eastern Pennsylvania, and had forbidden those people to make war or conduct their own relations with the whites. Furthermore, in the early years of the eighteenth century a stream of Tuscarora Indians, whom the colonists had defeated in North Carolina, had moved north and joined the New York Iroquois to form the Six Nations. The Iroquois had spread the protection of the League over all these peoples, but they had also spoken for them in councils and, in the case of the Delawares and Shawnees, had sold some of their lands to the Pennsylvania colonists. The latter two tribes had gradually retreated west of the Alleghenies, but, again, in the 1740's, the Iroquois had granted rights in the upper Ohio River country to colonial land speculators; by 1754, settlers were edging across the mountains. The hard-pressed Delawares and Shawnees stood their ground this time, and border warfare began in the western woods.

The frontier skirmishing became major war in a fight between Virginia and the French for the forks of the Ohio, the site of present-day Pittsburgh. On July 4, 1754, George Washington and his Virginians were forced to surrender Fort Necessity (near modern-day Uniontown, Pennsylvania) to an army of French and Indians. The next year Major General Edward Braddock, England's commander in chief in North America, set out with a column of 2,500 British regulars and Virginia militiamen, the latter again under Washington, to whip what Braddock called "naked Indians and Canadians." Near Fort Duquesne, on July 9, 1755, Delawares, Shawnees, Ottawas, and other tribes of the Ohio Valley joined the French in ambushing and cutting to pieces Braddock's force. The English defeat left the western frontier wide open to France's Indian allies, whose angry raids forced settlers to withdraw hurriedly to the east as much as a hundred miles. Frantic negotiations took place, and largely with the help of Christian Post, a Moravian missionary, and a friendly Delaware chief named Tedyuskung the English managed to make peace with many of the western tribes in 1758. In the same year, a new British force under Brigadier General John Forbes cut a road across the Pennsylvania wilderness and captured Fort Duquesne.

Fighting raged furiously also in northern New York, especially along the water route between Montreal and the upper Hudson. The theater of action was in Iroquois country, but during the hostilities the Iroquois, generally, remained "officially" neutral. In several ways, however, they gave both direct and indirect aid to the British. Their geographical position lay athwart the principal routes con-

necting eastern Canada with the French positions in the
Ohio Valley and Louisiana, and this fact hobbled French
strategy, movements, and command. At the same time, the
Iroquois controlled the water routes leading from the St.
Lawrence to the heart of the English colonies, and when
the French tried to use them, some of the Iroquois joined
the British forces in halting them. An important British
victory was won at Fort William Henry, near Lake George,
in 1755, when a Mohawk sachem named Hendrick, responding to an appeal from his friend, Sir William Johnson, England's agent among the Iroquois, led several hundred
warriors in helping the British turn back a French invasion
force.

The fall of Quebec in September 1759, and the final
triumph of the British in North America left the Iroquois in
a strong position. During the war the British government
had established a Northern and Southern Indian Department
to handle affairs with the tribes. Sir William Johnson, a
former fur trader who had married a Mohawk woman, had
been in charge of the Northern Department and had worked
skillfully to become a trusted friend of the Iroquois. His
influence greatly aided the British, and when the war was
over, he was able to assure the Iroquois respectful and
deferential treatment by the victors. But the interior tribes,
already demoralized by the collapse of the French whom
they had helped, had no intermediary. As British troops
moved into surrendered French forts at Detroit and elsewhere, English agents tried to reassure and win the loyalty
of the former French allies. The tribes, however, remained
fearful and suspicious, unable to believe that the French were
going for good, and certain that soldiers from New Orleans
or eastern Canada would soon appear to continue the war
against the English enemy. The situation was made harder
for the agents by General Jeffery Amherst, the Indian-hating
commander of British and colonial forces in America, who
issued strict new regulations that banned the credit and gifts
which the Indians had been accustomed to receiving from
the French. When the British agents in the West put the
rules into force, Indian resentments became intense.

An uprising against the British, led by a brilliant Ottawa
war leader named Pontiac, broke out suddenly in May 1763.
Failing to take Detroit by surprise, Pontiac organized a siege
of the fort that lasted until October—an unprecedented action in Indian military history. At the same time, he worked

furiously trying to forge Indian unity in the interior country and managed to induce many other tribes to join the war against the English. In a few weeks, Ottawas, Hurons, Delawares, Shawnees, Ojibwas, Potawatomis, Miamis, Weas, Senecas, Kickapoos, and others, many of them enraged by Amherst's orders as well as by the renewed movement of English settlers into lands west of the Alleghenies, overran every British-held post in the West except Fort Pitt and Detroit, and both of those were under siege. Although Pontiac held his unified forces together and kept the two forts surrounded through the summer, the stout resistance by the garrison at Detroit at last disheartened many of the Indians, and the so-called rebellion slowly fell apart. Finally, an English army under Colonel Henry Bouquet broke the siege of Fort Pitt. When British troops began to win victories elsewhere, white negotiators made determined efforts to wean tribes away from Pontiac. Faced by defections and a realization that the French were not going to return and join his war, Pontiac at last made peace with the English. A few years later, on April 20, 1769, he was murdered by a Peoria Indian in Cahokia in the Illinois country.

The Indian resentments that had caused the war, however, had meanwhile induced the British Crown to make a gesture in the tribes' behalf. On October 7, 1763, a royal proclamation reserved as hunting grounds for the Indians the country west of the Appalachian Mountains, directing all settlers to withdraw from unceded lands west of the mountains, and prohibiting all future purchases of land in that region unless approved in a public meeting between the Indian owners and representatives of the British government. The proclamation was expected to be enforced strictly by the provincial governors, and on occasion they sent troops west of the mountains to try to eject border jumpers. But the task was impossible, and the proclamation line itself was not intended to be permanent. Even as colonists raised an outcry over it, government agents and colonial land speculators negotiated treaties with the Iroquois at Fort Stanwix (1768) and with Cherokees at Hard Labor Creek (1768) and Lochaber (1770) that opened large areas of the trans-Appalachian country to the whites. With or without treaties, however, increasing numbers of settlers flowed across the mountains. Syndicates of land speculators, employing prospectors like Daniel Boone, led the way, focusing on the fertile lands of Kentucky and the upper Ohio Valley. The incursions again inflamed the

Indians, and various bands, including Shawnees led by Cornstalk and another group under Logan, an expatriate Iroquois halfblood and an able orator, tried to push back the whites. Kentucky, which became known as a "dark and bloody ground," was the scene of savage skirmishing that reached a climax in 1774 with the so-called Lord Dunmore's War, named for the royal governor of Virginia. At Point Pleasant in present-day West Virginia, Dunmore's forces finally won a decisive victory over the Indians and forced them to cede Kentucky's contested country.

The outbreak of the American Revolution in 1775 confronted the colonists with the necessity of making an abrupt about-face in their dealings with the Indians. To keep the tribes from helping the British, the Continental Congress ordered a halt to trespasses on Indian lands. In many places settlers were stopped and turned back, and the tribes were given gifts of gunpowder for their hunting. Peace came to some areas, but, in general, conflict continued. Occasional Indian raids occurred in Kentucky and along the upper Ohio. Farther west, the British at Detroit instigated Indian attacks on isolated American settlements until George Rogers Clark destroyed British power in the Ohio Valley with his capture of Lieutenant Colonel Henry Hamilton at Vincennes on February 25, 1779. Other violence stirred the borders of the Iroquois country in New York and Pennsylvania, where white settlements were more numerous. Although the Tuscaroras and Oneidas sided with the colonists, the Mohawks, Onondagas, Cayugas, and Senecas joined the British under the leadership of Thayendanegea, a Mohawk chief who was a nephew of one of William Johnson's Indian wives and was known as Joseph Brant. An intelligent, able, and well-educated Indian, whom Johnson had sent to school, Brant was also an outstanding leader and spokesman for his people. His statesmanlike qualities were obscured by the passionate events of the war that included savage raids and massacres of settlers at Cherry Valley, New York, and Wyoming, Pennsylvania. Both were blamed on Brant, although he may not have been present at Wyoming, where Delaware Indians joined the white settlers against the Iroquois and were also overwhelmed and slain.

Allied with Brigadier General Barry St. Leger in 1777, Brant and his Indians shared the British defeat at Oriskany, New York. The following year, American troops under General Johnson Sullivan launched a punitive expedition into

Iroquois country, burning the Indians' villages and destroying their crops and orchards. The Iroquois continued to make raids during the rest of the war, but they never fully recovered from Sullivan's campaign. When peace came, Brant and the pro-English Iroquois crossed into Canada and found permanent new homes for themselves in Ontario. The rest, under leaders like Red Jacket and Cornplanter, acknowledged the sovereignty of the new American nation and remained in New York and northwestern Pennsylvania. The power of the Six Nations, who during the Revolution had divided for the first time, was ended, although the member tribes, both in Canada and the United States, have continued in brotherly association to this day.

The new government of the United States made little change in Indian policy from that established by Great Britain. The tribes along the frontier were still powerful entities, susceptible to the intrigues of British agents and capable of diverting the energies of the struggling young nation. Expediency demanded a policy that would keep them peaceful and friendly to Americans, and Henry Knox, the first Secretary of War, spoke for the government when he asserted that the Indians possessed the right of the soil they occupied and could not be dispossessed without their consent. The nation's first Indian treaty, at Fort Stanwix, New York, in 1784, re-established peace with the Iroquois, who agreed to relinquish their claims to part of western New York, Pennsylvania, and Ohio.

The conduct of Indian affairs, in general, was placed under the War Department, and an agency system was devised. To maintain peace and order in the Indian trade, where the cheating of Indians, excesses of competition, and other activities often led to trouble, the government eventually established a chain of government-owned-and-operated "factories," or stores, in the Indian country to buy furs and sell trade goods. This system, by which the government controlled all trade through its agents or through licensed traders, lasted until 1822. Although it was designed to prevent conflicts with the Indians, it failed to halt the trade of unscrupulous persons who continued to cheat and otherwise anger the Indians. In the end, the system collapsed under the pressure of powerful private trading companies whose owners resented government competition.

In similar fashion, the assurances of the rights of the Indians in the Northwest Territory, contained in the Northwest Ordinance of 1787, could not be enforced. In the wake of the Revolution, settlers poured into the lands north of the Ohio River, ignoring Indian rights and demanding military protection if the Indians opposed them. Two American expeditions sent to restore peace failed; one of them, led by General Arthur St. Clair, suffered the worst defeat ever administered by Indians to U. S. troops, losing more than six hundred men on November 4, 1791, to a force of Shawnees and other Indians under Little Turtle. A punitive expedition under General Anthony Wayne finally defeated the Indians at Fallen Timbers, in northwestern Ohio, on August 20, 1794, and by the Treaty of Greenville (1795) Wayne forced a group of chastened chiefs to cede almost two thirds of the present state of Ohio, part of Indiana, and various strategic sites in other parts of the Northwest Territory. The treaty set a pattern for the westward movement of Americans. The peace that followed it could only be temporary: within a few years settlers filled up much of the ceded country and pushed on to threaten lands still held by the tribes.

Tension increased again during the first decade of the nineteenth century when Tecumseh, a Shawnee war chief, and his brother, the Prophet, urged Indians of all tribes to unite and refuse to cede any more land. Tecumseh, who has been called by some America's greatest Indian leader, was a talented and courageous fighter and an outstanding orator and diplomat. He was also a visionary who conceived of a separate Indian state or nation that white men would respect. Traveling tirelessly from the Great Lakes to the Gulf of Mexico, he pleaded with energy and passion for his dream, exhorting tribes to regard all unceded land as the common property of all tribes. No chief or individual tribe, he argued, has the right to sell any part of the land, and he called on the tribes to unite so that they might stand together in resisting further inroads by the whites. To win the respect of the white men, he also counseled the Indians to use methods that their American opponents would consider humane, and in warfare he practiced what he preached, winning high regard from many of his white foes.

Tecumseh's dream came too late in history and was doomed to failure. He was able to rally Ojibwas, Winnebagos, Potawatomis, and bands of many other tribes to stand with him, but still others refused to follow his leadership. Parts of the Indian domain continued to be nibbled

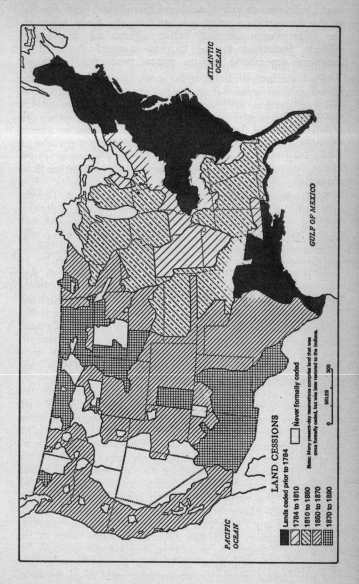

ATLANTIC OCEAN

GULF OF MEXICO

PACIFIC OCEAN

LAND CESSIONS

■ Lands ceded prior to 1784

☐ Never formally ceded

Note: Many present-day reservations comprise land that was once formally ceded, but was later restored to the Indians.

1784 to 1810

1810 to 1850

1850 to 1870

1870 to 1890

0   MILES   300

away, sold to whites by weak and venal chiefs. When Tecumseh refused to recognize the cessions, he incurred the hostility of William Henry Harrison, the governor of the Indiana Territory. Harrison was determined to remove all Indians from the Northwest Territory, and he used high-handed methods to achieve his goal. Losing patience with Tecumseh, he crossed into the Indians' unceded lands from his headquarters at Vincennes in 1811 and marched his army threateningly to the Tippecanoe River near the Prophet's village. In Tecumseh's absence, Indians who were concentrated there became panicky and during the night of November 6–7 attacked Harrison's army. Harrison drove off the Indians, burned the Prophet's town, and returned to Vincennes, claiming a great victory.

Soon afterward, when the War of 1812 broke out, Tecumseh with his Indian following joined the British, believing that an English triumph would allow him to establish the Indian state he envisioned. His military ability was of substantial value to the British, particularly at Detroit, where he played a leading role in bringing about the surrender of that fort by the American General William Hull on August 16, 1812. Defeats on Lake Erie and elsewhere finally forced the English to retreat from the western country, however, and Tecumseh and his Indians withdrew reluctantly with the British. At the Thames River in southern Canada, Tecumseh induced the irresolute English commander to stand and fight Harrison's pursuing army, and in the ensuing battle (October 5, 1813) the Indian leader was slain and his native following dispersed.

The return of peace sealed the fate of the tribes in the Northwest Territory. Bereft of power, and without British allies, they were coerced and cajoled into signing a series of treaties that extinguished their title to one large area after another. Frequently, settlers poured across their lands before treaty sessions could even be held; the tribes then had little choice but to sign and withdraw. In the meantime, pressure increased for a new national policy designed to remove all Indians to the prairies and plains west of the Mississippi River, which Major Stephen H. Long and other explorers had termed an "American Desert," unsuitable for farming or for habitation by whites. Gradually, many tribes in the Northwest Territory, now without hunting grounds and facing starvation, agreed to trade their homes for new ones on reservations which the government established for them on the prairies of eastern Kansas, and one by one the shattered peoples were shepherded west by government agents and missionaries. A few tribes connived desperately, and in the end were able to stay on greatly reduced—and unwanted—portions of their midwestern homelands, particularly in remote, forested areas of Wisconsin. Many of those who remained behind on the small reserves soon became paupers, and some took to drink to try to escape the hopelessness of their new life.

A final flurry of resistance was offered in 1832 by a band of Sauk and Foxes under their aged war chief, Black Hawk. A fiery rival of Keokuk, another Sauk chief who was ceding tribal land wholesale, Black Hawk refused to evacuate his village at Rock Island, Illinois, and move across the Mississippi to Iowa. Regular troops and militia finally chased him through northern Illinois and southern Wisconsin, and in a merciless massacre of his people at Bad Axe, Wisconsin, on the Mississippi River, August 3, 1832, ended what was called the Black Hawk War. The old chief surrendered and was taken to Washington to be shown the might of the American nation he had opposed. Then he was sent to Iowa, where he died in 1838.

In the southeastern region of the United States, events since the time of the first white settlements on the Atlantic coast had brought the various tribes, including the great confederacies, to a similar fate. Spanish missions of the sixteenth century had first acquainted many of the coastal tribes with the white man. In Florida and among the Guales of Georgia, it is estimated that Spain had as many as forty thriving missions by the early seventeenth century, overseeing the lives of perhaps 20,000 Christianized Indians. With the founding of permanent English settlements in the Carolinas, beginning in 1669, the Indians became embroiled inevitably in conflicts between the British and the Spaniards, and Creeks and various coastal tribes, like the Yuchis, traded with the English and helped them against the Spaniards, and raids and counterraids occurred. The Spaniards withdrew from Georgia, but in the early part of the eighteenth century expeditions of English, Creeks, and Yuchis invaded Florida, destroyed Spanish missions, and killed and enslaved vast numbers of Christian Indians, who had no guns because of Spanish policy against giving firearms to Indians. By 1745, many of the original Timucua, Apalachee, and Calusa Indians of Florida had become slaves of the Carolina colonists and the Creeks, and most of the rest had been removed to the West Indies by the Spaniards.

In the meantime, the British colonists had induced tribes in Georgia and South Carolina to war upon each other to secure captives to sell the whites as slaves. The rivalries among the tribes produced friction with the settlers, and one by one the individual tribes were destroyed by the whites, usually aided by native allies. Refugee groups of Hitchitis, Yamasees (beaten by the South Carolina settlers in the Yamasee War of 1715), Lower Creeks, Yuchis, and other Indians moved into the empty regions of Florida—where the Spaniards had once hoped to create a Christian Indian state under the care of missionaries—and, joined in time by many runaway Negro slaves from the English plantations, gave rise by the end of the eighteenth century to a new multiethnic tribe. Creeks gave the new groups in Florida the name Isty-Semole, which meant something like wild men and referred at first to the fact that they were essentially hunters, "attending but little to agriculture." Later, as the groups became preponderantly Creek and settled down in farming villages, their name was corrupted to Seminole, referring with new meaning to the fact that they were separatists or runaways from the Creek nation.

Members of the latter tribe, in the meantime, had welcomed James Oglethorpe's colonists to Georgia in 1732. Eager for white men's goods, the people of the interior towns of their powerful confederation, far removed from the pressure of land-hungry settlers, had grown prosperous in dealings with colonial traders, who visited them and even married Indian women and became influential leaders in the villages. Other tribes did not fare as well as the Creeks. In North Carolina, settlers repeatedly raided Indian villages for slaves and became involved in wars with the Tuscaroras, whom they forced eventually to emigrate north to Pennsylvania and the protection offered them by the Iroquois. Coastal tribes had aided the English against the Tuscaroras, but mistreatment by the colonists soon provoked them into conflict also. Beaten in 1715, the Yamasees fled to Florida, where the Yuchis had already gone; the Catawbas were overcome by disease, drink, and attacks by other Indians; and the Shawnees gradually withdrew from the area of the Savannah River (which was named for them—they had been called Savannahs in that region) and moved northward toward Kentucky and the upper Ohio Valley.

Farther west, on the lower Mississippi, meanwhile, French establishments had gradually engulfed or scattered various tribes, including the once-powerful Natchez. The growing strength of the French alarmed the English, and colonists on the Atlantic coast who were trading with the inland tribes tried to enlist the Cherokees, Chickasaws, Creeks, and Choctaws to help them halt the French. They achieved their principal successes with the Creeks and Chickasaws, who became firm allies of the English; but the Choctaws continually sided with the French, while the Cherokees—despite repeated British blandishments—avoided entanglements in the white men's rivalries. All four of the strong confederacies, however, prospered during most of the eighteenth century as a result of their trade with the whites. European traders continued to marry into the tribes, and some of their half-blood sons, bearing Scottish and English names, became chiefs. At the same time, the Indians adopted many civilized traits and began to amass wealth in white men's goods and livestock.

Serious pressure from speculators and settlers seeking Indian land was felt first by the Cherokees. After ceding some of their territory in 1755, they became involved in war with the colonists four years later. The fighting continued intermittently along the frontier until 1770, when the Indians relinquished more of their land by the Treaty of Lochaber. Some of the Cherokees sided with the colonists during the Revolution, but most of them, together with the Creeks, remained loyal to the English. After the war, intrigues by British and Spanish agents and traders based in Florida kept most of the Southeast tribes stirred up for years, although the new American government signed treaties with the principal nations and did its best to bring peace in the area. Much of the government's effort was undone by unscrupulous land speculators and by westward-moving settlers who cared nothing for the Indians' rights. Pressure was directed especially against the Creeks who were forced to cede large parts of their territory in Georgia. Once again, border warfare was common, and by the time of the War of 1812 many of the angered Creeks had responded eagerly to Tecumseh's appeals to stand fast and, along with other tribes, resist further white advances.

The attacks on white settlements, occurring principally in southern and eastern Alabama, were climaxed on August 30, 1813, when Upper Creeks, called Red Sticks in contrast to

White Sticks who remained loyal to the United States, over-ran Fort Mims and killed more than three hundred and fifty settlers and pro-white Indians. A civil war ensued be-tween the two factions of Creeks, and on the following March 27 a militia army led by Andrew Jackson, aided by White Sticks and pro-white Cherokees, almost wiped out the Red Stick forces under Menewa at Horseshoe Bend in eastern Alabama. Red Stick villages were attacked, and many of the people fled to Florida, where they joined bands of Seminoles. The remaining Red Sticks lost their power and stayed in hiding, while the White Sticks—in an ironic turn of justice for the aid they had given Jackson—were forced to sign a treaty in 1814, ceding almost two thirds of the Creek nation's territory, including large parts of the present states of Georgia and Alabama, to the United States.

As settlers moved into the new land, disturbances broke out along the Georgia-Florida border between anti-American Creeks and Georgia whites, who accused the Indians of harboring runaway Negro slaves in their settlements inside Spanish-owned Florida. Spanish authority was weak, and the Georgians demanded that troops go after the slaves and punish the Creeks who were now living with the Seminoles. In 1817, a U. S. force crossed the line to arrest a Seminole chief, and warfare began. The following year Andrew Jackson invaded the Spanish territory in the First Seminole War, dispersing the Indians, burning their villages, and seizing the Spanish towns of St. Marks and Pensacola. Spain ceded Florida to the United States in 1819, and soon afterward American agents persuaded the Seminoles to go onto a reservation in the interior of the Florida peninsula and permit settlers to move peaceably onto the lands the Indians gave up.

Conflict with the tribes in the Southeast, however, had only commenced. Settlers in greater numbers than ever before were on the move from Florida and Georgia to Mississippi, looking for fertile land for their cotton-and-slave economy, clamoring for lands still occupied by Indians, and demand-ing that the federal and state governments clear the natives out of the way. Georgia, Alabama, and Mississippi responded by passing laws that outlawed the tribal governments of the old confederacies and placed the Indians under the states rather than the national government. The new laws served to encourage injustices against the Indians, and the situation of the tribes deteriorated rapidly. Despite pleas by the Indians and various white friends, mostly in the North, the

U. S. government refused to help them, and on May 28, 1830, at the urging of President Andrew Jackson, who was dedicated to ridding the Southeast of Indians, Congress passed the Removal Bill, giving the President power to exchange land west of the Mississippi River for territory still held in the Southeast by the tribes.

The carrying out of the policy by Jackson and his successor, President Martin Van Buren, is one of the blackest chapters in American history. Tens of thousands of helpless Indians, many of whom had white blood, were wholly or partly civilized, and owned homes, livestock, and farms, suffered incredible hardships. Tribes were torn into factions that tried to determine the best policy for their people, whether to resist or accept removal peaceably. Some Indians became desperate and murdered their opponents; others turned to the law courts and addressed appeals to the conscience of the white American population. All their efforts to halt or reverse the government's policy failed, and in the end almost all the members of each of the tribes were removed to different areas in the present state of Oklahoma. Some of them went reluctantly but without defiance; others went in chains. Most of them streamed westward under the watchful eyes of troops who made sure that they kept moving. The first to go were the Choctaws who emigrated amid great hardship in November 1831. The Creeks delayed for four years, but when anguished violence began to spread among them, the army moved in, and in 1836 the entire membership of what was left of the once-mighty confederacy was marched west, some of the Indians in manacles. In 1837, the Chickasaws were removed. The Cherokees, under their leader John Ross, fought removal in the courts and thought they had won a victory when the Supreme Court, in a decision written by John Marshall, sustained their right to their Southeastern lands. But President Jackson refused to enforce the decision and in a final crushing blow to Cherokee hopes ordered the army to remove them. As the Indians prepared to go, their harassment by Georgia whites became savage. The trek west in 1838 and 1839—recalled as the "Trail of Tears"—was bitter, but almost a relief from the Georgians who had tormented and plundered them. As the troops pushed the Indians across the South to Oklahoma, nearly a fourth of the Cherokees died of disease, starvation, and hardship. A small band of several hundred Cherokees evaded the drive by hiding in the North Carolina mountains;

their descendants, known as the Eastern Cherokees, still live there.

The Seminoles of Florida, who had previously accepted a reservation for themselves on the peninsula, fought to stay where they were. Their resistance, aroused by a fiery young patriot named Osceola (Asi-Yaholo, which meant "black drink singer," referring to the serving attendant who sang during the purifying ritual of the Black Drink of the Muskogean-speaking peoples of the South), led to the Second Seminole War, begun in 1835. After suffering several disastrous defeats, the American troops treacherously seized Osceola during a parley under a white flag, and the young chief died in prison on January 30, 1838. Other Seminoles took up the fight, and the war dragged on until 1842, costing the lives of more than two thousand American soldiers, and between $40,000,000 and $60,000,000 in expenses. In the end, many of the Seminoles surrendered and were sent west, but a number held out in swamps of the lower part of the peninsula, and it is only recently that their descendants have made their peace with the whites.

It was the government's intention that the lands west of the Mississippi to which the Eastern tribes were removed would be guaranteed to them forever. But even as the tribes were being removed, white men were already across the Mississippi, and history was about to be repeated. The northern part of the trans-Mississippi country had been penetrated in 1804–6 by the Lewis and Clark Expedition, which in going all the way to the Pacific had been the first party of white men to appear to numerous Indian tribes, including the Flatheads, Nez Perces, and a host of Columbia Basin peoples. The Indian woman Sacajawea, wife of the expedition's French-Canadian interpreter Toussaint Charbonneau, was helpful to the Americans. She was a Shoshoni, and although it has been claimed erroneously that she guided the expedition, she became useful when the explorers met her brother and his people in present-day Idaho. The reports of rich western beaver country which the expedition publicized on its return to the East accelerated the movement of fur traders up the Missouri River beyond the Mandans to the high plains and mountain hunting grounds of the Blackfeet, Shoshonis, and other western tribes. At an earlier date (1778), members of the British exploring expedition of Captain James Cook had bartered bits of metal and trinkets to Pacific Northwest Indians for sea-otter furs that were abundant along the coast and had then sold the furs for high prices in China. It had led to a thriving trade between sea traders and Northwest Coast natives, particularly with Nootkas of Vancouver Island. Now, the two sources of fur wealth—the coast and the interior—attracted John Jacob Astor and other merchants and traders in the East. Astor sent expeditions overland and around Cape Horn in an attempt to establish a fur monopoly in the Columbia Basin, but the breaking out of the War of 1812 isolated his men in the Northwest and forced them to sell their posts, including Astoria at the mouth of the Columbia, to British North West Company traders who had entered the region by crossing the Canadian Rockies.

During the war, tribes under the influence of British agents closed the Missouri River to American traders, and the Oregon country fell firmly into the hands of the North West Company which organized the fur trade among Kutenais, Flatheads, Nez Perces, Cayuses, Shoshonis, and many other tribes of the Plateau and northern Rockies. With the return of peace, Americans managed to open the Missouri only temporarily; trade troubles with the Arikaras and the hostility of Blackfeet, who did not want Americans to trade with their enemies west of the mountains, again made the Missouri unsafe to them in the 1820's, and they had to find overland routes to the western fur lands. The Platte River route to South Pass and the Green River area of Wyoming was established, and by 1824 American trappers were again entering the upper Columbia Basin. The British Hudson's Bay Company, which had merged with the North West Company in 1821 and absorbed the fur trade in the Oregon country, maintained a strong control over the tribes in that region, however; and although a vigorous competition was waged between Americans and Englishmen for the furs of the Oregon country, the British generally held the upper hand until 1846, when the fur trade itself had declined and Oregon south of the forty-ninth parallel became American.

The interlude of the fur trade brought many changes to the western tribes. Those that participated in the trade became increasingly dependent on white men's goods. Entire tribes shifted their location to reside closer to the traders; after 1834, when Fort Laramie was built on the North Platte River, many bands of Teton Sioux moved from old hunting grounds in South Dakota to new ones in western Nebraska and eastern Wyoming, closer to the newly established post. The shifts sometimes brought tribes into conflict with others who were already hunting or living in the lands to which they moved, and the plains experienced new intertribal welfare. The tribes were the customers of the traders and trappers, who wanted nothing more from the Indians than their furs and permission to hunt and trap in their territories, and the small groups of whites generally got on well with most tribes, marrying Indian women and fathering half-blood children. Occasionally, the trappers became involved in intertribal rivalries and warfare, helping friendly tribes against their enemies, and incurring the hostility of other tribes—notably the members of the Blackfeet confederacy and the Atsinas, or Gros Ventres of Canada —who tried to stop their trade with the Flatheads, Nez Perces, and Shoshonis. White men's diseases also brought disasters to some of the tribes; in the late 1820's and early 1830's European illnesses almost wiped out the entire native population along the lower Columbia River and a smallpox epidemic practically exterminated the Mandan tribe on the middle Missouri in 1837, leaving less than 150 survivors who took refuge with the Hidatsas, and sweeping on to create havoc among the Blackfeet and other Plains tribes.

From the fur trappers and traders, also, some of the tribes learned of Christianity. Catholic Iroquois trappers from eastern Canada, who followed the British fur companies into the Oregon country, aroused an interest in the white man's religion among some of the Plateau tribes. Curiosity was increased when the Hudson's Bay Company sent the sons of a number of headmen of various Plateau tribes to an Anglican mission school at Red River near Lake Winnipeg. When the youths returned to their people after 1828 and preached the rudiments of Christianity to them, certain bands became intrigued with the white men's relations with the supernatural, believing that possession of knowledge of those relations would give their people power, influence, and prestige. Starting in 1831, the Nez Perces and Flatheads sent delegations across the plains to St. Louis with homeward-bound fur-trade caravans, charged with seeing if they could get religious instruction for their people. Missionaries of various denominations responded to their appearance and traveled to the Northwest to open missions. The best known were the Methodist Jason Lee, who settled in the Willamette Valley among the remnants of Chinookan-speaking tribes; Marcus and Narcissa Whitman and the

Henry Spaldings, all Presbyterians, who opened missions for the Cayuses and Nez Perces; and the Jesuit Father Pierre Jean De Smet, who built missions for the Flatheads and other Salish-speaking tribes. Their work enjoyed varying success. The Spaldings and Father De Smet converted some of the Indians, and the Spaldings, particularly, made progress in teaching the Nez Perces farming and white men's skills. But in the course of their labors they undermined tribal institutions and stability and created bitter factionalism that weakened the tribes and paved the way for their eventual loss of power and lands.

In addition, Jason Lee and the other Protestant missionaries soon became propagandists for American settlement of the Oregon country. Partly in response to their writings, which appeared in many widely read newspapers in the East, and to personal appeals during trips back East by some of the missionaries, settlers were attracted to Oregon. The newcomers, who began to arrive in growing numbers after 1840, settled first in the Willamette Valley, where few Indians remained. But after the United States acquired Oregon in 1846, the swelling tide of emigrants became a threat to the lands of the Northwest tribes. Apprehension grew among the Indians, and clashes occurred along the western end of the Oregon Trail. When an epidemic of measles broke out among some of the tribes in 1847, the Cayuses panicked and murdered the Whitmans and many other whites at the Whitman Mission of Waiilatpu. The episode led to the start of an era of Indian wars in the Northwest. The Spaldings, also threatened with death, hastily abandoned their mission among the Nez Perces, and soon afterward De Smet's successors, faced with defections by the Flatheads, temporarily withdrew from those Indians—although other priests managed to stay on with several tribes, including the Coeur d'Alenes and Yakimas.

A war fought by the Oregon settlers against the Cayuses ended inconclusively. In southwestern Oregon, Rogue River Indians became embroiled with miners, who were treating them highhandedly. And in southern Idaho, Shoshonis and Bannocks clashed with covered wagon trains of emigrants who were moving through their lands. A first round of punitive expeditions brought an uneasy truce to all the areas, but in 1854–5 the embers were stirred into fresh flames by I. I. Stevens, the newly arrived governor of Washington Territory. Impatient to ensure the safety of a route for a northern transcontinental railroad from St. Paul, Minnesota, to Puget Sound, and to acquire land for new settlers, Stevens harried the headmen of the various tribes around Puget Sound and in the interior into ceding large portions of their lands and accepting confining reservations for their people. The headmen smoldered over Stevens's methods of haste, coercion, and fraud, and the governor had scarcely announced the signing of treaties with the tribes when a series of wars erupted around the Sound and along the middle Columbia. The Puget Sound tribes were smashed quickly and confined to small reservations. In the interior, violence raged, off and on, until 1858, by which time the Yakimas, Cayuses, Walla-wallas, Spokans, Palouses, and Coeur d'Alenes had all been decisively defeated and most of their principal chiefs slain or hanged. With their power gone, the tribes were herded onto reservations, and the rest of their lands were thrown open to settlers.

At the same time, military units were active against bands of various tribes in southern Idaho and in parts of Oregon. Some tribes were pacified and put on reservations; others evaded a final settling of their fate. Under pressure, Modocs of southern Oregon retreated into hideouts in the lava beds of the Tule Lake area. A peace talk was arranged with them in 1872; during the meeting, the Indians killed two of the white negotiators, and the army renewed its war on the tribe, finally capturing and hanging the Modoc leaders, including Kintpuash, whom the whites called Captain Jack. The surrendered Modocs were sent to exile in Oklahoma, where their descendants still live. Trouble, in the meantime, was also flaring among the Nez Perces. Their many bands occupied a large area centering generally in the region where Washington, Oregon, and Idaho adjoin each other. The area had been guaranteed to them as a reservation in 1855, but intruders had discovered gold almost in the center of the reservation in 1860, and a rush of miners had overrun their lands. Government agents had used bribery and coercion to induce some of the Nez Perce headmen to sign a new treaty in 1863, binding all the bands to move onto a much smaller reservation. The chiefs who refused to sign argued that no one but themselves had the right to sign away the lands of their own bands, a point that was silently agreed to even by the headmen who signed the treaty. Nevertheless, the government took the position that the treaty was binding on the entire tribe. A crisis arose when the Joseph band of Nez Perces refused to leave its homeland in the Wallowa area of northeastern Oregon and move onto the new reservation.

When the government in 1877 threatened to use force to eject the Indians from the Wallowa, the band's leader, Chief Joseph, agreed reluctantly to go on the reservation. The band had started to move when several young warriors killed some settlers along Idaho's Salmon River. Troops immediately attacked the Indians who, fighting defensively, defeated them. Joseph's band, joined by several others that had earlier refused to move onto the reservation, was pursued by troops through central Idaho, western Montana, Yellowstone Park, and central and northern Montana until they were surrounded just south of the Canadian boundary, near the Bear Paw Mountains. They surrendered there to General Nelson A. Miles on October 5, 1877, after a five-day battle. During their long, fighting retreat, which eventually had turned into a desperate effort to reach the safety of Canada, they battled several armies of regular troops and militia bodies, defeating or staving off their pursuers each time until their final surrender. Credit for the skillful and courageous Nez Perce actions was given initially to Chief Joseph, who was called a "Red Napoleon." But it has since been realized that the Indian warriors were directed and led by more experienced war leaders, including Looking Glass and Joseph's younger brother, Ollokot, who were both killed in the final battle. Nevertheless, Joseph is recognized today as one of the greatest American Indians, a humane, philosophical and statesmanlike chief, who pled his people's cause, both before and after the war, with wisdom and ability. His words of surrender, ending, "Hear me, my chiefs, I am tired; my heart is sick and sad. From where the sun now stands, I will fight no more forever," are regarded by whites as among the most moving ever made by a vanquished leader. The surrendered Nez Perces were sent to exile in Oklahoma, rather than back to the Northwest as they had been promised when they agreed to give up the fight. On numerous occasions, Joseph pleaded forcefully for the Nez Perces' right to be returned to their Northwest homeland. Allowed to visit Washington in 1879, he spoke to a distinguished audience in the capital. His eloquent speech, which was printed by white sympathizers, included the following:

If the white man wants to live in peace with the Indian he can live in peace. . . . Treat all men alike. Give them all the same law. Give them all an even chance to live and grow. All men were made by the same Great Spirit Chief. They are all brothers. The earth is the mother of all people, and all people should have equal rights upon it. . . . Let me be a free man—free to travel, free to stop, free to work, free to trade, where I choose, free to choose my own teachers, free to follow the religion of my fathers, free to think and talk and act for myself—and I will obey every law, or submit to the penalty.

Finally, influential persons in the East took up Joseph's cause and, in time, effected the return of the Nez Perces to the Northwest. But Joseph and many of his followers were placed on the Colville Reservation, in Washington, and were never allowed to return to the Wallowa area from which they had been forced. The Nez Perces who had not been involved in the war were allowed to remain on their Idaho reservation.

Peace eventually came to the other tribes of the Plateau and the northern Rocky Mountain area, but not without trouble. Despite their protests, the Flatheads were forced to give up their homes in the Bitterroot Valley of western Montana and move peaceably onto a reservation farther north, where certain of their fellow tribesmen and other northwestern bands had previously been settled. Small bands in northeastern Washington were rounded up and placed on the Colville Reservation, and guaranteed lands were given the Spokans and Coeur d'Alenes. Violence flared with the Bannocks of southern Idaho in 1878, and the next year with a mixed group of Indians known as Sheepeaters, who lived in the mountains of central Idaho and made mountain sheep a principal part of their diet. Troops ended both clashes quickly; the Indians were placed on reservations, and native independence was a thing of the past in the North-west.

The breaking of Indian power elsewhere in the American West was stormier and more protracted. In the 1820's and 1830's, while trappers and traders had been moving into Indian lands in the Northwest and the Rocky Mountains, Americans, also from St. Louis, had been plying a busy overland trade to Santa Fe, from where some of them had been moving on through Southwest trapping grounds to the Mexican province of California. Along the trail to Santa Fe,

brushes with Comanches had been frequent; beyond Santa
Fe, Americans had skirmished repeatedly with Southwestern
tribes. Along the Colorado, they had incurred the hostility
of various Yuman tribes and had fought several battles with
them, one of the best known occurring in August 1827,
when Mohaves almost wiped out a trapping expedition under Jedediah Smith. Smith's men were victims of indiscre-
tions by an earlier group of trappers who had so outraged
the Mohaves that they sought revenge on the next party of
whites that entered their country. The pattern was a familiar one, and was repeated elsewhere. Trappers in the Great
Basin found sport in shooting defenseless Gosiute and Paiute
Indians who lived along the routes they took. Soon, those
impoverished Indians were annoying and pilfering from
any whites who came along.

The Americans who settled Texas included many persons
from the Southeast, who had helped to drive the Indians
from Georgia, Alabama, and Mississippi, and they carried
their hatred of Indians with them. In the first decade of
independence from Mexico, the Texans virtually wiped out
the Karankawas and many of the other tribes inhabiting
the areas in which they settled. On the northern and
western borders of their settlements, however, they found
Comanches, Kiowas, and various bands of Apaches more
formidable foes, and fought a desperate guerrilla-style war
with them, almost without pause, until the 1870's. The
best known Indian leaders on that frontier were three Kiowa
patriots, Set-Ankeah (known to the whites as Satank), Set-
Tainte (Satanta), and Addo-Eta (Big Tree), and Quanah
Parker, the son of a Comanche chief and a captured white
girl named Cynthia Ann Parker. Texas forces, sometimes
aided by U. S. Army troops, fought repeatedly against the
hard-riding Comanche and Kiowa warriors until 1867, when
both tribes agreed to settle in present-day Oklahoma, then
known as Indian Territory. White intruders on the Indians'
lands, however, provoked Quanah Parker and the Kiowa
chiefs into renewed hostilities in the early 1870's, and
skirmishing occurred across five states before troops finally
crushed the tribes and restored peace. During the turmoil,
Satank, who had been arrested, was murdered; later, Satanta,
made prisoner by the whites, committed suicide by jumping
out of a window.

In the Southwest, American sovereignty was extended over
many new tribes as a result of the Mexican War. Even before

that war ended, conflict began with the Indians. In 1847, just after the Americans had occupied the Santa Fe area, Pueblo Indians at Taos, instigated to some extent by Mexicans, rose up against the Americans. The Pueblos killed the acting American governor and a number of others, then fought troops and a unit of trappers who swiftly overcame them and hanged their leaders. It was the last violence engaged in by the usually peaceful Pueblos; although they were later subjected to injustices by settlers, and their entreaties were generally ignored by the government, they were powerless to defend themselves.

A harsher fate befell the Indians of the former Mexican Province of California. The closing of the missions by the Mexican government in 1834 had filled certain parts of the province with Christianized, partly acculturated, but economically impoverished and helpless "Mission Indians." Bands of unconverted native peoples, who had never been conquered, lived generally in the interior, populating the valleys, foothills, and mountainous regions of California. The whites of all nations who poured into California during the gold rush inundated the Indians in the northern and central parts of the state, obliterating their villages and overrunning their hunting and gathering grounds. Blown about like leaves in a storm, Indians struggled to survive. Their desperation turned some of them to robbery and the pilfering of miners, and the whites, in retaliation, formed posses and massacred the natives, guilty and innocent alike. In time, white attitudes, shaped generally by the ruffian elements of the mining regions, hardened against the Indians so that no excuse was needed for hostility against them. The white population viewed Indians as vermin who had to be eliminated from the California scene. Indian children were murdered with the explanation that "nits breed lice." Indian women were raped, forced into concubinage, or slain without mercy. Many adult males were rounded up and employed as slave labor. Disease had begun to cut down the Indian population even before the gold rush; now it quickened its work. It is estimated that as many as seventy thousand Indians died from one cause or another in California during the decade 1849–59. Some bands escaped annihilation by hiding in the mountains. In the southern part of the state, Indian groups near towns and settlements fared almost as badly as the natives in the north, though many bands in the desert evaded the whites. In the early 1850's the government went through the motions of extinguishing Indian titles to California land; cessions were wrung from the tribes and tribelets, and reservations were established for what were left of the native groups. On these reserves, generally in areas for which the whites had no use, population continued to decline. Disease and poverty were prevalent. The government's neglect of the California Indians eventually aroused the anger of reformers like Helen Hunt Jackson, who wrote *Ramona* (1884) and the more accusatory *A Century of Dishonor* (1881), the latter concerning the treatment of all Indians, and some steps were taken to ameliorate the natives' condition.

The conquest of the Navahos and Apaches was a different story. There were relatively few white settlements in the vast stretch of arid country lying between the Rio Grande towns and California. The Navahos dominated the countryside, menacing travelers and occasionally raiding outlying settlements. From 1847 on, units of American troops tried alternately to talk the Navahos into halting their raids and punish them for making the raids. Finally, during the winter of 1863-4, Colonel Kit Carson and an American force marched against the Navahos and trapped them in their Canyon de Chelly stronghold. After seizing their flocks and herds, destroying their gardens, and cutting down their peach orchards, the troops forced the entire tribe on a "long walk" of 300 miles to the Bosque Redondo, a reservation under the eye of Fort Sumner in eastern New Mexico. After four years of confinement, the chastened Navahos were sent back to a reservation established for them in northeastern Arizona. They settled down peaceably, never to make raids again. But their harsh and barren land confronted them with many economic problems that became increasingly severe as their population grew, and many of those problems have not yet been solved.

The conflict with the Apaches was more savage and protracted. Raiding Apache bands had fought with Spaniards and Mexicans for many years, the fierce warfare sometimes being generated by the activities of slave catchers from the south who seized Apaches and sold them into bondage. The Apaches were initially friendly to Americans; then clashes occurred, and cruelties began to be practiced on both sides. Warfare erupted in 1862, occasioned by two episodes of treachery and ill-conduct on the part of the Americans. Under the leadership of the huge Mangas Coloradas and Cochise, bands of Mimbreño and Chiricahua Apaches created a reign of terror for the whites and almost drove them from Arizona. Fighting went on for nine years, during which Mangas Coloradas was shot after being lured in for a peace talk by the Americans. Some three thousand California volunteers, aided by Pimas, Papagos, and Maricopas, as well as by Sonora and Chihuahua forces on the Mexican side of the border, finally forced the Apaches to make peace. But it was only temporary. The bands were placed on reservations, where new injustices were soon visited on them by hostile local citizens and corrupt and highhanded agents. Arbitrary removals of the bands to new reservations where they did not wish to go finally resulted in renewed hostilities in both Arizona and New Mexico. Raids by small, elusive bands, led by such men as Victorio, Nana, and Geronimo, brought the army into action again. At the head of a small group of Chiricahuas, Geronimo held out for many years in the wild, rocky country along the border, but finally surrendered in September 1886 and, with other Apaches, including scouts who had helped the army against him, was sent to prison in Florida. Eventually, he was transferred to Alabama and then to Fort Sill in Oklahoma. With his defeat, Indian resistance in the Southwest ended.

The most popularized Indian wars are probably those that crushed the proud warrior tribes of the Great Plains. Knowledge of the roots of those wars requires an understanding of the torturous course pursued by the federal government in trying to develop appropriate policies for dealing with the tribes. Beginning with Washington's administration, Indian affairs had been handled by the War Department, but in 1849 they were transferred to the newly established Department of Interior. Each administration had acknowledged the need to avoid or lessen conflict between the westward-moving population and the tribes that would be dispossessed. Giving much thought to the subject, Thomas Jefferson had hoped that government trading posts would encourage Indians to accumulate debts which they could pay off by ceding land. The government, he proposed, would then settle the Indians benignly on agricultural reservations where they would learn to farm and become like their white neighbors.

Jefferson's scheme was impractical. During his own administration, the just and fair treatment promised the Indians by the Northwest Ordinance was ignored by William Henry Harrison, whose coercive methods in dispossessing the tribes of the Northwest Territory set a pattern for future relations between the two races. The Presidents who succeeded Jefferson, notably James Monroe and John Quincy Adams, were persuaded that Indians would not change their ways of life quickly, or voluntarily, and that conflict between tribes that wanted large areas of land in which to hunt and whites who wanted the same land to farm was inevitable. "The hunter or savage state," wrote Monroe in 1817, "requires a greater extent of territory to sustain it than is compatible with the progress and just claims of civilized life . . . and must yield to it." The issue was drawn, and most whites, no matter how fair they wished to be to the Indians, took sides against them. It remained for Andrew Jackson to force the issue and carry out the removal of Indians wherever they occupied lands desired by whites. When Jackson moved, even most of the humanitarian whites in the North, upon whom the Southeast tribes had counted, fell silent, accepting the inevitable, and convincing themselves that removal would ultimately benefit the Indians who, on guaranteed lands west of the Mississippi far beyond the corrupting influences of whites, would have another chance to change into white men and blend harmoniously into the nation.

When the whites did not stop at the Mississippi, new policies had to be fashioned. The most practical solution was the establishment of reservations similar to those that already existed in parts of the East. Relations with individual tribes, at the same time, were guided by a policy, initiated under President Washington and confirmed by the Supreme Court under John Marshall, that recognized tribes as "distinct, independent, political communities" and "domestic dependent nations" with which the United States must deal legally by treaties. Tribes, in other words, were somewhat like separate nations with their own lands, over which the United States government exercised sovereignty. The tribes, too, held title to their lands, and treaties, ratified by the Senate, were the instruments by which title must pass from the tribes to the government. Lands, thus ceded, would be surveyed and disposed of by the government to settlers. Although many treaties had been forced upon tribes, they had been used to give a myth of legality to the removal of each of the tribes from the Northeast and the Southeast; now they would be used, also, to secure title to land west of the Mississippi and to force tribes to accept confinement on reservations.

The eastern part of Kansas, by the 1840's, already con-

tained a number of small reservations occupied by tribes
that had been removed there from the Northeast. Those
tribes were among the first to feel the new pressures, being
forced to make new cessions as settlers moved in on them.
Eventually, almost all those Indians made a final move to
Oklahoma, where they received land near the great confederacies that had been removed from the Southeast. For a time,
the settlers' frontier held on the fertile, watered eastern
fringe of the plains, and in 1850 the nomadic, buffalo-hunting Plains tribes still roamed in freedom from the edge of
the frontier to the Rocky Mountains, and from the Saskatchewan River in Canada to the border settlements of
Texas and New Mexico. When friction did develop, it
occurred along the white men's routes that ran through the
Indians' countries to the Far West and the Southwest. The
Indians complained that the great emigrant trains drove
the buffalo herds from their hunting grounds, and they
resented occasions when they received despotic or unfriendly
treatment from the white families passing through their
lands. Tension grew inevitably along the Oregon Trail, and
in September 1851, at Horse Creek, near Fort Laramie,
Wyoming, government agents induced some ten thousand
Plains Indians of many different tribes to sign a treaty
guaranteeing safety to white travelers on the Trail. The
hunting grounds of each tribe were defined, and promises
were made by tribal leaders to halt intertribal fighting on
the plains. In return, the government negotiators promised
to pay annuities to the tribes and to protect them with
troops against provocations by whites on the Trail.

Army units were stationed at Fort Laramie to protect
both the Indians and the whites, and peace was maintained
for three years. In 1854, however, a Mormon emigrant
claimed that Indians had killed one of his cows, and peace
was shattered when a small troop of soldiers under Lieutenant J. L. Grattan launched an impulsive punitive attack on
a Sioux encampment. The Indians killed Grattan's men
and scattered. The following year, General W. S. Harney,
determined to exact retribution on the Sioux, made a surprise
assault on a Brulé Sioux band at Blue Water Creek, east
of Fort Laramie, slaying men, women, and children. After
the battle, the Brulé chief Spotted Tail surrendered and was
imprisoned, and peace returned temporarily to the Sioux
country. Three years later, in 1857, hostilities flared in the
Cheyennes' country in southern Nebraska and Kansas. Again,

the trouble was occasioned by emigrants, this time by miners and settlers crossing the plains to Colorado and, in so doing, driving the buffalo herds from the Indians' hunting grounds. Troops were hurried into the area to protect the emigrants and punish the tribes.

With the coming of the Civil War, units of Army regulars were withdrawn from the plains for service in the bigger struggle, and the job of keeping the peace fell to bodies of state and territorial militiamen. For the moment, the plains became relatively quiet, but in 1862 an Indian war broke out suddenly in Minnesota. The Indians involved were Eastern, or Santee, Sioux, who in 1851 had ceded a large portion of their lands to the government, reserving for themselves a strip of territory along the Minnesota River. The ceded area around them had filled with whites, and grave injustices had been visited on the Indians by the government agents as well as by the settlers. The Indians' resentments had smoldered and finally burst out in an abrupt uprising and massacre of many of the settlers. The warfare that ensued in Minnesota and the Dakotas was savage. Army troops finally defeated and scattered the Indians, and the authorities executed many of the Sioux leaders in a public hanging. Little Crow, the principal instigator of the outbreak, escaped, but was later shot in a cornfield by a farmer who did not at first know his identity. The dispersed Sioux bands found refuge in Canada or on the Dakota plains where they joined the Teton Sioux tribes. The ferocity and suddenness of the uprising aroused the entire western country, which in the absence of regular troops feared similar outbreaks by other tribes. Volunteer troops from the western states and territories were dispatched to the Missouri, Platte, and Arkansas river valleys, but their appearance, in turn, only served to heighten tensions among the tribes. Inevitably, new troubles arose.

Hostilities broke out first in eastern Colorado, when Southern Cheyennes placed themselves athwart the lines of traffic between the Missouri River and the mountain mining regions. Skirmishes with troops led to a round of raids and retaliations until October 1864, when the Indians gave signs of wanting peace. Two Cheyenne leaders, Black Kettle and White Antelope, concluded an armistice and took their people into a peaceful camp at Sand Creek, 30 miles from Fort Lyon. A disastrous new provocation occurred, however, when Colonel J. M. Chivington and a force of Colorado militia, disregarding the Cheyennes' intentions, fell on the Sand Creek encampment on November 29 and massacred almost three hundred Indian men, women, and children. The surprise assault scattered the survivors, but sent the entire central plains into new warfare. In retaliation for Sand Creek, warrior bands of Cheyennes, Sioux, and Arapahos united and attacked settlements, ranches, and stage stations along the South Platte, destroying wagon trains, interrupting communications, and burning Julesburg twice. The fighting spread to the main Platte and its North Fork, where Sioux also raided settlements and defeated an army unit at Upper Platte Bridge on July 25–6, 1865. By then, the Civil War had ended, and regular troops were rushed to the plains. Although an expedition under General P. E. Conner, marching erratically through the Indian country, failed to find the war bands, the raids ended, and the Indians withdrew to their hunting grounds.

The Civil War had temporarily slowed the westward movement of whites. But with the fighting in the East now ended, new crises loomed for the tribes that were still free and in control of large areas of land. The plains were still unwanted, but west of them the nation was growing, and the Plains tribes stood like barriers across the whites' lines of communication. Construction began on the Union Pacific Railroad that would slice directly across the plains. At the same time, miners in western Montana were demanding a route, cutting through Sioux hunting grounds, that would connect them with the main Overland Trail along the Platte. To safeguard the building of the railroad and the use of a wagon route that John Bozeman had blazed from the Platte to the Montana mines, the government tried a new policy with the Plains Indians, offering them large gifts and annuities in return for guarantees of peace along the white men's avenues of traffic. Some of the tribes agreed and signed treaties with the government negotiators, but the Oglala Sioux under Red Cloud, fearful of losing some of their best hunting grounds, refused to allow the use of the Bozeman Trail. The government ignored the Sioux, sent troops up the trail to construct forts along it, and precipitated a new war. The Indians struck at wagon trains and soon stopped all traffic on the road. Shortly afterward, the troops at their isolated posts came under attack. Forts Phil Kearny, near present-day Sheridan, Wyoming, and C. F. Smith, farther north in Montana, were held almost constantly under siege.

On December 21, 1866, Captain William J. Fetterman and a unit of eighty men were lured onto the plains from Fort Phil Kearny and annihilated by Red Cloud's warriors. A fight occurred also outside of Fort C. F. Smith, and the next year a party of woodchoppers from Fort Phil Kearny fought off a bitter Sioux assault in the celebrated "wagon box fight," so named because the surrounded whites defended themselves from a corral made of wagon beds. Although the troops maintained their positions for more than a year, the steady Sioux harassment prohibited use of the road, and the government finally gave in to the Indians. The forts were abandoned, and on November 6, 1868, Red Cloud signed a treaty of peace at Fort Laramie.

The Platte Valley, along which the Union Pacific ran, was now freed of Indian interference, but farther south, along communication lines to Colorado and the Southwest, there were new troubles with Cheyennes, Arapahos, Kiowas, and Comanches. In the turmoil, another devastating blow was dealt Black Kettle's unfortunate band of Southern Cheyennes that had survived the Sand Creek massacre. Thinking themselves once again at peace with the whites, those Indians were attacked a second time by surprise, this time by Lieutenant Colonel George A. Custer's Seventh Cavalry, which fell on the Cheyennes' camp on the Washita River in Indian Territory and killed many Indians, including Black Kettle.

In the meantime, fundamental changes in the government's policy toward Indians were in the offing. Responding to population pressures and to the demand for more land for settlers, the Homestead Act had been passed in 1863, paving the way for the occupation of the plains. Settlers were already on the eastern fringes of what had once been called "the Great American Desert," and the need for Indian-held land was rising. Patience with the free, roaming tribes grew shorter, and efforts were accelerated to secure title to their countries and confine them on reservations. To speed their submission, encouragement was given to the slaughter of the big buffalo herds, the Indians' principal source of food; with their meat gone, it was believed, the tribes could be forced onto reservations by the promise of rations. At the same time, in 1871, Congress ended further treaty-making with tribes by a law that decreed that henceforth "no Indian nation or tribe within . . . the United States shall be acknowledged or recognized as an independent nation, tribe or power." All existing treaties, however, were considered as still binding on the government. Simultaneously, efforts were made to curb the graft and corruption of the Indian reservation agencies, which had reached scandalous proportions; the reservations were distributed among the major religious denominations, which, in an unprecedented delegation of power by the American government to church bodies, were given the right to nominate new agents and direct educational and other activities on the reservations. The change was motivated by the pressure of well-meaning, humanitarian reformers who convinced President Grant that their benign methods would also have more success than those of the military in hastening the pacification and assimilation of the tribes. Grant's experiment became known as his Peace Policy, but it failed. The church groups quarreled bitterly among themselves over the disposition of the reservations; too many of the agents they nominated were no improvement over the previous ones; and few of the religious groups gave adequate support to the undertaking. Politicians, who were eager to regain reservation jobs for office-seekers, finally helped to kill the policy under the Hayes administration. In the meantime, the Peace Policy left unhappy scars on the Indians: many reservations had come under the authority of what had amounted to stern missionary dictatorships whose fanatic zealousness had crushed Indian culture and institutions, suppressed religious and other liberties, and punished Indians for the least show of independence. Nor had the Peace Policy brought peace. On the reservations, the agents had had to rely frequently on the military to enforce their orders. Where there were still no reservations, tribes had continued to roam in freedom across unceded lands.

The attempt to round up the Plains tribes reached a climax in the mid-1870's. The Treaty of 1868 with Red Cloud had recognized South Dakota's Black Hills, called *Paha Sapa* by the Tetons and held sacred by them, as part of a great Sioux reservation. Ignoring the treaty, however, a column of troops under Custer invaded the Black Hills in 1874 on a reconnaissance tour. Custer suspected he would find gold in the area, and when he did, he took no pains to conceal the discovery. A gold rush ensued, and although troops interfered, the miners refused to leave the Sioux grounds. When the Indians threatened war, the government tried in vain to purchase the area from the Sioux. The latter refused to sell, and the government in desperation ordered the Indians onto reservations, in effect condemning the Sioux title to the

Black Hills. The tribes were given a deadline to report to reservation agencies, but large groups of Sioux and Northern Cheyennes either would not or could not appear at the agencies within the time given them. In March 1876, the government ordered General George Crook to lead an army north from the Platte River and round up the bands.

The scene was set for the most dramatic of all the Plains wars. Marching north, some of Crook's cavalry came on a group of Northern Cheyennes who were on their way to give up at an agency. The cavalry attacked the Indians, but during the fight the Cheyennes were reinforced by Oglala Sioux who arrived under their veteran young war leader, Crazy Horse. The battle, fought in the middle of March, was inconclusive. The Indians got away, and Crook's column, suffering without shelter in the cold weather, gave up its mission and returned to the Platte River.

The Northern Cheyennes, embittered by Crook's assault, now joined the Sioux. With the return of warm weather, the army launched a three-pronged invasion of the Indians' country, determined to find and whip the tribes. On June 17, the southern prong, again led by General Crook and advancing north from the Platte River, was stopped by Crazy Horse and his Oglalas in a fierce battle on Rosebud Creek in south-central Montana. As Crook withdrew, Crazy Horse led his warriors across country to a large Sioux and Cheyenne encampment on the Little Bighorn River. Farther north, on the Yellowstone River, meanwhile, the two other prongs of the army, one coming from the west and one from the east, had met and decided to move south, intending to trap the Indians between themselves and Crook, of whose repulse they were still ignorant. A scouting unit of six hundred troopers of the Seventh Cavalry was sent south in advance of the main columns. Custer, in command of the Seventh, learned of the Indian encampment on the Little Bighorn, and on June 25 rashly attacked it. In a savage fight, the Sioux and Northern Cheyennes under Crazy Horse, Sitting Bull, Gall, and other tribal leaders killed Custer and some two hundred and twenty-five of his men, letting the rest of the troopers barely escape with their lives.

The nation was shocked by Custer's defeat, and efforts were redoubled to clear the plains of the Indians. As the bands dispersed for the winter, army units trudged determinedly after them, wearing them down and rounding them up, one by one. Hounded by troopers, Sitting Bull and some of his Hunkpapa Sioux crossed into Canada where they found sanctuary under the eye of Canadian authorities. (In 1881, Sitting Bull returned peacefully to the United States, and later, before he again had trouble with the army, he toured the country as the star attraction of Buffalo Bill's Wild West Show.) Other Indians, including Crazy Horse's Oglalas, fought on desperately until forced by hunger to give up. Crazy Horse's surrender occurred at Fort Robinson in May 1877; that September, when rumors spread that he was planning to escape, he was taken to a guard room and in a scuffle was bayoneted to death.

The peace that settled over the plains after the confinement of the last Sioux bands was broken occasionally by desperate attempts of various groups to regain their freedom. The Northern Cheyennes were exiled to malarial country in Oklahoma. In 1878, they evaded their captors and under the leadership of Morning Star (known sometimes as Dull Knife) and Little Wolf headed north, trying to return to their old hunting grounds in Montana. Their trek became an epic as they fought off pursuing armies. Some of them were captured, but broke out again. They suffered great hardships, but in the end were overtaken by troops who killed many of them before the rest surrendered. In 1879, Utes rose up against white tormentors in western Colorado, and were put down forcibly. The anguished rebellions against the intolerable conditions on reservations gradually became fewer, and many Indians turned, instead, to making appeals for help from the supernatural. It was futile. The Ghost Dance, which promised the return of the buffalo and the disappearance of white men, spread from the Nevada Paiutes, where it had originated, to the Plains reservations. In 1890, it was crushed out sternly with the murder of Sitting Bull and the massacre of a Sioux band at Wounded Knee, South Dakota. The episode marked the completion of the white man's conquest of the Indian in the United States.

In Canada, relations between the Indians and the whites had been marked by considerably less conflict and violence than in the U.S. In the East, the French had put few pressures on the Indians. What clashes occurred usually stemmed from the fur trade or from the imperial rivalries between France and England. Many Frenchmen married into the Algonquian-speaking tribes, and their descendants became gradually assimilated into the white culture. Conflicts between settlers and Indians over land were practically nonexistent; very early, reserves were guaranteed to different bands, and abundant land was available elsewhere to the relatively sparse white population. Economic, rather than military, problems beset many of the Indians. The Ojibwas and various tribes of the beaver countries from north of the St. Lawrence to Lake Winnipeg enjoyed prosperity in the years of the fur trade, but when that trade declined, they were left without an economic base. By renouncing their Indianness, they were free to enter white society and try to make their own way in the nation's economic life, but many of them preferred to cling to their reserves where their status as wards of the government entitled them to certain minimal economic benefits.

Farther west, the Plains tribes and those in the mountains were scourged on occasion by white men's diseases, but were generally unmolested until the second half of the nineteenth century. Numerous Métis, halfbreed French-Indians, were concentrated in the Red River Valley of central Canada, but were spread also farther west across the plains, living at times in association with Assiniboines, Crees, and Blackfeet. The Métis's frequent clashes with Canadian authorities, stemming sometimes from their French Catholic attitudes of defiance to Protestant officialdom, led to two revolts, in 1870, and again in 1885. Some of the Indians, made restless by disease and starvation, sided with them in a cause that promised the establishment of a separate, independent half-breed and Indian state in central Canada to be called Assiniboia. Troops and Mounted Police put down the revolts, and after the second one, the Métis's fiery leader, Louis Riel, was tried and executed.

As the buffalo disappeared and settlers moved west across the Canadian plains, the system of guaranteed reserves gave protection to the western tribes, though it did not begin to meet their subsistence problems. Despite a generally paternal attitude on the part of Canadian authorities, many bands suffered great hardships as civilization closed in around them. Gradually, some individuals began to prosper as ranchers and small farmers. Others, however, including Indians of the Plateau and the Northwest Coast, could not easily adjust to new conditions. Poverty was widespread, and tribal population generally declined. With the passage of time, conditions improved, but the economic situation of many Canadian Indians has continued until today to be a hard and uncertain one.

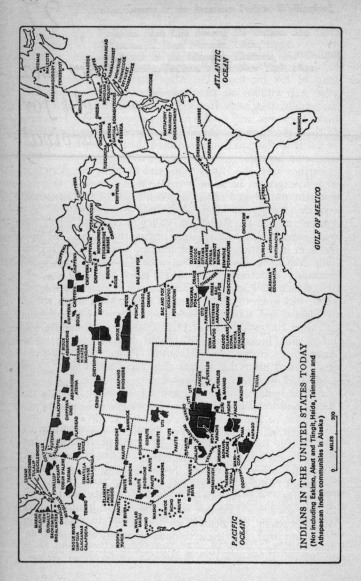

INDIANS IN THE UNITED STATES TODAY
(Not including Eskimo, Aleut and Tlingit, Haida, Tsimshian and
Athapascan Indian communities in Alaska)

27

Indians Today and Their Fight for Survival

In early days we were close to nature. We judged time, weather conditions, and many things by the elements—the good earth, the blue sky, the flying of geese, and the changing winds. We looked to these for guidance and answers. Our prayers and thanksgiving were said to the four winds—to the East, from whence the new day was born; to the South, which sent the warm breeze which gave a feeling of comfort; to the West, which ended the day and brought rest; and to the North, the Mother of winter whose sharp air awakened a time of preparation for the long days ahead. We lived by God's hand through nature and evaluated the changing winds to tell us or warn us of what was ahead.

Today we are again evaluating the changing winds. May we be strong in spirit and equal to our Fathers of another day in reading the signs accurately and interpreting them wisely. May Wah-Kon-Tah, the Great Spirit, look down upon us, guide us, inspire us, and give us courage and wisdom. Above all, may He look down upon us and be pleased.

The speaker, an Indian leader, addressing a convention in the mid-1960's of the National Congress of American Indians, composed of delegates from many tribes in the United States, was pointing out an old story: the Indians faced new challenges to their survival. At the same time, his words were testimony to one of the most miraculous facts of the mid-twentieth century. Despite almost five hundred years of a history marked generally by attempts to exterminate American Indians or force them, by one means or another, to adopt the cultures of their conquerors, they—and their attachment to their Indian heritage—are far from extinct.

Since 1492, Indians have been uninterruptedly on the defensive, fighting for their lives, their homes, their means of sustenance, their societies, and their religions. During that time, on both continents, many of them were assimilated into the white men's civilizations. Some of them ceased entirely to be Indians, but others, through blood, pride, and continued association with Indian groups, retained Indian identification. Almost everywhere, to be sure, acculturation—the adoption of elements of European culture—occurred and, save among the few remaining "wild" tribes, Indian life today is totally different from what it was prior to the arrival of the white man. Most tribes adopted numerous elements of the white men's ways of life, but they also kept many of their own ways which they found useful and worth retaining, in frequent instances blending the old with the new. Many Indians in Middle and South America possess communal or privately owned sewing machines, radio sets, and other manufactured goods, but they also live in pre-Columbian-style dwellings and favor the same foods their ancestors ate hundreds of years ago. Pueblo Indians of the Southwest have added glass windows, wooden doors, and factory-made furniture to their traditional adobe and stone houses; and their youths, wearing the latest teen-age hair and clothing styles, enjoy rock-and-roll music, but also participate devoutly in ancient Pueblo ceremonial dances and rituals. The garb of some Indians includes ponchos, parkas, moccasins, cushmas, or other elements of pre-Columbian clothing together with European-influenced "Panama" hats and manufactured wool and cotton shirts, blue jeans, dresses, and shoes. Digging sticks and other centuries-old tools and methods of farming are often combined with the use of oxen, steel-edged plows, packaged fertilizers, and newly learned soil-testing techniques. Many highland Indians in Peru tile their roofs in Spanish style; Eskimos and tribes of river fishermen drive their boats and dugouts with outboard engines; and shamans, wearing sunglasses to help their trachoma-troubled eyes, travel to curing ceremonies in automobiles. In addition, Indian societies, social and political systems, and religious beliefs and rituals have all, to a greater or lesser degree, changed under the impact of the white man, although in most places they have been modified or combined with new concepts rather than abandoned entirely. Especially in Latin America, Indian culture as a whole has been generally intermixed with European and, in some places, where large numbers of Negro slaves were introduced, with African culture.

Nevertheless, the Indian has survived, still posing to the white conqueror a challenge that not all non-Indians, particularly in the United States, wish happily to tolerate, even, indeed, if they understand it: acceptance of the right to be Indian. That right suggests, at heart, the right to be different, which in the United States runs counter to a traditional drive of the dominant society. Ideally, the American Dream in the United States offers equal opportunities to all persons; but in practice the opportunities imply a goal of sameness, and the Indians, clinging to what seems right and best for them, have instinctively resisted imposed measures by non-Indians designed to make them give up what they want to keep and adopt what they have no desire to acquire. That has been—and continues to be—the core of the so-called "Indian problem" in the United States, which many Indians characteristically refer to as "the white man's problem." Essentially, the Indian recognizes the problem better than the white man. The best-meant aim of the non-Indian is to get the Indian thoroughly assimilated into white society. As years go by, and the Indian is still not assimilated (and, like the white man, enjoying the fruits of the white man's society), the non-Indian loses patience, first with the office-holders who are supposedly charged with getting the Indians assimilated, and then with the Indians themselves. Altruism falls away, and tolerance disappears for the Indians "who don't want to be like everyone else." Moreover, difference, to most non-Indians in the United States implies being inferior, and most people with a guilt complex about Indians wish they would stop being inferior so the guilt complex would go away! To the Indian, the concept that being different means being inferior remains—as it has for almost five hundred years—one of the principal obstacles to his survival. But, ironically, he now views it increasingly—with one eye on the rest of the world—as a concept which the white man must soon shed if he, the white man, expects to survive.

There are other facets to the Indians' resistance to assimilation. To many of them, the argument that they should assimilate (implying detribalization, loss of cultural heritage, and dispersion) is not alone an appeal for them to give up their identity as Indians, but an excuse for the taking of the rest of their lands from them and the ending of their treaty rights and guarantees. The white man may insist that he has other motives that can only be achieved by assimilation: he wants to raise the Indians' standards of living; he wants to give them education, technological know-how, managerial ability, and purchasing power with which to share the white man's affluence. To such arguments, Indians remain deaf: assimilation still means dispossession. Moreover, while most Indians want also to raise their standards of living, they do not see that assimilation is required to do so. More real to them is the need for a new point of view by white men which accepts the right of Indians to manage their own affairs in communities (i.e., reservations) of their own. It is not a new concept. Indians have pleaded in its behalf for years. But they have had little or no response from the non-Indian population, in or out of government, which has failed to recognize the inhibitions, deadening of initiative, and lack of motivation that exist inevitably when an individual or an institution is not vested with responsibility for success or failure

In contrast to what most Indians would consider a realistic appraisal of the roots of their stagnation, non-Indians generally have made no change for almost a century in their basic point of view concerning the nature of "the Indian problem," but still endorse a national policy founded on the maxims that reservations are intolerable enclaves of different peoples within the nation's boundaries, and that Indians who choose to remain unassimilated on the reservations are incapable of managing their own affairs. As a result of adherence, ultimately, to these ideas, the history of federal-Indian relations, since the final pacification of the Plains tribes, reflects a self-defeating, zigzag course of constantly altering programs, all of them designed to lead to Indian assimilation, rather than to the establishment of viable economic bases for the growth of healthy, self-governing, self-sustaining Indian communities within the body politic of the American nation. That history, one of vexation to the American government and degradation and demoralization to the tribes, underscores the failure of the American Dream of equal opportunities to all, as it applies to Indians. Vivid in the memories of most tribes (although it is little known to most non-Indians), it portrays an unrelieved series of frustrations and provides insights into present-day Indian resistance to suggestions of assimilation.

Immediately after their military defeat, tribes were placed

on reservations policed by the Army and administered by the Department of Interior, sometimes through bureaucratic agents, sometimes through missionaries carrying the credentials of agents. The Indians were relegated "out of sight and out of mind" to the American people except for church and charitable agencies, sympathetic private groups, students of the Indians, and rapacious non-Indians on the borders of the reservations who still sought every opportunity to acquire Indian land. The first decades of reservation life were harsh, marked by murders of Indians, systematic persecution of Indian leaders, withholding of rations, and other punishments designed to break the spirit of the people and force them to conform to the orders of the agents and missionaries. Traditional methods of self-government were undermined and destroyed, and in their place was substituted dictatorship by the agents.

From one administration to the next, Congress dutifully, but with little interest, appropriated funds necessary to feed the Indians, meet treaty obligations, and finance in a minimal way policies hopefully fashioned to hasten assimilation. The programs changed impatiently in almost each administration, being carried out by commissioners and agents who also changed with a rapidity that caused confusion and further defeatism to the tribes. While acculturation occurred slowly, the Indians, with minor exceptions, did not become assimilated. For a long time the Indians, regarded as wards of the government, were confined to their reservations— sometimes behind barbed wire—and were often forbidden to leave them without a permit. Far from being given an opportunity to learn to manage their own affairs, they were treated as prisoners or children; the smallest detail was directed and handled for them by the agent. Their religious practices, ceremonies, and organizations were banned, and their children were taken from them, sometimes forcibly, and sent to distant all-Indian schools like Carlisle in Pennsylvania, where they were taught the white men's ways. Some of these Indians, as adults, eventually became assimilated into the white culture; others returned to Indian life on the reservations, and still others became hopelessly lost, unable to make their way successfully among non-Indians, and out of place and scorned when they tried to return to their own people. On the reservations, strong efforts were made to end tribal cultures and ways of life, but no satisfactory substitutes were offered. Traditional means of livelihood had disappeared, but no suitable new economy was introduced. The hunters and warriors, stripped of their dignity and self-respect, were given few manly diversions, and many of them, losing the respect of the women and children, sank into an indolence that withered their souls and turned them, ultimately, to alcohol as an escape and violence as an outlet for their hurts. At the same time, corruption and graft on the part of many agents and hostility and pressures from neighboring whites added to the demoralization of the beaten peoples.

Intrigues to acquire what Indian lands remained were common and were frequently disguised in proposals that would hasten assimilation by forcing the Indians off their reservations and into white society, where they would quickly have to become like everyone else. Such excuses were sometimes made by well-meaning friends of the Indians who genuinely sought methods for hurrying what they considered to be the economic and social improvement of the Indians. In 1887, the Dawes General Allotment Act, initiated and supported by many persons who were sympathetic to the Indians, was passed with the argument that it would give each Indian his own private plot of land and encourage him to become an industrious farmer. The law was tailored to hasten assimilation: it provided for the end of tribal relationships and stipulated that reservations were to be surrendered and divided into family-sized farms which would be allotted to each Indian. Each adult was to receive 160 acres and each minor child 80 acres. The allotted lands would be held in trust for twenty-five years by the government, after which the Indian would be granted outright ownership and thereafter could sell the land if he wished to do so. Meanwhile, whatever reservation acreage was left over after the allotments were made would be declared "surplus" and offered for sale to whites.

Some tribes resisted allotment, and in the Southwest it was scarcely put into practice. Elsewhere it cut deeply into Indian land holdings and caused further hardships and problems for the Indians, although in the end it failed either to break up the tribes or to convert large numbers of Indians into farmers. In 1887 some 138 million acres were held by the Indians; approximately 90 million of them had passed to white ownership under the Dawes Act by 1932. The Allotment Act further failed to recognize that many Indians, particularly those who traditionally had been nomadic

hunters and gatherers, could not or would not become farmers overnight; they had neither the cultural background for
the new way of life nor the necessary training. Furthermore,
much of the land allotted to them was too poor to farm,
and they received no financial credit nor little help of any
other kind. Many Indians, totally estranged from non-Indian
economic motivations and customs, leased or sold their lands
to whites at bargain prices; others were swindled out of
their holdings; and poverty, drunkenness, and debauchery
increased.

The Dawes Act did not apply at once to the "Five Civilized Tribes"—the Creeks, Choctaws, Cherokees, Chickasaws, and Seminoles—who since their removal from the
Southeast had possessed the rights to large portions of the
Indian Territory that now constitutes part of Oklahoma.
During the Civil War, some members of those tribes had
joined the Confederate forces (the last Confederate general
officer to surrender was Stand Watie, a Cherokee), and after
the war punishment had been visited upon them by the
Federal government. On April 22, 1889, some "unassigned
lands" in the center of the Indians' country was thrown open
to white settlers in the first "Oklahoma run." Other lands
in the western part of the Territory were also opened to
land-hungry whites during the next sixteen years, and by
1905 the Five Civilized Tribes had been persuaded to allot
their lands under the Dawes Act, accept citizenship, and
join their white neighbors in preparing a state constitution.
On January 16, 1907, Oklahoma entered the Union.

Under the Dawes Act, conditions on reservations eventually became scandalous. Indian life was marked by poverty,
squalor, disease, and hopelessness. In general, Indians received little or no education and were still treated as wards,
incapable of self-government or making decisions for themselves. Whatever revenues the tribes received from land
sales were dissipated, with virtually none of them going to
assist the Indians to create sound foundations for the development of the human and economic resources of the reservation. The situation demanded reforms. In 1924, as an
acknowledgment of the country's gratitude to Indians who
had volunteered for service in the armed forces during
World War I, the Snyder Act conferred citizenship on all
Indians. Two years later, a special group under Lewis
Meriam investigated Indian conditions for the Department
of Interior and proposed a sweeping list of reforms, includ-

ing a halt to allotments which, in bringing about a drastic
reduction of reservation land, was finally recognized as one
of the prime causes of the Indians' impoverishment and
continued demoralization. The Wheeler-Howard Act of
1934, better known as the Indian Reorganization Act, stemming from the Meriam survey and administered by Indian
Commissioner John Collier, brought an end to the allotment
policy, encouraged tribal self-government, extended financial
credit to the tribes, began an improvement in educational
and medical facilities, restored freedom of religion for
Indians, and promoted a revival of Indian culture.

The Indian Reorganization Act was an admission that
assimilation was still far off, but essentially it represented a
substitution of slower-acting and more considerate methods
that were still designed, ultimately, to achieve the national
policy of guiding Indians to assimilation. At the same time,
it conferred on the Indians greater freedom to proceed
toward assimilation at a rate of speed and under conditions
of their own choosing. In confirming Indian self-government,
it returned to them the right to organize their own institutions and manage their own affairs, although the Department of the Interior, through the Indian agents, still retained
a veto power over many reservation details, including, most
importantly, financial matters. The Indian response to the
new rights and responsibilities was generally slow; after
so many years of wardship, most tribes could not easily adjust to the new policy. Nevertheless, tribal governments were
formed, Indian inhibitions and fears began to disappear, the
initiative and energies of the peoples began to stir, and conditions started gradually to improve.

During World War II, approximately twenty-five thousand Indians served in the armed forces of the United States.
Some were employed in communications teams, where they
spoke their own languages on field telephones and walkie-
talkie radios to confuse enemy interceptors. Many Indian
servicemen mixed in the non-Indian world for the first time
and returned to their reservations anxious to bring more of
the white man's technology to their own people. At the
same time, some Indians who had served in the war, together
with others who had left the reservations to work in war
plants and shipyards, preferred to continue living in the
white men's cities, and many of them gradually became
assimilated into non-Indian life, though they retained their
Indian identity and their attachments to their people.

Soon after World War II, impatience with the speed of Indian assimilation, motivated in part by concern over how long the taxpayer would have to continue paying for treaty-guaranteed services to Indians, led to a violent reversal of government policy that brought new demoralization to the tribes. Underlying the change was hostility to the Indian Reorganization Act, which did not seem to be moving Indians toward assimilation quickly enough. Actually, the aims of the Act were being delayed by administrative short-comings, including the failure of Indian Bureau officials to aid the Indians to take advantage of the benefits of the Act and to trust their ability to learn to handle their own affairs, and by the inadequacy of Congressional appropriations for credit facilities and other activities necessary to make the Act work. At any rate, in 1953, two measures—an act authorizing states to assume jurisdiction over criminal and civil matters on reservations without approval by the tribes, and a resolution declaring Congress's intent to terminate Federal relations with the tribes at the earliest possible time —were adopted. The ultimate goal of both measures was, again, to speed the assimilation of Indians and break down the remaining tribal and cultural bonds that supposedly interfered with their economic progress and hindered their becoming like all other citizens. Making use of misleading appeals, including "free the Indians from the reservations" (implying to the uninformed that reservations were concentration camps and that Indians were still held as prisoners upon them), the proponents of the second measure, particularly, brought new confusion to the tribes who had barely begun to make use of the rights and responsibilities of the Indian Reorganization Act.

Under the determined pressure of Senator Arthur Watkins of Utah, one of the chief spokesmen in Congress for the "termination" policy, a number of tribes, including the Klamaths of Oregon, the Menominees of Wisconsin, four bands of Paiutes and some Utes of Utah, various western Oregon tribes, and the Alabamas and Coushattas of the South, felt the impact of termination, which, in the case of the Klamaths and Menominees particularly, was carried out in an ill-conceived fashion and over the opposition of many of the tribal members. The reasons behind the selections of the terminated tribes differed, from the explanation that a tribe was financially well off (the Menominees, who owned a profitably operating commercial forest) to the assertion that tribes could not be worse off under any condition (the Paiutes in Utah). The hurried termination brought new confusion and hardship to most of the terminated peoples and, in the case of the Menominees, economic disaster. Almost overnight, many millions of dollars of tribal assets disappeared in the rush to transform the Menominee reservation into a self-supporting county. The need to finance the usual hospital, police, and other services of a county and pay taxes imperiled the tribe's sawmill and forest holdings, alienated tribal lands, threatened many Indians with the loss of their homes and life savings, and saddled Wisconsin with a huge welfare problem which it could not underwrite and which had to be met by desperate appeals for help from the same federal government that had thought it had washed its hands of the Menominees.

In the 1950's also, the Indian Bureau, again attempting to improve the Indian's economic status and hasten assimilation, gave increased emphasis to a "relocation" program that sent Indians to certain cities where homes and jobs were found for them. The Indians were first screened on the reservations, and those who seemed to possess the best chance for adjustment were sent to such cities as Chicago, Denver, and Los Angeles. Many Indians made the change successfully and have continued to live in white society. But the program was severely criticized because it was not balanced by efforts to develop the economies on reservations, and because in numerous cases the government abandoned interest in the "relocated" Indians after they had been in the cities a short time. When they lost their jobs or housing, the Indians tended to become stranded persons in alien societies. Some of them ended on skid rows, while others gravitated for help to church and welfare groups. Although numbers of "relocated" Indians returned to their reservations, the program was never formally abandoned. It tapered off after 1960, and under the administrations of Presidents Kennedy and Johnson greater efforts were made to help the Indians relocate more successfully.

On the other hand, many tribes benefited by still another post-war federal program. In 1946, the government established a special Indian Claims Commission, designed to bring to an end all Indian claims of unjust land dealings in the past by hearing whatever evidence the tribes wished to present and awarding payments where fairness demanded restitution for lands taken illegally or for less than proper payment. The Indians lodged more than 580 claims, and by 1964 almost $100,000,000 had been paid to settle 50 out of 158 claims decided, some of the awards being made with injunctions to the tribes to use the funds to prepare for termination. The life of the commission was extended periodically by Congress to continue liquidating the claims.

As a result of the opposition of the tribes, and the difficulties encountered by the Klamaths and Menominees, the termination policy, while continuing to be understood as the ultimate intent of Congress, was all but abandoned in the latter part of the 1950's and the early 1960's. In 1961, the Kennedy administration, dropping talk of termination, showed an intention of reemphasizing the most beneficial aspects of the Indian Reorganization Act as the best road along which the Indians could travel. A survey by a special task force appointed by Secretary of the Interior Stewart L. Udall, as well as a statement of aims and goals by a conference of Indians in Chicago in the summer of 1961, pointed the way to greatly accelerated progress in the future. Under Commissioner of Indian Affairs Philleo Nash, new programs of education, vocational training, housing, and economic development on reservations were inaugurated, some of them receiving assistance from other government agencies and from legislation like the Area Redevelopment Act of 1961, which did not apply solely to Indians. In addition, progress in meeting reservation health and sanitation problems was made by the U. S. Public Health Service, which in 1955 had taken over responsibility for providing medical care and health services to the Indians. Overall improvement in the economic conditions of the Indians, however, came more slowly than desired by the Johnson administration or the termination-minded members of Congress, and in 1966 Commissioner Nash was replaced by Robert L. Bennett, an Oneida Indian from Wisconsin who had risen through the ranks of the Bureau of Indian Affairs.

To stave off congressional pressure for a renewal of the termination policy, administration energies were directed toward fashioning fresh programs to hasten the economic development of the reservations and lifting the standards of living of the Indians. In the spate of legislation designed to bring about the Great Society, envisioned by President Johnson, Indians were included with the general population, and many benefits, together with funds, became available to them for the first time from various health, housing, educational, manpower development and vocational training, and other programs administered by agencies other than the Department of the Interior. At the same time, new methods were sought to provide capital and credit for the use of tribes and individual Indians and for the relaxation, and eventual withering away, of the government's managerial functions, particularly over the financial affairs of the tribes and individual Indians. Following a Capital Conference on Indian Poverty in Washington in 1964, a momentous breakthrough had occurred via the operations on reservations of the antipoverty programs of the Office of Economic Opportunity. Once reservation poverty programs, suggested by Indians, had been approved, funds were made available to the Indians who ran the programs themselves. It was the first time that Indians generally had been allowed to assume the full responsibility for the management of, and the use of funds for, programs on reservations, and, by and large, the Indians showed that they were able to carry out functions which, up to then, had been supervised for them by their agents. Part of the success, moreover, stemmed from the fact that the programs were ones which the Indians themselves wanted and planned according to the needs as they saw them.

The lessons of the Community Action, Operation Headstart, Neighborhood Youth Corps, Vista, and other antipoverty programs on reservations were not lost on the Indians who, through such organizations of their own as the National Congress of American Indians and the National Indian Youth Council, increased their demand for the right of Indians to participate in the designing of programs for them and to manage their own affairs on the reservations. The first test came in 1966 in an attempt by the administration to shape an "omnibus bill" of new economic legislation for presentation to Congress in 1967 as an Indian Resources Development Act. In response to the Indians' demands, Commissioner Bennett and Department of the Interior officials met with Indian leaders to learn what kind of legislation the tribes wanted. Nevertheless, Department officials, still not trusting the Indians to know what was best for them and continuing to try to impose their own ideas on them, sent a final draft of the bill to Congress which many tribes claimed did not reflect the needs or desires that the Indians had expressed in their meetings with Commissioner Bennett. By the end of 1967 opposition to the bill by many tribes had doomed it. In the process, however, a forward step may have been taken, for once again the Indians had demonstrated their growing initiative in matters concerning their people; and in the government (which in early 1968 introduced new legislation more closely tailored to Indian thinking), as well as among private groups of non-Indians who had been used to imposing their own ideas on Indians in their efforts to aid them, there were signs of an increasing willingness to listen to the Indians and try to support what the tribes themselves proposed.

At the same time, other developments were occurring. A White House task force, reporting directly to the President in 1966, recommended the transfer of the Bureau of Indian Affairs to the Department of Health, Education and Welfare. Pending action on the proposal, which was opposed by many tribes as well as by various congressmen, the Bureau took steps to upgrade its Educational Division and plan for a thoroughgoing reform of Indian education which would meet the many special problems in that field and bring the education of Indian youths into line with the level of American education generally. The new thinking included such ideas as instilling Indian pride among Indian youths by instructing them in their own history and culture, by using their own languages in classrooms, and by involving their own people in the administration of the schools, even to the extent of letting tribes run the schools. The role of the Bureau itself, in education as well as in other matters, came under scrutiny too: with the benefits, aids, and funds of so many other governmental, foundation, and private agencies becoming available to tribes, the Bureau, said Commissioner Bennett in 1967, should no longer be "the sole source of funds and technical resources for Indian assistance. Its function should be shifting from one exclusive responsibility for Indians to the role of 'finder' and 'coordinator' of other sources of aid." Agreeing with him, many of the tribes looked forward to agents on reservations becoming coordinating service officers, bringing the tribes together with industrial, technological, and other specialists who could aid them in their economic development.

Despite the tribes' almost unanimous opposition to termination as a national policy, the ending of Federal relations with tribes may, in the long run, be inevitable. Some of the members of certain tribes and reservations, like those of the Colville Reservation in Washington, are asking for it themselves, although the demand usually comes from the Indians who have moved off the reservations and, trying to make a life for themselves in white society, no longer have an interest in maintaining the reservations but want the tribal resources liquidated and divided among the people. Certain congressmen, too, have not abandoned their interest in seeing termination hurried, and occasionally attach termination riders to bills appropriating claims awards or other special funds to tribes. After the Army Engineers won the right to build Kinzua Dam and inundate a large part of the Senecas' reservation in western New York State in the early 1960's, compensatory funds were not voted for the Indians until the Senecas had agreed to a demand that they prepare a program for the termination of all future relations between themselves and the federal government.

At the same time, if termination is inevitable, it is now generally recognized that most tribes are far from ready for it, and that the government for a long time still to come must help the Indians develop the human and economic resources of the reservations. In this view, no tribe would be terminated until its members felt they were ready to manage their own affairs and compete on equal terms with non-Indian society. To many Indian leaders, the attainment of such a status by their people will result not so much from assimilation as from a restoration of their pride in themselves as Indians. The goal of Indian youths, according to many tribal leaders, should no longer be "either-or" (either become a white man and be able to compete, or stay an Indian and suffer). Presupposing that even after termination tribal corporations and other unifying influences will be able to maintain the reservations intact for the people, such leaders assert that their youths should be educated and trained to be comfortable in the societies of both the whites and the Indians, able to make their way easily on and off the reservations, knowledgeable about the white men's ways and yet proud of their Indian heritage, with a foot, so to speak, planted firmly in each culture.

In the meantime, the harsh facts of present-day Indian life, made ever more difficult to cope with because of rapidly increasing Indian populations on reservations, often demand measures that are little more than emergency in nature. Most Indians are still among the poorest of all the American people. A few tribes at one time enjoyed financial windfalls and received spectacular publicity: oil leases in Oklahoma enriched some of the Osages, and land rights in the Cali-

fornia desert resort of Palm Springs brought wealth to some
Cahuilla Indians. But they are the exceptions. Oil, gas,
helium, uranium, and vanadium have all been found in the
Navahos' country in the Southwest and have provided the
tribal council with large amounts of capital, which has been
invested in corporate enterprises and other projects to benefit
the entire tribe. But the plight of the Navahos, resulting
from a rapidly increasing population that cannot sustain
itself on the barren land of the reservation, continues to
hover close to the critical point; and despite the efforts of
able and visionary Navaho leaders, great problems remain
to be solved. Almost everywhere else, tribes have an economic standard well below that of surrounding white communities, and in some areas, conditions of extreme poverty,
near-starvation at certain seasons, and political helplessness
demand the best efforts of the government and tribal leaders.
Some statistics of 1967 make the situation graphic: The
average Indian family income in the United States was
$1500. Unemployment on reservations ranged from 45 per
cent up, reaching 80 per cent on some reservations at certain seasons. Some 90 per cent of Indian housing on reservations was unacceptable by any standards. Some 70 per cent
of the people on reservations still hauled their water one mile
or more from its source. Average schooling of Indian children
was five years. The average school drop-out rate was 50
per cent, compared with a national average of 29 per cent.

Today the Indian population of the United States, including Eskimos, is approximately 600,000, with some
380,000 of them living on or near reservations and eligible
to participate in programs of the Bureau of Indian Affairs.
By treaty and other obligations, the Bureau's jurisdiction
includes 284 separate Indian land units (reservations,
colonies, rancherias, and communities) and 35 groups of scattered public-domain allotments and other off-reservation
lands. In addition, the Bureau has some service relationship
with 147 Alaskan Native communities and many scattered,
Native-owned town lots in Alaska.

The largest centers of Indian population in the United
States today are Arizona with more than 85,000; Oklahoma
with more than 65,000; New Mexico with some 57,000;
Alaska with approximately 50,000; California and North
Carolina, each with about 40,000; South Dakota with about
30,000; and Montana and Washington, each with about
22,000. Since the Reorganization Act of 1934, some tribes

have been able to increase their land holdings, and tribal lands now total almost 40 million acres, with nearly 12 million more acres in allotted land. Individual reservations range in size from small settlements, or rancherias, of a few acres in California (California's Strawberry Valley Rancheria in Yuba County, with one acre, is the smallest) to the Navaho reservation of more than 15 million acres (about the size of West Virginia) in Arizona, New Mexico, and Utah. In the eastern states, particularly, are many small communities of Indians, like Pequots in Connecticut, Shinnecocks on Long Island, and Mattaponys in Virginia, who have almost blended into the surrounding white society, but still maintain their unity and their own cohesive settlements and, in some cases, enjoy recognition as Indians by the governments of the states in which they live. Many other persons, also, count themselves Indians by blood and cultural heritage, although their tribes are almost extinct, they have no reservations, and they live entirely like white men in urban or rural areas.

Despite acculturation, numerous Indian ways of life survive in the United States, especially in the larger centers of Indian population. The Hopis and many other Pueblo peoples of the Southwest maintain their priesthoods, dances, and religious, social, and political organizations and customs with remarkably little change, and one group of Hopis gives determined leadership to Indians of many different tribes who seek the strengthening of traditional Indian values and ways of life. These Hopis, following the customs of their ancestors in seeking peace and harmony with the cosmos, urge Indians to avoid the non-Indian world of turmoil and competitiveness, and have opposed moves of their own people to grant oil leases on their lands or allow factories to be built in Hopi country. Among the Navahos, who have been torn between progressive and traditionalist factions over how far to go in accepting the white man's civilization, healing ceremonies that make use of sand, or dry paintings, and traditional prayers, are still in common use. Non-Christian Iroquois Indians of New York, some of whom work regularly on structural steel building projects in urban centers, still follow the precepts of Handsome Lake, who more than a century ago revised the ancient Iroquois faith. An example of change is the Native American Church, a widespread religion that incorporates Indian beliefs and

Christianity. An important rite of this religion, presided over by native priests, is the eating of peyote, a nonaddictive drug that produces hallucinations. Peyote is made by cutting off and drying the tip of the mescal cactus. The members of the Native American Church eat it to induce contact with the supernatural. The pantheon of the religion includes both Indian and Christian spiritual beings, and the rituals make use of eagle-bone whistles, water drums, gourd rattles, and other Indian elements. Many Indians, including the Ojibwas (now generally known as the Chippewas) and certain Plains and Plateau tribes, still prefer to live in wigwams and tipis, at least during the summer months. Elements of Indian garb are still used in dress; sweat baths are still taken; and hunting and fishing in seasonal round are still pursued by many tribes, sometimes over the objections of non-Indian sportsmen whose hunting and fishing seasons are limited by state laws to periods of shorter duration. In addition, almost all tribes have shown a renewed interest in their dances, songs, and stories, and some have revived long-abandoned crafts and arts and set up classes in their own languages for young and old.

In Canada, the conduct of Indian affairs has been characterized generally by a colonialist adherence to a policy that originated with the Proclamation of 1763, which prohibited the displacement of Indians from their lands except with their consent and with Crown approval. Relatively few treaties were required with the tribes; those that were made usually formalized the setting aside of lands reserved for the exclusive use of Indians, the establishment of perpetual trusteeship by the Crown, and the promise of the payment of annuities and the providing of schools and services. Under the Indian Act of 1876, individual Indians—or the members of a band by a majority vote—could ask for enfranchisement (in effect, citizenship), which entailed the voluntary renunciation of a person's status and rights and privileges as an Indian. Between 1876 and 1951 various acts enabled the government to take the initiative in enfranchising certain Indians. The Indian Act of 1951 went further, making Indians generally subject to the same laws as all other Canadians and enabling them to vote in national elections. Adult Indians in Canada may now become full citizens, but only by presenting character references and evidence that they have lived away from reserves for a certain length of time and have steady employment. Upon enfranchisement, the Indians receive their share of band assets in cash and give up all their legal rights as Indians.

In general, most Canadian Indians have resisted enfranchisement and, as in the United States, have remained unassimilated. Today there are some 225,000 Indians in Canada, 215,000 of them living on 2,260 reserves, ranging in size from a few acres to 500 square miles. The Indians are organized in bands, rather than tribes, the largest of more than 550 bands in the nation being that of the Six Nations (Iroquois), with 7,000 members, living near Brantford, Ontario. The Indian Act is administered by the Department of Indian Affairs, which looks after education, provides social-welfare services, administers trust monies from the sale and lease of reserve lands, aids with the securing of housing and loans, and helps Indians find employment both on and off the reserves through a placement program.

In recent years, the Canadian government has awakened to the realization that Canadian Indians have the same economic problems as those in the United States. Indians derive income from trapping, commercial fishing, hunting, lumbering, craftwork, guiding sportsmen and vacationers, frog catching for food markets, fruit and berry picking, working as itinerant farm and ranch hands, and from small farms and enterprises of their own. But many jobs are seasonal, and unemployment is often widespread. Some educated Indians, as in the United States, have become businessmen and have entered the professions. But fewer than 15 per cent of the Indian homes in Canada have flush toilets, running water, or telephones; fewer than 50 per cent have electricity; and three out of four Indian families earn $2,000 or less per year. In 1966, as Indian restlessness increased over economic conditions on many of the reserves, the government moved to pay more attention to improving the lot of the various bands. Most of the bands have elected band councils. Varying in size, they include one chief and from two to twelve councilors, depending on the band's population. None of the bands or band councils, however, possessed the legal right to conduct business with outsiders. As a result, new changes in Canada's Indian Act pointed to the freeing of reserves from federal government interference or influence, and permitting the bands to become legal entities in their own rights, able to lease land, levy taxes, and otherwise conduct their own affairs. All reserve land would continue to be vested in the Crown, but the Indians could make all their own decisions, even to turning the reserves into corporate municipalities. Such self-determination might free Indian energies and, with continued government assistance, hasten an improvement in the economies of the bands.

In Latin America, the Indian situation varies almost from country to country. In remote areas of South America, a few so-called wild tribes with relatively pure Indian cultures still exist, mostly in the Amazon River Basin. Other "wild" tribes dwell along the upper tributaries of the Orinoco River in eastern Colombia and Venezuela, in parts of Paraguay and eastern Brazil, and on the eastern slopes of the Peruvian and Ecuadorean Andes. Some are tropical forest farmers, and some are nomadic fishermen, hunters, and gatherers. Among them are such peoples as the Cariban-speaking Motilones of Colombia; a few Guaraní tribes in Paraguay and Brazil; various Ge-speaking bands on the tributaries of the Xingú River in Brazil; and the Jívaros, Campas, and others in Ecuador and Peru. Occasionally they are visited by missionaries, and sometimes they become embroiled in clashes with frontier oil workers and others who invade their home areas. Not a few times in recent years, whites have struck savagely at some of these Indians, using modern weapons to massacre certain groups.

Aside from the relatively few pure Indians remaining in Latin America, the question of who are, and who are not, Indians is frequently difficult to determine. In a population of approximately 12 million in the Central Andean nations of Peru and Bolivia, at least 6 million are classed as Indians. Yet this is a cultural, rather than a biological, classification, and it counts only those who have not yet abandoned many of their distinctly Indian patterns of life. Similarly, in Paraguay, only about 60,000, or roughly 3 per cent of the total population, are considered Indians, although by a racial reckoning hundreds of thousands of others would qualify as Indians. Between these "cultural" Indians and the whites in most Latin American countries is a large mestizo class composed of persons who have lost their distinctive Indian ways, yet who have not been thoroughly assimilated into the dominant white, Hispanic patterns. Many of the mestizos are urban artisans and laborers or peasant farmers.

In the Central Andean highlands, where Indians who speak Quechua and Aymara still comprise the majority of the rural population from Ecuador to southern Bolivia and northwestern Argentina, most people continue to dwell in pre-Columbian style, one-family sod or stone huts. In addition, they still raise potatoes, corn, and quinoa as their principal crops; herd llamas and alpacas (but now also possess sheep and pigs); wear woolen ponchos and headpieces; and make music on Indian panpipes. Fundamental economic changes, however, have affected their social organizations and concepts of family, property, and inheritance. Many whose lands proved insufficient to support them have become hacienda employees, bound to large landholders as sharecroppers, tenant farmers, or laborers, and are compelled by indebtedness to renew their contracts annually with the hacienda owners. They are generally very poor and live within the social and economic framework of a single hacienda. In recent years, inter-American aid programs, like the Alliance for Progress, as well as small political revolutionary movements, have had as their aim the bettering of the condition of people like these.

Many other highland Indians live in small, autonomous peasant communities, self-sufficient, self-contained, and fairly isolated from the rest of society. They retain many of their Indian traits, but often the settlements show white—especially Spanish—influences. The communities usually consist of several patrilineal families related to one another by marriage. People generally are suspicious and afraid of outsiders, Indian as well as white, and forbid the sale of land to them. Community lands are divided into family plots; but national laws, supporting individual rather than community ownership of land, have caused changes within the communities and have led to conflicts between traditional and European concepts of land tenure. Each year, the arable land is reallocated among the families of the community in official ceremonies; but the idea of individual ownership is gradually being accepted and is disrupting the extended families. The attractiveness of private ownership of land has been increased by the pressure of overpopulation, which creates competition for land, and the growing of crops that can be taken to market and sold for cash with which to purchase manufactured goods. However, ancient farming implements, including the digging stick, are still employed, and low yields, often insufficient to meet local needs, are frequently the rule. In some regions, the national governments have attempted to transform the communities into more productive cooperatives. To supplement their income people also make and sell various handicrafts. As in many parts of Latin America, Catholicism was overlaid on, or added to, elements of earlier religious beliefs and practices of the Quechuas and Aymarás. Religion is a basic part of daily social, political, and economic life and today is only slightly connected to the Roman Catholic Church. An unofficial sort of politico-religious leadership within many communities is provided by elders who are often shamans and who perform cures and various forms of sorcery.

In Paraguay, a strong cultural nationalism is based on the fact that more than half of the country's almost 2 million people, particularly in the more densely populated regions, still speak the Guaraní Indian language, although many of them are bilingual and also speak Spanish. The use of Guaraní has helped to further belief that the country also possesses a Guaraní culture and race, although this is erroneous. The aboriginal Guaraní culture has virtually disappeared, and most of the people are descendants of a few original Spanish settlers and their many native wives. The Guaraní culture today is heavily Hispanicized, although lack of capital and other economic problems have kept most people on substantially a lower-class level. Paraguayan peasants are mostly self-sufficient, growing their own food and making the goods they require for their daily needs. Indian crops are supplemented by sugar cane, wheat, and oranges, which were introduced by Europeans; and cattle, horses, pigs, and chickens, also brought by the white man, are raised. Indian products, including hammocks and maté, are still in wide use, and some homes are pre-Columbian and others European in style. The people are Catholic but sometimes maintain only loose relationships to the Church. Marriages are easily ended, and kinship bonds, called *compadrazgo*, or co-parenthood, based on close ties between the parents and godparents of a child, and common in various parts of Latin America, are often established outside of the Church.

Despite the tendency of the white and mestizo parts of the population in most Latin American nations to look down on Indians, an Indianist movement has spread through many of those countries since the first decades of the twentieth century and has given rise to a strong national interest in the Indian past and in the welfare of Indian tribes that still exist. The movement has perhaps been strongest in Mexico, where it has influenced artistic and intellectual life, as well as the political forces that grouped around the "Revolutionary" movement which, born in 1910, received a major part of its inspiration from Mexico's Indian leader of the mid-nineteenth century, Benito Juárez, and reached its latter-day climax under another Indian leader, President Lázaro Cárdenas, in the 1930's. In Guatemala, also, Indian interests, from time to time, have been identified with political movements, while in other countries the Indianist movement has attempted to enfold "wild" and only slightly acculturated native peoples in modern national life and, at the same time, encourage the preservation of tribal cultural elements. In Brazil, an Indian Protective Service was founded in 1911 to halt the destruction of Indian communities and Indian cultural values in the Amazon Basin. For a time, the Service guarded the Indians' interests zealously. But in 1968, shocking disclosures revealed that for twenty years many officials of the Service had been systematically annihilating entire tribes for their lands. Hundreds of officials were arrested or dismissed, and a new National Indian Foundation, dedicated to the original purposes of the Service, was set up.

In a rapidly diminishing world, the future of the Indians on both continents is one of accelerating acculturation. But complete and final assimilation is still so remote a prospect as to make certain the Indians' own pronouncement: "We are here, and we will be here for many generations yet to come."

BIBLIOGRAPHY

THE LITERATURE ON AMERICAN INDIANS IS VOLUMINOUS. IT INCLUDES numerous journals, diaries, letters, reports, and other writings, many of extreme ethnohistorical importance, by explorers, traders, missionaries, colonists, government agents, and others who met Indian tribes and wrote about them before the full impact of European ways had begun to change them. Later, an increasing flow of studies, based on field, laboratory, and documentary research, began to come from anthropologists, archeologists, historians, and other specialists, many of them examining small but significant aspects of the full Indian story. Through the years an outpouring of general works has also appeared, some—but not all—of them tending to go out of date with new findings of research and study. In recent years the tide of both research papers and general studies has swelled, and a flood of serious and commendable works, ranging from archeological reports on prehistoric cultures to popular syntheses of histories of tribes and of Indian-white relations, is being added to the literature each year.

This bibliography represents a selective culling of works that are most likely to be of major assistance and interest to the nonspecialist. For additional aid to those who would read further, the titles of published works are listed under four categories, reflecting the principal emphasis of the material with which they deal. Some, while out of date today, are of continuing ethnological or historical interest. Others, though quite specialized in subject or presentation, nevertheless encompass material that should interest the general reader. Many of the works contain valuable bibliographies of their own that will guide the more demanding reader to detailed studies of individual tribes and to more specific areas and aspects of Indian life and history.

In addition, mention should be made of the numerous museums, libraries, and national, state, and local historical societies and other institutions in the United States, as well as in other countries, that contain important collections, including unpublished manuscript materials, relating to American Indians. I have listed those with which I am familiar. Finally, I have noted certain publications that appear—or have appeared in the past—with some regularity and have been helpful to me.

Institutions With Important Materials Pertaining to Indians

Alaska Historical Library and Museum, Juneau

American Antiquarian Society, Worcester, Massachusetts

American Museum of Natural History, New York

American Philosophical Society, Philadelphia

Archives of Ontario, Toronto

Archivo General de Indias, Seville

Archivo Historico Nacional, Madrid

Arizona Pioneers Historical Society, Tucson

Arizona State Museum, Tucson

Bancroft Library, University of California, Berkeley

Bibliothèque Nationale, Paris

British Museum, London

Brooklyn Museum, Brooklyn, New York

John Carter Brown Library, Providence, Rhode Island

California Historical Society, San Francisco

Chicago Historical Society, Chicago

Chicago Natural History Museum, Chicago

Denver Museum of Natural History, Denver

Detroit Public Library, Detroit

El Museo Nacional de Antropología y Arqueología, Peru

Thomas Gilcrease Institute of American History and Art, Tulsa, Oklahoma

Glenbow Foundation, Calgary, Alberta

Haffenreffer Museum, Bristol, Rhode Island

Hudson's Bay Company, London and Winnipeg

Henry E. Huntington Library and Art Gallery, San Marino, California

Idaho Historical Society, Boise

Kansas State Historical Society, Topeka

Library of Congress, Washington, D.C.

Los Angeles County Museum, Los Angeles

Manitoba Historical Society, Winnipeg

Minnesota Historical Society, St. Paul

Missouri Historical Society, St. Louis

Montana Historical Society, Helena

Museo Nacional de Antropología, Mexico City

Museo Naval, Madrid

Museum für Völkerkunde, Vienna

Museum of New Mexico, Santa Fe

Museum of Northern Arizona, Flagstaff

Museum of the American Indian, Heye Foundation, New York

National Archives, Washington, D.C.

National Museum of Canada, Ottawa

Nebraska State Historical Society, Lincoln

Newberry Library, Chicago

The New-York Historical Society, New York

New York Public Library, New York

New York State Museum, Albany

Oklahoma Historical Society, Oklahoma City

Oregon Historical Society, Portland

Peabody Museum of Archaeology and Ethnology, Harvard University

Provincial Archives of British Columbia, Victoria

Provincial Museum, Victoria

Public Archives of Canada, Ottawa

Royal Ontario Museum, Toronto

Sheldon Jackson Museum, Sitka, Alaska

State Historical Society of Colorado, Denver

Smithsonian Institution and National Museum, Washington, D.C.

South Dakota State Historical Museum, Pierre

Southwest Museum, Los Angeles

Texas Memorial Museum, University of Texas, Austin

University Museum, University of Pennsylvania, Philadelphia

Utah State Historical Society, Salt Lake City

Washington State Historical Society, Tacoma

Wisconsin State Historical Society, Madison

Yale University Library, New Haven, Connecticut

Periodic Publications with Information on Indians

ABC Americans Before Columbus, Schurz, Nevada (newspaper of the National Indian Youth Council)

American Anthropologist, Chicago

American Antiquity, Salt Lake City

Annual Reports and *Bulletins*, Bureau of American Ethnology, Smithsonian Institution, Washington, D.C.

Annual Reports, Commissioner of Indian Affairs, Washington, D.C.

Ethnohistory, Bloomington, Indiana

Indian Affairs, Association on American Indian Affairs, New York

Indian Historian, American Indian Historical Society, San Francisco

Indian Voices, University of Chicago, Chicago

Indian Truth, Indian Rights Association, Inc., Philadelphia

NCAI Sentinel, National Congress of American Indians, Washington, D.C.

Newspapers and bulletins of various Indian tribes, including the Navahos, Nez Perces, Rosebud Sioux, and Utes

Periodic publications on Indians today issued by the Bureau of Indian Affairs and the Indian Arts and Crafts Board, Department of the Interior, Washington, D.C.; the U.S. Public Health Service, Washington, D.C.; and the Indian Affairs Branch, Department of Citizenship and Immigration, Ottawa.

Periodic publications on Indians and New World archeology: American Museum of Natural History, New York; Chicago Natural History Museum, Chicago; Idaho State Museum, Pocatello; Museum of the American Indian, Heye Foundation, New York; Peabody

Museum of Archeology and Ethnology, Harvard University; Southwest Museum, Los Angeles; University of California, Berkeley.

Periodic *Reports on Indian Legislation*, Friends Committee on National Legislation, Washington, D.C.

Newsletter, Survival of American Indians Association, Inc., Tacoma, Washington

The Amerindian, Chicago

Tundra Times, Fairbanks, Alaska

Books and Articles

A. *Works that pertain essentially to Early Man in the Americas and to Indian cultures and civilizations that existed in the Western Hemisphere prior to the arrival of the white man.*

Amsden, Charles A. *Prehistoric Southwesterners from Basketmaker to Pueblo.* Los Angeles: Southwest Museum; 1949.

Baumhoff, Martin A. "Ecological Determinants of Aboriginal California Populations." *University of California Publications in American Archaeology and Ethnology*, Vol. XLIX, No. 2. Berkeley and Los Angeles, 1963, pp. 155–235.

Bennett, Wendell C. *Ancient Arts of the Andes.* New York: Museum of Modern Art; 1954.

——— and Bird, Junius S. *Andean Culture History.* 2nd edn. Garden City, N.Y., 1964.

Brush, C. F. "Pox Pottery: Earliest Identified Mexican Ceramic." *Science*, Vol. CXLIX (1965), pp. 194–5.

Bryan, Alan Lyle. *Paleo-American Prehistory.* Occasional Papers, No. 16, Pocatello: Idaho State University Museum; 1965.

Butler, B. R. *The Old Cordilleran Culture in the Pacific Northwest.* Occasional Papers, No. 5. Pocatello: Idaho State University Museum; 1961.

———. *Contributions to the Prehistory of the Columbia Plateau.* Occasional Papers, No. 9. Pocatello: Idaho State University Museum; 1962.

Campbell, J. M., ed. *Prehistoric Cultural Relations Between the Arctic and Temperate Zones of North America.* Technical Papers, No. 11. Montreal: Arctic Institute of North America; 1962.

Coe, M. D. "La Victoria, an Early Site on the Pacific Coast of Guatemala." *Papers*, Vol. LIII. Cambridge, Mass.: Peabody Museum; 1961.

———; Diehl, Richard A.; and Stuiver, Minze. "Olmec Civilization, Veracruz, Mexico: Dating of the San Lorenzo Phase." *Science*, Vol. CLV, No. 3768 (March 17, 1967), pp. 1399–1401.

Collins, Henry B., Jr. *The Origin and Antiquity of the Eskimo.* 1950 Annual Report. Washington, D.C.: Smithsonian Institution; 1951, pp. 423–67.

Covarrubias, Miguel. *Indian Art of Mexico and Central America.* New York, 1957.

———. *The Eagle, the Jaguar, and the Serpent: Indian Art of the Americas.* New York, 1954.

Cressman, Luther S., and others. "Cultural Sequences at The Dalles, Oregon." *Transactions,* Vol. L, Pt. 10. American Philosophical Society, Philadelphia.

Daugherty, R. D. "The Intermontane Western Tradition." *American Antiquity,* Vol. XXVIII, No. 2 (1962), pp. 144–50.

Dockstader, Frederick J. *Indian Art in Middle America.* New York, 1964.

Early Indian Farmers and Villages and Communities. Theme Study of the National Survey of Historic Sites and Buildings, National Park Service, Washington, D.C., 1963.

Emmerich, André. *Sweat of the Sun and Tears of the Moon: Gold and Silver in Pre-Columbian Art.* Seattle, 1965.

Esplendor del México Antiguo. Noriega, Raúl, Carmen Cook de Leonard, and Julio Rodolfo Moctezuma, eds., with other contributors. 2 vols. Mexico, D.F.: Centro de Investigaciones Antropológicas de México; 1959.

Flannery, Kent V.; Kirkby, Anne V. T.; Kirkby, Michael J.; and Williams, Aubrey W., Jr. "Farming Systems and Political Growth in Ancient Oaxaca." *Science,* Vol. CLVIII, No. 3800 (October 27, 1967), pp. 445–54.

Ford, James A. "Early Formative Cultures in Georgia and Florida." *American Antiquity,* Vol. XXXI, No. 6 (October 1966), pp. 781–99.

Giddings, J. Louis. *Ancient Men of the Arctic.* New York, 1967.

———. *The Archaeology of Cape Denbigh.* Providence, R.I., 1964.

Greenberg, Joseph H. "The General Classification of Central and South American Languages," in *Men and Cultures,* A. F. C. Wallace, ed., *Selected Papers, 5th International Congress of Anthropological and Ethnological Sciences.* Philadelphia, 1960, pp. 791–4.

Griffin, James B., ed. *Archaeology of Eastern United States.* Chicago, 1952.

———. "Eastern North American Archaeology: A Summary." *Science,* Vol. CLVI, No. 3772 (April 14, 1967), pp. 175–91.

Gruhn, Ruth. "Two Early Radiocarbon Dates from the Lower Levels of Wilson Butte Cave, South Central Idaho." *Tebiwa,* The Journal of the Idaho State University Museum, Vol. VIII, No. 2. Pocatello, 1965, p. 57.

Handbook of Middle American Indians, ed. by Robert Wauchope, with other contributors. Vols. 1–3. Austin, Texas, 1964–5.

Hibben, Frank C. "Mexican Features of Mural Paintings at Pottery Mound." *Archaeology,* Vol. XX, No. 2 (April 1967), pp. 84–7.

Hopewellian Studies, ed. by Joseph R. Caldwell and Robert L. Hall.

Scientific Papers No. 12. Springfield, Ill.: Illinois State Museum; 1964.

Hopkins, David M., ed. *The Bering Land Bridge*. Stanford, Calif., 1967.

Hopkins, Nicholas A. "Great Basin Prehistory and Uto-Aztecan." *American Antiquity*, Vol. XXXI, No. 1 (July 1965), pp. 48–60.

Hurt, Wesley R. "New and Revised Radiocarbon Dates from Brazil." *Museum News*, W. H. Over Museum, State University of South Dakota, Vol. XXIII, Nos. 11, 12. Vermillion, 1962.

———. "Recent Radiocarbon Dates for Central and Southern Brazil." *American Antiquity*. Vol. XXX, No. 1 (July 1964), pp. 25–33.

Jennings, J. D. "Danger Cave." *Memoirs of the Society for American Archaeology*, No. 14. Salt Lake City, 1957.

———, and Norbeck, Edward. "Great Basin Prehistory: A Review." *American Antiquity*, Vol. XXI, No. 1 (1955), pp. 1–11.

———, and ———, eds. *Prehistoric Man in the New World*. Chicago, 1964.

Keleman, Pál. *Medieval American Art*. New York, 1956.

Kidder, Alfred V. *An Introduction to the Study of Southwestern Archaeology with a Preliminary Account of the Excavations at Pecos*. With an Introduction on "Southwestern Archaeology Today" by Irving Rouse. New Haven, Conn., 1962.

Lamb, Sidney M. "Linguistic Prehistory in the Great Basin." *International Journal of American Linguistics*, Vol. XXIV, No. 2. Baltimore, 1958, pp. 95–100.

Lanning, Edward P. "A Pre-Agricultural Occupation on the Central Coast of Peru." *American Antiquity*, Vol. XXVIII, No. 3 (1963), pp. 360–71.

———. "Early Man in Peru." *Scientific American*, Vol. CXIII, No. 4 (October 1965), pp. 68–76.

———, and Patterson, Thomas C. "Early Man in South America." *Scientific American*, Vol. CCXVII, No. 5 (November 1967), pp. 44–50.

Leonhardy, Frank C., ed., with other contributors. "Domebo: A Paleo-Indian Mammoth Kill in the Prairie-Plains." *Contributions of the Museum of the Great Plains*, No. 1. Lawton, Okla., 1966.

Lewis, T. M. N., and Lewis, Madeline Kneberg. *Eva, an Archaic Site*. Knoxville: University of Tennessee; 1961.

Lothrop, S. K., with others. *Pre-Columbian Art*. New York, 1957.

Lynch, Thomas F. "Quishqui Puncu: A Preceramic Site in Highland Peru." *Science*, Vol. CLVIII, No. 3802 (November 10, 1967), pp. 780–3.

———. *The Nature of the Central Andean Preceramic*. Occasional Papers, No. 21. Pocatello, Idaho State University Museum, 1967.

Macgowan, Kenneth, and Hester, Joseph A., Jr. *Early Man in the New World*. Garden City, N.Y., 1962.

MacNeish, Richard S. "Ancient Mesoamerican Civilization." *Science*, Vol. CXLIII (February 7, 1964), pp. 531–7.

———. "The Origins of New World Civilization." *Scientific American*, Vol. CCXI, No. 5 (November 1964), pp. 29–37.

McKusick, Marshall. *Men of Ancient Iowa as Revealed by Archaeological Discoveries*. Ames, Iowa, 1964.

Mangelsdorf, P. C., and Reeves, R. G. "The Origin of Corn—Five Papers Commemorating the Darwin Centennial." *Botanical Museum Leaflets*, Vol. 18, Nos. 7–10, Cambridge, Mass., 1959, pp. 329–440.

Martin, Paul S.; Quimby, George I.; and Collier, Donald. *Indians Before Columbus*. Chicago, 1947.

Mayer-Oakes, William J. "El Inga Projectile Points." *American Antiquity*, Vol. XXXI, No. 5, Pt. I (1966), pp. 644–61.

Meggers, Betty J., and Evans, Clifford. *Archaeological Investigations at the Mouth of the Amazon*. Bureau of American Ethnology, Bulletin 167. Washington, D.C., 1957.

———, and ———, eds. "Aboriginal Cultural Development in Latin America: An Interpretive Review." *Smithsonian Miscellaneous Collections*, Vol. CXLVI, No. 1. Washington, D.C.: Smithsonian Institution; 1963.

———, ———, and Estrada, Emilio. *Early Formative Period of Coastal Ecuador: The Valdivia and Machalilla Phases*. Smithsonian Contributions to Anthropology, Vol. I. Washington, D.C., 1965.

Michels, Joseph W. "Archeology and Dating by Hydration of Obsidian." *Science*, Vol. CLVIII, No. 3798 (October 13, 1967), pp. 211–14.

Millon, R. F., and Bennyhoff, J. A. "A Long Architectural Sequence at Teotihuacán." *American Antiquity*, Vol. XXVI (1961), pp. 516–23.

Morley, S. G., and Brainerd, G. W. *The Ancient Maya*, 3rd edn. Palo Alto, Calif., 1956.

Paddock, John, ed. *Ancient Oaxaca*. Stanford, Calif., 1966.

Parsons, James J., and Denevan, William M. "Pre-Columbian Ridged Fields." *Scientific American*, Vol. CCXVII, No. 1 (July 1967), pp. 93–100.

Prehistoric Hunters and Gatherers. Theme Study of the National Survey of Historic Sites and Buildings. Washington, D.C.: National Park Service; 1960.

Quimby, George I. *Indian Life in the Upper Great Lakes, 11,000 B.C. to A.D. 1800*. Chicago, 1960.

Reichel-Dolmatoff, G. "Jungle Gods of San Agustín." *Natural History* (December 1966), pp. 42–8.

Ritchie, William A. *The Archaeology of New York State*. Garden City, N.Y., 1965.

Rouse, Irving. "Archaeology in Lowland South America and the

Caribbean, 1935–60." *American Antiquity*, Vol. XXVII (1961), pp. 56–62.

Roys, Ralph L. *The Indian Background of Colonial Yucatán.* Carnegie Institution of Washington, Publication 548. Washington, D.C., 1943.

Sahagún, Fray Bernardino de. *Florentine Codex: General History of the Things of New Spain*, trans. from the Aztec by Arthur J. O. Anderson and Charles E. Dibble. Santa Fe and Salt Lake City, 1950–8.

Sapir, E. "Central and North American Indian Languages." *Encyclopaedia Britannica*, 14th edn., Vol. 5. New York, 1929.

Sauer, Carl O. "Agricultural Origins and Dispersals." New York: The American Geographic Society; 1952.

Schroeder, Albert H. "Pattern Diffusion From Mexico Into the Southwest After A.D. 600." *American Antiquity*, Vol. XXXI, No. 5, Pt. 1 (July 1966), pp. 683–704.

——. "The Hakataya Cultural Tradition." *American Antiquity*, Vol. XXIII, No. 2 (1957), pp. 176–8.

——. "The Hohokam, Sinagua, and Hakataya." *Archives of Archaeology*, No. 5. Madison: Society for American Archaeology and the University of Wisconsin Press; 1960.

——. "Unregulated Diffusion From Mexico Into the Southwest Prior to A.D. 700." *American Antiquity*, Vol. XXX, No. 3 (January 1965), pp. 297–309.

Spinden, H. J. *Maya Art and Civilization.* Indian Hills, Colo., 1957.

Stephens, John Lloyd. *Incidents of Travel in Yucatán*, ed. by Victor W. von Hagen. 2 vols. Norman, Okla., 1962.

Swadesh, Morris. "Linguistic Relations Across Bering Strait." *American Anthropologist*, Vol. LXIV, No. 6 (1962), pp. 1262–91.

Swanson, E. H., Jr. *The Emergence of Plateau Culture.* Occasional Papers, No. 8. Pocatello: Idaho State College Museum; 1962.

Tax, Sol, ed. "The Civilizations of Ancient America." *Selected Papers of the 29th International Congress of Americanists*, Vol. I. Chicago, 1951.

Taylor, Walter W "Archaeology and Language in Western North America." *American Antiquity*, Vol. XXVII, No. 1 (1961), pp. 71–81.

Thompson, J. Eric. *The Rise and Fall of Maya Civilization.* Norman, Okla., 1954.

Vaillant, George. *Aztecs of Mexico.* New York, 1941.

Wallace, W. J. "Prehistoric Cultural Development in the Southern California Deserts." *American Antiquity*, Vol. XXVIII, No. 2 (1962).

Wauchope, Robert. "Archaeological Survey of Northern Georgia." *Memoirs of the Society for American Archaeology*, No. 21. Salt Lake City, 1966.

——. *Lost Tribes and Sunken Continents.* Chicago, 1962.

Wedel, Waldo R. *Prehistoric Man on the Great Plains*. Norman, Okla., 1961.

Wicke, Charles R. "Pyramids and Temple Mounds: Mesoamerican Ceremonial Architecture in Eastern North America." *American Antiquity*, Vol. XXX, No. 4 (April 1965), pp. 409–20.

Willey, Gordon R. *An Introduction to American Archaeology. Volume One: North and Middle America*. Englewood Cliffs, N.J., 1966.

——. "The Interrelated Rise of the Native Cultures of Middle and South America." New Interpretations of Aboriginal American Culture History. *75th Anniversary Volume of the Anthropological Society of Washington*. Washington, D.C., 1955.

——, and Phillips, Philip. "New Discoveries at Altar de Sacrificios, Guatemala." *Archaeology*, Vol. XVI, No. 2 (1963). Cambridge, Mass., pp. 83–9.

Wormington, H. M. *Ancient Man in North America*, 4th edn. rev. Denver Museum of Natural History "Popular Series" No. 4. Denver, 1957.

B. *Works that pertain especially to the cultures and ways of life of particular tribes, groups of tribes, or Indians in general.*

Alexander, Hartley Burr. *The World's Rim: Great Mysteries of the North American Indians*. Lincoln, Nebr., 1953.

Astrov, Margot, ed. *The Winged Serpent*. New York, 1946. (Indian prose and poetry.)

Baker, Paul E. *The Forgotten Kutenai*. Boise, Idaho, 1955.

Baldwin, Gordon C. *The Warrior Apaches*. Tucson, Ariz., 1965.

Barbeau, Marius. "Indian Days on the Western Prairies." *Bulletin No. 163, Anthropological Series No. 46*. Ottawa: Department of Northern Affairs and National Resources, National Museum of Canada; 1959.

——. "Medicine Men on the North Pacific Coast." *Bulletin No. 152*. Ottawa: National Museum of Canada; 1958.

——. "Tsimsyan Myths." *Bulletin No. 174*. Ottawa: National Museum of Canada; 1961.

——. "Totem Poles." 2 vols. *Bulletin No. 119*. Ottawa: National Museum of Canada; n.d.

Barnett, Homer G. *The Coast Salish of British Columbia*. Eugene, Ore., 1955.

Berthrong, Donald J. *The Southern Cheyennes*. Norman, Okla., 1963.

Boas, Franz. *Handbook of American Indian Languages*. Washington, D.C.: Bureau of American Ethnology, Bulletin 40; 1911.

——. *Race, Language and Culture*. New York, 1949.

Brown, Joseph Epes. *The Sacred Pipe*. Norman, Okla., 1953.

————. *The Spiritual Legacy of the American Indian.* Wallingford, Pa., 1964.

Catlin, George. *Episodes from Life Among the Indians* and *Last Rambles,* ed. by Marvin C. Ross. Norman, Okla., 1959.

————. *Letters and Notes on the Manners, Customs, and Condition of the North American Indians.* 2 vols. New York, 1842.

————. *O-Kee-Pa. A Religious Ceremony and Other Customs of the Mandans,* ed. by John C. Ewers, New Haven, Conn., 1967.

Clark, Ella Elizabeth. *Indian Legends From the Northern Rockies.* Norman, Okla., 1966.

————. *Indian Legends of Canada.* Toronto, 1960.

————. *Indian Legends of the Pacific Northwest.* Berkeley, Calif., 1953.

Collier, John. *The Indians of the Americas.* New York, 1947.

Colson, Elizabeth. *The Makah Indians.* St. Paul, 1953.

Corwin, Hugh D. *The Kiowa Indians: Their History and Life Stories.* Lawton, Okla., 1958.

Culin, Stewart. *Games of the North American Indians.* 24th Annual Report, Bureau of American Ethnology. Washington, D.C., 1907.

Day, A. Grove. *The Sky Clears.* New York, 1951. (Indian poetry.)

De Angulo, Jaime. *Indian Tales.* New York, 1962.

Denig, Edwin T. *Five Indian Tribes of the Upper Missouri: Sioux, Arikaras, Assiniboines, Crees, Crows,* ed. by John C. Ewers. Norman, Okla., 1961.

Densmore, Frances. *Music of the Maidu Indians of California.* Los Angeles: Southwest Museum; 1958.

————. *The American Indians and Their Music.* New York, 1926.

Dockstader, Frederick J. *Indian Art in America.* Greenwich, Conn., 1961.

Driver, Harold E. *Indians of North America.* Chicago, 1961.

————, and Massey, William C. "Comparative Studies of North American Indians." *Transactions of the American Philosophical Society,* Vol. XLVII (1957), pp. 165–456.

Drucker, Philip. *Indians of the Northwest Coast.* New York, 1955.

Dusenberry, Verne. *The Rocky Boy Indians.* Montana Heritage Series, No. 3. Helena, 1954.

Eggan, Fred. *The American Indian.* Chicago, 1966.

Embree, Edwin R. *Indians of the Americas.* Boston, 1939.

Ewers, John C. *The Blackfeet.* Norman, Okla., 1958.

————. *The Horse in Blackfoot Indian Culture.* Bureau of American Ethnology, Bulletin 159. Washington, D.C., 1955.

Feldman, Susan, ed. *The Story Telling Stone: Myths and Tales of the American Indian.* New York, 1965.

Fenton, William N. "Problems Arising from the Historic Northeastern Position of the Iroquois." *Essays in Historical Anthropology of North America,* Smithsonian Miscellaneous Collections, Vol. C (1940), pp. 159–251.

Forbes, Jack D. *Warriors of the Colorado: The Yumas of the Quechan Nation and Their Neighbors.* Norman, Okla., 1965.

Foreman, Grant. *Sequoyah.* Norman, Okla., 1938.

———. *The Five Civilized Tribes.* Norman, Okla., 1934.

Grant, Campbell. *The Rock Paintings of the Chumash. A Study of a California Indian Culture.* Berkeley, Calif., 1965.

Grinnell, George Bird. *By Cheyenne Campfires.* New Haven, Conn., 1926.

———. *Pawnee, Blackfoot and Cheyenne.* New York, 1961.

———. *Pawnee Hero Stories and Folk-Tales.* Lincoln, Nebr., 1961.

———. *The Fighting Cheyennes.* Norman, Okla., 1956.

Hagan, William T. *American Indians.* Chicago, 1961.

———. *The Sac and Fox Indians.* Norman, Okla., 1958.

Handbook of American Indians North of Mexico, ed. by Frederick W. Hodge, with many contributors. 2 vols. Bureau of American Ethnology, Bulletin 30. Washington, D.C., 1910. Reprinted in New York, 1959.

Handbook of South American Indians, ed. by Julian H. Steward, with other contributors. 6 vols. Bureau of American Ethnology, Bulletin 143. Washington, D.C., 1946–50.

Hassrick, Royal B. *The Sioux: Life and Customs of a Warrior Society.* Norman, Okla., 1964.

Hawthorn, Harry B.; Belshaw, Cyril S.; and Jamieson, Stuart M. *The Indians of British Columbia.* Berkeley, Calif., 1958.

Heizer, Robert F. "The California Indians." *The California Historical Society Quarterly,* Vol. XLI, No. 1 (March 1962), pp. 1–28.

Hoebel, E. Adamson. *The Cheyennes: Indians of the Great Plains.* New York, 1960.

Jenness, Diamond. *The Indians of Canada.* Canadian Department of Mines, Bulletin 65. Ottawa: National Museum of Canada; 1932.

Jones, Louis Thomas. *Aboriginal American Oratory.* Los Angeles: Southwest Museum; 1964.

Kluckhohn, Clyde, and Leighton, Dorothea. *The Navaho.* Rev. edn. in paperback, with revisions by Lucy H. Wales and Richard Kluckhohn. Garden City, N.Y., 1962.

Krause, Aurel. *The Tlingit Indians,* trans. by Erna Gunther. Seattle, 1956.

Kroeber, Alfred L. *Cultural and Natural Areas of Native North America.* Berkeley, Calif., 1939.

———. *Ethnography of the Cahuilla Indians.* University of California Publications in American Archaeology and Ethnology, Vol. VIII, No. 2 (1908).

———. *Handbook of the Indians of California.* Bureau of American Ethnology, Bulletin 78. Washington, D.C., 1925.

LaFarge, Oliver. *A Pictorial History of the American Indian.* New York, 1956.

Leekley, Thomas B. *The World of Manabozho: Tales of the Chippewa Indians.* New York, 1964.

Long, James Larpenteur. *The Assiniboines: From the Accounts of the Old Ones Told to First Boy*, ed. by Michael Kennedy. Norman, Okla., 1961.

Lowie, Robert H. *Indians of the Plains*. New York, 1954.

———. *The Crow Indians*. New York, 1935.

Lurie, Nancy O., ed. *Mountain Wolf Woman, Sister of Crashing Thunder*. Ann Arbor, Mich., 1961. (Autobiography of a Winnebago Indian.)

Massey, W. C. "Tribes and Languages of Baja California." *Southwestern Journal of Anthropology*, Vol. V, No. 3. Albuquerque, 1949, pp. 272–307.

Mathews, John Joseph. *The Osages*. Norman, Okla., 1961.

McKenney, Thomas L., and Hall, James. *The Indian Tribes of North America*, ed. by Frederick W. Hodge, 3 vols. Edinburgh, 1933.

McReynolds, Edwin C. *The Seminoles*. Norman, Okla., 1957.

Mooney, James. *The Ghost Dance Religion*. Bureau of American Ethnology, Annual Report, Vol. XIV, No. 2. Washington, D.C., 1896.

Morgan, L. H. *League of the Ho-de-no-sau-nee or Iroquois*. New York, 1904.

———. *The Indian Journals, 1859–62*, ed. by Leslie A. White, Ann Arbor, Mich., 1959.

Murdock, George Peter. *Ethnographic Bibliography of North America*. 3rd edn. Human Relations Area Files. New Haven, Conn., 1960.

National Geographic Society. *Indians of the Americas*. Washington, D.C., 1961.

Neihardt, John G. *Black Elk Speaks*. New York, 1932.

Newcomb, W. W., Jr. *The Indians of Texas*. Austin, 1961.

Oswalt, Wendell H. *This Land Was Theirs*. New York, 1966.

Owen, Roger C.; Deetz, James J. F.; and Fisher, Anthony D. *The North American Indians*. New York, 1967.

Powell, J. W. *Indian Linguistic Families North of Mexico*. Annual Report, Bureau of American Ethnology, Vol. 7. Smithsonian Institution, Washington, D.C., 1891.

Radin, Paul. *The Story of the American Indian*. New York, 1957.

Ray, Verne F. *Cultural Relations in the Plateau Region of Northwestern America*. Los Angeles, 1939.

———. *Primitive Pragmatists; the Modoc Indians of Northern California*. Seattle, 1963.

Relander, Click. *Drummers and Dreamers*. Caldwell, Idaho, 1956.

Roe, Frank G. *The Indian and the Horse*. Norman, Okla., 1955.

Ruby, Robert H. and John A. Brown. *Half-Sun on the Columbia*. Norman, Okla., 1965.

Schoolcraft, Henry R. *The Indian of the United States*. Parts I–VI. Philadelphia, 1851–7.

————. *The Literary Voyager or Muzzeniegun,* ed. by Philip P. Mason. East Lansing, Mich., 1962.

Smith, M. W. *The Puyallup-Nisqually.* Columbia University Contributions to Anthropology, Vol. XXXII. New York, 1940.

Sonnichsen, C. L. *The Mescalero Apaches.* Norman, Okla., 1958.

Speck, F. G. *Naskapi.* Norman, Okla., 1935.

Spencer, Robert F.; Jennings, Jesse D.; and others. *The Native Americans.* New York, 1965.

Stands In Timber, John, and Liberty, Margot. *Cheyenne Memories.* New Haven, Conn., 1967.

Stern, Theodore. *The Klamath Tribe.* Seattle, 1965.

Steward, Julian H., and Faron, Louis C. *Native Peoples of South America.* New York, 1959.

Stirling, Matthew W. *Historical and Ethnographical Material on the Jívaro Indians.* Bureau of American Ethnology, Bulletin 117. Washington, D.C., 1938.

Stone, Eric. *Medicine Among the American Indians.* New York, 1932.

Strong, William D. *Aboriginal Society in Southern California.* University of California Publications in American Archaeology and Ethnology, Vol. XXVI. 1929.

Swanton, John R. *Indian Tribes of the Lower Mississippi Valley and Adjacent Coast of the Gulf of Mexico.* Bureau of American Ethnology, Bulletin 43. Washington, D.C., 1911.

————. *Indian Tribes of North America.* Bureau of American Ethnology, Bulletin 145. Washington, D.C., 1952.

————. *The Indians of the Southeastern United States.* Bureau of American Ethnology, Bulletin 137. Washington, D.C., 1946.

Teit, James A. *The Salishan Tribes of the Western Plateaus,* ed. by Franz Boas. 45th Annual Report of the Bureau of American Ethnology. Washington, D.C., 1930.

The Incas of Pedro de Cieza de Léon, trans. by Harriet de Onís and ed. by Victor W. von Hagen. Norman, Okla., 1959.

Thompson, Laura. *Culture in Crisis.* New York, 1950. (On the Hopis.)

Thwaites, Reuben Gold, ed. *The Original Journals of the Lewis and Clark Expedition.* 8 vols. New York, 1904–5.

Titiev, Mischa. *Old Oraibi.* Papers of the Peabody Museum of American Archaeology and Ethnology, Vol. XXII, No. 1 (1944).

Tomorrow: Quarterly Review of Psychical Research. Vol. IV, No. 3 (Spring 1956). (Special issue on American Indians.)

Underhill, Ruth. *Indians of the Pacific Northwest.* Washington, D.C.: Bureau of Indian Affairs, Department of the Interior; 1944.

————. *Red Man's America.* Chicago, 1953.

————. *Red Man's Religion: Beliefs and Practices of the Indians North of Mexico.* Chicago, 1965.

————. *The Papago Indians of Arizona and Their Relatives the*

Pima. Sherman Pamphlets, No. 3. Washington, D.C.: Bureau of Indian Affairs; n.d.

Van Steensel, Maja, ed., *People of Light and Dark.* Department of Indian Affairs and Northern Development. Ottawa, 1966.

Verrill, A. Hyatt. *Foods America Gave the World.* New York, 1937.

Wallace, Ernest, and Hoebel, E. Adamson. *The Comanches.* Norman, Okla., 1952.

Wallace, Paul A. W. *Indians in Pennsylvania.* Harrisburg, Pa., 1961.

Wallis, Wilson D., and Wallis, Ruth Sawtell. *The Micmac Indians of Eastern Canada.* St. Paul, Minn., 1955.

Waters, Frank. *The Book of the Hopi.* New York, 1963.

Weslager, C. A. *A Brief Account of the Indians of Delaware.* Newark, Dela., 1953.

Weyer, Edward M. *The Eskimos: Their Environment and Folkways.* New Haven, Conn., 1962.

Williams, Samuel Cole, ed. *Adair's History of the American Indians.* New York, 1966.

Wissler, Clark. *Indians of the United States: Four Centuries of Their History and Culture.* New York, 1940. Rev. edn., Garden City, N.Y., 1966.

Wright, Muriel. *A Guide to the Indian Tribes of Oklahoma.* Norman, Okla., 1951.

C. Works with particular emphasis on the history of Indian-white relations in the Americas.

Andrist, Ralph K. *The Long Death.* New York, 1964. (Plains wars.)

Arciniegas, Germán. *Amerigo and the New World.* New York, 1955. (Vespucci.)

Bailey, L. R. *The Long Walk.* Los Angeles, 1964. (Navahos.)

Bancroft, Hubert Howe. *The Works of Hubert Howe Bancroft,* Vols. 1–5, *Native Races.* San Francisco, 1886–90.

Blumenthal, Walter Hart. *American Indians Dispossessed.* Philadelphia, 1955.

Brandon, William. *The American Heritage Book of Indians,* ed. by Alvin M. Josephy, Jr. New York, 1961.

Burns, Robert I. *The Jesuits and the Indian Wars of the Northwest.* New Haven, Conn., 1966.

Colden, Cadwallader. *The History of the Five Nations.* Ithaca, N.Y., 1958.

Coues, Elliott, ed. *New Light on the Early History of the Greater Northwest.* 3 vols. New York, 1897.

Debo, Angie. *The Rise and Fall of the Choctaw Republic.* Norman, Okla., 1961.

DeForest, John W. *History of the Indians of Connecticut.* Hartford, Conn., 1851.

DeVoto, Bernard. *Course of Empire*. Boston, 1952.

Díaz del Castillo, Bernal. *The Discovery and Conquest of Mexico*. New York, 1956.

Dockstader, Frederick J. *The Kachina and the White Man*. Cranbrook Institute of Science, Bulletin 35. Bloomfield Hills, Mich., 1954.

Dunn, Jacob P., Jr., *Massacres of the Mountains*. New York, 1886.

Emmitt, Robert. *The Last War Trail. The Utes and the Settlement of Colorado*. Norman, Okla., 1954.

Fenton, William N. *American Indian and White Relations to 1830*, with bibliography compiled by L. H. Butterfield, Wilcomb E. Washburn and William N. Fenton. Chapel Hill, N.C., 1957.

Filler, Louis, and Guttman, Allen, eds. *Removal of the Cherokee Nation: Manifest Destiny or National Dishonor?* Boston, 1962.

Forbes, Jack D. *Apache, Navaho, and Spaniard*. Norman, Okla., 1960.

Foreman, Grant. *Advancing the Frontier, 1830–1860*. Norman, Okla., 1933.

———. *Indians and Pioneers*. Norman, Okla., 1936.

———. *Indian Removal*. Norman, Okla., 1953.

Garcilaso de la Vega. *The Florida of the Inca*, trans. by John Grier Varner and Jeannette Johnson Varner. Austin, Tex., 1951.

Gibson, Charles. *Spain in America*. New York, 1966.

Giddings, Joshua R. *Exiles of Florida*, ed. by A. W. Thompson. Gainesville, Fla., 1964.

Hallowell, A. Irving. *The Backwash of the Frontier: The Impact of the Indian on American Culture*. Annual Report, Smithsonian Institution. Washington, D.C., 1958, pp. 447–72.

———. "The Impact of the American Indian on American Culture." *American Anthropologist*, Vol. LIX, pp. 201–17.

Horgan, Paul. *Great River*. 2 vols. New York, 1954.

Howard, Joseph Kinsey. *Strange Empire*. New York, 1952. (Métis.)

Hunt, George T. *The Wars of the Iroquois*. Madison, Wis., 1940.

Hyde, George E. *Indians of the High Plains*. Norman, Okla., 1959.

———. *Red Cloud's Folk*. Norman, Okla., 1957.

———. *Spotted Tail's Folk: A History of the Brulé Sioux*. Norman, Okla., 1961.

Innis, Harold A. *The Fur Trade In Canada*. New Haven, Conn., 1962.

Jackson, Donald, ed. *Black Hawk: An Autobiography*. Urbana, Ill., 1955.

Jackson, Helen Hunt. *A Century of Dishonor*. New York, 1881.

Josephy, Alvin M., Jr. *The Nez Perce Indians and the Opening of the Northwest*. New Haven, Conn., 1965.

———. *The Patriot Chiefs*. New York, 1961.

Kappler, Charles J. *Indian Affairs: Laws and Treaties*. 5 vols. Washington, D.C.: Government Printing Office; 1903–40.

Kroeber, Theodora. *Ishi in Two Worlds*. Berkeley, Calif., 1961.

Las Casas, Bartolomé de. *Historia de las Indias,* ed. by Gonzalo de Reparaz. Madrid, 1927.

————. *The Tears of the Indians,* trans. by John Phillips. Stanford, Calif., n.d.

Lauber, Almon W. *Indian Slavery in Colonial Times Within the Present Limits of the United States.* New York, 1913.

Leach, Douglas E. *Flintlock and Tomahawk.* New York, 1959.

————. *The Northern Colonial Frontier, 1607–1763.* New York, 1966.

MacLeod, William C. *The American Indian Frontier.* New York, 1928.

McNickle, D'Arcy. *The Indian Tribes of the United States.* New York, 1962.

————. *They Came Here First.* Philadelphia, 1949.

Morison, Samuel Eliot. *Admiral of the Ocean Sea.* 2 vols. Boston, 1946.

Murray, Keith A. *The Modocs And Their War.* Norman, Okla., 1965.

Olson, James C. *Red Cloud and the Sioux Problem.* Lincoln, Nebr., 1965.

Oviedo, Gonzalez Fernández de. *Natural History of the West Indies,* trans. and ed. by Sterling A. Stoudemire. Chapel Hill, N.C., 1959.

Porter, C. Fayne. *Our Indian Heritage.* Philadelphia, 1964.

Prescott, William H. *History of the Conquest of Mexico and History of the Conquest of Peru.* Modern Library edn. New York, 1936.

Priest, Loring B. *Uncle Sam's Stepchildren: The Reformation of United States Indian Policy, 1865–87.* New Brunswick, N.J., 1942.

Prucha, F. P. *American Indian Policy in the Formative Years.* Cambridge, Mass., 1962.

Rich, E. E. *The History of the Hudson's Bay Company, 1670–1870.* 2 vols. London, 1958–9.

Royce, Charles C. *Indian Land Cessions in the United States.* Bureau of American Ethnology, 18th Annual Report, Part 2. Washington, D.C., 1899.

Schmitt, Martin F., and Brown, Dee. *Fighting Indians of the West.* New York, 1948.

Simpson, Lesley Byrd, trans. *The Laws of Burgos of 1512–1513.* San Francisco, 1960.

Sirmans, M. Eugene. *Colonial South Carolina.* Chapel Hill, N.C., 1966.

Spicer, Edward H. *Cycles of Conquest.* Tucson, Ariz., 1962.

————, ed. *Perspectives in American Indian Cultural Change.* Chicago, 1961.

Thornbrough, Gayle, ed. *Letter Book of the Indian Agency at Fort Wayne, 1809–1815.* Indianapolis, 1961.

Thwaites, Reuben Gold, ed. *Jesuit Relations and Allied Documents.* 73 vols. Cleveland, 1896–1901.

Trelease, Allen W. *Indian Affairs in Colonial New York: The Seventeenth Century.* Ithaca, N.Y., 1960.

Turner, Frederick Jackson. *The Frontier in American History.* New York, 1920.

Utley, Robert, ed. *Battlefield and Classroom.* New Haven, Conn., 1964.

———. *The Last Days of the Sioux Nation.* New Haven, Conn., 1963.

Van Every, Dale. *Disinherited.* New York, 1966.

Vaughan, Alden T. *The New England Frontier: Puritans and Indians, 1620–1675.* Boston, 1965.

Washburn, Wilcomb E., ed. *The Indian and the White Man.* Garden City, N.Y., 1964.

D. *Works pertaining essentially to Indians in recent times.*

Cohen, Felix S. *Handbook of Federal Indian Law.* Washington, D.C.: Government Printing Office, 1945.

Declaration of Indian Purpose. The American Indian Chicago Conference, Chicago, 1961.

Federal Indian Law. U. S. Department of the Interior, Office of the Solicitor. Washington, D.C.: Government Printing Office; 1958.

Fey, Harold E., and McNickle, D'Arcy. *Indians and Other Americans.* New York, 1959.

Fritz, Henry L. *The Movement for Indian Assimilation.* Philadelphia, 1963.

Gridley, Marion E., ed. and comp. *Indians of Today.* 3rd edn. Chicago, 1960.

Horsman, Reginald. *Expansion and American Indian Policy.* East Lansing, Mich., 1966.

Liberty, Margot. "Suppression and Survival of the Northern Cheyenne Sun Dance." *The Minnesota Archaeologist*, Vol. XXVII, No. 4 (1965), pp. 121–43.

Meriam, Lewis. *The Problem of Indian Administration.* Baltimore, 1928.

Reference Encyclopedia of the American Indian, ed. by Bernard Klein and Daniel Icolari. New York, 1967.

Report on Indians Taxed and Indians Not Taxed in the United States (Except Alaska) at the Eleventh Census: 1890. Washington, D.C.: Government Printing Office; 1894.

Report to the Secretary of the Interior By the Task Force on Indian Affairs, July 10, 1961.

Report to the Secretary of the Interior By the Task Force on Alaska Native Affairs, December 28, 1962.

Shimony, Annemarie A. *Conservatism Among the Iroquois at the Six Nations Reserve.* Yale University Publications in Anthropology, No. 65. 1961.

Simpson, George E., and Yinger, John M., eds. "American Indians and American Life." *The Annals of the American Academy of Political and Social Science,* Vol. CCCXI (May 1957).

The Indian—America's Unfinished Business. Report of the Commission on the Rights, Liberties, and Responsibilities of the American Indian. Comp. by William A. Brophy and Sophie D. Aberle. Norman, Okla., 1966.

United States Government. House Report No. 2503, Calendar No. 790, 82nd Congress, 2nd Session. *Report with respect to the House Resolution authorizing the Committee on Interior and Insular Affairs to conduct an investigation of the Bureau of Indian Affairs.* Washington, D.C.: Government Printing Office; 1952.

Wilson, Edmund. *Apologies to the Iroquois.* New York, 1959.

Index

ABOUT THE AUTHOR

ALVIN M. JOSEPHY, JR. was born in 1915 in Woodmere, New York. He attended Harvard University and has been a foreign correspondent, a Hollywood script writer, and an Associate Editor of *Time*. During World War II he served with the Office of War Information and as a combat correspondent in the Pacific. In 1960, Mr. Josephy joined American Heritage, where he is now Editor of General Books and responsible for the entire adult American Heritage and Horizon book programs.

Mr. Josephy's deep interest in Indian history and contemporary life has brought him close to the people of numerous tribes. He has served with various organizations in the field of Indian affairs, was a consultant to Secretary of the Interior Stewart L. Udall, and in 1966 was appointed a commissioner of the Indian Arts and Crafts Board of the Department of the Interior. He edited *The American Heritage Book of Indians* and also wrote *The Patriot Chiefs: A Chronicle of American Leadership* and *The Nez Perce Indians and the Opening of the Northwest*.

BANTAM BESTSELLERS

OUTSTANDING BOOKS NOW AVAILABLE
AT A FRACTION
OF THEIR ORIGINAL COST!

If you think this book was good, wait 'til you see what *else* we've got in store for you!

Send for your FREE catalog of Bantam Bestsellers today!

This money-saving catalog lists hundreds of best-sellers originally priced from $3.75 to $15.00—yours now in Bantam paperback editions for just 50¢ to $1.95! Here is a great opportunity to read the good books you've missed and add to your private library at huge savings! The catalog is FREE! So don't delay—send for yours today!